Praise for the First Edition

From the first edition of *Unity in Action* by Joseph Hocking

"The text is clear and concise, and the examples are outstanding. As a new user, I found this book to be an invaluable resource."

—Dan Kacenjar Sr., Cornerstone Software

"All the roadblocks evaporated, and I took my game from concept to build in short order."

—Philip Taffet, SOHOsoft LLC

"Gets you up and running in no time."

—Sergio Arbeo, codecantor

"Covers all the key elements for using Unity effectively."

—Shiloh Morris, Southern Nevada Water Authority

"Useful and to the point! You will learn the basics and more to start developing your own games"

—Victor M. Perez, Software developer

"Recommended for anyone starting out with Unity."

—Alex Lucas, Independent Contractor

"Teaches with good clean code and gives ideas on how to alter it for more interesting results."

—Amazon reader

Unity in Action

Multiplatform game development in C#

SECOND EDITION

JOSEPH HOCKING

MANNING
SHELTER ISLAND

Manning Publications Co.
20 Baldwin Road
PO Box 761
Shelter Island, NY 11964

Development editor:	Candace West
Technical development editor:	René van den Berg
Review editor:	Ivan Martinovic
Project editor:	David Novak
Copy editor:	Safis Editing
Proofreader:	Elizabeth Martin
Technical proofreader:	Shiloh Morris
Typesetter:	Happenstance Type-O-Rama
Cover designer:	Marija Tudor

ISBN 9781617294969
Printed in the United States of America
1 2 3 4 5 6 7 8 9 10 - EBM - 22 21 20 19 18

brief contents

contents

foreword

I started programming games in 1982. It wasn't easy. We had no internet. Resources were limited to a handful of mostly terrible books and magazines that offered fascinating but confusing code fragments, and as for game engines—well, there weren't any! Coding games was a massive uphill battle.

How I envy you, reader, holding the power of this book in your hands. The Unity engine has done so much to open game programming up to so many people. Unity has managed to strike an excellent balance by being a powerful, professional game engine that's still affordable and approachable for someone just getting started.

Approachable, that is, with the right guidance. I once spent time in a circus troupe run by a magician. He was kind enough to take me in and helped guide me toward becoming a good performer. "When you stand on a stage," he pronounced, "you make a promise. And that promise is 'I will not waste your time.'"

What I love most about *Unity in Action* is the "action" part. Joe Hocking wastes none of your time and gets you coding fast—and not just nonsense code, but interesting code that you can understand and build from, because he knows you don't just want to read his book, and you don't just want to program his examples—you want to be coding *your own game.*

And with his guidance, you'll be able to do that sooner than you might expect. Follow Joe's steps, but when you feel ready, don't be shy about diverging from his path and

xv

breaking out on your own. Skip to what interests you most—try experiments, be bold and brave! You can always return to the text if you get too lost.

But let's not dally in this foreword—the entire future of game development is impatiently waiting for you to begin! Mark this day on your calendar, for today is the day that everything changed. It will be forever remembered as the day you started making games.

From the First Edition
JESSE SCHELL
CEO of Schell Games
Author of The *Art of Game Design*
www.amazon.com/Art-Game-Design
-Lenses-Second/dp/1466598646/

preface

I've been programming games for quite some time, but only started using Unity relatively recently. Unity didn't exist when I first started developing games; the first version was released in 2005. Right from the start, it had a lot of promise as a game development tool, but it didn't come into its own until several versions later. In particular, platforms like iOS and Android (collectively referred to as "mobile") didn't emerge until later, and those platforms factor heavily into Unity's growing prominence.

Initially, I viewed Unity as a curiosity, an interesting development tool to keep an eye on but not actually use. During that time, I was programming games for both desktop computers and websites and doing projects for a range of clients. I was using tools like Blitz3D and Flash, which were great to program in but were limiting in a lot of ways. As those tools started to show their age, I kept looking for better ways to develop games.

I started experimenting with Unity around version 3, and then completely switched to it for my development work at Synapse Games. At first, I worked for Synapse on web games, but we eventually moved over to mobile games. And then we came full circle because Unity enabled us to deploy to the web in addition to mobile, all from one codebase!

I've always seen sharing knowledge as important, and I've taught game development for several years. A large part of why I do this is the example set for me by the many mentors and teachers I've had. (Incidentally, you may even have heard of one of my teachers because he was such an inspiring person: Randy Pausch delivered *The Last Lecture* shortly before he passed away in 2008.) I've taught classes at several schools, and I've always wanted to write a book about game development.

In many ways, what I've written here is the book I wish had existed back when I was first learning Unity. Among Unity's many virtues is a huge treasure trove of learning resources, but those resources tend to take the form of unfocused fragments (like the script reference or isolated tutorials) and require much digging to find what you need. Ideally, I'd have a book that wrapped up everything I needed to know in one place and presented it in a clear and logical manner, so now I'm writing such a book for you. I'm targeting people who already know how to program but who are newcomers to Unity, and possibly new to game development in general. The choice of projects reflects my experience of gaining skills and confidence by doing a variety of freelance projects in rapid succession.

In learning to develop games using Unity, you're setting out on an exciting adventure. For me, learning how to develop games meant putting up with a lot of hassle. You, on the other hand, have the advantage of a single coherent resource to learn from: this book!

acknowledgments

I would like to thank Manning Publications for giving me the opportunity to write this book. The editors I worked with, including Robin de Jongh and especially Dan Maharry, helped me throughout this undertaking, and the book is much stronger for their feedback. Candace West took over as primary editor for the second edition. My sincere thanks also to the many others who worked with me during the development and production of the book.

My writing benefited from the scrutiny of reviewers every step of the way. Thanks to Alex Lucas, Craig Hoffman, Dan Kacenjar, Joshua Frederick, Luca Campobasso, Mark Elston, Philip Taffet, René van den Berg, Sergio Arbeo Rodríguez, Shiloh Morris, Victor M. Perez, Christopher Haupt, Claudio Caseiro, David Torribia Iñigo, Dean Tsaltas, Eric Williams, Nickie Buckner, Robin Dewson, Sergey Evsikov, and Tanya Wilke. Special thanks to the notable review work by technical development editor Scott Chaussee and by technical proofreader Christopher Haupt, with René van den Berg and Shiloh Morris stepping into those roles for the 2nd edition. And I also want to thank Jesse Schell for writing the foreword to my book.

Next, I'd like to recognize the people who've made my experience with Unity a fruitful one. That, of course, starts with Unity Technologies, the company that makes Unity (the game engine). I am indebted to the community at gamedev.stackexchange.com/; I visit that QA site almost daily to learn from others and to answer questions. And the biggest push for me to use Unity came from Alex Reeve, my boss at Synapse Games.

Similarly, I've picked up tricks and techniques from my coworkers, and they all show up in the code I write.

Finally, I want to thank my wife, Virginia, for her support during the time I was writing the book. Until I started working on it, I never really understood how much a book project takes over your life and affects everyone around you. Thank you so much for your love and encouragement.

about this book

Unity in Action, Second Edition is a book about programming games in Unity. Think of it as an intro to Unity for experienced programmers. The goal of this book is straightforward: to take people who have some programming experience but no experience with Unity and teach them how to develop a game using Unity.

The best way of teaching development is through example projects, with students learning by doing, and that's the approach this book takes. I'll present topics as steps toward building sample games, and you'll be encouraged to build these games in Unity while exploring the book. We'll go through a selection of different projects every few chapters, rather than one monolithic project developed over the entire book. (Sometimes other books take the "one monolithic project" approach, but that can make it hard to jump into the middle if the early chapters aren't relevant to you.)

This book will have more rigorous programming content than most Unity books (especially beginners' books). Unity is often portrayed as a list of features with no programming required, which is a misleading view that won't teach people what they need to know in order to produce commercial titles. If you don't already know how to program a computer, I suggest going to a resource like Codecademy first (the computer programming lessons at Khan Academy work well, too) and then come back to this book after learning how to program.

Don't worry about the exact programming language; C# is used throughout this book, but skills from other languages will transfer quite well. Although the first part of the book will take its time introducing new concepts and will carefully and deliberately step you through developing your first game in Unity, the remaining chapters will move a lot faster in order to take readers through projects in multiple game genres. The book will end with a chapter describing deployment to various platforms like the web and mobile, but the main thrust of the book won't make any reference to the ultimate deployment target because Unity is wonderfully platform-agnostic.

As for other aspects of game development, extensive coverage of art disciplines would water down how much the book can cover and would be largely about software external to Unity (for example, the animation software used). Discussion of art tasks will be limited to aspects specific to Unity or that all game developers should know. (Note, though, that there is an appendix about modeling custom objects.)

Roadmap

Chapter 1 introduces you to Unity, the cross-platform game development environment. You'll learn about the fundamental component system underlying everything in Unity, as well as how to write and execute basic scripts.

Chapter 2 progresses to writing a demo of movement in 3D, covering topics like mouse and keyboard input. Defining and manipulating both 3D positions and rotations are thoroughly explained.

Chapter 3 turns the movement demo into a first-person shooter, teaching you raycasting and basic AI. Raycasting (shooting a line into the scene and seeing what it intersects) is a useful operation for all sorts of games.

Chapter 4 covers art asset importing and creation. This is the one chapter of the book that does not focus on code, because every project needs (basic) models and textures.

Chapter 5 teaches you how to create a 2D puzzle game in Unity. Although Unity started exclusively for 3D graphics, there's now excellent support for 2D graphics.

Chapter 6 expands the 2D game explanations with platform game mechanics. In particular, we'll implement controls, physics, and animation for the player.

Chapter 7 introduces you to the latest GUI functionality in Unity. Every game needs a UI, and the latest versions of Unity feature an improved system for creating UIs.

Chapter 8 shows how to create another movement demo in 3D, only seen from third-person perspective this time. Implementing third-person controls will demonstrate a number of key 3D math operations, and you'll learn how to work with an animated character.

Chapter 9 goes over how to implement interactive devices and items within your game. The player will have a number of ways of operating these devices, including touching them directly, touching triggers within the game, or pressing a button on the controller.

Chapter 10 covers how to communicate with the internet. You'll learn how to send and receive data using standard internet technologies, like HTTP requests to get XML data from a server.

Chapter 11 teaches how to program audio functionality. Unity has great support for both short sound effects and long music tracks; both sorts of audio are crucial for almost all video games.

Chapter 12 walks you through bringing together pieces from different chapters into a single game. In addition, you'll learn how to program point-and-click controls and how to save the player's game.

Chapter 13 goes over building the final app, with deployment to multiple platforms like desktop, web, mobile, and even VR. Unity is wonderfully platform-agnostic, enabling you to create games for every major gaming platform!

There are also four appendixes with additional information about scene navigation, external tools, Blender, and learning resources.

Code conventions, requirements, and downloads

All the source code in the book, whether in code listings or snippets, is in a `fixed-width font like this`, which sets it off from the surrounding text. In most listings, the code is annotated to point out key concepts, and numbered bullets are sometimes used in the text to provide additional information about the code. The code is formatted so that it fits within the available page space in the book by adding line breaks and using indentation carefully.

The only software required is Unity; this book uses Unity 2017.1, which is the latest version as I write this. Certain chapters do occasionally discuss other pieces of software, but those are treated as optional extras and not core to what you're learning.

> **WARNING** Unity projects remember which version of Unity they were created in and will issue a warning if you attempt to open them in a different version. If you see that warning while opening this book's sample downloads, click Continue and ignore it.

The code listings sprinkled throughout the book generally show what to add or change in existing code files; unless it's the first appearance of a given code file, don't replace the entire file with subsequent listings. Although you can download complete working sample projects to refer to, you'll learn best by typing out the code listings and only looking at the working samples for reference. Those downloads are available from the publisher's website (www.manning.com/books/unity-in-action-second-edition) and on GitHub (https://github.com/jhocking/uia-2e).

Author Online

Purchase of *Unity in Action, Second Edition* includes free access to a private web forum run by Manning Publications where you can make comments about the book, ask technical questions, and receive help from the author and from other users. To access the forum, go to https://forums.manning.com/forums/unity-in-action-second-edition. You can also learn more about Manning's forums and the rules of conduct at https://forums.manning.com/forums/about.

Manning's commitment to our readers is to provide a venue where a meaningful dialogue between individual readers and between readers and the author can take place. It is not a commitment to any specific amount of participation on the part of the author, whose contribution to the forum remains voluntary (and unpaid). We suggest you try asking the author some challenging questions lest his interest stray! The forum and the archives of previous discussions will be accessible from the publisher's website as long as the book is in print.

about the author

JOSEPH HOCKING is a software engineer who specializes in interactive media development. He currently works for InContext Solutions and wrote the first edition while working for Synapse Games. He has also taught classes at the University of Illinois at Chicago, the School of the Art Institute of Chicago, and Columbia College Chicago. His website is www.newarteest.com.

about the cover illustration

The figure on the cover of *Unity in Action, Second Edition* is captioned "Habit of the Master of Ceremonies of the Grand Signior." The Grand Signior was another name for a sultan of the Ottoman Empire. The illustration is taken from Thomas Jefferys' *A Collection of the Dresses of Different Nations, Ancient and Modern* (4 volumes), London, published between 1757 and 1772. The title page states that these are hand-colored copperplate engravings, heightened with gum arabic. Thomas Jefferys (1719–1771), was called "Geographer to King George III." An English cartographer who was the leading map supplier of his day, Jeffreys engraved and printed maps for government and other official bodies and produced a wide range of commercial maps and atlases, especially of North America. His work as a mapmaker sparked an interest in local dress customs of the lands he surveyed, which are brilliantly displayed in this four-volume collection.

Fascination with faraway lands and travel for pleasure were relatively new phenomena in the late eighteenth century and collections such as this one were popular, introducing both the tourist as well as the armchair traveler to the inhabitants of other countries. The diversity of the drawings in Jeffreys' volumes speaks vividly of the uniqueness and individuality of the world's nations some 200 years ago. Dress codes have changed since then and the diversity by region and country, so rich at the time, has faded away. It is now hard to tell the inhabitant of one continent apart from another. Perhaps, trying to view it optimistically, we have traded a cultural and visual diversity for a more varied personal life, or a more varied and interesting intellectual and technical life.

At a time when it is hard to tell one computer book from another, Manning cele-brates the inventiveness and initiative of the computer business with book covers based on the rich diversity of regional life of two centuries ago, brought back to life by Jeffreys' pictures.

Part 1

First steps

It's time to take your first steps in using Unity. If you don't know anything about Unity, that's okay! I'm going to start by explaining what Unity *is*, including the fundamentals of how to program games in it. Then we'll walk through a tutorial about developing a simple game in Unity. This first project will teach you a number of specific game development techniques, as well as giving you a good overview of how the process works.

Onward to chapter 1!

Getting to know Unity

This chapter covers

- What makes Unity a great choice
- Operating the Unity editor
- Programming in Unity
- Comparing C# and JavaScript

If you're anything like me, you've had developing a video game on your mind for a long time. But it's a big jump from playing games to making them. Numerous game development tools have appeared over the years, and we're going to discuss one of the most recent and most powerful of these tools. Unity is a professional-quality game engine used to create video games targeting a variety of platforms. Not only is it a professional development tool used daily by thousands of seasoned game developers, it's also one of the most accessible modern tools for novice game developers. Until recently, a newcomer to game development would face lots of imposing barriers right from the start, but Unity makes it easy to start learning these skills.

Because you're reading this book, chances are you're curious about computer technology and you've either developed games with other tools or built other kinds of software, such as desktop applications or websites. Creating a video game isn't fundamentally different from writing any other kind of software; it's mostly a difference

3

of degree. For example, a video game is a lot more interactive than most websites, and thus involves very different sorts of code, but the skills and processes involved in creating both are similar. If you've already cleared the first hurdle on your path to learning game development, having learned the fundamentals of programming software, then your next step is to pick up some game development tools and translate that programming knowledge into the realm of gaming. Unity is a great choice of game development environment to work with.

A warning about terminology

This book is about programming in Unity and is therefore primarily of interest to coders. Although many other resources discuss other aspects of game development and Unity, this is a book where programming takes front and center.

Incidentally, note that the word *developer* may have an unfamiliar meaning in the context of game development: *developer* is a synonym for *programmer* in disciplines like web development, but in game development the word *developer* often refers to anyone who works on a game, with *programmer* being a specific role within that. Other kinds of game developers are artists and designers, but this book focuses on programming.

To start, go to www.unity3d.com to download the software. This book uses Unity 2017.1, which is the latest version as of this writing. The URL is a leftover from Unity's original focus on 3D games; support for 3D games remains strong, but Unity works great for 2D games as well, and this book covers both. Indeed, even when demonstrated on a 3D demo, many topics (saving data, playing audio, and so on) apply to both. Meanwhile, although there are also paid versions, the base version is free. Everything in this book works in the free version, and none of it requires the paid versions of Unity, which differ mainly in commercial licensing terms.

1.1   *Why is Unity so great?*

Let's take a closer look at that description from the beginning of the chapter: Unity is a professional-quality game engine used to create video games targeting a variety of platforms. That's a fairly straightforward answer to the straightforward question: "What is Unity?" But, what exactly does that answer mean, and why is Unity so great?

1.1.1   *Unity's strengths and advantages*

Game engines provide a plethora of features that are useful across many different games. A game implemented using a particular engine will get all those features, while adding custom art assets and gameplay code specific to that game. Unity has physics simulation, normal maps, screen space ambient occlusion (SSAO), dynamic shadows . . . and the list goes on. Many game engines boast such features, but Unity has two main advantages over similar cutting-edge game development tools: an extremely productive visual workflow and a high degree of cross-platform support.

The visual workflow is a fairly unique design, different from most other game development environments. Whereas other game development tools are often a complicated mishmash of disparate parts that must be wrangled, or perhaps a programming library that requires you to set up your own integrated development environment (IDE), build-chain, and whatnot, the development workflow in Unity is anchored by a sophisticated visual editor. The editor is used to lay out the scenes in your game and to tie together art assets and code into interactive objects. The beauty of this editor is that it enables professional-quality games to be built quickly and efficiently, giving developers tools to be incredibly productive, while still using an extensive list of the latest technologies in video gaming.

> **NOTE** Most other game development tools that have a central visual editor are also saddled with limited and inflexible scripting support, but Unity doesn't suffer from that disadvantage. Although everything created for Unity ultimately goes through the visual editor, this core interface involves a lot of linking projects to custom code that runs in Unity's game engine. That's not unlike linking in classes in the project settings for an IDE like Visual Studio or Eclipse. Experienced programmers shouldn't dismiss this development environment, mistaking it for some click-together game creator with limited programming capability!

The editor is especially helpful for doing rapid iteration, honing the game through cycles of prototyping and testing. You can adjust objects in the editor and move things around even while the game is running. Plus, Unity allows you to customize the editor itself by writing scripts that add new features and menus to the interface.

Besides the editor's significant productivity advantages, the other main strength of Unity's toolset is a high degree of cross-platform support. Not only is Unity multiplatform in terms of deployment targets (you can deploy to PC, web, mobile, or consoles), but it's also multiplatform in terms of development tools (you can develop a game on Windows or macOS). This platform-agnostic nature is largely because Unity started as Mac-only software and was later ported to Windows. The first version launched in 2005, but now Unity is past its fifth major version (with lots of minor updates released frequently). Initially, Unity supported only Mac for both development and deployment, but within months Unity had been updated to work on Windows as well. Successive versions gradually added more deployment platforms, such as a cross-platform web player in 2006, iPhone in 2008, Android in 2010, and even game consoles like Xbox and PlayStation. More recently, they've added deployment to WebGL, the new framework for 3D graphics in web browsers, and there's even support for VR platforms like Oculus Rift and Vive. Few game engines support as many deployment targets as Unity, and none make deploying to multiple platforms so simple.

In addition to these main strengths, a third, more subtle, benefit comes from the modular component system used to construct game objects. In a component system, *components* are mix-and-match packets of functionality, and objects are built up as a collection of components, rather than as a strict hierarchy of classes. A component system is a different (and usually more flexible) approach to doing object-oriented programming (OOP), where game objects are constructed through composition rather than inheritance. Figure 1.1 diagrams an example comparison.

Figure 1.1   Inheritance vs. components

In a component system, objects exist on a flat hierarchy and different objects have different collections of components, rather than an inheritance structure where different objects are on completely different branches of the tree. This arrangement facilitates rapid prototyping, because you can quickly mix and match different components rather than having to refactor the inheritance chain when objects change.

Although you could write code to implement a custom component system if one didn't exist, Unity already has a robust component system, and this system is even integrated with the visual editor. Rather than only being able to manipulate components in code, you can attach and detach components within the visual editor. Meanwhile, you aren't limited to only building objects through composition; you still have the option of using inheritance in your code, including all the best-practice design patterns that have emerged based on inheritance.

1.1.2 Downsides to be aware of

Unity has many advantages that make it a great choice for developing games, and I highly recommend it, but I'd be remiss if I didn't mention its weaknesses. In particular, the combination of the visual editor and sophisticated coding, though very effective with Unity's component system, is unusual and can create difficulties. In complex scenes, you can lose track of which objects in the scene have specific components attached. Unity does provide a search feature for finding attached scripts, but it could be more robust; sometimes you still encounter situations where you need to manually inspect everything in the scene in order to find script linkages. This doesn't happen often, but when it does happen, it can be tedious.

Another disadvantage that can be surprising and frustrating for experienced programmers is that Unity doesn't support linking in external code libraries. Necessary libraries must be manually copied into every project that they'll be used in, as opposed to referencing one central shared location. The lack of a central location for libraries can make it awkward to share functionality between multiple projects. This disadvantage can be worked around with clever use of version control systems, but Unity doesn't support external code libraries out of the box.

> **NOTE** Difficulty working with version control systems (such as Subversion, Git, and Mercurial) used to be a significant weakness of Unity, but more recent versions work fine. You may find out-of-date resources telling you that Unity doesn't work with version control, but newer resources will describe which files and folders in a project need to be put in the repository and which don't. To start out, read Unity's documentation (http://mng.bz/BbhD) or look at the .gitignore file maintained by GitHub (http://mng.bz/g7nl).

A third weakness has to do with working with prefabs. Prefabs are a concept specific to Unity and are explained in chapter 3; for now, all you need to know is that prefabs are a flexible approach to visually defining interactive objects. The concept of prefabs is both powerful and unique to Unity (and yes, the concept of prefabs only makes sense in the context of Unity's component system), but it can be surprisingly awkward to edit prefabs. Considering that prefabs are such a useful and central part of working with Unity, I hope that future versions improve the workflow for editing them.

1.1.3 Example games built with Unity

You've heard about the pros and cons of Unity, but you might still need convincing that the development tools in Unity can give first-rate results. Visit the Unity gallery at http://unity3d.com/showcase/gallery to see a constantly updated list of hundreds of games and simulations developed using Unity. This section explores a handful of games, showcasing a number of genres and deployment platforms.

DESKTOP (WINDOWS, MAC, AND LINUX)

Because the Unity editor runs on the same platform, deployment to Windows or Mac is often the most straightforward target platform. Here are a couple of examples of desktop games in different genres:

- *Guns of Icarus Alliance* (figure 1.2), a first-person shooter developed by Muse Games

Figure 1.2   *Guns of Icarus Alliance*

- *Gone Home* (figure 1.3), an exploration adventure developed by The Fullbright Company

Figure 1.3   *Gone Home*

MOBILE (IOS AND ANDROID)

Unity can also deploy games to mobile platforms like iOS (iPhones and iPads) and Android (phones and tablets). Here are three examples of mobile games in different genres:

- *Lara Croft GO* (figure 1.4), a 3D puzzle game developed by Square Enix

Figure 1.4 *Lara Croft GO*

- *INKS* (figure 1.5), a 2D puzzle game developed by State of Play

Figure 1.5 *INKS*

- *Tyrant Unleashed* (figure 1.6), a collectible card game developed by Synapse Games

Figure 1.6   *Tyrant Unleashed*

CONSOLE (PLAYSTATION, XBOX, AND SWITCH)

Unity can even deploy to game consoles, although the developer must obtain licensing from Sony, Microsoft, or Nintendo. Because of this requirement and Unity's easy cross-platform deployment, console games are often available on desktop computers as well. Here are a couple of examples of console games in different genres:

- *Yooka-Laylee* (figure 1.7), a 3D platformer developed by Playtonic Games

Figure 1.7 *Yooka-Laylee*

- *Shadow Tactics* (figure 1.8), a stealth game developed by Mimimi Productions

Figure 1.8 *Shadow Tactics*

As you can see from these examples, Unity's strengths can definitely translate into commercial-quality games. But even with Unity's significant advantages over other game development tools, newcomers may misunderstand the involvement of programming in the development process. Unity is often portrayed as a list of features with no programming required, which is a misleading view that won't teach people what they need to know in order to produce commercial titles. Though it's true that you can click together a fairly elaborate prototype using pre-existing components even without a programmer being involved (which is itself a pretty big feat), rigorous programming is required to move beyond an interesting prototype to a polished game ready for release.

1.2   How to use Unity

The previous section talked a lot about the productivity benefits of Unity's visual editor, so let's go over what the interface looks like and how it operates. If you haven't done so, download the program from www.unity3d.com/ and install it on your computer (be sure to include Example Project if that's unchecked in the installer). After you install it, launch Unity to start exploring the interface.

You probably want an example to look at, so open the included example project; a new installation should open the example project automatically, but you can also select File > Open Project to open it manually. The example project is installed in the shared user directory, which is something like C:\Users\Public\Documents\Unity Projects\ on Windows, or Users/Shared/Unity/ on macOS. You may also need to open the example scene, so double-click the Car scene file (highlighted in figure 1.9; scene files have the Unity cube icon), which is found by going to SampleScenes/Scenes/ in the file browser at the bottom of the editor. You should see a screen similar to figure 1.9.

Scene and Game are tabs for viewing the 3D scene and playing the game, respectively.

The whole top area is the Toolbar. To the left are buttons for looking around and moving objects, and in the middle is the Play button.

The inspector fills the right side. This displays information about the currently selected object (a list of components mostly).

Hierarchy shows a text list of all objects in the scene, nested according to how they're linked together. Drag objects in the hierarchy to link them.

Project and Console are tabs for viewing all files in the project and messages from the code, respectively.

Navigate folders on the left, then double-click the Car example scene.

Figure 1.9   Parts of the interface in Unity

The interface in Unity is split into sections: the Scene tab, the Game tab, the Toolbar, the Hierarchy tab, the Inspector, the Project tab, and the Console tab. Each section has a different purpose, but all are crucial to the game building lifecycle.

- You can browse through all the files in the Project tab.
- You can place objects in the 3D scene being viewed using the Scene tab.
- The Toolbar has controls for working with the scene.
- You can drag and drop object relationships in the Hierarchy tab.
- The Inspector lists information about selected objects, including linked code.
- You can test playing in Game view while watching error output in the Console tab.

This is the default layout in Unity; all of the views are in tabs and can be moved around or resized, docking in different places on the screen. Later, you can play around with customizing the layout, but for now, the default layout is the best way to understand what all the views do.

1.2.1 Scene view, Game view, and the Toolbar

The most prominent part of the interface is the Scene view in the middle. This is where you can see what the game world looks like and move objects around. Mesh objects in the scene appear as, well, their mesh (defined in a moment). You can also see a number of other objects in the scene, represented by icons and colored lines: cameras, lights, audio sources, collision regions, and so forth. Note that the view you're seeing here isn't the same as the view in the running game—you're able to look around the scene at will without being constrained to the game's view.

> **DEFINITION** A *mesh object* is a visual object in 3D space. Visuals in 3D are constructed out of lots of connected lines and shapes; hence the word *mesh*.

The Game view isn't a separate part of the screen but rather another tab located right next to Scene (look for tabs at the top left of views). A couple of places in the interface have multiple tabs like this; if you click a different tab, the view is replaced by the new active tab. When the game is running, what you see in this view is the game. It isn't necessary to manually switch tabs every time you run the game, because the view automatically switches to Game when the game starts.

> **TIP** While the game is running, you can switch back to the Scene view, allowing you to inspect objects in the running scene. This capability is extremely useful for seeing what's going on while the game is running and is a helpful debugging tool that isn't available in most game engines.

Speaking of running the game, that's as simple as hitting the Play button just above the Scene view. That whole top section of the interface is referred to as the Toolbar, and Play is located right in the middle. Figure 1.10 breaks apart the full editor interface to show only the Toolbar at the top, as well as the Scene/Game tabs right underneath.

Figure 1.10   Editor screenshot cropped to show Toolbar, Scene, and Game

At the left-hand side of the Toolbar are buttons for scene navigation and transforming objects—how to look around the scene and how to move objects. I suggest you spend time practicing these, because they are two of the most important activities you'll do in Unity's visual editor. (They're so important that they get their own section following this one.) The right-hand side of the Toolbar is where you'll find drop-down menus for layouts and layers. As mentioned earlier, the layout of Unity's interface is flexible, so the Layouts menu allows you to switch between layouts. As for the Layers menu, that's advanced functionality that you can ignore for now (layers will be mentioned in future chapters).

1.2.2   *Using the mouse and keyboard*

Scene navigation is primarily done using the mouse, along with a few modifier keys used to modify what the mouse is doing. The three main navigation maneuvers are Move, Orbit, and Zoom. The specific mouse movements, because they vary depending on which mouse you're using, are described in appendix A. The three different movements involve clicking-and-dragging while holding down a combination of Alt (or Option on Mac) and Ctrl. Spend a few minutes moving around in the scene to understand what Move, Orbit, and Zoom do.

> **TIP**   Although Unity can be used with one- or two-button mice, I highly recommend getting a three-button mouse (and yes, a three-button mouse works fine on Mac OS X).

Transforming objects is also done through three main maneuvers, and the three scene navigation moves are analogous to the three transforms: Translate, Rotate, and Scale (figure 1.11 demonstrates the transforms on a cube).

Translate   Rotate   Scale

Figure 1.11   Applying the three transforms: Translate, Rotate, and Scale. (The lighter lines are the previous state of the object before it was transformed.)

When you select an object in the scene, you can then move it around (the mathematically accurate technical term is *translate*), rotate it, or scale how big it is. Relating back to scene navigation maneuvers, Move is when you Translate the camera, Orbit is when you Rotate the camera, and Zoom is when you Scale the camera. Besides the buttons on the Toolbar, you can switch between these functions by pressing W, E, or R on the keyboard. When you activate a transform, you'll notice that a set of color-coded arrows or circles appears over the object in the scene; this is the Transform gizmo, and you can click-and-drag this gizmo to apply the transformation.

There's a fourth tool next to the transform buttons. Called the Rect tool, it's designed for use with 2D graphics. This one tool combines movement, rotation, and scaling. These operations have to be separate tools in 3D but are combined in 2D because there's one less dimension to worry about. Unity has a host of other keyboard shortcuts for speeding up a variety of tasks. Refer to appendix A to learn about them. And with that, on to the remaining sections of the interface!

1.2.3   *The Hierarchy view and the Inspector panel*

Looking at either side of the screen, you'll see the Hierarchy tab on the left and the Inspector tab on the right (see figure 1.12). Hierarchy is a list view with the name of every object in the scene listed, with the names nested together according to their hierarchy linkages in the scene. Basically, it's a way of selecting objects by name instead of hunting them down and clicking them within Scene. The Hierarchy linkages group objects together, visually grouping them like folders and allowing you to move the entire group as one.

Figure 1.12   Editor screenshot cropped to show the Hierarchy and Inspector tabs

The Inspector shows you information about the currently selected object. Select an object and the Inspector is then filled with information about that object. The information shown is pretty much a list of components, and you can even attach or remove components from objects. All game objects have at least one component, Transform, so you'll always at least see information about positioning and rotation in the Inspector. Often, objects will have several components listed here, including scripts attached to them.

1.2.4   *The Project and Console tabs*

At the bottom of the screen, you'll see Project and Console (see figure 1.13). As with Scene and Game, these aren't two separate portions of the screen, but rather tabs that you can switch between. Project shows all the assets (art, code, and so on) in the project. Specifically, on the left-hand side of the view is a listing of the directories in the project; when you select a directory, the right side of the view shows the individual files in that directory. The directory listing in Project is similar to the list view in Hierarchy, but Hierarchy shows objects in the scene; Project shows files that may not be contained within any specific scene (including scene files—when you save a scene, it shows up in Project!).

Figure 1.13   Editor screenshot cropped to show the Project and Console tabs

TIP Project view mirrors the Assets directory on disk, but generally, you shouldn't move or delete files directly by going to the Assets folder. If you do those things within the Project view, Unity will keep in sync with that folder.

The Console is the place where messages from the code show up. Some of these messages will be debug output that you placed deliberately, but Unity also emits error messages if it encounters problems in the script you wrote.

1.3   *Getting up and running with Unity programming*

Now let's look at how the process of programming works in Unity. Although art assets can be laid out in the visual editor, you need to write code to control them and make the game interactive. Unity supports multiple programming languages, in particular JavaScript and C#. Both have their pros and cons, but you'll be using C# throughout this book.

Why choose C# over JavaScript?

All of the code listings in this book use C# because it has a number of advantages over JavaScript and fewer disadvantages, particularly for professional developers (it's certainly the language I use at work).

One benefit is that C# is strongly typed, whereas JavaScript is not. Now, there are lots of arguments among experienced programmers about whether or not dynamic typing is a better approach for, say, web development, but programming for certain gaming platforms (such as iOS) often benefits from or even requires static typing. Unity has even added the directive #pragma strict to force static typing within JavaScript. Technically this works, but it breaks one of the bedrock principles of how JavaScript operates, and if you're going to do that, then you're better off using a language that's intrinsically strongly typed.

This is just one example of how JavaScript within Unity isn't quite the same as JavaScript elsewhere. JavaScript in Unity is certainly similar to JavaScript in web browsers, but there are lots of differences in how the language works in each context. Many developers refer to the language in Unity as UnityScript, a name that indicates similarity to but separateness from JavaScript. This similar-but-different state can create issues for programmers,

> *(continued)*
>
> both in terms of bringing in knowledge about JavaScript from outside Unity, and in terms of applying programming knowledge gained by working in Unity.
>
> Meanwhile, for these reasons, Unity is in the process of removing JavaScript/UnityScript support. As explained on its blog, the support is gradually being phased out: http://mng .bz/B9au.

Let's walk through an example of writing and running some code. Launch Unity and create a new project; choose New in Unity's starting window, or File > New Project if Unity was already running. Type a name for the project, leave the default 3D setting (future chapters will mention 2D), and then choose where you want to save it. A Unity project is simply a directory full of various asset and settings files, so save the project anywhere on your computer. Click Create Project and then Unity will briefly disappear while it sets up the project directory.

> **WARNING** Unity projects remember which version of Unity they were created in and will issue a warning if you attempt to open them in a different version. Sometimes it doesn't matter (for example, ignore the warning if it appears while opening this book's sample downloads), but sometimes you will want to back up your project before opening it.

> **WARNING** Along similar lines, Unity may emit the following message when you open the sample downloads: Rebuilding Library because the asset database could not be found! This literally refers to the project's Library folder; that folder contains files generated by Unity and used while working, but it is not necessary to distribute those files.

When Unity reappears, you'll be looking at a blank project. Next, let's discuss how programs get executed in Unity.

1.3.1   How code runs in Unity: script components

All code execution in Unity starts from code files linked to an object in the scene. Ultimately, it's all part of the component system described earlier; game objects are built up as a collection of components, and that collection can include scripts to execute.

> **NOTE** Unity refers to the code files as scripts, using a definition of "script" that's most commonly encountered with JavaScript running in a browser: the code is executed within the Unity game engine, as opposed to compiled code that runs as its own executable. But don't get confused, because many people define the word differently; for example, "scripts" often refer to short, self-contained utility programs. Scripts in Unity are more akin to individual OOP classes, and scripts attached to objects in the scene are object instances.

As you've probably surmised from this description, in Unity, scripts *are* components—not all scripts, mind you, only scripts that inherit from MonoBehaviour, the base class for script components. `MonoBehaviour` defines the invisible groundwork for how components attach to game objects, and (as shown in listing 1.1) inheriting from it provides a couple of automatically run methods that you can implement. Those methods include `Start()`, called once when the object becomes active (which is generally as soon as the level with that object has loaded), and `Update()`, which is called every frame. Your code is run when you put it inside these predefined methods.

> **DEFINITION** A *frame* is a single cycle of the looping game code. Nearly all video games (not only in Unity, but video games in general) are built around a core game loop, where the code executes in a cycle while the game is running. Each cycle includes drawing the screen; hence the name *frame* (like the series of still frames of a movie).

Listing 1.1 Code template for a basic script component

```
using UnityEngine;                                  Include namespaces for Unity
using System.Collections;                           and Mono classes.
using System.Collections.Generic;

public class HelloWorld : MonoBehaviour {           The syntax for inheritance
    void Start() {
        // do something once                        Put code in here that runs once.
    }

    void Update() {
        // do something every frame                 Put code in here that runs every frame.
    }
}
```

This is what the file contains when you create a new C# script: the minimal boilerplate code that defines a valid Unity component. Unity has a script template tucked away in the bowels of the application, and when you create a new script it copies that template and renames the class to match the name of the file (which is HelloWorld.cs in my case). There are also empty shells for `Start()` and `Update()`, because those are the two most common places to call your custom code from.

To create a script, select C# Script from the Create menu, which you access either under the Assets menu (note that Assets and GameObjects both have listings for Create but they're different menus) or by right-clicking in the Project view. Type in a name for the new script, such as HelloWorld. As explained later in the chapter (see figure 1.15), you'll click-and-drag this script file onto an object in the scene. Double-click the script and it'll automatically be opened in another program for editing, as discussed next.

1.3.2 *Using MonoDevelop, the cross-platform IDE*

Programming isn't done within Unity exactly, but rather code exists as separate files that you point Unity to. Script files can be created within Unity, but you still need to use a text editor or IDE to write all the code within those initially empty files. Unity comes bundled with MonoDevelop, an open source, cross-platform IDE for C# (figure 1.14 shows what it looks like). You can visit www.monodevelop.com/ to learn more about this software, but the version to use is the version bundled along with Unity, rather than a version downloaded from its website, because some modifications were made to the base software in order to better integrate it with Unity.

Don't hit the Run button within MonoDevelop; hit Play in Unity to run the code.

Document Outline may not be showing by default. Select it under View > Pads and then drag the tab to where you want it.

Script files open as tabs in the main viewing area. Multiple script files can be open at once.

Solution view shows all script files in the project.

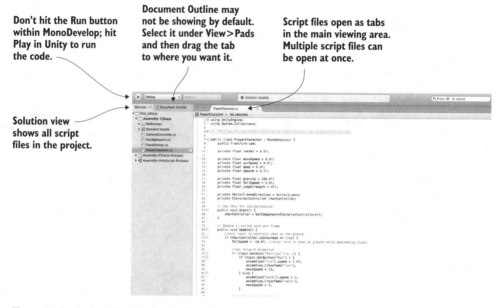

Figure 1.14   Parts of the interface in MonoDevelop

NOTE MonoDevelop organizes files into groupings called a *solution*. Unity automatically generates a solution that has all the script files, so you usually don't need to worry about that.

Because C# originated as a Microsoft product, you may be wondering whether you can use Visual Studio to do programming for Unity. The short answer is yes, you can. Support tools are available for using Visual Studio with Unity (particularly so that debugging and breakpoints work properly). To see if this support is already installed, check the Debug menu for the option Attach Unity Debugger. If it isn't installed, simply run the Visual Studio Installer to modify your install and look for the Unity game development module.

I generally use MonoDevelop, but if you're already using Visual Studio to do programming, then you could keep using it and not have any problems following along with this book. (Beyond this introductory chapter, I'm not going to talk about the IDE.) Tying your workflow to Windows, though, would run counter to one of the biggest advantages of using Unity. Although C# originated as a Microsoft product, and thus

only worked on Windows with the .NET Framework, C# has now become an open language standard and there's a significant cross-platform framework: Mono. Unity uses
Mono for its programming backbone, and using MonoDevelop allows you to keep the
entire development workflow cross-platform.

> **WARNING** MonoDevelop is the IDE bundled with Unity 2017.1, but as
> explained on Unity's blog http://mng.bz/9HR8, this will be changed in
> Unity 2018.1.

Always keep in mind that, although the code is written in Visual Studio or MonoDevelop, the code isn't run there. The IDE is pretty much a fancy text editor, and the
code is run when you hit Play within Unity.

1.3.3 Printing to the console: Hello World!

All right, you already have an empty script in the project, but you also need an object
in the scene to attach the script to. Recall figure 1.1 depicting how a component system
works; a script is a component, so it needs to be set as one of the components on an
object.

Select GameObject > Create Empty, and a blank GameObject will appear in the Hierarchy list. Now drag the script from the Project view over to the Hierarchy view and drop
it on the empty GameObject. As shown in figure 1.15, Unity will highlight valid places to
drop the script, and dropping it on the GameObject will attach the script to that object.
To verify that the script is attached to the object, select the object and look at the Inspector view. You should see two components listed: the Transform component, which is the
basic position/rotation/scale component all objects have and which can't be removed,
and below that, your script.

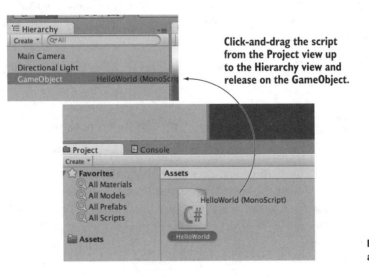

Click-and-drag the script
from the Project view up
to the Hierarchy view and
release on the GameObject.

**Figure 1.15   How to link
a script to a GameObject**

NOTE   Eventually, this action of dragging objects from one place and dropping them on other objects will feel routine. A lot of different linkages in Unity are created by dragging things on top of each other, not only attaching scripts to objects.

When a script is linked to an object, you'll see something like figure 1.16, with the script showing up as a component in the Inspector. Now the script will execute when you play the scene, although nothing is going to happen yet, because you haven't written any code. Let's do that next!

Figure 1.16   Linked script being displayed in the Inspector

Open the script in MonoDevelop to get back to listing 1.1. The classic place to start when learning a new programming environment is having it print the text "Hello World!", so add this line inside the Start() method.

> **Listing 1.2   Adding a console message**

```
...
void Start() {
    Debug.Log("Hello World!");          ◄—— Add the logging command here.
}
...
```

What the Debug.Log() command does is print a message to the Console view in Unity. Meanwhile, that line goes in the Start() method because, as was explained earlier, that method is called as soon as the object becomes active. Start() will be called once, as soon as you hit Play in the editor. Once you've added the log command to your script (be sure to save the script), hit Play in Unity and switch to the Console view. You'll see the message "Hello World!" appear. Congratulations, you've written your first Unity script! Of course, the code will be more elaborate in later chapters, but this is an important first step.

"Hello World!" steps in brief

Let's reiterate and summarize the steps from the last few pages:

1. Create a new project.

2. Create a new C# script.

3. Create an empty GameObject.

4. Drag the script onto the object.

5. Add the log command to the script.

6. Press Play!

You could now save the scene; that would create a .unity file with the Unity icon. The scene file is a snapshot of everything currently loaded in the game so that you can reload this scene later. It's hardly worth saving this scene because it's so simple (a single empty GameObject), but if you don't save the scene, then you'll find it empty again when you come back to the project after quitting Unity.

Errors in the script

To see how Unity indicates errors, purposely put a typo in the HelloWorld script. For example, if you type an extra parenthesis symbol, an error message will appear in the Console with a red error icon.

Summary

- Unity is a multiplatform development tool.
- Unity's visual editor has several sections that work in concert.
- Scripts are attached to objects as components.
- Code is written inside scripts using MonoDevelop.

Building a demo that puts you in 3D space

This chapter covers

- Understanding 3D coordinate space
- Putting a player in a scene
- Writing a script that moves objects
- Implementing FPS controls

Chapter 1 concluded with the traditional "Hello World!" introduction to a new programming tool; now it's time to dive into a nontrivial Unity project, a project with interactivity and graphics. You'll put some objects into a scene and write code to enable a player to walk around that scene. Basically, it'll be *Doom* without the monsters (something like what figure 2.1 depicts). The visual editor in Unity enables new users to start assembling a 3D prototype right away, without needing to write a lot of boilerplate code first (for things like initializing a 3D view or establishing a rendering loop).

It's tempting to immediately start building the scene in Unity, especially with such a simple (in concept!) project. But it's always a good idea to pause at the beginning and plan out what you're going to do, and this is especially important right now because you're new to the process.

Figure 2.1 Screenshot of the 3D demo (basically, *Doom* without the monsters)

NOTE Remember, the project for this (and all chapters) can be downloaded from the book's website. Open the project in Unity, then open Scene to run it. While you're learning, I recommend you type out all the code yourself and only use the downloaded sample for reference. The website's address is www. manning.com/books/unity-in-action-second-edition.

2.1 Before you start ...

Unity makes it easy for a newcomer to get started, but let's go over a couple of points before you build the complete scene. Even when working with a tool as flexible as Unity, you do need to have some sense of the goal you're working toward. You also need a grasp of how 3D coordinates operate, or you could get lost as soon as you try to position an object in the scene.

2.1.1 Planning the project

Before you start programming anything, you always want to pause and ask yourself, "So what am I building here?" Game design is a huge topic in itself, with many impressively large books focused on how to design a game. Fortunately for our purposes, you only need a brief outline of this simple demo in mind in order to develop a basic learning project. These initial projects won't be terribly complex designs anyway, in order to avoid distracting you from learning programming concepts; you can (and should!) worry about higher-level design issues after you've mastered the fundamentals of game development.

For this first project, you'll build a basic FPS (first-person shooter) scene. There will be a room to navigate around, players will see the world from their character's point of view, and the player can control the character using the mouse and keyboard. All the interesting complexity of a complete game can be stripped away for now in order to concentrate on the core mechanic: moving around in a 3D space. Figure 2.2 depicts the roadmap for this project, laying out the checklist I built in my head:

1 Set up the room: create the floor, outer walls, and inner walls.
2 Place the lights and camera.
3 Create the player object (including attaching the camera on top).
4 Write movement scripts: rotate with the mouse and move with the keyboard.

1. Set up the boundaries of the room. First create the floor, then the outer walls, and then place the inner walls.

2. Players need to be able to see the room. Put some lights around the room, and place the camera that will be the player's view.

3. Create the primitive shape for the player. Attach the camera to the top of this, so that as this object moves the camera moves with it.

4. Write movement scripts for the player. First write code to rotate with the mouse, then write code to move with keyboard.

Figure 2.2   Roadmap for the 3D demo

Don't be scared off by everything in this roadmap! It sounds like there's a lot in this chapter, but Unity makes it easy. The upcoming sections about movement scripts are so extensive only because we'll be going through every line in order to understand all the concepts in detail. This project is a first-person demo in order to keep the art requirements simple; because you can't see yourself, it's fine for "you" to be a cylindrical shape with a camera on top! Now you only need to understand how 3D coordinates work, and it will be easy to place everything in the visual editor.

2.1.2   Understanding 3D coordinate space

If you think about the simple plan we're starting with, there are three aspects to it: a room, a view, and controls. All of these items rely on you understanding how positions and movements are represented in 3D computer simulations, and if you're new to working with 3D graphics you might not already know that stuff.

It all boils down to numbers that indicate points in space, and the way those numbers correlate to the space is through coordinate axes. If you think back to math class, you've probably seen and used X- and Y-axes (see figure 2.3) for assigning coordinates to points on the page, which is referred to as a Cartesian coordinate system.

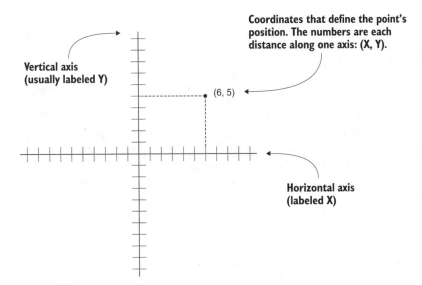

Coordinates that define the point's position. The numbers are each distance along one axis: (X, Y).

Vertical axis (usually labeled Y)

(6, 5)

Horizontal axis (labeled X)

Figure 2.3   Coordinates along the X- and Y-axes define a 2D point.

Two axes give you 2D coordinates, with all points in the same plane. Three axes are used to define 3D space. Because the X-axis goes along the page horizontally and the Y-axis goes along the page vertically, we now imagine a third axis that sticks straight into and out of the page, perpendicular to both the X- and Y- axes. Figure 2.4 depicts the X-, Y-, and Z-axes for 3D coordinate space. Everything that has a specific position in the scene will have XYZ coordinates: the position of the player, the placement of a wall, and so forth.

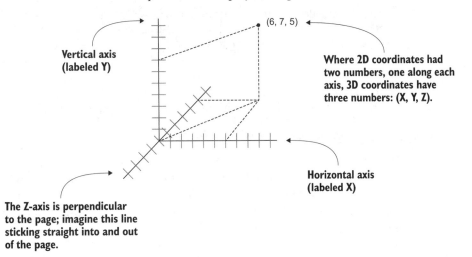

Vertical axis (labeled Y)

(6, 7, 5)

Where 2D coordinates had two numbers, one along each axis, 3D coordinates have three numbers: (X, Y, Z).

Horizontal axis (labeled X)

The Z-axis is perpendicular to the page; imagine this line sticking straight into and out of the page.

Figure 2.4   Coordinates along the X-, Y-, and Z-axes define a 3D point.

In Unity's Scene view, you can see these three axes displayed, and in the Inspector you can type in the three numbers required to position an object. Not only will you write code to position objects using these three-number coordinates, but you can also define movements as a distance to move along each axis.

Left-handed vs. right-handed coordinates

The positive and negative direction of each axis is arbitrary, and the coordinates still work no matter in which direction the axes point. You simply need to maintain consistency within a given 3D graphics tool (animation tool, game development tool, and so forth).

But in almost all cases, X goes to the right and Y goes up; what differs between different tools is whether Z goes into or comes out of the page. These two directions are referred to as "left-handed" or "right-handed"; as this figure shows, if you point your thumb along the X-axis and your index finger along the Y-axis, then your middle finger points along the Z-axis.

The Z-axis points in a different direction on the left hand versus the right hand.

Unity uses a left-handed coordinate system, as do many 3D art applications. Many other tools use right-handed coordinate systems (OpenGL, for example), so don't get confused if you ever see different coordinate directions.

Now that you have a plan in mind for this project and you know how coordinates are used to position objects in 3D space, it's time to start building the scene.

2.2   *Begin the project: place objects in the scene*

Let's create and place objects in the scene. First, you'll set up all the static scenery—the floor and walls. Then you'll place lights around the scene and position the camera. Lastly, you'll create the object that will be the player, the object to which you'll attach scripts to walk around the scene. Figure 2.5 shows what the editor will look like with everything in place.

Lights—Both directional and point lights are in this scene.

Camera view— The camera object is located right on top of the player; these angled white lines indicate the camera's field of view.

Player—This is a basic capsule object.

Figure 2.5   Scene in the Editor with floor, walls, lights, a camera, and the player

Chapter 1 showed how to create a new project in Unity, so you'll do that now. Remember: Choose New (or File > New Project) and then name your new project in the window that pops up. After creating the new project, immediately save the current empty default scene, because the project doesn't have any Scene files initially. The scene starts out empty, and the first objects to create are the most obvious ones.

2.2.1   *The scenery: floor, outer walls, and inner walls*

Select the GameObject menu at the top of the screen, and then hover over 3D Object to see that drop-down menu. Select Cube to create a new cube object in the scene (later, we'll use other shapes, like Sphere and Capsule). Adjust the position and scale of this object, as well as its name, in order to make the floor; figure 2.6 shows which values the floor should be set to in the Inspector (it's only a cube initially, before you stretch it out).

> **NOTE** The numbers for position can be any units you want, as long as you're consistent throughout the scene. The most common choice for units is meters, and that's what I generally choose, but I also use feet sometimes, and I've even seen other people decide that the numbers are inches!

Repeat the same steps in order to create outer walls for the room. You can create new cubes each time, or you can copy and paste existing objects using the standard shortcuts. Move, rotate, and scale the walls to form a perimeter around the floor. Experiment with different numbers (for example, 1, 4, 50 for scale) or use the transform tools first seen in section 1.2.2 (remember that the mathematical term for moving and rotating in 3D space is *transform*).

At the top you can type
in a name for the object.
For example, call the
floor object "Floor."

Position and scale the
cube in order to create
a floor for the room. Or
rather "cube," since it
won't look like a cube
anymore after being
stretched out with
differing scale values
on different axes.

Meanwhile the position
is lowered very slightly
to compensate for the
height; we set the Y scale
to 1, and the object is
positioned around
its center.

The remaining components
filling the view come with a
new Cube object but don't
need to be adjusted right
now. These components
include a Mesh Filter (to
define the geometry of the
object), a Mesh Renderer
(to define the material on the
object), and a Box Collider (so
that the object can be collided
with during movement).

Figure 2.6   Inspector view for the floor

TIP   Recall the navigation controls to view the scene from different angles or
zoom out for a bird's-eye view. If you ever get lost in the scene, press F to reset
the view on the currently selected object.

The exact transform values the walls end up with will vary depending on how you rotate
and scale the cubes to fit, and on how the objects are linked together in the Hierarchy
view. For example, in figure 2.7 the walls are all children of an empty root object, so
that the Hierarchy list will look organized. If you need an example to copy working values from, download the sample project and refer to the walls there.

**Figure 2.7   The Hierarchy view showing the walls and floor organized
under an empty object**

TIP Drag objects on top of each other in the Hierarchy view to establish link-ages. Objects that have other objects attached are referred to as *parents*; objects attached to other objects are referred to as *children*. When the parent object is moved (or rotated or scaled), the child objects are transformed along with it.

TIP Empty game objects can be used to organize the scene in this way. By link-ing visible objects to a root object, their Hierarchy list can be collapsed. Be warned: before linking any child objects to it, you need to reset the transform (position and rotation 0 0 0, scale 1 1 1) of the empty root object to avoid any positioning oddities later.

What is GameObject?

All scene objects are instances of the `GameObject` class, similar to how all script compo-nents inherit from the `MonoBehaviour` class. This fact was more explicit with the empty object actually named `GameObject`, but is still true regardless of whether the object is named `Floor`, `Camera`, or `Player`.

`GameObject` is really a container for a bunch of components. The main purpose of `Game-Object` is so that `MonoBehaviour` has something to attach to. What exactly the object is in the scene depends on what components have been added to that `GameObject`. `Cube` objects have a Cube component, `Sphere` objects have a Sphere component, and so on.

Once the outer walls are in place, create some inner walls to navigate around. Position the inner walls however you like; the idea is to create some hallways and obstacles to walk around once you write code for movement.

Now the scene has a room in it, but we still need to set up the lighting. Let's take care of that next.

2.2.2 Lights and cameras

Typically, you light a 3D scene with a directional light and then a series of point lights. Start with a directional light; the scene probably already has one by default, but if not, then create one by choosing GameObject > Light and selecting Directional Light.

Types of lights

You can create several types of light sources, defined by how and where they project light rays. The three main types are point, spot, and directional.

Point lights are a kind of light source where all the light rays originate from a single point and project out in all directions, like a lightbulb in the real world. The light is brighter up close because the light rays are bunched up.

Spot lights are a kind of light source where all the light rays originate from a single point but only project out in a limited cone. No spot lights are used in the current project, but these lights are commonly used to highlight parts of a level.

Directional lights are a kind of light source where all the light rays are parallel and project evenly, lighting everything in the scene the same way. This is like the sun in the real world.

The position of a directional light doesn't affect the light cast from it, only the rotation the light source is facing, so technically, you could place that light anywhere in the scene. I recommend placing it high above the room so that it intuitively feels like the sun and so that it's out of the way when you're manipulating the rest of the scene. Rotate this light and watch the effect on the room; I recommend rotating it slightly on both the X- and Y-axes to get a good effect. You will see an Intensity setting when you look in the Inspector (see figure 2.8). As the name implies, that setting controls the brightness of the light. If this were the only light, it'd have to be more intense, but because you'll add a bunch of point lights as well, this directional light can be pretty dim, like 0.6 Intensity.

The remaining settings don't need to be adjusted right now. These settings include the color of the light, shadows cast by the light, and even a silhouette projection (think of the Bat signal).

Here is where you control the light's brightness, from 0 for completely dark.

Figure 2.8 Directional light settings in the Inspector

As for point lights, create several using the same menu and place them in dark spots around the room in order to make sure all the walls are lit. You don't want too many (performance will degrade if the game has lots of lights), but one near each corner should be fine (I suggest raising them to the tops of the walls), plus one placed high above the scene (like a Y of 18) to give variety to the light in the room. Note that point lights have a setting for Range added to the Inspector (see figure 2.9). This controls how far away the light reaches; whereas directional lights cast light evenly throughout the entire scene, point lights are brighter when an object is closer. The point lights closer to the floor should have a range of around 18, but the light placed high up should have a range of around 40 in order to reach the entire room.

Other than Range, the settings for point lights are the same as for directional lights.

Here is where you control light range, with the same units as position and scale.

(If you see an error about "realtime not supported," just ignore it or switch Baking to Mixed.)

Figure 2.9 Point light settings in the Inspector

The other kind of object needed in order for the player to see the scene is a camera, but the "empty" scene came with a main camera, so you'll use that. If you ever need to create new cameras (such as for split screen views in multiplayer games), Camera is another choice in the same GameObject menu as Cube and Lights. The camera will be positioned around the top of the player so that the view appears to be the player's eyes.

2.2.3   *The player's collider and viewpoint*

For this project, a simple primitive shape will do to represent the player. In the GameObject menu (remember, hover over 3D Object to expand the menu), click Capsule. Unity creates a cylindrical shape with rounded ends; this primitive shape will represent the player. Position this object at 1.1 on the Y-axis (half the height of the object, plus a bit to avoid overlapping the floor). You can move the object along X and Z wherever you like, as long as it's inside the room and not touching any walls. Name the object Player.

In the Inspector, you'll notice that this object has a capsule collider assigned to it. That's a logical default choice for a capsule object, just like cube objects had a box collider by default. But this particular object will be the player and thus needs a slightly different sort of component than most objects. Remove the capsule collider by clicking the gear icon toward the top-right of that component, shown in figure 2.10; that will display a menu that includes the option Remove Component. The collider is a green mesh surrounding the object, so you'll see the green mesh disappear after deleting the capsule collider.

Figure 2.10   Removing a component in the Inspector

Instead of a capsule collider, we're going to assign a character controller to this object. At the bottom of the Inspector, there's a button labeled Add Component; click that button to open a menu of components that you can add. In the Physics section of this menu, you'll find Character Controller; select that option. As the name implies, this component will allow the object to behave like a character.

You need to complete one last step to set up the player object: attaching the camera. As mentioned in the earlier section on floors and walls, objects can be dragged onto each other in the Hierarchy view. Drag the camera object onto the player capsule to attach the camera to the player. Now position the camera so that it'll look like the player's eyes (I suggest a position of 0, 0.5, 0). If necessary, reset the camera's rotation to 0, 0, 0 (this will be off if you've rotated the capsule).

You've created all the objects needed for this scene. What remains is writing code to move the player object.

2.3 Making things move: a script that applies transforms

To have the player walk around the scene, you'll write movement scripts attached to the player. Remember, components are modular bits of functionality that you add to objects, and scripts are a kind of component. Eventually, those scripts will respond to keyboard and mouse input, but first you'll make the player spin in place. This modest beginning will teach you how to apply transforms in code. Remember that the three transforms are Translate, Rotate, and Scale; spinning an object means changing the rotation. But there's more to know about this task than only "this involves rotation."

2.3.1 Visualizing how movement is programmed

Animating an object (such as making it spin) boils down to moving it a small amount every frame, with the frames playing over and over. By themselves, transforms apply instantly, as opposed to visibly moving over time. But applying the transforms over and over causes the object to visibly move, like a series of still drawings in a flipbook. Figure 2.11 illustrates how this works.

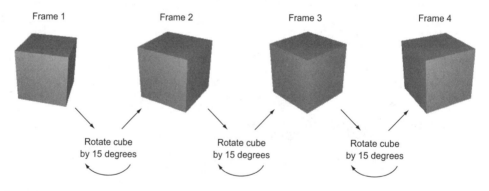

Figure 2.11   The appearance of movement: cyclical process of transforming between still pictures

Recall that script components have an Update() method that runs every frame. To spin the cube, add code inside Update() that rotates the cube a small amount. This code will run over and over every frame. Sounds pretty simple, right?

2.3.2 Writing code to implement the diagram

Now let's put in action the concepts we've just discussed. Create a new C# script (remember, it's in the Create submenu of the Assets menu), name it Spin, and write in this code (don't forget to save the file after typing in it!).

Listing 2.1 Making the object spin

```
using UnityEngine;
using System.Collections;
public class Spin : MonoBehaviour {          Declare a public variable
    public float speed = 3.0f;               for the speed of rotation.

    void Update() {                          Put the Rotate command here so that it
        transform.Rotate(0, speed, 0);       runs every frame.
    }
}
```

To add the script component to the player object, drag the script up from the Project view and drop it onto Player in the Hierarchy view. Now hit Play, and you'll see the view spin around; you've written code to make an object move! This code is pretty much the default template for a new script plus two new added lines, so let's examine what those two lines do.

First, there's the variable for speed added toward the top of the class definition (the f after the number tells the computer to treat this as a float value; otherwise, C# treats decimal numbers as a double). The rotation speed is defined as a variable rather than a constant because Unity does something handy with public variables in script components, as described in the following tip:

> **TIP** Public variables are exposed in the Inspector so that you can adjust the component's values after adding a component to a game object. This is referred to as *serializing* the value, because Unity saves the modified state of the variable.

Figure 2.12 shows what the script component looks like in the Inspector. You can type in a new number, and then the script will use that value instead of the default value defined in the code. This is a handy way to adjust settings for the component on different objects, working within the visual editor instead of hardcoding every value.

Figure 2.12 The Inspector displaying a public variable declared in the script

The second line to examine from listing 2.1 is the `Rotate()` method. That's inside `Update()` so that the command runs every frame. `Rotate()` is a method of the Transform class, so it's called with dot notation through the transform component of this object (as in most object-oriented languages, `this.transform` is implied if you type `transform`). The transform is rotated by `speed` degrees every frame, resulting in a smooth spinning movement. But why are the parameters to `Rotate()` listed as `(0, speed, 0)` as opposed to, say, `(speed, 0, 0)`?

Recall that there are three axes in 3D space, labeled X, Y, and Z. It's fairly intuitive to understand how these axes relate to positions and movements, but these axes can also be used to describe rotations. Aeronautics describes rotations in a similar way, so programmers working with 3D graphics often use a set of terms borrowed from aeronautics: pitch, yaw, and roll. Figure 2.13 illustrates what these terms mean; pitch is rotation around the X-axis, yaw is rotation around the Y-axis, and roll is rotation around the Z-axis.

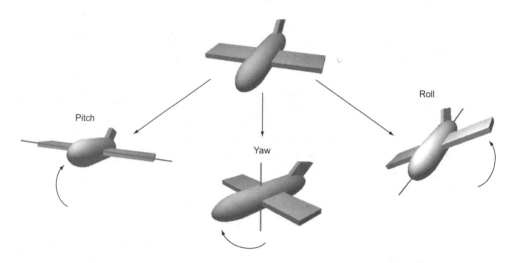

Figure 2.13   Illustration of pitch, yaw, and roll rotation of an aircraft

Given that we can describe rotations around the X-, Y-, and Z-axes, that means the three parameters for `Rotate()` are X, Y, and Z rotation. Because we only want the player to spin around sideways, as opposed to tilting up and down, there should only be a number given for the Y rotation, and 0 for X and Z rotation. Hopefully you can guess what will happen if you change the parameters to (`speed, 0, 0`) and then play it. Try that now!

There's one other subtle point to understand about rotations and 3D coordinate axes, embodied in an optional fourth parameter to the `Rotate()` method.

2.3.3   *Local vs. global coordinate space*

By default, the `Rotate()` method operates on what are called local coordinates. The other kind of coordinates you could use are global. You tell the method whether to use local or global coordinates using an optional fourth parameter by writing either `Space.Self` or `Space.World` like so:

```
Rotate(0, speed, 0, Space.World)
```

Refer to the explanation about 3D coordinate space earlier in this chapter, and ponder these questions: Where is (0, 0, 0) located? Which direction is the X-axis pointing in? Can the coordinate system itself move around?

It turns out that every single object has its own origin point, as well as its own direction for the three axes, and this coordinate system moves around with the object. This is referred to as local coordinates. The overall 3D scene also has its own origin point and its own direction for the three axes, and this coordinate system never moves. This is referred to as global coordinates. Therefore, when you specify local or global for the `Rotate()` method, you're telling it whose X-, Y-, and Z-axes to rotate around (see figure 2.14).

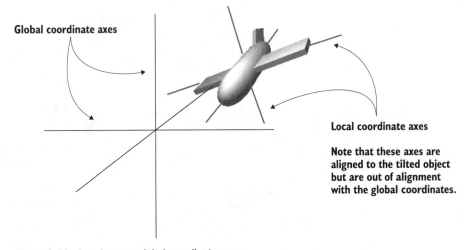

Global coordinate axes

Local coordinate axes

Note that these axes are aligned to the tilted object but are out of alignment with the global coordinates.

Figure 2.14   Local versus global coordinate axes

If you're new to 3D graphics, this is somewhat of a mind-bending concept. The different axes are depicted in figure 2.14 (notice how "left" to the plane is a different direction than "left" to the world), but the easiest way to understand local and global is through an example.

Select the player object and then tilt it a bit (something like 30 for the X rotation). This will throw off the local coordinates so that local and global rotations will look different. Now try running the Spin script both with and without `Space.World` added to the parameters; if it's too hard for you to visualize what's happening, try removing the spin component from the player object and instead spin a tilted cube placed in front of the player. You'll see the object rotating around different axes when you set the command to local or global coordinates.

2.4   *Script component for looking around: MouseLook*

Now you'll make rotation respond to input from the mouse (that is, rotation of the object this script is attached to, which in this case will be the player). You'll do this in several steps, progressively adding new movement abilities to the character. First, the player will only rotate side to side, and then the player will only rotate up and down. Eventually, the player will be able to look around in all directions (rotating horizontally and vertically at the same time), a behavior referred to as *mouse-look*.

Given that there will be three different types of rotation behavior (horizontal, vertical, and both), you'll start by writing the framework for supporting all three. Create a new C# script, name it MouseLook, and write in this code.

Listing 2.2 **MouseLook framework with enum for the Rotation setting**

```csharp
using UnityEngine;
using System.Collections;
public class MouseLook : MonoBehaviour {          Define an enum data structure
  public enum RotationAxes {                        to associate names with settings.
    MouseXAndY = 0,
    MouseX = 1,
    MouseY = 2
  }                                                 Declare a public variable
  public RotationAxes axes = RotationAxes.MouseXAndY;   to set in Unity's editor.

  void Update() {
    if (axes == RotationAxes.MouseX) {              Put code here for
      // horizontal rotation here                   horizontal rotation only.
    }
    else if (axes == RotationAxes.MouseY) {         Put code here for
      // vertical rotation here                     vertical rotation only.
    }
    else {                                          Put code here for both
      // both horizontal and vertical rotation here  horizontal and vertical rotation.
    }
  }
}
```

Notice that an enum is used to choose horizontal or vertical rotation for the MouseLook script. Defining an enum data structure allows you to set values by name, rather than typing in numbers and trying to remember what each number means (is 0 horizontal rotation? Is it 1?). If you then declare a public variable typed to that enum, that will display in the Inspector as a drop-down menu (see figure 2.15), which is useful for selecting settings.

Figure 2.15 **The Inspector displays public enum variables as a drop-down menu.**

Remove the Spin component (the same way you removed the capsule collider earlier) and attach this new script to the player object instead. Use the Axes drop-down menu in the Inspector to switch the direction of rotation. With the horizontal/vertical rotation setting in place, you can fill in code for each branch of the conditional statement.

2.4.1 *Horizontal rotation that tracks mouse movement*

The first and simplest branch is horizontal rotation. Start by writing the same rotation command you used in listing 2.1 to make the object spin. Don't forget to declare a public variable for the rotation speed; declare the new variable after axes but before

Update(), and call the variable sensitivityHor because speed is too generic a name once you have multiple rotations involved. Increase the value of the variable to 9 this time, because that value needs to be bigger once the code starts scaling it (which will be soon). The adjusted code should look like this.

Listing 2.3   Horizontal rotation, not yet responding to the mouse

```
...
public RotationAxes axes = RotationAxes.MouseXAndY;       ◄── Italicized code was already in
                                                              script; it's shown here for reference.
public float sensitivityHor = 9.0f;       ◄── Declare a variable for
                                              the speed of rotation.

void Update() {
  if (axes == RotationAxes.MouseX) {
    transform.Rotate(0, sensitivityHor, 0);       ◄── Put the Rotate command here
  }                                                   so that it runs every frame.
...
```

Set the Axes menu of the MouseLook component to horizontal rotation and play the script; the view will spin as before. The next step is to make the rotation react to mouse movement, so let's introduce a new method: Input.GetAxis(). The Input class has a bunch of methods for handling input devices (such as the mouse) and the GetAxis() method returns numbers correlated to the movement of the mouse (positive or negative, depending on the direction of movement). GetAxis() takes the name of the axis desired as a parameter, and the horizontal axis is called Mouse X.

If you multiply the rotation speed by the axis value, the rotation will respond to mouse movement. The speed will scale according to mouse movement, scaling down to zero or even reversing direction. The Rotate command now looks like this.

Listing 2.4   Rotate command adjusted to respond to the mouse

```
...
transform.Rotate(0, Input.GetAxis("Mouse X") * sensitivityHor, 0);       ◄──
...
                                                          Note the use of GetAxis()
                                                          to get mouse input.
```

Hit Play and then move the mouse around. As you move the mouse from side to side, the view will rotate from side to side. That's pretty cool! The next step is to rotate vertically instead of horizontally.

2.4.2   Vertical rotation with limits

For horizontal rotation we've been using the Rotate() method, but we'll take a different approach with vertical rotation. Although that method is convenient for applying transforms, it's also kind of inflexible. It's only useful for incrementing the rotation without limit, which was fine for horizontal rotation, but vertical rotation needs limits on how much the view can tilt up or down. This listing shows the vertical rotation code for MouseLook; a detailed explanation of the code will immediately follow.

Listing 2.5   Vertical rotation for `MouseLook`

```
...
public float sensitivityHor = 9.0f;           ─── Declare variables used
public float sensitivityVert = 9.0f;              for vertical rotation.

public float minimumVert = -45.0f;
public float maximumVert = 45.0f;
                                              ─── Declare a private variable
private float _rotationX = 0;                     for the vertical angle.

                                                         Increment the
void Update() {                                          vertical angle based
  if (axes == RotationAxes.MouseX) {                     on the mouse.
    transform.Rotate(0, Input.GetAxis("Mouse X") * sensitivityHor, 0);
  }
  else if (axes == RotationAxes.MouseY) {
    _rotationX -= Input.GetAxis("Mouse Y") * sensitivityVert;  ◄───
    _rotationX = Mathf.Clamp(_rotationX, minimumVert, maximumVert);

    float rotationY = transform.localEulerAngles.y;

    transform.localEulerAngles = new Vector3(_rotationX, rotationY, 0); ◄─
  }
...
```

Clamp the vertical angle between minimum and maximum limits.

Keep the same Y angle (i.e., no horizontal rotation).

Create a new vector from the stored rotation values.

Set the Axes menu of the `MouseLook` component to vertical rotation and play the new script. Now the view won't rotate sideways, but it'll tilt up and down when you move the mouse up and down. The tilt stops at upper and lower limits.

There are several new concepts in this code that need to be explained. First off, we're not using `Rotate()` this time, so we need a variable (called `_rotationX` here, because vertical rotation goes around the X-axis) in which to store the rotation angle. The `Rotate()` method increments the current rotation, whereas this code sets the rotation angle directly. It's the difference between saying "add 5 to the angle" and "set the angle to 30." We do still need to increment the rotation angle, but that's why the code has the `-=` operator: to subtract a value from the rotation angle, rather than set the angle to that value. By not using `Rotate()` we can manipulate the rotation angle in various ways aside from only incrementing it. The rotation value is multiplied by `Input.GetAxis()`, like in the code for horizontal rotation, except now we ask for `Mouse Y` because that's the vertical axis of the mouse.

The rotation angle is manipulated further on the next line. We use `Mathf.Clamp()` to keep the rotation angle between minimum and maximum limits. Those limits are public variables declared earlier in the code, and they ensure that the view can only tilt 45 degrees up or down. The `Clamp()` method isn't specific to rotation, but is generally useful for keeping a number variable between limits. To see what happens, try commenting out the `Clamp()` line; now the tilt doesn't stop at upper and lower limits, allowing you to even rotate completely upside down! Clearly, viewing the world upside down is undesirable, hence the limits.

Because the angles property of `transform` is a Vector3, we need to create a new Vector3 with the rotation angle passed in to the constructor. The `Rotate()` method was automating this process for us, incrementing the rotation angle and then creating a new vector.

DEFINITION A *vector* is multiple numbers stored together as a unit. For example, a Vector3 is three numbers (labeled x, y, z).

WARNING The reason why we need to create a new Vector3 instead of changing values in the existing vector in the transform is because those values are read-only for transforms. This is a common mistake that can trip you up.

Euler angles vs. quaternion

You're probably wondering why the property is called `localEulerAngles` and not `localRotation`. First, you need to know about a concept called *quaternions*.

Quaternions are a different mathematical construct for representing rotations. They're distinct from Euler angles, which is the name for the X-, Y-, Z-axes approach we've been taking. Remember the whole discussion of pitch, yaw, and roll? Well, that method of representing rotations is Euler angles. Quaternions are . . . different. It's hard to explain quaternions, because they're an obscure aspect of higher math, involving movement through four dimensions. For a detailed explanation, go to www.flipcode.com/documents/matrfaq.html - Q47.

It's a bit easier to explain why quaternions are used to represent rotations: interpolating between rotation values (that is, going through a bunch of in-between values to gradually change from one value to another) looks smoother and more natural when using quaternions.

To return to the initial question, it's because `localRotation` is a quaternion, rather than Euler angles. Unity also provides the Euler angles property to make manipulating rotations easier to understand; the Euler angles property is converted to and from quaternion values automatically. Unity handles the harder math for you behind the scenes, so you don't have to worry about handling it yourself.

There's one more rotation setting for `MouseLook` that needs code: horizontal and vertical rotation at the same time.

2.4.3 *Horizontal and vertical rotation at the same time*

This last chunk of code won't use `Rotate()` either, for the same reason: The vertical rotation angle is clamped between limits after being incremented. That means the horizontal rotation needs to be calculated directly now. Remember, `Rotate()` was automating the process of incrementing the rotation angle, shown here.

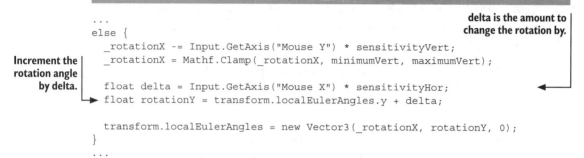

The first couple of lines, dealing with _rotationX, are exactly the same as in listing 2.5. Remember that rotating around the object's X-axis is vertical rotation. Because horizontal rotation is no longer being handled using the Rotate() method, that's what the delta and rotationY lines are doing. *Delta* is a common mathematical term for "the amount of change," so our calculation of delta is the amount that rotation should change. That amount of change is then added to the current rotation angle to get the desired new rotation angle.

Finally, both angles, vertical and horizontal, are used to create a new vector that's assigned to the transform component's angle property.

Disallow physics rotation on the player

Although this doesn't matter quite yet for this project, in most modern FPS games there's a complex physics simulation affecting everything in the scene. This will cause objects to bounce and tumble around; this behavior looks and works great for most objects, but the player's rotation needs to be solely controlled by the mouse and not affected by the physics simulation.

For that reason, mouse input scripts usually set the freezeRotation property on the player's Rigidbody. Add this Start() method to the MouseLook script:

```
...
void Start() {
    Rigidbody body = GetComponent<Rigidbody>();
    if (body != null)                          ←—— Check if this component exists.
        body.freezeRotation = true;
}
```

(A Rigidbody is an additional component an object can have. The physics simulation acts on Rigidbodys and manipulates objects they're attached to.)

In case you've gotten lost on where to make the various changes and additions we've gone over, this listing has the full finished script. Alternatively, download the example project.

Listing 2.7   The finished `MouseLook` script

```
using UnityEngine;
using System.Collections;

public class MouseLook : MonoBehaviour {
  public enum RotationAxes {
    MouseXAndY = 0,
    MouseX = 1,
    MouseY = 2
  }
  public RotationAxes axes = RotationAxes.MouseXAndY;

  public float sensitivityHor = 9.0f;
  public float sensitivityVert = 9.0f;

  public float minimumVert = -45.0f;
  public float maximumVert = 45.0f;

  private float _rotationX = 0;

  void Start() {
    Rigidbody body = GetComponent<Rigidbody>();
    if (body != null)
        body.freezeRotation = true;
  }

  void Update() {
    if (axes == RotationAxes.MouseX) {
      transform.Rotate(0, Input.GetAxis("Mouse X") * sensitivityHor, 0);
    }
    else if (axes == RotationAxes.MouseY) {
      _rotationX -= Input.GetAxis("Mouse Y") * sensitivityVert;
      _rotationX = Mathf.Clamp(_rotationX, minimumVert, maximumVert);

      float rotationY = transform.localEulerAngles.y;

      transform.localEulerAngles = new Vector3(_rotationX, rotationY, 0);
    }
    else {
      _rotationX -= Input.GetAxis("Mouse Y") * sensitivityVert;
      _rotationX = Mathf.Clamp(_rotationX, minimumVert, maximumVert);

      float delta = Input.GetAxis("Mouse X") * sensitivityHor;
      float rotationY = transform.localEulerAngles.y + delta;

      transform.localEulerAngles = new Vector3(_rotationX, rotationY, 0);
    }
  }
}
```

When you set the Axes menu and run the new code, you're able to look around in all directions while moving the mouse. Great! But you're still stuck in one place, looking around as if mounted on a turret. The next step is moving around the scene.

2.5   *Keyboard input component: first-person controls*

Looking around in response to mouse input is an important part of first-person controls, but you're only halfway there. The player also needs to move in response to keyboard input. Let's write a keyboard controls component to complement the mouse controls component; create a new C# script called FPSInput and attach that to the player (alongside the MouseLook script). For the moment, set the MouseLook component to horizontal rotation only.

> **TIP**   The keyboard and mouse controls explained here are split into separate scripts. You don't have to structure the code this way, and you could have everything bundled into a single player controls script, but a component system (such as the one in Unity) tends to be most flexible and therefore most useful when you have functionality split into several smaller components.

The code you wrote in the previous section affected rotation only, but now we'll change the object's position instead. Refer to listing 2.1; type that into FPSInput, but change Rotate() to Translate(). When you hit Play, the view slides up instead of spinning around. Try changing the parameter values to see how the movement changes (in particular, try swapping the first and second numbers); after experimenting with that for a bit, you can move on to adding keyboard input.

Listing 2.8   Spin code from the first listing, with a couple of minor changes

```
using UnityEngine;
using System.Collections;

public class FPSInput : MonoBehaviour {          Not required, but you probably
  public float speed = 6.0f;                     want to increase the speed.

  void Update() {
    transform.Translate(0, speed, 0);            Change Rotate() to Translate().
  }
}
```

2.5.1   *Responding to keypresses*

The code for moving according to keypresses is similar to the code for rotating according to the mouse. The GetAxis() method is used as well, and in a similar way. This listing demonstrates how to use it.

Listing 2.9   Positional movement responding to keypresses

```
...
void Update() {
  float deltaX = Input.GetAxis("Horizontal") * speed;
  float deltaZ = Input.GetAxis("Vertical") * speed;
  transform.Translate(deltaX, 0, deltaZ);
}
...
```

"Horizontal" and "Vertical" are indirect names for keyboard mappings.

As before, the GetAxis() values are multiplied by speed in order to determine the amount of movement. Whereas before the requested axis was always "Mouse something," now we pass in either "Horizontal" or "Vertical". These names are abstractions for input settings in Unity; if you look in the Edit menu under Project Settings and then look under Input, you'll find a list of abstract input names and the exact controls mapped to those names. Both the left/right arrow keys and the letters A/D are mapped to "Horizontal", whereas both the up/down arrow keys and the letters W/S are mapped to "Vertical".

Note that the movement values are applied to the X and Z coordinates. As you probably noticed while experimenting with the Translate() method, the X coordinate moves from side to side and the Z coordinate moves forward and backward.

Put in this new movement code and you should be able to move around by pressing either the arrow keys or WASD letter keys, the standard in most FPS games. The movement script is nearly complete, but we have a few more adjustments to go over.

2.5.2 Setting a rate of movement independent of the computer's speed

It's not obvious right now because you've only been running the code on one computer (yours), but if you ran it on different machines it'd run at different speeds. That's because some computers can process code and graphics faster than others. Right now, the player would move at different speeds on different computers because the movement code is tied to the computer's speed. That is referred to as *frame rate dependent*, because the movement code is dependent on the frame rate of the game.

Imagine you run this demo on two different computers, one that gets 30 fps (frames per second) and one that gets 60 fps. That means Update() would be called twice as often on the second computer, and the same speed value of 6 would be applied every time. At 30 fps, the rate of movement would be 180 units/second, and the movement at 60 fps would be 360 units/second. For most games, movement speed that varies like this would be bad news.

The solution is to adjust the movement code to make it *frame rate independent*. That means the speed of movement is not dependent on the frame rate of the game. The way to achieve this is by not applying the same speed value at every frame rate. Instead, scale the speed value higher or lower depending on how quickly the computer runs. This is achieved by multiplying the speed value by another value called deltaTime.

Listing 2.10 Frame rate independent movement using deltaTime

```
...
void Update() {
  float deltaX = Input.GetAxis("Horizontal") * speed;
  float deltaZ = Input.GetAxis("Vertical") * speed;
  transform.Translate(deltaX * Time.deltaTime, 0, deltaZ * Time.deltaTime);
}
...
```

That was a simple change. The Time class has a number of properties and methods that are useful for timing, and one of those properties is deltaTime. We know that *delta* means the amount of change, so that means deltaTime is the amount of change in time. Specifically, deltaTime is the amount of time between frames. The time between frames varies at different frame rates (for example, 30 fps is a deltaTime of 1/30th of a second), so multiplying the speed value by deltaTime will scale the speed value on different computers.

Now the movement speed will be the same on all computers. But the movement script is still not quite done; when you move around the room you can pass through walls, so we need to adjust the code further to prevent that.

2.5.3   *Moving the CharacterController for collision detection*

Directly changing the object's transform doesn't apply collision detection, so the character will pass through walls. To apply collision detection, what we want to do instead is use CharacterController, a component that makes the object move more like a character in a game, including colliding with walls. Recall that, back when we set up the player, we attached a CharacterController, so now we'll use that component with the movement code in FPSInput.

Listing 2.11   **Moving** CharacterController **instead of** Transform

```
...
private CharacterController _charController;          ← Variable for referencing
                                                       the CharacterController
void Start() {
  _charController = GetComponent<CharacterController>();   ← Access other
}                                                            components attached
                                                             to the same object.
void Update() {
  float deltaX = Input.GetAxis("Horizontal") * speed;
  float deltaZ = Input.GetAxis("Vertical") * speed;      ← Limit diagonal movement
  Vector3 movement = new Vector3(deltaX, 0, deltaZ);        to the same speed as
  movement = Vector3.ClampMagnitude(movement, speed);      movement along an axis.

  movement *= Time.deltaTime;
  movement = transform.TransformDirection(movement);   ← Transform the movement
  _charController.Move(movement);                        vector from local to global
}                                                        coordinates.
...                                                    ← Tell the CharacterController
                                                         to move by that vector.
```

This code excerpt introduces several new concepts. The first concept to point out is the variable for referencing the CharacterController. This variable creates a local reference to the object (code object, that is—not to be confused with scene objects); multiple scripts can have references to this one CharacterController instance.

That variable starts out empty, so before you can use the reference, you need to assign an object for it to refer to. This is where GetComponent comes into play; that method returns other components attached to the same GameObject. Rather than passing a parameter inside the parentheses, you use the C# syntax of defining the type inside angle brackets, <>.

Once you have a reference to the `CharacterController`, you can call `Move()` on the controller. Pass in a vector to that method, similar to how the mouse rotation code used a vector for rotation values. Also, similar to how rotation values were limited, use `Vector3.ClampMagnitude()` to limit the vector's magnitude to the movement speed; the clamp is used because, otherwise, diagonal movement would have a greater magnitude than movement directly along an axis (picture the sides and hypotenuse of a right triangle).

But there's one tricky aspect to the movement vector here, and it has to do with local versus global, as we discussed earlier for rotations. We'll create the vector with a value to move, say, to the left. That's the *player's* left, though, which may be a completely different direction from the *world's* left. That is, we're talking about left in local space, not global space. We need to pass a movement vector defined in global space to the `Move()` method, so we're going to need to convert the local space vector into a global space vector. Doing that conversion is extremely complex math, but fortunately for us, Unity takes care of that math for us, and we simply need to call the `TransformDirection()` method in order to, well, transform the direction.

> **DEFINITION**   *Transform* in this context means to convert from one coordinate space to another (refer to section 2.3.3 if you don't remember what a coordinate space is). Don't get confused with the other definitions of transform, including both the `Transform` component and the action of moving the object around the scene. It's sort of an overloaded term, because all these meanings refer to the same underlying concept.

Test playing the movement code now. If you haven't done so already, set the `MouseLook` component to both horizontal and vertical rotation. You can look around the scene fully and fly around the scene using keyboard controls. This is pretty great if you want the player to fly around the scene, but what if you want the player walking instead of flying?

2.5.4   *Adjusting components for walking instead of flying*

Now that collision detection is working, the script can have gravity and the player will stay down against the floor. Declare a `gravity` variable and use that value for the Y-axis.

Listing 2.12   Adding gravity to the movement code

```
...
public float gravity = -9.8f;
...
void Update() {
  ...
  movement = Vector3.ClampMagnitude(movement, speed);
  movement.y = gravity;                                    Use the gravity value
  ...                                                      instead of just 0.
```

Now there's a constant downward force on the player, but it's not always pointed straight down, because the player object can tilt up and down with the mouse. Fortunately, everything we need to fix that is already in place, so we need only to make minor adjustments to how components are set up on the player. First, set the MouseLook component on the player object to horizontal rotation only. Add the MouseLook component to the camera object, and set that one to vertical rotation only. That's right; you're going to have two different objects responding to the mouse!

Because the player object now only rotates horizontally, there's no longer any problem with the downward force of gravity being tilted. The camera object is parented to the player object (remember when we did that in the Hierarchy view?), so even though it rotates vertically independently from the player, the camera rotates horizontally along with the player.

Polishing the finished script

Use the RequireComponent() method to ensure that other components needed by the script are also attached. Sometimes other components are optional (that is, code that says "If this other component is also attached, then..."), but sometimes you want to make the other components mandatory. Add the method to the top of the script in order to enforce that dependency and give the required component as a parameter.

Similarly, if you add the AddComponentMenu method to the top of your scripts, that script will be added to the component menu in Unity's editor. Tell the command the name of the menu item you want to add, and then the script can be selected when you click Add Component at the bottom of the Inspector. Handy!

A script with both methods added to the top would look something like this:

```
using UnityEngine;
using System.Collections;

[RequireComponent(typeof(CharacterController))]
[AddComponentMenu("Control Script/FPS Input")]
public class FPSInput : MonoBehaviour {
...
```

Listing 2.13 shows the full finished script. Along with the small adjustments to how components are set up on the player, the player can walk around the room. Even with the gravity variable being applied, you can still use this script for flying movement by setting Gravity to 0 in the Inspector.

Listing 2.13   The finished FPSInput script

```
using UnityEngine;
using System.Collections;

[RequireComponent(typeof(CharacterController))]
[AddComponentMenu("Control Script/FPS Input")]
public class FPSInput : MonoBehaviour {
  public float speed = 6.0f;
  public float gravity = -9.8f;
```

```
  private CharacterController _charController;

  void Start() {
    _charController = GetComponent<CharacterController>();
  }

  void Update() {
    float deltaX = Input.GetAxis("Horizontal") * speed;
    float deltaZ = Input.GetAxis("Vertical") * speed;
    Vector3 movement = new Vector3(deltaX, 0, deltaZ);
    movement = Vector3.ClampMagnitude(movement, speed);

    movement.y = gravity;

    movement *= Time.deltaTime;
    movement = transform.TransformDirection(movement);
    _charController.Move(movement);
  }
}
```

Congratulations on building this 3D project! We covered a lot of ground in this chapter, and now you're well-versed in how to code movement in Unity. As exciting as this first demo is, it's still a long way from being a complete game. After all, the project plan described this as a basic FPS scene, and what's a shooter if you can't shoot? So, give yourself a well-deserved pat on the back for this chapter's project, and then get ready for the next step.

Summary

- 3D coordinate space is defined by X-, Y-, and Z-axes.
- Objects and lights in a room set the scene.
- The player in a first-person scene is essentially a camera.
- Movement code applies small transforms repeatedly in every frame.
- FPS controls consist of mouse rotation and keyboard movement

Adding enemies and projectiles to the 3D game

This chapter covers

- Taking aim and firing, both for the player and for enemies
- Detecting and responding to hits
- Making enemies that wander around
- Spawning new objects in the scene

The movement demo from the previous chapter was pretty cool, but still not really a game. Let's turn that movement demo into a first-person shooter. If you think about what else we need now, it boils down to the ability to shoot, and things to shoot at. First, we're going to write scripts that enable the player to shoot objects in the scene. Then, we're going to build enemies to populate the scene, including code to both wander around aimlessly and react to being hit. Finally, we're going to enable the enemies to fight back, emitting fireballs at the player. None of the scripts from chapter 2 need to change; instead, we'll add scripts to the project—scripts that handle the additional features.

I've chosen a first-person shooter for this project for a couple of reasons. One is simply that FPS games are popular; people like shooting games, so let's make a shooting game. A subtler reason has to do with the techniques you'll learn; this project is a great way to learn about several fundamental concepts in 3D simulations. For example, shooting games are a great way to teach *raycasting*. In a bit, we'll get into the specifics of what *raycasting* is, but for now, you only need to know that it's a tool that's useful for many different tasks in 3D simulations. Although raycasting is useful in a wide variety of situations, it happens that using raycasting makes the most intuitive sense for shooting.

Creating wandering targets to shoot at gives us a great excuse to explore code for computer-controlled characters, as well as to use techniques for sending messages and spawning objects. In fact, this wandering behavior is another place that raycasting is valuable, so we're already going to be looking at a different application of the technique after having first learned it with shooting. Similarly, the approach to sending messages that's demonstrated in this project is also useful elsewhere. In future chapters, you'll see other applications for these techniques, and even within this one project we'll go over alternative situations.

Ultimately, we'll approach this project one new feature at a time, with the game always playable at every step but also always feeling like there's a missing part to work on next. This roadmap breaks down the steps into small, understandable changes, with only one new feature added in each step.

1 Write code enabling the player to shoot into the scene.
2 Create static targets that react to being hit.
3 Make the targets wander around.
4 Spawn the wandering targets automatically.
5 Enable the targets/enemies to shoot fireballs at the player.

NOTE This chapter's project assumes you already have a first-person movement demo to build on. We created a movement demo in chapter 2, but if you skipped straight to this chapter then you will need to download the sample files for chapter 2.

3.1 Shooting via raycasts

The first new feature to introduce into the 3D demo is shooting. Looking around and moving are certainly crucial features for a first-person shooter, but it's not a game until players can affect the simulation and apply their skills. Shooting in 3D games can be implemented with a few different approaches, and one of the most important approaches is raycasting.

3.1.1 What is raycasting?

As the name indicates, raycasting is when you cast a ray into the scene. Clear, right? Well, okay, so what exactly is a *ray*?

DEFINITION A *ray* is an imaginary or invisible line in the scene that starts at a point of origin and extends out in a specific direction.

Raycasting is when you create a ray and then determine what intersects that ray; figure 3.1 illustrates the concept. Consider what happens when you fire a bullet from a gun: the bullet starts at the position of the gun and then flies forward in a straight line until it hits something. A ray is analogous to the path of the bullet, and raycasting is analogous to firing the bullet and seeing what it hits.

A ray projected through a 3D scene

Origin of the ray (imagine a gun)

Point of intersection (where the ray hit)

Figure 3.1   **A ray is an imaginary line, and raycasting is finding where that line intersects.**

As you can imagine, the math behind raycasting often gets complicated. Not only is it tricky to calculate the intersection of a line with a 3D plane, but you need to do that for all polygons of all mesh objects in the scene (remember, a mesh object is a 3D visual constructed from lots of connected lines and shapes). Fortunately, Unity handles the difficult math behind raycasting, but you still have to worry about higher-level concerns like where the ray is being cast from and why.

In this project, the answer to the latter question (why) is to simulate a bullet being fired into the scene. For a first-person shooter, the ray generally starts at the camera position and then extends out through the center of the camera view. In other words, you're checking for objects straight in front of the camera; Unity provides commands to make that task simple. Let's look at these commands.

3.1.2   *Using the ScreenPointToRay command for shooting*

You'll implement shooting by projecting a ray that starts at the camera and extends forward through the center of the view. Projecting a ray through the center of the camera view is a special case of an action referred to as *mouse picking*.

> **DEFINITION**   *Mouse picking* is the action of picking out the spot in the 3D scene directly under the mouse cursor.

Unity provides the ScreenPointToRay() method to perform this action. Figure 3.2 illustrates what happens when it's invoked. The method creates a ray that starts at the camera and projects at an angle passing through the given screen coordinates. Usually, the coordinates of the mouse position are used for mouse picking, but for first-person shooting the center of the screen is used. Once you have a ray, it can be passed to the `Physics.Raycast()` method to perform raycasting using that ray.

The camera is the origin of this ray, similar to the gun previously.

The screen (the camera's window into the 3D scene)

Ray projects from the camera through this point on the screen

Figure 3.2 `ScreenPointToRay()` projects a ray from the camera through the given screen coordinates.

Let's write code that uses the methods we just discussed. In Unity, create a new C# script, call it RayShooter, attach that script to the camera (not the player object), and then write the code from this listing in it.

Listing 3.1 `RayShooter` **script to attach to the camera**

```
using UnityEngine;
using System.Collections;

public class RayShooter : MonoBehaviour {
  private Camera _camera;

  void Start() {
    _camera = GetComponent<Camera>();            ← Access other components
  }                                                 attached to the same object.

  void Update() {                                 Respond to the mouse button.
    if (Input.GetMouseButtonDown(0)) {        ←
      Vector3 point = new Vector3(_camera.pixelWidth/2, _camera.
      pixelHeight/2, 0);
      Ray ray = _camera.ScreenPointToRay(point);
      RaycastHit hit;                             The raycast fills a referenced
      if (Physics.Raycast(ray, out hit)) {    ← variable with information.
        Debug.Log("Hit " + hit.point);     ←
      }
    }                              Retrieve coordinates where the ray hit.
  }
}
```

The middle of the screen is half its width and height.

Create the ray at that position using ScreenPointToRay().

You should note a number of things in this code listing. First, the `Camera` component is retrieved in `Start()`, just like the `CharacterController` in the previous chapter. Then, the rest of the code is put in `Update()` because it needs to check the mouse repeatedly, as opposed to just one time. The `Input.GetMouseButtonDown` method returns `true` or `false` depending on whether the mouse has been clicked, so putting that command in a conditional means the enclosed code runs only when the mouse has been clicked. You want to shoot when the player clicks the mouse; hence the conditional check of the mouse button.

A vector is created to define the screen coordinates for the ray (remember that a vector is several related numbers stored together). The camera's `pixelWidth` and `pixelHeight` values give you the size of the screen, so dividing those values in half gives you the center of the screen. Although screen coordinates are 2D, with only horizontal and vertical components and no depth, a `Vector3` was created because `ScreenPointToRay()` requires that data type (presumably because calculating the ray involves arithmetic on 3D vectors). `ScreenPointToRay()` was called with this set of coordinates, resulting in a Ray object (a code object, that is, not a game object; the two can be confused sometimes).

The ray is then passed to the `Raycast()` method, but it's not the only object passed in. There's also a `RaycastHit` data structure; `RaycastHit` is a bundle of information about the intersection of the ray, including where the intersection happened and what object was intersected. The C# syntax `out` ensures that the data structure manipulated within the command is the same object that exists outside the command, as opposed to the objects being separate copies in the different function scopes.

With those parameters in place, the `Physics.Raycast()` method can do its work. This method checks for intersections with the given ray, fills in data about the intersection, and returns `true` if the ray hit anything. Because a Boolean value is returned, this method can be put in a conditional check, just as you used `Input.GetMouseButton-Down()` earlier.

For now, the code emits a console message to indicate when an intersection occurred. This console message displays the 3D coordinates of the point where the ray hit (the XYZ values we discussed in chapter 2). But it can be hard to visualize where exactly the ray hit; similarly, it can be hard to tell where the center of the screen is (that is, where the ray shoots through). Let's add visual indicators to address both problems.

3.1.3   Adding visual indicators for aiming and hits

Our next step is to add two kinds of visual indicators: an aiming spot at the center of the screen and a mark in the scene where the ray hit. For a first-person shooter, the latter is usually bullet holes, but for now, you're going to put a blank sphere on the spot (and use a coroutine to remove the sphere after one second). Figure 3.3 shows what you'll see.

> **DEFINITION**   *Coroutines* are a way of handling tasks that execute incrementally over time, as opposed to how most functions make the program wait until they finish.

First, let's add indicators to mark where the ray hits. This listing shows the script after making this addition. Run around the scene shooting; it's pretty fun seeing the sphere indicators!

Target point
in the center
of the screen

Sphere indicates
where the wall
was hit

Figure 3.3 Shooting repeatedly after adding visual indicators for aiming and hits

Listing 3.2 `RayShooter` script with sphere indicators added

```
using UnityEngine;
using System.Collections;

public class RayShooter : MonoBehaviour {
  private Camera _camera;

  void Start() {
    _camera = GetComponent<Camera>();
  }

  void Update() {
    if (Input.GetMouseButtonDown(0)) {
      Vector3 point = new Vector3(_camera.pixelWidth/2, _camera.
    pixelHeight/2, 0);
      Ray ray = _camera.ScreenPointToRay(point);
      RaycastHit hit;
      if (Physics.Raycast(ray, out hit)) {
        StartCoroutine(SphereIndicator(hit.point));
      }
    }
  }

  private IEnumerator SphereIndicator(Vector3 pos) {
    GameObject sphere = GameObject.CreatePrimitive(PrimitiveType.Sphere);
    sphere.transform.position = pos;

    yield return new WaitForSeconds(1);

    Destroy(sphere);
  }
}
```

This function is mostly the same raycasting code from listing 3.1.

Launch a coroutine in response to a hit.

Coroutines use IEnumerator functions.

The yield keyword tells coroutines where to pause.

Remove this GameObject and clear its memory.

The new method is SphereIndicator(), plus a one-line modification in the existing Update() method. This method creates a sphere at a point in the scene and then removes that sphere a second later. Calling SphereIndicator() from the raycasting code ensures that there will be visual indicators showing exactly where the ray hit. This function is defined with IEnumerator, and that type is tied in with the concept of coroutines.

Technically, coroutines aren't asynchronous (asynchronous operations don't stop the rest of the code from running; think of downloading an image in the script of a website), but through clever use of enumerators, Unity makes coroutines behave similarly to asynchronous functions. The secret sauce in coroutines is the yield keyword; that keyword causes the coroutine to temporarily pause, handing back the program flow and picking up again from that point in the next frame. In this way, coroutines seemingly run in the background of a program, through a repeated cycle of running partway and then returning to the rest of the program.

As the name implies, StartCoroutine() sets a coroutine in motion. Once a coroutine is started, it keeps running until the function is finished; it pauses along the way. Note the subtle but significant point that the method passed to StartCoroutine() has a set of parentheses following the name: this syntax means you're calling that function, as opposed to passing its name. The called function runs until it hits a yield command, at which point the function pauses.

SphereIndicator() creates a sphere at a specific point, pauses for the yield statement, and then destroys the sphere after the coroutine resumes. The length of the pause is controlled by the value returned at yield. A few types of return values work in coroutines, but the most straightforward is to return a specific length of time to wait. Returning WaitForSeconds(1) causes the coroutine to pause for one second. Create a sphere, pause for one second, and then destroy the sphere: that sequence sets up a temporary visual indicator.

Listing 3.2 gave you indicators to mark where the ray hits. But you also want an aiming spot in the center of the screen.

Listing 3.3   Visual indicator for aiming

```
...
void Start() {
  _camera = GetComponent<Camera>();

  Cursor.lockState = CursorLockMode.Locked;          Hide the mouse cursor at
  Cursor.visible = false;                            the center of the screen.
}

void OnGUI() {
  int size = 12;
  float posX = _camera.pixelWidth/2 - size/4;
  float posY = _camera.pixelHeight/2 - size/2;                  The GUI.Label() command
  GUI.Label(new Rect(posX, posY, size, size), "*");            displays text on screen.
}
...
```

Another new method has been added to the RayShooter class, called OnGUI(). Unity comes with both a basic and more advanced UI system; because the basic system has a lot of limitations, we'll build a more flexible advanced UI in future chapters, but for now, it's much easier to display a point in the center of the screen using the basic UI. Much like Start() and Update(), every MonoBehaviour automatically responds to an OnGUI() method. That function runs every frame right after the 3D scene is rendered, resulting in everything drawn during OnGUI() appearing on top of the 3D scene (imagine stickers applied to a painting of a landscape).

> **DEFINITION** *Render* is the action of the computer drawing the pixels of the 3D scene. Although the scene is defined using XYZ coordinates, the actual display on your monitor is a 2D grid of colored pixels. In order to display the 3D scene, the computer needs to calculate the color of all the pixels in the 2D grid; running that algorithm is referred to as *rendering*.

Inside OnGUI() the code defines 2D coordinates for the display (shifted slightly to account for the size of the label) and then calls GUI.Label(). That method displays a text label; because the string passed to the label is an asterisk (*), you end up with that character displayed in the center of the screen. Now it's much easier to aim in our nascent FPS game!

Listing 3.3 also added cursor settings to the Start() method. All that's happening is that the values are being set for cursor visibility and locking. The script will work perfectly fine if you omit the cursor values, but these settings make first-person controls work a bit more smoothly. The mouse cursor will stay in the center of the screen, and to avoid cluttering the view it will turn invisible and will only reappear when you press Esc.

> **WARNING** Always remember that you can press Esc to unlock the mouse cursor in order to move it away from the middle of the Game view. While the mouse cursor is locked, it's impossible to click the Play button and stop the game.

That wraps up the first-person shooting code . . . well, that wraps up the player's end of the interaction, anyway, but we still need to take care of targets.

3.2 Scripting reactive targets

Being able to shoot is all well and good, but at the moment, players don't have anything to shoot at. We're going to create a target object and give it a script that will respond to being hit. Or rather, we'll slightly modify the shooting code to notify the target when hit, and then the script on the target will react when notified.

3.2.1 Determining what was hit

First, you need to create a new object to shoot at. Create a new cube object (Game-Object > 3D Object > Cube) and then scale it up vertically by setting the Y scale to 2 and leaving X and Z at 1. Position the new object at 0, 1, 0 to put it on the floor in the middle of the room, and name the object Enemy. Create a new script called ReactiveTarget and attach that to the newly created box. Soon, you'll write code for this script, but leave it as the default for now; you're only creating the script file because the next code listing requires it to exist in order to compile. Go back to RayShooter.cs and modify the raycasting code according to the following listing. Run the new code and shoot the new target; debug messages appear in the console instead of sphere indicators in the scene.

Listing 3.4   Detecting whether the target object was hit

```
...
if (Physics.Raycast(ray, out hit)) {
  GameObject hitObject = hit.transform.gameObject;        ◄─── Retrieve the object the ray hit
  ReactiveTarget target = hitObject.GetComponent<ReactiveTarget>();
  if (target != null) {
    Debug.Log("Target hit");        ◄─── Check for the ReactiveTarget
  } else {                                component on the object
    StartCoroutine(SphereIndicator(hit.point));
  }
}
...
```

Notice that you retrieve the object from RaycastHit, just like the coordinates were retrieved for the sphere indicators. Technically, the hit information doesn't return the game object hit; it indicates the Transform component hit. You can then access game-Object as a property of transform.

Then, you use the GetComponent() method on the object to check whether it's a reactive target (that is, if it has the ReactiveTarget script attached). As you saw previously, that method returns components of a specific type that are attached to the Game-Object. If no component of that type is attached to the object, then GetComponent() won't return anything. You check whether null was returned and run different code in each case.

If the hit object is a reactive target, the code emits a debug message instead of starting the coroutine for sphere indicators. Now let's inform the target object about the hit so that it can react.

3.2.2   Alert the target that it was hit

All that's needed in the code is a one-line change, as shown next.

Listing 3.5   Sending a message to the target object

```
...
if (target != null) {                    Call a method of the target instead of
  target.ReactToHit();        ◄───        just emitting the debug message
} else {
  StartCoroutine(SphereIndicator(hit.point));
}
...
```

Now the shooting code calls a method of the target, so let's write that target method. In the ReactiveTarget script, write in the code from the next listing. The target object will fall over and disappear when you shoot it; refer to figure 3.4.

Listing 3.6 `ReactiveTarget` **script that dies when hit**

```
using UnityEngine;
using System.Collections;

public class ReactiveTarget : MonoBehaviour {

  public void ReactToHit() {            ◄──── Method called by the shooting script
    StartCoroutine(Die());
  }                                           Topple the enemy, wait 1.5
                                              seconds, then destroy the enemy.
  private IEnumerator Die() {          ◄──
    this.transform.Rotate(-75, 0, 0);

    yield return new WaitForSeconds(1.5f);

    Destroy(this.gameObject);             Object can destroy itself
  }                                   ◄──── just like a separate object.
}
```

Most of this code should be familiar to you from previous scripts, so we'll only go over it briefly. First, you define the ReactToHit() method, because that's the method name called in the shooting script. This method starts a coroutine that's similar to the sphere indicator code from earlier; the main difference is that it operates on the object of this script rather than creating a separate object. Expressions like this.gameObject refer to the GameObject that this script is attached to (and the this keyword is optional, so code could refer to gameObject without anything in front of it).

Figure 3.4   The target object falling over when hit

The first line of the coroutine function makes the object tip over. As discussed in chapter 2, rotations can be defined as an angle around each of the three coordinate axes, X, Y, and Z. Because we don't want the object to rotate side to side, leave Y and Z as 0 and assign an angle to the X rotation.

> **NOTE** The transform is applied instantly, but you may prefer seeing the movement when objects topple over. Once you start looking beyond this book for more advanced topics, you might want to look up *tweens*, systems used to make objects move smoothly over time.

The second line of the method uses the `yield` keyword that's so significant to coroutines, pausing the function there and returning the number of seconds to wait before resuming. Finally, the game object destroys itself in the last line of the function. `Destroy(this.gameObject)` is called after the wait time, just like the code called `Destroy(sphere)` before.

> **WARNING** Be sure to call `Destroy()` on `this.gameObject` and not simply `this`! Don't get confused between the two; `this` only refers to this script component, whereas `this.gameObject` refers to the object the script is attached to.

The target now reacts to being shot; great! But it doesn't do anything else on its own, so let's add more behavior to make this target a proper enemy character.

3.3 Basic wandering AI

A static target isn't terribly interesting, so let's write code that'll make the enemy wander around. Code for wandering around is pretty much the simplest example of AI; *artificial intelligence* (AI) refers to computer-controlled entities. In this case, the entity is an enemy in a game, but it could also be a robot in the real world, or a voice that plays chess, for example.

3.3.1 Diagramming how basic AI works

There are a number of different approaches to AI (seriously, AI is a major area of research for computer scientists), but for our purposes we'll stick with a simple one. As you become more experienced and your games get more sophisticated, you'll probably want to explore the various approaches to AI.

Figure 3.5 depicts the basic process. In every frame, the AI code will scan around its environment to determine whether it needs to react. If an obstacle appears in its way, the enemy turns to face a different direction. Regardless of whether the enemy needs to turn, it will always move forward steadily. As such, the enemy will ping-pong around the room, always moving forward and turning to avoid walls.

The actual code will look pretty familiar, because it moves enemies forward using the same commands as moving the player forward. The AI code will also use raycasting, similar to, but in a different context from, shooting.

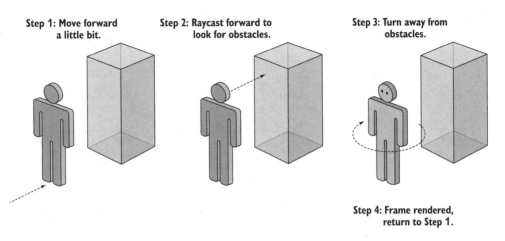

Step 1: Move forward a little bit.

Step 2: Raycast forward to look for obstacles.

Step 3: Turn away from obstacles.

Step 4: Frame rendered, return to Step 1.

Figure 3.5   Basic AI: cyclical process of moving forward and avoiding obstacles

3.3.2 *"Seeing" obstacles with a raycast*

As you saw in the introduction to this chapter, raycasting is a technique that's useful for a number of tasks within 3D simulations. One easily grasped task is shooting, but another task raycasting can be useful for is scanning around the scene. Given that scanning around the scene is a step in AI code, that means raycasting is used in AI code.

Earlier, you created a ray that originated from the camera, because that's where the player was looking from; this time, you'll create a ray that originates from the enemy. The first ray shot out through the center of the screen, but this time the ray will shoot forward in front of the character; figure 3.6 illustrates this. Then, just like the shooting code used `RaycastHit` information to determine whether anything was hit and where, the AI code will use `RaycastHit` information to determine whether anything is in front of the enemy and, if so, how far away.

For every frame the AI character projects a ray in front of it in order to detect obstacles. Here the character is facing a wall, so the raycast will detect a close obstacle.

Figure 3.6   Using raycasting to "see" obstacles

One difference between raycasting for shooting and raycasting for AI is the radius of the ray detected against. For shooting, the ray was treated as infinitely thin, but for AI, the ray will be treated as having a large cross section; in terms of the code, this means using the SphereCast() method instead of Raycast(). The reason for this difference is that bullets are tiny, whereas to check for obstacles in front of the character, we need to account for the width of the character.

Create a new script called WanderingAI, attach that to the target object (alongside the ReactiveTarget script), and write the code from the next listing. Play the scene now and you should see the enemy wandering around the room; you can still shoot the target and it will react the same way as before.

Listing 3.7   Basic WanderingAI script

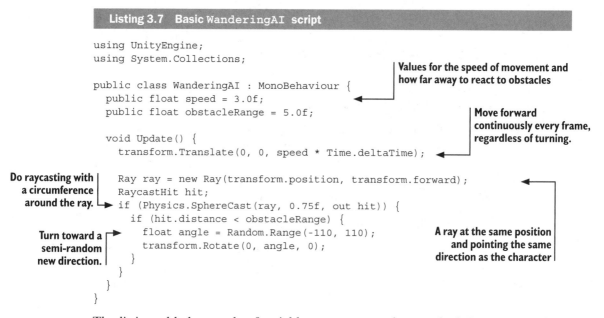

```
using UnityEngine;
using System.Collections;

public class WanderingAI : MonoBehaviour {
    public float speed = 3.0f;
    public float obstacleRange = 5.0f;

    void Update() {
        transform.Translate(0, 0, speed * Time.deltaTime);

        Ray ray = new Ray(transform.position, transform.forward);
        RaycastHit hit;
        if (Physics.SphereCast(ray, 0.75f, out hit)) {
            if (hit.distance < obstacleRange) {
                float angle = Random.Range(-110, 110);
                transform.Rotate(0, angle, 0);
            }
        }
    }
}
```

Values for the speed of movement and how far away to react to obstacles

Move forward continuously every frame, regardless of turning.

Do raycasting with a circumference around the ray.

Turn toward a semi-random new direction.

A ray at the same position and pointing the same direction as the character

The listing added a couple of variables to represent the speed of movement and the distance at which the AI reacts to obstacles. Then, a Translate() method was added in the Update() method in order to move forward continuously (including the use of deltaTime for frame rate–independent movement). In Update(), you'll also see raycasting code that looks a lot like the shooting script from earlier; again, the same technique of raycasting is being used here to see instead of shoot. The ray is created using the enemy's position and direction, instead of using the camera.

As explained earlier, the raycasting calculation was done using the Physics.Sphere-Cast() method. This method takes a radius parameter to determine how far around the ray to detect intersections, but in every other respect it's exactly the same as Physics.Raycast(). This similarity includes how the command fills in hit information, checks for intersections just like before, and uses the distance property to be sure to react only when the enemy gets near an obstacle (as opposed to a wall across the room).

When the enemy has a nearby obstacle right in front of it, the code rotates the character a semi-random amount toward a new direction. I say semi-random because the values are constrained to the minimum and maximum values that make sense for this situation. Specifically, we use the `Random.Range()` method which Unity provides for obtaining a random value between constraints. In this case, the constraints were just slightly beyond an exact left or right turn, allowing the character to turn sufficiently to avoid obstacles.

3.3.3 *Tracking the character's state*

One oddity of the current behavior is that the enemy keeps moving forward after falling over from being hit. That's because, right now, the `Translate()` method runs every frame no matter what. Let's make small adjustments to the code in order to keep track of whether or not the character is alive—or to put it in another (more technical) way, we want to track the alive state of the character. Having the code keep track of and respond differently to the current state of the object is a common code pattern in many areas of programming, not just AI. More sophisticated implementations of this approach are referred to as *state machines*, or possibly even *finite state machines.*

> **DEFINITION** *A finite state machine (FSM)* is a code structure in which the current state of the object is tracked, well-defined transitions exist between states, and the code behaves differently based on the state.

We're not going to implement a full FSM, but it's no coincidence that a common place to see the initials FSM is in discussions of AI. A full FSM would have many states for all the different behaviors of a sophisticated AI, but in this basic AI, we need only to track whether or not the character is alive. The next listing adds a Boolean value, `_alive`, toward the top of the script, and the code needs occasional conditional checks of that value. With those checks in place, the movement code only runs while the enemy is alive.

Listing 3.8 `WanderingAI` script with alive state added

```
...
private bool _alive;                                          Boolean value to track
                                                             whether the enemy is alive

void Start() {
  _alive = true;                                             Initialize that value.
}

void Update() {
  if (_alive) {                                              Only move if the character is alive.
    transform.Translate(0, 0, speed * Time.deltaTime);
    ...
  }
}
                                                             Public method allowing outside code to
                                                             affect the "alive" state
public void SetAlive(bool alive) {
  _alive = alive;
}
...
```

The `ReactiveTarget` script can now tell the `WanderingAI` script whether the enemy is or isn't alive.

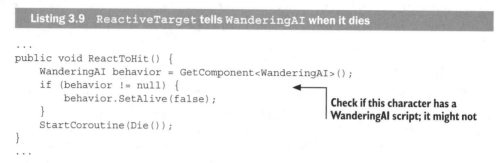

Listing 3.9 ReactiveTarget tells WanderingAI when it dies

```
...
public void ReactToHit() {
    WanderingAI behavior = GetComponent<WanderingAI>();
    if (behavior != null) {                            ◄──── Check if this character has a
        behavior.SetAlive(false);                              WanderingAI script; it might not
    }
    StartCoroutine(Die());
}
...
```

AI code structure

The AI code in this chapter is contained within a single class so that learning and under-standing it is straightforward. This code structure is perfectly fine for simple AI needs, so don't be afraid that you've done something wrong and that a more complex code struc-ture is an absolute requirement. For more complex AI needs (such as a game with a wide variety of highly intelligent characters), a more robust code structure can help facilitate developing the AI.

As alluded to in chapter 1's example for composition versus inheritance, sometimes you'll want to split chunks of the AI into separate scripts. Doing so will enable you to mix and match components, generating unique behavior for each character. Think about the similarities and differences between your characters, and those differences will guide you as you design your code architecture. For example, if your game has some enemies that move by charging headlong at the player and some that slink around in the shadows, you may want to make `Locomotion` a separate component. Then you can create scripts for both `LocomotionCharge` and `LocomotionSlink`, and use different `Locomotion` components on different enemies.

The exact AI code structure you want depends on the design of your specific game; there's no one right way to do it. Unity makes it easy to design flexible code architectures like this.

3.4 Spawning enemy prefabs

At the moment, there's only one enemy in the scene, and when it dies, the scene is empty. Let's make the game spawn enemies so that whenever the enemy dies, a new one appears. This is easily done in Unity using a concept called *prefabs*.

3.4.1 What is a prefab?

Prefabs are a flexible approach to visually defining interactive objects. In a nutshell, a prefab is a fully fleshed-out game object (with components already attached and set up) that doesn't exist in any specific scene but rather exists as an asset that can be copied into any scene. This copying can be done manually, to ensure that the enemy object (or other prefab) is the same in every scene. More importantly, though, prefabs can also be spawned from code; you can place copies of the object into the scene using commands in scripts and not only by doing so manually in the visual editor.

> **DEFINITION** An *asset* is any file that shows up in the Project view; these could be 2D images, 3D models, code files, scenes, and so on. I mentioned the term *asset* briefly in chapter 1, but I didn't emphasize it until now.

The term for one of these copies of a prefab is an *instance*, analogous to how the word instance refers to a specific code object created from a class. Try to keep the terminology straight: *prefab* refers to the game object existing outside of any scene; *instance* refers to a copy of the object that's placed in a scene.

> **DEFINITION** Also analogous to object-oriented terminology, *instantiate* is the action of creating an instance.

3.4.2 Creating the enemy prefab

To create a prefab, first create an object in the scene that will become the prefab. Because our enemy object will become a prefab, we've already done this first step. Now all we do is drag the object down from the Hierarchy view and drop it in the Project view; this will automatically save the object as a prefab (see figure 3.7). Back in the Hierarchy view, the original object's name will turn blue to signify that it's now linked to a prefab. If you wanted to edit the prefab further (such as by adding new components), you'd make those changes on the object in the scene and then select Game-Object > Apply Changes To Prefab. But we don't want the object in the scene anymore (we're going to spawn the prefab, not use the instance already in the scene), so delete the enemy object now.

Drag the object from Hierarchy view into Project view to create a prefab.

Figure 3.7   Drag objects from Hierarchy to Project in order to create prefabs.

> **WARNING** The interface for working with prefabs is somewhat awkward, and the relationship between prefabs and their instances in scenes can be brittle. For example, you often have to drag a prefab into a scene to edit it, and then

delete the object once you're done editing. In chapter 1, I mentioned this as a downside to Unity, and I hope the workflow with prefabs improves in future versions of Unity.

Now we have the actual prefab object to spawn in the scene, so let's write code to create instances of the prefab.

3.4.3   *Instantiating from an invisible SceneController*

Although the prefab itself doesn't exist in the scene, there has to be an object in the scene for the enemy spawning code to attach to. What we'll do is create an empty game object; we can attach the script to that, but the object won't be visible in the scene.

> **TIP**   The use of empty `GameObjects` for attaching script components is a common pattern in Unity development. This trick is used for abstract tasks that don't apply to any specific object in the scene. Unity scripts are intended to be attached to visible objects, but not every task makes sense that way.

Choose GameObject > Create Empty, rename the new object `Controller`, and then set its position to `0, 0, 0`. (Technically the position doesn't matter because the object isn't visible, but putting it at the origin will make life simpler if you ever parent anything to it.) Create a script called `SceneController`.

Listing 3.10   `SceneController` that spawns the enemy prefab

```
using UnityEngine;
using System.Collections;                          Serialized variable for linking
                                                   to the prefab object
public class SceneController : MonoBehaviour {
  [SerializeField] private GameObject enemyPrefab;
  private GameObject _enemy;                        Private variable to keep track of
                                                    the enemy instance in the scene
  void Update() {
    if (_enemy == null) {
      _enemy = Instantiate(enemyPrefab) as GameObject;      Method that copies
      _enemy.transform.position = new Vector3(0, 1, 0);     the prefab object
      float angle = Random.Range(0, 360);
      _enemy.transform.Rotate(0, angle, 0);
    }
  }
}
```

Only spawn a new enemy if there isn't already one in the scene.

Attach this script to the controller object, and in the Inspector you'll see a variable slot for the enemy prefab. This works similarly to public variables, but there's an important difference.

> **WARNING**   I recommend private variables with `SerializeField` to reference objects in Unity's editor, because you want to expose that variable in the Inspector but don't want the value to be changed by other scripts. As explained in chapter 2, public variables show up in the Inspector by default (in other words,

they're serialized by Unity), so most tutorials and sample code you'll see use public variables for all serialized values. But these variables can also be modified by other scripts (these are public variables, after all); in many cases, you don't want the value to be modified in code but only set in the Inspector.

Drag the prefab asset up from Project to the empty variable slot. When the mouse gets near, you should see the slot highlight to indicate that the object can be linked there (see figure 3.8). Once the enemy prefab is linked to the `SceneController` script, play the scene in order to see the code in action. An enemy will appear in the middle of the room just like before, but now if you shoot the enemy, it will be replaced by a new enemy. Much better than just one enemy that's gone forever!

Drag the prefab from Project view to a slot in the Inspector.

Figure 3.8   Link the enemy prefab to the script's prefab slot.

TIP   This approach of dragging objects onto the Inspector's variable slots is a handy technique that comes up in a lot of different scripts. Here we linked a prefab to the script, but you can also link to objects in the scene, or even specific components (because the code needs to call public methods in that specific component). In future chapters, we'll use this technique again.

The core of this script is the `Instantiate()` method, so take note of that line. When we instantiate the prefab, that creates a copy in the scene. By default, `Instantiate()` returns the new object as a generic `Object` type, but `Object` is pretty useless directly and we need to handle it as a `GameObject`. In C#, use the as keyword for typecasting to convert from one type of code object into another type (written with the syntax `original-object as new-type`).

The instantiated object is stored in _enemy, a private variable of the `GameObject` type. (Keep the distinction between a prefab and an instance of the prefab straight: `enemyPrefab` stores the prefab; _enemy stores the instance.) The `if` statement that checks the stored object ensures that `Instantiate()` is called only when _enemy is empty (or `null`, in coder-speak). The variable starts out empty, so the instantiating code runs once right from the beginning of the session. The object returned by `Instantiate()` is then stored in _enemy so that the instantiating code won't run again.

Because the enemy destroys itself when shot, that empties the _enemy variable and causes Instantiate() to be run again. In this way, there's always an enemy in the scene.

Destroying GameObjects and memory management

It's somewhat unexpected for existing references to become null when an object destroys itself. In a memory-managed programming language like C#, normally you aren't able to directly destroy objects; you can only dereference them so that they can be destroyed automatically. This is still true within Unity, but the way GameObjects are handled behind the scenes makes it look like they were destroyed directly.

To display objects in the scene, Unity has to have a reference to all objects in its scene graph. As such, even if you removed all references to the GameObject in your code, there would still be this scene graph reference preventing the object from being destroyed automatically. Because of this, Unity provides the Destroy() method to tell the game engine "Remove this object from the scene graph." As part of that behind-the-scenes functionality, Unity also overloads the == operator to return true when checking for null. Technically, that object still exists in memory, but it may as well not exist any longer, so Unity has it appearing as null. You could confirm this by calling GetInstanceID() on the destroyed object.

Note, that the developers of Unity have considered changing this behavior to more standard memory management. If they do, then the spawning code will need to change as well, probably by swapping the (_enemy==null) check with a new parameter like (_enemy.isDestroyed).

(If most of this discussion was Greek to you, just don't worry about it; this was a tangential technical discussion for people interested in these obscure details.)

3.5   *Shooting by instantiating objects*

All right, let's add another bit of functionality to the enemies. Much as we did with the player, first we made them move—now let's make them shoot! As I mentioned back when introducing raycasting, that was just one of the approaches to implementing shooting. Another approach involves instantiating prefabs, so let's take that approach to making the enemies shoot back. The goal of this section is to see figure 3.9 when playing.

3.5.1   *Creating the projectile prefab*

This time shooting will involve a projectile in the scene. Shooting with raycasting was basically instantaneous, registering a hit the moment the mouse was clicked, but this time enemies are going to emit fireballs that fly through the air. Admittedly, they'll be moving pretty fast, but it won't be instantaneous, giving the player a chance to dodge out of the way. Instead of using raycasting to detect hits, we'll use collision detection (the same collision system that keeps the moving player from passing through walls).

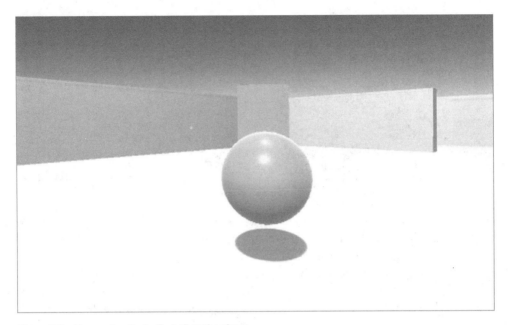

Figure 3.9   Enemy shooting a fireball at the player.

The code will spawn fireballs in the same way that enemies spawn: by instantiating a prefab. As explained in the previous section, the first step when creating a prefab is to create an object in the scene that will become the prefab, so let's create a fireball. To start, choose GameObject > 3D Object > Sphere. Rename the new object Fireball. Now create a new script, also called Fireball, and attach that script to this object. Eventually, we'll write code in this script, but leave it as default for now while we work on a few other parts of the Fireball object. So that it appears like a fireball and not just a gray sphere, we're going to give the object a bright orange color. Surface properties such as color are controlled using materials.

> **DEFINITION**   A *material* is a packet of information that defines the surface properties of any 3D object that the material is attached to. These surface properties can include color, shininess, and even subtle roughness.

Choose Assets > Create > Material. Name the new material something like Flame and drag it onto the object in the scene. Select the material in the Project view in order to see the material's properties in the Inspector. As figure 3.10 shows, click the color swatch labeled Albedo (that's a technical term that refers to the main color of a surface). Clicking that will bring up a color picker in its own window; slide both the rainbow-colored bar on the right-hand side and the main picking area to set the color to orange.

Click the color
swatch to bring
up color picker.

Adjust hue on the
right side and value
in the main area.

**Figure 3.10   Setting the color of
a material**

We're also going to brighten the material to make it look more like fire. Adjust the
Emission value (one of the other attributes in the Inspector). It defaults to 0, so type in
.3 to brighten up the material.

Now you can turn the fireball object into a prefab by dragging the object down from
Hierarchy into Project, just as you did with the enemy prefab. Great, we have a new prefab to use as a projectile! Next up is writing code to shoot using that projectile.

3.5.2   Shooting the projectile and colliding with a target

Let's make adjustments to the enemy in order to emit fireballs. Because code to recognize the player will require a new script (just like ReactiveTarget was required by the
code to recognize the target), first create a new script and name it PlayerCharacter.
Attach this script to the player object in the scene.

Now open up WanderingAI and add to the code from this listing.

Listing 3.11   WanderingAI additions for emitting fireballs

```
...
[SerializeField] private GameObject fireballPrefab;        ◀─  Add these two fields
private GameObject _fireball;                                   before any methods, just
...                                                             like in SceneController.
if (Physics.SphereCast(ray, 0.75f, out hit)) {
  GameObject hitObject = hit.transform.gameObject;
  if (hitObject.GetComponent<PlayerCharacter>()) {        ◀─  Player is detected
    if (_fireball == null) {                                   in the same way as
      _fireball = Instantiate(fireballPrefab) as GameObject;   the target object in
      _fireball.transform.position =                           RayShooter.
      transform.TransformPoint(Vector3.forward * 1.5f);
      _fireball.transform.rotation = transform.rotation;   ◀─  Place the fireball in front
    }                                                          of the enemy and point in
  }                                                            the same direction.
  else if (hit.distance < obstacleRange) {
    float angle = Random.Range(-110, 110);
    transform.Rotate(0, angle, 0);
  }
}
...
```

**Same null
GameObject
logic as
SceneController**

**Instantiate()
method here is
just like it was in
SceneController.**

You'll notice that all the annotations in this listing refer to similar (or the same) bits in previous scripts. Previous code listings showed everything needed for emitting fireballs; now we're mashing together and remixing bits of code to fit in the new context. Just like in `SceneController`, you need to add two `GameObject` fields toward the top of the script: a serialized variable for linking the prefab to, and a private variable for keeping track of the instance copied by the code. After doing a raycast, the code checks for the `PlayerCharacter` on the object hit; this works just like when the shooting code checked for `ReactiveTarget` on the object hit. The code that instantiates a fireball when there isn't already one in the scene works like the code that instantiates an enemy. The positioning and rotation are different, though; this time, you place the instance just in front of the enemy and point it in the same direction.

Once all the new code is in place, a new Fireball Prefab slot will appear when you view the component in the Inspector, like the Enemy Prefab slot in the `SceneController` component. Click the enemy prefab in the Project view and the Inspector will show that object's components, as if you'd selected an object in the scene. Although the earlier warning about interface awkwardness often applies when editing prefabs, the interface makes it easy to adjust components on the object, and that's all we're doing. As shown in figure 3.11, drag the fireball prefab from Project onto the Fireball Prefab slot in the Inspector (again, just as you did with `SceneController`).

Drag the prefab from Project view to a slot in the Inspector.

Figure 3.11 Link the fireball prefab to the script's prefab slot.

Now the enemy will fire at the player when the player is directly ahead of it . . . well, try to fire; the bright orange sphere appears in front of the enemy, but it just sits there because we haven't written its script yet. Let's do that now.

Listing 3.12 `Fireball` script that reacts to collisions

```
using UnityEngine;
using System.Collections;

public class Fireball : MonoBehaviour {
  public float speed = 10.0f;
  public int damage = 1;

  void Update() {
```

```
      transform.Translate(0, 0, speed * Time.deltaTime);
  }

  void OnTriggerEnter(Collider other) {
    PlayerCharacter player = other.GetComponent<PlayerCharacter>();
    if (player != null) {
      Debug.Log("Player hit");
    }
    Destroy(this.gameObject);
  }
}
```

Called when another object collides with this trigger

Check if the other object is a PlayerCharacter

The crucial new bit to this code is the `OnTriggerEnter()` method, called automatically when the object has a collision, such as with the walls or with the player. At the moment, this code won't work entirely; if you run it, the fireball will fly forward thanks to the `Translate()` line, but the trigger won't run, queuing up a new fireball by destroying the current one. There need to be a couple of other adjustments made to components on the `Fireball` object. The first change is making the collider a trigger. To adjust that, click the Is Trigger check box in the Sphere Collider component.

TIP A Collider component set as a trigger will still react to touching/overlapping other objects, but it will no longer stop other objects from physically passing through.

The fireball also needs a Rigidbody, a component used by the physics system in Unity. By giving the fireball a Rigidbody component, you ensure that the physics system is able to register collision triggers for that object. In the Inspector, click Add Component and choose Physics > Rigidbody. In the component that's added, deselect Use Gravity (see figure 3.12) so that the fireball won't be pulled down by gravity.

Uncheck this value.

Figure 3.12   Turn off gravity in the Rigidbody component.

Play now, and fireballs are destroyed when they hit something. Because the fireball-emitting code runs whenever there isn't already a fireball in the scene, the enemy will shoot more fireballs at the player. Now there's just one more thing remaining for shooting at the player: making the player react to being hit.

3.5.3   *Damaging the player*

Earlier, you created a `PlayerCharacter` script but left it empty. Now you'll write code to have it react to being hit.

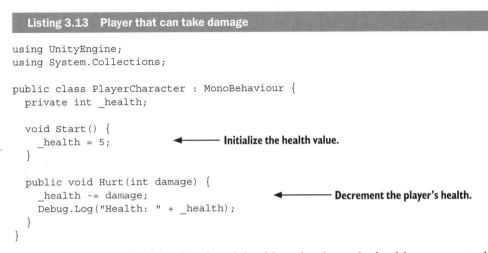

Listing 3.13 Player that can take damage

```
using UnityEngine;
using System.Collections;

public class PlayerCharacter : MonoBehaviour {
  private int _health;

  void Start() {
    _health = 5;                                    ◄──────── Initialize the health value.
  }

  public void Hurt(int damage) {
    _health -= damage;                                ◄──────── Decrement the player's health.
    Debug.Log("Health: " + _health);
  }
}
```

The listing defines a field for the player's health and reduces the health on command. In later chapters, we'll go over text displays to show information on the screen, but for now, we can only display information about the player's health using debug messages.

Now you need to go back to the `Fireball` script to call the player's `Hurt()` method. Replace the debug line in the `Fireball` script with `player.Hurt(damage)` to tell the player they've been hit. And that's the final bit of code we needed!

Whew! That was a pretty intense chapter, with lots of code introduced. Between the previous chapter and this one, you now have most of the functionality in place for a first-person shooter.

Summary

- A ray is an imaginary line projected into the scene.
- For both shooting and sensing obstacles, do a raycast with that line.
- Making a character wander around involves basic AI.
- New objects are spawned by instantiating prefabs.
- Coroutines are used to spread out functions over time.

Developing graphics
for your game

4

We've been focusing mostly on how the game functions and not as much on how the game looks. That was no accident—this book is mostly about programming games in Unity. Still, it's important to understand how to work on and improve the visuals. Before we get back to the book's main focus on coding different parts of the game, let's spend a chapter learning about game art so that your projects won't always end up with just blank boxes sliding around.

All of the visual content in a game is made up of what are called *art assets*. But what exactly does that mean?

4.1 Understanding art assets

An art asset is an individual unit of visual information (usually a file) used by the game. It's an overarching umbrella term for all visual content; image files are art assets, 3D models are art assets, and so on. Indeed, the term *art asset* is simply a specific case of an asset, which you've learned is any file used by the game (such as a script)—hence the main Assets folder in Unity. Table 4.1 lists and describes the five main kinds of art assets used in building a game.

Table 4.1 Types of art assets

Type of art asset	Definition of this type
2D image	Flat pictures. To make a real-world analogy, 2D images are like paintings and photographs.
3D model	3D virtual objects (almost a synonym for *mesh objects*). To make a real-world analogy, 3D models are like sculptures.
Material	A packet of information that defines the surface properties of any object that the material is attached to. These surface properties can include color, shininess, and even subtle roughness.
Animation	Packets of information that define the movement of the associated object. These are detailed movement sequences created ahead of time, as opposed to code that calculates positions on the fly.
Particle system	An orderly mechanism for creating and controlling large numbers of small moving objects. Many visual effects, like fire, smoke, or spraying water, are created this way.

Creating art for a new game generally starts with either 2D images or 3D models because those assets form a base on which everything else relies. As the names imply, 2D images are the foundation of 2D graphics, whereas 3D models are the foundation of 3D graphics. Specifically, 2D images are flat pictures; even if you have no previous familiarity with game art, you're probably already familiar with 2D images from the graphics used on websites. Three-dimensional models, on the other hand, may need to be defined for a newcomer.

> **DEFINITION** A *model* is a 3D virtual object. In chapter 1, you were introduced to the term *mesh object*; *3D model* is practically a synonym. The terms are frequently used interchangeably, but *mesh object* strictly refers to the geometry of the 3D object (the connected lines and shapes), whereas *model* is a bit more ambiguous and often includes other attributes of the object.

The next two types of assets on the list are materials and animations. Unlike 2D images and 3D models, materials and animations don't do anything in isolation and are much harder for newcomers to understand. 2D images and 3D models are easily understood through real-world analogs: paintings for the former, sculptures for the latter. Materials and animations aren't as directly relatable to the real world. Instead, both are abstract packets of information that layer onto 3D models. In fact, materials were already introduced in a basic sense in chapter 3.

> **DEFINITION**   A *material* is a packet of information that defines the surface properties (color, shininess, etc.) of any object that it's attached to. Defining surface properties separately enables multiple objects to share a material (all the castle walls, for example).

Continuing the art analogy, you can think of a material as the medium (clay, brass, marble, and so on) that the sculpture is made of. Similarly, an animation is also an abstract layer of information that's attached to a visible object.

> **DEFINITION**   An *animation* is a packet of information that defines the movement of the associated object. Because these movements can be defined independently from the object itself, they can be used in a mix-and-match way with multiple objects.

For a concrete example, think about a character walking around. The overall position of the character is handled by the game's code (for example, the movement scripts you wrote in chapter 2). But the detailed movements of feet hitting the ground, arms swinging, and hips rotating are an animation sequence that's being played back; that animation sequence is an art asset.

To help you understand how animations and 3D models relate, let's make an analogy with puppeteering: the 3D model is the puppet, the animator is the puppeteer who makes the puppet move, and the animation is a recording of the puppet's movements. The movements defined this way are created ahead of time and are usually small-scale movements that don't change the overall positioning of the object. This is in contrast to the sort of large-scale movements that were done in code in previous chapters. The final kind of art asset from table 4.1 is a particle system.

> **DEFINITION**   A *particle system* is an orderly mechanism for creating and controlling large numbers of moving objects. These moving objects are usually small—hence the name *particle*—but they don't have to be.

Particle systems are useful for creating visual effects, like fire, smoke, or spraying water. The particles (that is, the individual objects under the control of a particle system) can be any mesh object that you choose, but for most effects the particles will be a square displaying a picture (a flame spark or a smoke puff, for example).

Much of the work of creating game art is done in external software, not within Unity itself. Materials and particle systems are created within Unity, but the other art assets are created using external software. Refer to appendix B to learn more about external tools; a variety of art applications are used for creating 3D models and animation. 3D models created in an external tool are then saved as an art asset that's imported by Unity. I use Blender when explaining how to model in appendix C (download it from www.blender.org/), but that's just because Blender is open source and thus available to all readers.

> **NOTE** The project download for this chapter includes a folder named `scratch`. Although that folder is in the same place as the Unity project, it's not part of the Unity project; that's where I put extra external files.

As you work through the project for this chapter, you'll see examples of most of these types of art assets (animations are a bit too complex for now and will be addressed later in the book). You're going to build a scene that uses 2D images, 3D models, materials, and a particle system. In some cases, you'll bring in already existing art assets and learn how to import them into Unity, but at other times (especially with the particle system) you'll create the art asset from scratch within Unity.

This chapter only scratches the surface of game art creation. Because this book focuses on how to program in Unity, extensive coverage of art disciplines would reduce how much the book could cover. Creating game art is a giant topic in and of itself, easily able to fill several books. In most cases, a game programmer would need to partner with a game artist who specializes in that discipline. That said, it's extremely useful for game programmers to understand how Unity works with art assets and possibly even create their own rough stand-ins to be replaced later (commonly known as *programmer art*).

> **NOTE** Nothing in this chapter directly requires projects from the previous chapters. But you'll want to have movement scripts like the ones from chapter 2 so that you can walk around the scene you'll build. If necessary, you can grab the player object and scripts from the project download. Similarly, this chapter ends with moving objects that are similar to the ones created in previous chapters.

4.2 Building basic 3D scenery: whiteboxing

The first content creation topic we'll go over is whiteboxing. This process is usually the first step in building a level on the computer (after designing the level on paper). As the name implies, you block out the walls of the scene with blank geometry (that is, white boxes). Looking at the list of different art assets, this blank scenery is the most basic sort of 3D model, and it provides a base on which to display 2D images. If you think back to the primitive scene you created in chapter 2, that was basically whiteboxing (you just hadn't learned the term yet). Some of this section will be a rehash of work done in the beginning of chapter 2, but we'll cover the process a lot faster this time, as well as discussing more new terminology.

> **NOTE** Another term that is frequently used is *grayboxing*. It means the same thing. I tend to use whiteboxing because that was the term I first learned, but others use grayboxing which is just as accepted. The actual color used varies anyway, similar to how blueprints aren't necessarily blue.

4.2.1   Whiteboxing explained

Blocking out the scene with blank geometry serves a couple of purposes. First, this process enables you to quickly build a sketch that will be progressively refined over time. This activity is closely associated with level design and/or level designers.

> DEFINITION   *Level design* is the discipline of planning and creating scenes (or levels) in the game. A level designer is a practitioner of level design.

As game development teams have grown in size and team members have become more specialized, a common level-building workflow is for the level designer to create a first version of the level through whiteboxing. This rough level is then handed over to the art team for visual polish. But even on a tiny team, where the same person is both designing levels and creating art for the game, this workflow of first doing whiteboxing and then polishing the visuals generally works best; you have to start somewhere, after all, and whiteboxing gives a clear foundation on which to build up the visuals.

A second purpose served by whiteboxing is that the level reaches a playable state very quickly. It may not be finished (indeed, a level right after whiteboxing is *far* from finished), but this rough version is functional and can support gameplay. At a minimum, the player can walk around the scene (think of the demo from chapter 2). In this way, you can test to make sure the level is coming together well (for example, are the rooms the right size for this game?) before investing a lot of time and energy in detailed work. If something is off (say you realize the spaces need to be bigger), then it's much easier to change and retest while you're at the whiteboxing stage.

Moreover, being able to play the under-construction level is a huge morale boost. Don't discount this benefit: Building all the visuals for a scene can take a great deal of time, and it can start to feel like a slog if you have to wait a long time before you can experience any of that work in the game. Whiteboxing builds a complete (if primitive) level right away, and it's exciting to then play the game as it continually improves.

All right, so you understand why levels start with whiteboxing; now let's build a level!

4.2.2   Drawing a floor plan for the level

Building a level on the computer follows designing the level on paper. We're not going to get into a huge discussion about level design; just as chapter 2 noted about game design, level design (which is a subset of game design) is a large discipline that could fill an entire book by itself. For our purposes, we're going to draw a basic level, with little design going into the plan, in order to give us a target to work toward.

Figure 4.1 is a top-down drawing of a simple layout with four rooms connected by a central hallway. That's all we need for a plan right now: a bunch of separated areas and interior walls to place. In a real game, your plan would be more extensive and include things like enemies and items.

Figure 4.1   Floor plan for the level: four rooms and a central corridor

You could practice whiteboxing by building this floor plan, or you could draw your own simple level to practice that step, too. The specifics of the room layout matters little for this exercise. The important thing for our purposes is to have a floor plan drawn so that we can move forward with the next step.

4.2.3   *Laying out primitives according to the plan*

Building the whitebox level in accordance with the drawn floor plan involves positioning and scaling a bunch of blank boxes to be the walls in the diagram. As described in section 2.2.1, select GameObject > 3D Object > Cube to create a blank box that you can position and scale as needed.

> **NOTE** It isn't required, but instead of cube objects you may want to use the QuadsBox object in the project download. This object is a cube constructed of six separate pieces to give you more flexibility when applying materials. Whether or not you use this object depends on your desired workflow; for example, I don't bother with QuadsBox because all the whitebox geometry will be replaced by new art later anyway.

Level editing with CSG

In the workflow featured in this chapter, the level is first blocked out with primitives, and then the final level geometry is built in an external 3D art tool. But a different approach to editing the level is called CSG (Constructive Solid Geometry). In that approach, you don't use Unity's primitives but instead use shapes referred to as *brushes*, and everything from the initial prototype to final level geometry is built within Unity.

There are multiple CSG add-ons for Unity. One option is SabreCSG, an open source set of CSG tools. Go to sabrecsg.com for more information.

The first object will be the floor of the scene; in the Inspector, rename the object and lower it to -.5 Y in order to account for the height of the box itself (figure 4.2 depicts this). Then stretch the object along the X- and Z-axes.

Name of the object

Position of the floor (lowered slightly to account for thickness)

Scale out on X and Z.

Figure 4.2   Inspector view of the box positioned and scaled for the floor

Repeat these steps to create the walls of the scene. You probably want to clean up the Hierarchy view by making walls children of a common base object (remember, position the root object at 0, 0, 0, and then drag objects onto it in Hierarchy), but that's not required. Also put a few simple lights around the scene so that you can see it; referring to chapter 2, create lights by selecting them in the Light submenu of the GameObject menu. The level should look something like figure 4.3 once you're done with whiteboxing.

A room (blocked out with interior walls)

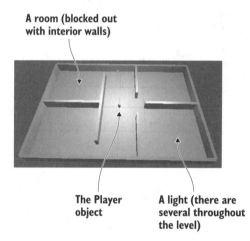

Figure 4.3   Whitebox level of the floor plan in figure 4.1

The Player object

A light (there are several throughout the level)

Set up your player object or camera to move around (create the player with a character controller and movement scripts; refer to chapter 2 if you need a full explanation). Now you can walk around the primitive scene in order to experience your work and test it out. And that's how you do whiteboxing! Pretty simple—but all you have right now is blank geometry, so let's dress up the geometry with pictures on the walls.

Exporting whitebox geometry to external art tools

Much of the work when adding visual polish to the level is done in external 3D art applications like Blender. Because of this, you may want to have the whitebox geometry in your art tool to refer to. By default, there's no export option for primitives laid out within Unity. But third-party scripts that add this functionality to the editor are available. Most of these scripts allow you to select the geometry and then hit an Export button.

These custom scripts usually export geometry as an OBJ file. (OBJ is one of several file types discussed later in this chapter.) On the Unity3D website, click the Search button and type `obj exporter`. Or you can go here for one option: http://wiki.unity3d.com/index.php?title=ObjExporter.

4.3 Texture the scene with 2D images

The level at this point is a rough sketch. It's playable, but clearly a lot more work needs to be done on the visual appearance of the scene. The next step in improving the look of the level is applying textures.

> **DEFINITION** A *texture* is a 2D image being used to enhance 3D graphics. That's literally the totality of what the term means; don't confuse yourself by thinking that any of the uses of textures are part of how the term is defined. No matter how the image is being used, it's still referred to as a texture.

> **NOTE** The word *texture* is routinely used as both a verb and a noun. In addition to the noun definition, the word describes the action of using 2D images in 3D graphics.

Textures have a number of uses in 3D graphics, but the most straightforward use is to be displayed on the surface of 3D models. Later in this chapter, we'll discuss how this works for more complex models, but for our whiteboxed level, the 2D images will act as wallpaper covering the walls (see figure 4.4).

Before texturing
(only shading from lights)

After applying textures
(1 floor texture, 1 on all walls)

Figure 4.4   Comparing the level before and after textures

As you can see from the comparison in figure 4.4, textures turn what was an obviously unreal digital construct into a brick wall. Other uses for textures include masks to cut out shapes and normal maps to make surfaces bumpy. Later, you may want to look up more information about textures in the resources mentioned in appendix D.

4.3.1   Choosing a file format

A variety of file formats is available for saving 2D images, so which should you use? Unity supports the use of many different file formats, so you could choose any of the ones shown in table 4.2.

Table 4.2   2D image file formats supported by Unity

File type	Pros and cons
PNG	Commonly used on the web. Lossless compression; has an alpha channel.
JPG	Commonly used on the web. Lossy compression; no alpha channel.
GIF	Commonly used on the web. Lossy compression; no alpha channel. (Technically, the loss isn't from compression; rather, data is lost when the image is converted to 8-bit. Ultimately, it amounts to the same thing.)
BMP	Default image format on Windows. No compression; no alpha channel.
TGA	Commonly used for 3D graphics; obscure everywhere else. No or lossless compression; has an alpha channel.
TIFF	Commonly used for digital photography and publishing. No or lossless compression; no alpha channel.
PICT	Default image format on old Macs. Lossy compression; no alpha channel.
PSD	Native file format for Photoshop. No compression; has an alpha channel. The main reason to use this file format would be the advantage of using Photoshop files directly.

DEFINITION   The *alpha channel* is used to store transparency information in an image. The visible colors come in three *channels* of information: Red, Green, and Blue. Alpha is an additional channel of information that isn't visible but controls the visibility of the image.

Although Unity will accept any of the images shown in table 4.2 to import and use as a texture, the file formats vary considerably in what features they support. Two factors are particularly important for 2D images imported as textures: How is the image compressed, and does it have an alpha channel? The alpha channel is a straightforward consideration: Because the alpha channel is used often in 3D graphics, it's better when the image has an alpha channel. Image compression is a slightly more complicated consideration, but it boils down to "lossy compression is bad." Both no compression and lossless compression preserve the image quality, whereas lossy compression reduces the image quality (hence the term *lossy*) as part of reducing the file size.

Between these two considerations, the two file formats I recommend for Unity textures are either PNG or TGA. Targas (TGA) used to be the favorite file format for texturing 3D graphics, before PNG had become widely used on the internet. These days, PNG is almost equivalent technologically but is much more widespread, because it's useful both on the web and as a texture. PSD is also commonly recommended for Unity textures, because it's an advanced file format and it's convenient that the same file you work on in Photoshop also works in Unity. But I tend to prefer keeping work files separate from "finished" files that are exported over to Unity (this same mind-set comes up again later with 3D models).

The upshot is that all the images I provide in the example projects are PNG, and I recommend that you work with that file format as well. With this decision made, it's time to bring some images into Unity and apply them to the blank scene.

4.3.2 Importing an image file

Let's start creating/preparing the textures we'll use. The images used to texture levels are usually tileable so that they can be repeated across large surfaces like the floor.

> **DEFINITION** A *tileable* image (sometimes referred to as a *seamless tile*) is an image where opposite edges match up when placed side by side. This way, the image can be repeated without any visible seams between the repeats. The concept for 3D texturing is just like wallpapers on web pages.

You can obtain tileable images in several different ways, like manipulating photographs or even painting them by hand. Tutorials and explanations of these techniques can be found in numerous books and websites, but we don't want to get bogged down with that right now. Instead, let's grab a couple of tileable images from one of the many websites that offer a catalog of such images for 3D artists to use. I obtained a couple of images from www.textures.com/ (see figure 4.5) to apply to the walls and floor of the level; find a couple of images you think look good for the floor and walls.

Figure 4.5 Seamlessly tiling stone and brick images obtained from textures.com

Download the images you want and prepare them for use as textures. Technically, you could use the images directly as they were downloaded, but those images aren't ideal for use as textures. Although they're certainly tileable (the important aspect of why you're using these images), they aren't the right size and they're the wrong file format. Textures should be sized in powers of 2. For reasons of technical efficiency, graphics chips like to handle textures in sizes that are 2^N: 4, 8, 16, 32, 64, 128, 256, 512, 1024, 2048 (the next number is 4096, but at that point the image is too big to use as a texture). In your image editor (Photoshop, GIMP, or whatever; refer to appendix B), scale the downloaded image to 256 x 256, and save it as a PNG.

Now drag the files from their location in the computer into the Project view in Unity. This will copy the files into your Unity project (see figure 4.6), at which point they're imported as textures and can be used in the 3D scene. If dragging the file over would be awkward, you could instead right-click in Project and select Import New Asset to get a file picker.

Figure 4.6   Drag images from outside Unity to import them into the Project view.

TIP   Organizing your assets into separate folders is probably a good idea as your projects start to get more complex. In the Project view, create folders for Scripts and Textures and then move assets into the appropriate folders. Simply drag files to their new folder.

WARNING   Unity has several keywords that it responds to in folder names, with special ways of handling the contents of these special folders. Those keywords are Resources, Plugins, Editor, and Gizmos. Later in the book, we'll go over what some of these special folders do, but for now, avoid naming any folders with those words.

Now the images are imported into Unity as textures, ready to use. But how do we apply the textures to objects in the scene?

4.3.3   *Applying the image*

Technically, textures aren't applied to geometry directly. Instead, textures can be part of materials, and materials are applied to geometry. As explained in the introduction, a material is a set of information defining the properties of a surface; that information can include a texture to display on that surface. This indirection is significant because the same texture can be used with multiple materials. That said, typically each texture goes with a different material, so for convenience Unity allows you to drop a texture onto an object and then it creates a new material automatically. If you drag a texture from Project view onto an object in the scene, Unity will create a new material and apply the new material to the object; figure 4.7 illustrates the maneuver. Try that now with the texture for the floor.

Assets ▸ **Textures**

BrickRound0067 (Texture2D)

BrickLargeBa... BrickRound0

Figure 4.7   One way to apply textures is by dragging them from Project onto Scene objects.

Besides this convenience method of automatically creating materials, the "proper" way to create a material is through the Create submenu of the Assets menu; the new asset will appear in the Project view. Now select the material to show its properties in the Inspector (you'll see something like figure 4.8) and drag a texture to the main texture slot; the setting is called Albedo (that's a technical term for the base color) and the texture slot is the square to the side of the panel. Meanwhile, drag the material up from Project onto an object in the scene to apply the material to that object. Try these steps now with the texture for the wall: create a new material, drag the wall texture into this material, and drag the material onto a wall in the scene.

Assets ▸ **Textures**

BrickLargeBa... BrickRound0...

ⓘ Inspector

BrickLargeBare0032

Shader Standard

Rendering Mode   Opaque

Main Maps
BrickLargeBare0032 (Texture2D)
○ Albedo

○ Metallic

Smoothness

○ Normal Map

○ Height Map

Figure 4.8   Select a material to see it in the Inspector, then drag textures to the material properties.

You should now see the stone and brick images appear on the surface of the floor and wall objects, but the images look rather stretched-out and blurry. What's happening is the single image is being stretched out to cover the entire floor. What you want instead is for the image to repeat a few times over the floor surface. You can set this using the tiling property of the material; select the material in Project and then change the tiling number in the Inspector (with separate X and Y values for tiling in each direction).

Make sure you're setting the tiling of the main map and not the secondary map (this material supports a secondary texture map for advanced effects). The default tiling is 1 (that's no tiling, with the image being stretched over the entire surface); change the number to something like 8 and see what happens in the scene. Change the numbers in both materials to tiling that looks good.

> **NOTE**   Adjusting the tiling property like this is only useful for texturing white-box geometry; in a polished game, the floor and walls will be built with more intricate art tools, and that includes setting up their textures.

Great, now the scene has textures applied to the floor and walls! You can also apply textures to the sky of the scene; let's look at that process.

4.4   *Generating sky visuals using texture images*

The brick and stone textures gave a much more natural look to the walls and floor. Yet the sky is currently blank and unnatural; we also want a realistic look for the sky. The most common approach to this task is a special kind of texturing using pictures of the sky.

4.4.1   *What is a skybox?*

By default, the camera's background color is dark blue. Ordinarily, that color fills in any empty area of the view (for example, above the walls of this scene), but it's possible to render pictures of the sky as background. This is where the concept of a *skybox* comes in.

> **DEFINITION**   A *skybox* is a cube surrounding the camera with pictures of the sky on each side. No matter what direction the camera is facing, it's looking at a picture of the sky.

Properly implementing a skybox can be tricky; figure 4.9 shows a diagram of how a skybox works. A number of rendering tricks are needed for the skybox to appear as a distant background. Fortunately, Unity already takes care of all that for you.

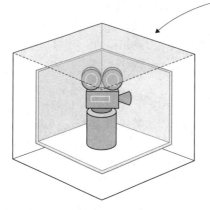

The skybox – functionality needed:

Render behind everything else in the scene.

Stay centered on the camera, so that it will seem too far away for the player's movements to affect it.

Full brightness with no shading applied, to avoid any lighting differences between sides of the cube.

Figure 4.9   Diagram of a skybox

New scenes come with a very simple skybox already assigned to them. This is why the sky has a gradient from light to dark blue, rather than being a flat dark blue. If you open the lighting window (Window > Lighting > Settings), the first setting is Skybox Material and the slot for that setting says Default. This setting is in the Environment Lighting panel; this window has a number of settings panels related to the advanced lighting system in Unity, but for now, we only care about the first setting.

Just like the brick textures earlier, skybox images can be obtained from a variety of websites. Search for *skybox textures*; for example, I obtained several great skyboxes from https://93i.de/, including the TropicalSunnyDay set. Once this skybox is applied to the scene, you will see something like figure 4.10.

Figure 4.10   Scene with background pictures of the sky

As with other textures, skybox images are first assigned to a material, and that gets used in the scene. Let's examine how to create a new skybox material.

4.4.2   Creating a new skybox material

First, create a new material (as usual, either right-click and Create, or choose Create from the Assets menu) and select it to see settings in the Inspector. Next, you need to change the shader used by this material. The top of the material settings has a Shader menu (see figure 4.11). In section 4.3, we pretty much ignored this menu because the default works fine for most standard texturing, but a skybox requires a special shader.

> **DEFINITION**   A *shader* is a short program that outlines instructions for how to draw a surface, including whether to use any textures. The computer uses these instructions to calculate the pixels when rendering the image. The most common shader takes the color of the material and darkens it according to the light, but shaders can also be used for all sorts of visual effects.

Every material has a shader that controls it (you could think of a material as an instance of a shader). New materials are set to the Standard shader by default. This shader displays the color of the material (including the texture) while applying basic dark and light across the surface.

For skyboxes, there's a different shader. Click the menu in order to see the dropdown list (see figure 4.11) of all the available shaders. Move down to the Skybox section and choose 6 Sided in the submenu.

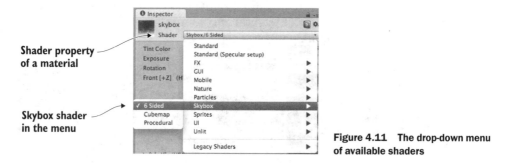

Shader property of a material

Skybox shader in the menu

Figure 4.11   **The drop-down menu of available shaders**

With this shader active, the material now has six large texture slots (instead of only the small Albedo texture slot that the standard shader has). These six texture slots correspond to the six sides of a cube, so these images should match up at the edges in order to appear seamless. For example, figure 4.12 shows the images for the sunny skybox.

Skybox images from 93i.de: up, down, front, back, left, right

Figure 4.12   **Six sides of a skybox—images for top, bottom, front, back, left, and right**

Import the skybox images into Unity the same way you brought in the brick textures: drag the files into the Project view or right-click in Project and select Import New Asset. There's one subtle import setting to change; click the imported texture to see its properties in the Inspector, and change the Wrap Mode setting (shown in figure 4.13) from Repeat to Clamp (don't forget to click Apply when you're done). Ordinarily, textures can be tiled repeatedly over a surface; for this to appear seamless, opposite edges of the image bleed together. But this blending of edges can create faint lines in the sky where images meet, so the Clamp setting (similar to the `Clamp()` function in chapter 2) will limit the boundaries of the texture and get rid of this blending.

Faint lines may be visible at the edges of the skybox images ...

... so change the Wrap Mode of the textures from Repeat to Clamp.

Figure 4.13   Correct faint edge lines by adjusting the Wrap mode.

Now you can drag these images to the texture slots of the skybox material. The names of the images correspond to the texture slot to assign them to (such as left or front). Once all six textures are linked up, you can use this new material as the skybox for the scene. Open the lighting window again and set this new material to the Skybox slot; either drag the material to that slot, or click the tiny circle icon to bring up a file picker.

> **TIP**   By default, Unity will display the skybox (or at least its main color) in the editor's Scene view. You may find this color distracting while editing objects, so you can toggle the skybox on or off. Across the top of the Scene view's pane are buttons that control what's visible; look for the Effects button to toggle the skybox on or off.

Woo-hoo, you've learned how to create sky visuals for your scene! A skybox is an elegant way to create the illusion of a vast atmosphere surrounding the player. The next step in polishing the visuals in your level is to create more complex 3D models.

4.5   *Working with custom 3D models*

In the previous sections, we looked at applying textures to the large flat walls and floors of the level. But what about more detailed objects? What if you want, say, interesting furniture in the room? You can accomplish that by building 3D models in external 3D art apps. Recall the definition from the introduction to this chapter: 3D models are the mesh objects in the game (that is, the three-dimensional shapes). Well, you're going to import a 3D mesh of a simple bench.

Applications widely used for modeling 3D objects include Autodesk's Maya and 3ds Max. Those are both expensive commercial tools, so the sample for this chapter uses the open source app Blender. The sample download includes a `.blend` file that you can use; figure 4.14 depicts the bench model in Blender. If you're interested in learning how to model your own objects, you'll find an exercise in appendix C about modeling this bench in Blender.

This includes both the 3D mesh geometry
and a texture applied to the mesh.

Figure 4.14   The bench model in Blender

Besides custom-made models created by yourself or an artist you're working with, many 3D models are available for download from game art websites. One great resource for 3D models is Unity's Asset Store: https://www.assetstore.unity3d.com.

4.5.1   Which file format to choose?

After you obtain a model made in an external art tool, you need to export the asset from that software. Just as with 2D images, a number of different file formats are available for you to use when exporting the 3D model, and these file types have various pros and cons. Table 4.3 lists the 3D file formats that Unity supports.

Table 4.3   3D Model file formats supported by Unity

File type	Pros and cons
FBX	Mesh and Animation; recommended option when available.
Collada (DAE)	Mesh and Animation; another good option when FBX isn't available.
OBJ	Mesh only; this is a text format, so sometimes useful for streaming over the internet.
3DS	Mesh only; a pretty old and primitive model format.
DXF	Mesh only; a pretty old and primitive model format.
Maya	Works via FBX; requires this application to be installed.
3ds Max	Works via FBX; requires this application to be installed.
Blender	Works via FBX; requires this application to be installed.

Choosing an option boils down to whether or not the file supports animation. Because Collada and FBX are the only two options that include animation data, those are the two options to choose. Whenever it's available (not all 3D tools have it as an export option), FBX export tends to work best, but if you're using a tool without FBX export, then Collada works well, too. In our case, Blender supports FBX export, so we'll use that file format.

Note that the bottom of table 4.3 lists several 3D art applications. Unity allows you to directly drop those application's files into your project, which seems handy at first, but that functionality has some caveats. For starters, Unity doesn't load those application files directly; instead, it exports the model behind the scenes and loads that exported file. Because the model is being exported to FBX or Collada anyway, it's preferable to do that step explicitly. Furthermore, this export requires you to have the relevant application installed. This requirement is a big hassle if you plan to share files among multiple computers (for example, a team of developers working together). I don't recommend using 3D art application files directly in Unity.

4.5.2 Exporting and importing the model

All right, it's time to export the model from Blender and then import it into Unity. First, open the bench in Blender and then choose File > Export > FBX. Once the file is saved, import it into Unity the same way that you import images. Drag the FBX file from the computer into Unity's Project view or right-click in Project and choose Import New Asset. The 3D model will be copied into the Unity project and show up ready to be put in the scene.

> **NOTE** The sample download includes the .blend file so that you can practice exporting the FBX file from Blender; even if you don't end up modeling anything yourself, you may need to convert downloaded models into a format Unity accepts. If you want to skip all steps involving Blender, use the provided FBX file.

There are a few default settings used to import the model that you want to change immediately. First, Unity defaults imported models to a very small scale (refer to figure 4.15, which shows what you see in the Inspector when you select the model); change the Scale Factor to 100 to partially counteract the .01 File Scale. You may also want to click the Generate Colliders check box, but that's optional; without a collider you can walk through the bench. Then, switch to the Animation tab in the import settings and deselect Import Animation (you didn't animate this model).

Optional: Generate a collider or you can walk through the bench.

Default size is too small so set scale to 100.

Turn off animation because the bench is static.

Figure 4.15   Adjust import settings for the 3D model.

That takes care of the imported mesh. Now for the texture; when Unity imported the FBX file, it also created a material for the bench. This material defaults to blank (just like any new material), so assign the bench texture (the image in figure 4.16) in the same way that you assigned bricks to the walls earlier: drag the texture image into Project to import it into Unity, and then drag the imported texture onto the texture slot of the bench material. The image looks somewhat odd, with different parts of the image appearing on different parts of the bench; the model's texture coordinates were edited to define this mapping of image-to-mesh.

This image relates to the model using "texture coordinates."

To understand the concept of texture coordinates, refer to appendix C.

Figure 4.16   The 2D image for the bench texture

DEFINITION   *Texture coordinates* are an extra set of values for each vertex that assign polygons to areas of the texture image. Think about it like wrapping paper; the 3D model is the box being wrapped, the texture is the wrapping paper, and the texture coordinates represent where on the wrapping paper each side of the box will go.

NOTE   Even if you don't want to model the bench, you may want to read the detailed explanation of *texture coordinates* in appendix C. The concept of texture coordinates (as well as other related terms like UVs and mapping) can be useful to know when programming games.

New materials are often too shiny, so you may want to reduce the Smoothness setting (smoother surfaces are more shiny) to 0. Finally, having adjusted everything as needed, you can put the bench in the scene. Drag the model up from the Project view and place it in one room of the level; as you drag the mouse, you should see it in the scene. Once you drop it in place, you should see something like figure 4.17. Congratulations; you've created a textured model for the level!

NOTE   We're not going to do it in this chapter, but typically, you'd also replace the whitebox geometry with models created in an external tool. The new geometry might look essentially identical, but you'll have much more flexibility in controlling the texture.

Figure 4.17 The imported bench in the level

Animating characters with Mecanim

The model you created is static, sitting still where placed. You can also animate in Blender and then play the animation in Unity. The process of creating 3D animation is long and involved, but this isn't a book about animation so we're not going to discuss that here. As has already been mentioned for modeling, there are a lot of existing resources if you want to learn more about 3D animation. But be warned: it is a *huge* topic. There's a reason "animator" is a specialized role within game development.

Unity has a sophisticated system for managing animations on models, a system called *Mecanim*. The special name Mecanim identifies the newer, more advanced animation system that was added to Unity as a replacement for the older animation system. The older system is still around, identified as legacy animation. But the legacy animation system may be phased out in a future version of Unity, at which point Mecanim will be *the* animation system.

Although we don't work with any animations in this chapter, we'll play animations on characters in future chapters.

4.6   *Creating effects using particle systems*

Besides 2D images and 3D models, the remaining type of visual content that game artists create are particle systems. The definition in this chapter's introduction explained
that particle systems are orderly mechanisms for creating and controlling large numbers of moving objects. Particle systems are useful for creating visual effects, like fire,
smoke, or spraying water. The fire effect in figure 4.18 was created using a particle
system.

Figure 4.18   Fire effect created using a particle system

Whereas most other art assets are created in external tools and imported into the project, particle systems are created within Unity itself. Unity provides some flexible and
powerful tools for creating particle effects.

> **NOTE**   Much like the situation with the Mecanim animation system, there used
> to be an older legacy particle system and the newer system had a special name,
> Shuriken. At this point, the legacy particle system has been phased out, so the
> separate name is no longer necessary.

To begin, create a new particle system and watch the default effect play. From the
GameObject menu, choose Particle System, and you'll see basic white puffballs spraying upward from the new object. Or rather, you'll see particles spraying upward while
you have the object selected; when you select a particle system, the particle playback
panel is displayed in the corner of the screen and indicates how much time has elapsed
(see figure 4.19).

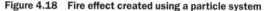

Pause or reset the particle effect playing in the scene.

Click and drag the label Playback Time to play back and forth.

Figure 4.19 Playback panel for a particle system

The default effect looks pretty neat already, but let's go through the extensive list of parameters you can use to customize the effect.

4.6.1 *Adjusting parameters on the default effect*

Figure 4.20 shows the entire list of settings for a particle system. We're not going to go through every single setting in that list; instead, we'll look at those relevant to making the fire effect. Once you understand how a few of the settings work, the rest should be fairly self-explanatory. Each setting's labels is in fact a whole information panel. Initially, only the first information panel is expanded; the rest of the panels are collapsed. Click on the setting's label to expand that information panel.

> **TIP** Many of the settings are controlled by a curve displayed at the bottom of the Inspector. That curve represents how the value changes over time: the left side of the graph is when the particle first appears, the right side is when the particle is gone, the bottom is a value of 0, and the top is the maximum value. Drag points around the graph and double-click or right-click on the curve to insert new points.

Adjust parameters of the particle system as indicated in figure 4.20 and it'll look more like a jet of flame.

4.6.2 *Applying a new texture for fire*

Now the particle system looks more like a jet of flame, but the effect still needs the particles to look like flame, not white blobs. That requires importing a new image into Unity. Figure 4.21 depicts the image I painted; I made an orange dot and used the Smudge tool to draw out the tendrils of the flame (and then I drew the same thing in yellow). Whether you use this image from the sample project, draw your own, or download a similar one, you need to import the image file into Unity. As explained previously, drag image files into the Project view, or choose Assets > Import New Asset.

Looping: The particle system keeps playing forever; leave default.

Lifetime: How long the particle exists; reduce to 3.

Speed: How fast the particle is moving; reduce to 1.

Size: How big the particle is; leave default.

Rotation: The orientation of the particle; click the arrow menu to change to Between Constants, set to 0 and 180.

Color: Tint the particles. You want a dim orange, like RGB values 182, 101, 58.

Local simulation space is fine for a still particle system, but World may be better for a system that's moving.

Emission: How quickly particles are emitted; leave default.

Shape: The shape of the area emitted from. The default is a wide cone, but we want a small box to make a tight jet of flame (set Box, all numbers 0.2).

Size over Lifetime: The particle grows and shrinks while it moves. The default is off; turn this on and click the arrow to set a curve that quickly grows from 0 and then slowly shrinks back to 0 (as illustrated here).

Rotation over Lifetime: The particle rotates while it moves. The default is off. Turn this on and set Random Between to −80 and 80 to make different particles rotate in different directions.

Renderer: Set what each particle looks like. You could even set this to a mesh, but leave it as Billboard and drag in a new material (explained shortly).

Add points to the curve by double-clicking or right-click and select Add Key.

Particle System	
Duration	5.00
Looping	☑
Prewarm	☐
Start Delay	0
Start Lifetime	3
Start Speed	1
3D Start Size	☐
Start Size	1
3D Start Rotation	☐
Start Rotation	0 180
Randomize Rotation Direc	0
Start Color	
Gravity Modifier	0
Simulation Space	World
Scaling Mode	Shape
Play On Awake*	☑
Max Particles	1000
Auto Random Seed	☑
✓ Emission	
✓ Shape	
Velocity over Lifetime	
Limit Velocity over Lifetime	
Inherit Velocity	
Force over Lifetime	
Color over Lifetime	
Color by Speed	
✓ Size over Lifetime	
Separate Axes	☐
Size	
Size by Speed	
✓ Rotation over Lifetime	
Rotation by Speed	
External Forces	
Collision	
Triggers	
Sub Emitters	
Texture Sheet Animation	
✓ Renderer	

Particle System Curves

1.0

Figure 4.20 The Inspector displays settings for a particle system (pointing out settings for the fire effect).

Figure 4.21   The image used for fire particles

Just like with 3D models, textures aren't applied to particle systems directly; you add the texture to a material and apply that material to the particle system. Create a new material and then select it to see its properties in the Inspector. Drag the fire image from Project up to the texture slot. That links the fire texture to the fire material, so now you want to apply the material to the particle system. Figure 4.22 shows how to do this; select the particle system, expand Renderer at the bottom of the settings, and drag the material onto the Material slot.

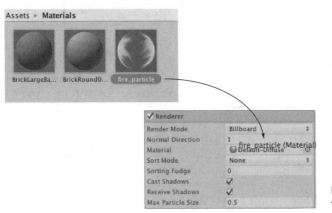

Figure 4.22   Assign a material to the particle system.

As you did for the skybox material, you need to change the shader for a particle material. Click the Shader menu near the top of the material settings to see the list of available shaders. Instead of the standard default, a material for particles needs one of the shaders under the Particles submenu. As shown in figure 4.23, in this case, we want Additive (Soft). This will make the particles appear to be hazy and brighten the scene, just like a fire.

Figure 4.23   **Setting the shader for the fire particle material**

DEFINITION   *Additive* is a shader that adds the color of the particle to the color behind it, as opposed to replacing the pixels. This makes the pixels brighter and makes black on the particle turn invisible. The opposite is *Multiply*, which makes everything darker; these shaders have the same visual effect as the Additive and Multiply layer effects in Photoshop.

With the fire material assigned to the fire particle effect, it'll now look like the effect shown in figure 4.18. This looks like a pretty convincing jet of flame, but the effect doesn't only work when sitting still; next, let's attach it to an object that moves around.

4.6.3   Attaching particle effects to 3D objects

Create a sphere (remember, GameObject > 3D Object > Sphere). Create a new script called `BackAndForth` and attach it to the new sphere.

> **Listing 4.1   Moving an object back and forth along a straight path**

```
using UnityEngine;
using System.Collections;

public class BackAndForth : MonoBehaviour {
    public float speed = 3.0f;
    public float maxZ = 16.0f;
    public float minZ = -16.0f;

    private int _direction = 1;
```

These are the positions the object moves between.

Which direction is the object currently moving in?

```
void Update() {
    transform.Translate(0, 0, _direction * speed * Time.deltaTime);

    bool bounced = false;
    if (transform.position.z > maxZ || transform.position.z < minZ) {
        _direction = -_direction;
        bounced = true;
    }
    if (bounced) {
        transform.Translate(0, 0, _direction * speed * Time.deltaTime);
    }
}
}
```

Make an extra movement this frame if the object switched directions.

Toggle the direction back and forth.

Run this script and the sphere glides back and forth in the central corridor of the level. Now you can make the particle system a child of the sphere and the fire will move with the sphere. Just like with the walls of the level, in the Hierarchy view, drag the particle object onto the sphere object.

> **WARNING** You usually have to reset the position of an object after making it the child of another object. For example, we want the particle system at 0, 0, 0 (this is relative to the parent). Unity will preserve the placement of an object from before it was linked as a child.

Now the particle system moves along with the sphere. However, the fire isn't deflecting from the movement, which looks unnatural. That's because, by default, particles move correctly only in the local space of the particle system. To complete the flaming sphere, find Simulation Space in the particle system settings (it's in the top panel of figure 4.20) and switch from Local to World.

> **NOTE** In this script, the object moves back and forth in a straight line, but video games commonly have objects moving around complex paths. Unity comes with support for complex navigation and paths; see https://docs.unity3d.com/Manual/Navigation.html to read about it.

I'm sure that, at this point, you're itching to apply your own ideas and add more content to this sample game. You should do that—you could create more art assets, or even test your skills by bringing in the shooting mechanics developed in chapter 3. In the next chapter, we'll switch gears to a different game genre and start over with a new game. Even though future chapters will switch to different game genres, everything from these first four chapters will still apply and will be useful.

Summary

- *Art asset* is the term for all individual graphics.
- Whiteboxing is a useful first step for level designers to block out spaces.
- Textures are 2D images displayed on the surface of 3D models.
- 3D models are created outside Unity and imported as FBX files.
- Particle systems are used to create many visual effects (fire, smoke, water, and so on).

part 2

Getting comfortable

You've built your first game prototypes in Unity, so now you're ready to stretch yourself by tackling other game genres. At this point, the rhythms of working in Unity should feel familiar: create a script with such and such function, drag this object to that slot in the Inspector, and so forth. You're not tripping over details of the interface so much anymore, which means the remaining chapters don't need to rehash the basics.

Let's run through a succession of additional projects that will progressively teach you more and more about developing games in Unity.

Building a Memory game using Unity's 2D functionality

This chapter covers

- Displaying 2D graphics in Unity
- Making objects clickable
- Loading new images programmatically
- Maintaining and displaying state using UI text
- Loading levels and restarting the game

Up to now, we've been working with 3D graphics, but you can also work with 2D graphics in Unity. So in this chapter, you'll build a 2D game to learn about that. You're going to develop the classic children's game Memory: you'll display a grid of card backs, reveal the card front when it's clicked, and score matches. These mechanics cover the basics you need to know in order to develop 2D games in Unity.

Although Unity originated as a tool for 3D games, it's used often for 2D games as well. Later versions of Unity (starting with version 4.3, released near the end of 2013) have added the ability to display 2D graphics, but even before then 2D games were already being developed in Unity (especially mobile games that took advantage of Unity's cross-platform nature). In prior versions of Unity, game developers required a third-party framework (such as 2D Toolkit from Unikron Software) to emulate 2D graphics within Unity's 3D scenes. Eventually, the core editor and game engine were modified to incorporate 2D graphics, and this chapter will teach you about that newer functionality.

The 2D workflow in Unity is more or less the same as the workflow to develop a 3D game: import art assets, drag them into a scene, and write scripts to attach to the objects. The primary kind of art asset in 2D graphics is called a *sprite*.

> **DEFINITION**   *Sprites* are 2D images displayed directly on the screen, as opposed to images displayed on the surface of 3D models (that is, *textures*).

You can import 2D images into Unity as sprites in much the same way you can import images as textures (see chapter 4). Technically, these sprites will be objects in 3D space, but they'll be flat surfaces all oriented perpendicular to the Z-axis. Because they'll all face the same direction, you can point the camera straight at the sprites and players will only be able to discern their movements along the X- and Y-axes (that is, two dimensions).

In chapter 2, we discussed the coordinate axes: having three dimensions adds a Z-axis perpendicular to the X- and Y-axes you were already familiar with. Two dimensions are just those X- and Y-axes (that's what your teacher was talking about in math class!).

5.1   *Setting everything up for 2D graphics*

You're going to create the classic game of Memory. For those unfamiliar with this game, a series of cards will be dealt out facedown. Every card will have a matching card located somewhere else, but the player will see only the reverse side of the card. The player can turn over two cards at a time, attempting to find matching cards; if the two cards chosen aren't a match, they'll flip back and then the player can guess again.

Figure 5.1 shows a mock-up of the game we're going to build; compare this to the roadmap diagram from chapter 2.

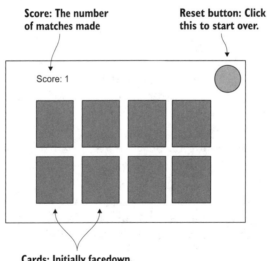

Score: The number
of matches made

Reset button: Click
this to start over.

Score: 1

Cards: Initially facedown,
show image when clicked

Figure 5.1   Mock-up of what the Memory
game will look like

Note that the mock-up this time depicts exactly what the player will see (whereas the mock-up for a 3D scene depicted the space around the player and then where the camera went for the player to see through). Now that you know what you'll be building, it's time to get to work!

5.1.1 Preparing the project

The first step is to gather up and display graphics for our game. In much the same way as building the 3D demo previously, you want to start the new game by putting together the minimum set of graphics for the game to operate, and after that's in place, you can start programming the functionality.

That means you'll need to create everything depicted in figure 5.1: card backs for hidden cards, a series of card fronts for when they turn over, a score display in one corner, and a reset button in the opposite corner. We also need a background for the screen, so all together, our art requirements sum up to figure 5.2.

Card back

Background (table top)

Card front (four different symbols)

Start   Reset button

Figure 5.2   Art assets required for the Memory game

> **TIP**   As always, a finished version of the project, including all necessary art assets, can be downloaded from www.manning.com/books/unity-in-action-second-edition, this book's website. You can copy the images from there to use in your own project.

Gather together the required images, and then create a new project in Unity. In the New Project window that comes up, you'll notice a couple of buttons at the bottom (shown in figure 5.3) that let you switch between 2D and 3D mode. In previous chapters, we've worked with 3D graphics, and because that's the default value we haven't been concerned with this setting. In this chapter, though, you'll want to switch to 2D mode when creating a new project.

2D setting at the bottom of the window

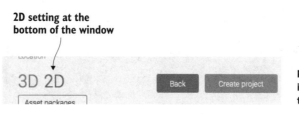

Figure 5.3   Create new projects in either 2D or 3D mode with these buttons.

2D Editor mode and 2D Scene view

The 2D/3D setting for new projects adjusts two different settings within Unity's editor, both of which you can adjust manually later if you wish. Those two settings are the 2D Editor mode and the 2D Scene view. The 2D Scene view controls how the scene is displayed within Unity; toggle the 2D button along the top of the Scene view.

2D view toggle button

2D Scene view toggle

You set 2D Editor mode by opening the Edit menu and selecting Editor from the Project Settings drop-down menu. Within those settings, you'll see the Default Behavior Mode setting with selections for either 3D or 2D.

Editor Settings

Unity Remote
Device   None
Compression   JPEG
Resolution   Normal
Joystick Source   Remote

Version Control
Mode   Hidden Meta Files

WWW Security Emulation
Enable Webplayer Secu ☐
Host URL   http://www.mydomain.com/myg

Asset Serialization
Mode   Mixed

Default Behavior Mode
Mode   2D   ← **2D/3D Behavior Mode menu**

Sprite Packer
Mode   Always Enabled
Padding Power   1

C# Project Generation
Additional extensions   txt;xml;fnt;cd
Root namespace

Default Behavior Mode setting within Edit > Project Settings > Editor

Setting the editor to 2D mode causes imported images to be set to Sprite; as you saw in chapter 4, images normally import as textures. 2D Editor mode also causes new scenes to lack the default 3D lighting setup; this lighting doesn't harm 2D scenes, but it's unnecessary. If you ever need to remove it manually, delete the directional light that comes with new scenes and turn off the skybox in the lighting window (click the tiny circle icon for a file picker and choose None from the list).

With the new project for this chapter created and set for 2D, we can start putting our images into the scene.

5.1.2 Displaying 2D images (aka sprites)

Drag all the image files into the Project view to import them; make sure the images are imported as sprites and not textures. (This is automatic if the editor is set to 2D. Select an asset to see its import settings in the Inspector.) Now drag the table_top sprite (our background image) up from the Project view into the empty scene. As with mesh objects, in the Inspector there's a Transform component for the sprite; type 0, 0, 5 to position the background image.

> **TIP** Another import setting to take note of is Pixels-Per-Unit. Because Unity was previously a 3D engine that has recently had 2D graphics grafted in, one unit in Unity isn't necessarily one pixel in the image. You could set the Pixels-To-Units setting to 1:1, but I recommend leaving it at the default of 100:1 (because the physics engine doesn't work properly at 1:1, and the default is better for compatibility with others' code).

Creating atlases using Sprite Packer

Although we're going to use separate images in this project, you can have multiple sprites laid out in a single image. The image is usually called a *sprite sheet* when numerous frames of an animation are combined into one image, but the more general term for multiple images combined into one is an *atlas*.

Animated sprites are common in 2D games, and those will be implemented in the next chapter. Multiple frames can be imported as multiple images, but games usually have all the frames of animation laid out in a sprite sheet. Basically, all the separate frames appear as a grid on one large image.

In addition to keeping frames of animation together, sprite atlases are also often used for still images. That's because atlases can optimize the performance of sprites in two ways: (1) by reducing the amount of wasted space in images by packing them tightly, and (2) by reducing the draw calls of the video card (every new image that's loaded causes a bit more work for the video card).

Sprite atlases can be created using external tools like TexturePacker (see appendix B) and that approach will certainly work. But Unity includes a Sprite Packer, which packs together multiple sprites automatically. To use this feature, enable Sprite Packer in Editor settings (found under Edit > Project Settings). Now write a name in the Packing Tag option when looking at the Import settings of a sprite image; Unity will pack together sprites with the same packing tag into one atlas. For more information, look at Unity's documentation: http://docs.unity3d.com/Manual/SpritePacker.html.

The 0s for the X and Y positions are straightforward (this sprite will fill the entire screen, so you want it at the center), but that 5 for the Z position might seem odd. For 2D graphics, shouldn't only X and Y matter? Well, X and Y are the only coordinates that matter for positioning the object on the 2D screen; Z coordinates still matter for stacking objects, though. Lower Z values are closer to the camera, so sprites with lower Z values are displayed on top of other sprites (refer to figure 5.4). Accordingly, the background sprite should have the highest Z value. You'll set your background to a positive Z position, and then give everything else a 0 or negative Z position.

Stacked sprites seen in 2D (orthographic) view

3D (perspective) view

Sprites

Z axis

Figure 5.4   How sprites stack along the Z-axis

Other sprites will be positioned with values with up to two decimal places because of the Pixels-To-Units setting mentioned earlier. A ratio of 100:1 means that 100 pixels in the image are 1 unit in Unity; put another way, 1 pixel is .01 units. But before you put any more sprites into the scene, let's set up the camera for this game.

5.1.3   Switching the camera to 2D mode

Now let's adjust settings on the main camera in the scene. You might think that because the Scene view is set to 2D, what you see in Unity is what you'll see in the game. Somewhat unintuitively, though, that isn't the case.

> **WARNING**   Whether or not the Scene view is set to 2D has nothing to do with the camera view in the running game.

It turns out that, regardless of whether the Scene view is set to 2D mode, the camera in the game is set independently. This can be handy in many situations so that you can toggle the Scene view back to 3D in order to work on certain effects within the scene. This disconnect does mean that what you see in Unity isn't necessarily what you see in the game, and it can be easy for beginners to forget this.

The most important camera setting to adjust is Projection. The camera projection is probably already correct because you created the new project in 2D mode, but this is still important to know about and worth double-checking. Select the camera in Hierarchy to show its settings in the Inspector, and then look for the Projection setting (see figure 5.5). For 3D graphics the setting should be Perspective, but for 2D graphics the camera projection should be Orthographic.

Background color

Perspective/orthographic projection

Camera size (half the screen height)

Figure 5.5 Camera settings to adjust for 2D graphics

DEFINITION *Orthographic* is the term for a flat camera view that has no apparent perspective. This is the opposite of a Perspective camera, where closer objects appear larger and lines recede into the distance.

Although the Projection mode is the most important camera setting for 2D graphics, there are a few other settings for us to adjust as well. Next, we'll look at Size; that setting is under Projection. The camera's orthographic size determines the size of the camera view from the center of the screen up to the top of the screen. In other words, set Size to half the pixel dimensions of the screen you want. If you later set the resolution of the deployed game to the same pixel dimensions, you'll get pixel-perfect graphics.

DEFINITION *Pixel-perfect* means one pixel on the screen corresponds to one pixel in the image (otherwise, the video card will make the images subtly blurry while scaling up to fit the screen).

Let's say you want a pixel-perfect 1024 x 768 screen. That means the camera height should be 384 pixels. Divide that by 100 (because of the pixels-to-units scale) and you get 3.84 for the camera size. Again, that math is SCREEN_SIZE / 2 / 100f (f as in float, rather than an int value). Given that the background image is 1024 x 768 (select the asset to check its dimensions), then clearly this value of 3.84 is what we want for our camera.

The two remaining adjustments to make in the Inspector are the camera's background color and Z position. As mentioned previously for sprites, higher Z positions are further away into the scene. As such, the camera should have a pretty low Z position; set the position of the camera to 0, 0, -100. The camera's background color should probably be black; the default color is blue, and that'll look odd displayed along the sides if the screen is wider than the background image (which is likely). Click the color swatch next to Background and set the color picker to black.

Now save the scene as Scene and hit Play; you'll see the Game view filled with our tabletop sprite. As you saw, getting to this point wasn't completely straightforward (again, that's because Unity was a 3D game engine that has recently had 2D graphics grafted in). But the tabletop is completely bare, so our next step is to put a card on the table.

5.2   *Building a card object and making it react to clicks*

Now that the images are all imported and ready to use, let's build the card objects that form the core of this game. In Memory, all the cards are initially face down, and they're only face up temporarily when you choose a pair of cards to turn over. To implement this functionality, you're going to create objects that consist of multiple sprites stacked on top of one another. Then, you'll write code that makes the cards reveal themselves when clicked with the mouse.

5.2.1   *Building the object out of sprites*

Drag one of the card images into the scene. Use one of the card fronts, because you'll add a card back on top to hide the image. Technically, the position right now doesn't matter, but eventually it will, so you may as well position the card at -3, 1, 0. Now drag the card_back sprite into the scene. Make this new sprite a child of the previous card sprite (remember, in the Hierarchy, drag the child object onto the parent object) and then set its position to 0, 0, -.1 (Keep in mind that this position is relative to the parent, so this means "Put it at the same X and Y but move it closer on Z.")

> **TIP**   Instead of the Move, Rotate, and Scale tools that we used in 3D, in 2D mode we use a single manipulation tool called the *Rect Tool*. In 2D mode, this tool is selected automatically, or you can click the rightmost navigation button in the top-left corner of Unity. With this tool active, click and drag objects to do all three operations (move/rotate/scale) in two dimensions.

With the card back in place, as depicted in figure 5.6, the graphics are in place for a reactive card that can be revealed.

Card back is a child of
the card front sprite.

Position slightly in front
of the parent sprite.

(Remember, this is the
local position relative
to the parent.)

Figure 5.6   Hierarchy linking and position for the card back sprite

5.2.2　*Mouse input code*

In order to respond when the player clicks on them, the card sprites need to have a collider component. New sprites don't have a collider by default, so they can't be clicked on. You're going to attach a collider to the root card object, but not to the card back, so that only the card front and not the card back will receive mouse clicks. To do this, select the root card object in Hierarchy (don't click the card in the scene, because the card back is on top and you'll select that part instead) and then click the Add Component button in the Inspector. Select Physics 2D (not Physics, because that system is for 3D physics and this is a 2D game), and then choose a box collider.

Besides a collider, the card needs a script in order to be reactive to the player clicking on it, so let's write some code. Create a new script called `MemoryCard.cs` and attach this script to the root card object (again, not the card back). This listing shows the code that makes the card emit debug messages when clicked.

Listing 5.1　Emitting debug messages when clicked

```
using UnityEngine;
using System.Collections;

public class MemoryCard : MonoBehaviour {
    public void OnMouseDown() {
        Debug.Log("testing 1 2 3");
    }
}
```

Function is called when the object is clicked.

Just emit a test message to the console for now.

> **TIP**　If you're not in this habit yet, organizing your assets into separate folders is probably a good idea; create folders for scripts and drag files within the Project view. Be careful to avoid the special folder names Unity responds to: Resources, Plugins, Editor, and Gizmos. Later in the book, we'll go over what some of these special folders do, but for now avoid naming any folders with those words.

Nice, we can click on the card now! Just like `Update()`, `OnMouseDown()` is another function provided by `MonoBehaviour`, this time responding when the object is clicked on. Play the game and watch messages appear in the console. But this only prints to the console for testing; we want the card to be *revealed*.

5.2.3　*Revealing the card on click*

Rewrite the code to match this listing (the code won't run quite yet but don't worry).

Listing 5.2　Script that hides the back when the card is clicked

```
using UnityEngine;
using System.Collections;

public class MemoryCard : MonoBehaviour {
    [SerializeField] private GameObject cardBack;
```

Variable that appears in the Inspector

```
public void OnMouseDown() {
    if (cardBack.activeSelf) {
        cardBack.SetActive(false);
    }
}
}
```

> Only run deactivate code if the object is currently active/visible.

> Set the object to inactive/invisible.

There are two key additions to the script: a reference to an object in the scene, and the SetActive() method that deactivates that object. The first part, the reference to an object in the scene, is similar to what we've done in previous chapters: mark the variable as serialized, and then drag the object from Hierarchy over to the variable in the Inspector. With the object reference set, the code will now affect the object in the scene.

The second key addition to the code is the SetActive command. That command will deactivate any GameObject, making that object invisible. If we now drag card_back in the scene to this script's variable in the Inspector, when you play the game the card back disappears when you click the card. Hiding the card back will reveal the card front; we've accomplished yet another important task for the Memory game! But this is still only one card, so now let's create a bunch of cards.

5.3   *Displaying the various card images*

We've programmed a card object that initially shows the card back but reveals itself when clicked. That was a single card, but the game needs a whole grid of cards, with different images on most cards. We'll implement the grid of cards using a couple of concepts seen in previous chapters, along with some concepts you haven't seen before. Chapter 3 included the notions of (1) using an invisible SceneController component and (2) instantiating clones of an object. The SceneController will apply different images to different cards this time.

5.3.1   *Loading images programmatically*

There are four card images in the game we're creating. All eight cards on the table (two for each symbol) will be created by cloning the same original, so initially, all cards will have the same symbol. We'll have to change the image on the card in the script, loading different images programmatically.

To examine how images can be assigned programmatically, let's write simple test code (that will be replaced later) to demonstrate the technique. First, add this code to the MemoryCard script.

Listing 5.3   Test code to demonstrate changing the sprite image

```
...
[SerializeField] private Sprite image;
void Start() {
    GetComponent<SpriteRenderer>().sprite = image;
}
...
```

> Reference to the Sprite asset that will be loaded

> Set the sprite for this SpriteRenderer component.

After you save this script, the new `image` variable will appear in the Inspector because it has been set as serialized. Drag a sprite up from the Project view (pick one of the card images, and not the same as the image already in the scene) and drop it on the Image slot. Now run the scene, and you'll see the new image on the card.

The key to understanding this code is to know about the `SpriteRenderer` component. You'll notice in figure 5.7 that the card back object has just two components, the standard `Transform` component on all objects in the scene, and a new component called `SpriteRenderer`. This component makes it a sprite object and determines which sprite asset will be displayed. Note that the first property in the component is called `Sprite` and links to one of the sprites in the Project view; the property can be manipulated in code, and that's precisely what this script does.

Sprite asset displayed on this Sprite object

Color that tints this Sprite object (default is white for no tint)

Figure 5.7 A sprite object in the scene has the `SpriteRenderer` component attached to it.

As it did with `CharacterController` and custom scripts in previous chapters, the `GetComponent()` method returns other components on the same object, so we use it to reference the `SpriteRenderer` object. The `sprite` property of `SpriteRenderer` can be set to any sprite asset, so this code sets that property to the `Sprite` variable declared at the top (which we filled with a sprite asset in the editor).

Well, that wasn't too hard! But it's only a single image; we have four different images to use, so now delete the new code from listing 5.3 (it was only a demonstration of how the technique works) to prepare for the next section.

5.3.2 *Setting the image from an invisible SceneController*

Recall how, in chapter 3, we created an invisible object in the scene to control spawning objects. We're going to take that approach here as well, using an invisible object to control more abstract features that aren't tied to any specific object in the scene. First, create an empty `GameObject` (remember, select menu GameObject > Create Empty). Then create a new script, `SceneController.cs`, in the Project view, and drag this script asset onto the controller `GameObject`. Before writing code in the new script, first add the contents of the next listing to the `MemoryCard` script instead of what you saw in listing 5.3.

Listing 5.4 New public methods in MemoryCard.cs

```
...
[SerializeField] private SceneController controller;

private int _id;
public int id {
    get {return _id;}
}

public void SetCard(int id, Sprite image) {
    _id = id;
    GetComponent<SpriteRenderer>().sprite = image;
}
...
```

- Added getter function (an idiom common in languages like C# and Java)
- Public method that other scripts can use to pass new sprites to this object
- SpriteRenderer code line just like in the deleted example code

The primary change from previous listings is that we're now setting the sprite image in SetCard() instead of Start(). Because that's a public method that takes a sprite as a parameter, you can call this function from other scripts and set the image on this object. Note that SetCard() also takes an ID number as a parameter, and the code stores that number. Although we don't need the ID quite yet, soon we'll write code that compares cards for matches, and that comparison will rely on the IDs of the cards.

> **NOTE** Depending on what programming languages you've used in the past, you may not be familiar with the concept of *getters* and *setters*. Long story short, they are functions that run when you attempt to access the property associated with them (for example, retrieving the value of card.id). There are multiple reasons to use getters and setters, but in this case the id property is read-only because there's only a function to get the value and not set it.

Finally, note that the code has a variable for the controller; even as SceneController starts cloning card objects to fill the scene, the card objects also need a reference to the controller to call its public methods. As usual, when the code references objects in the scene, drag the controller object in Unity's editor to the variable slot in the Inspector. Do this once for this single card and all of the copies to come later will have the reference as well.

With that additional code now in MemoryCard, write this code in SceneController.

Listing 5.5 First pass at SceneController for the Memory game

```
using UnityEngine;
using System.Collections;

public class SceneController : MonoBehaviour {
    [SerializeField] private MemoryCard originalCard;
    [SerializeField] private Sprite[] images;

    void Start() {
        int id = Random.Range(0, images.Length);
```

- Reference for the card in the scene
- An array for references to the sprite assets

```
        originalCard.SetCard(id, images[id]);
    }
}
```
◄─────┐ **Call the public method we**
      └ **added to MemoryCard.**

For now, this is a short snippet to demonstrate the concept of manipulating cards from `SceneController`. Most of this should already be familiar to you (for example, in Unity's editor, drag the card object to the variable slot in the Inspector), but the array of images is new. As shown in figure 5.8, in the Inspector you can set the number of elements. Type in 4 for the array length, and then drag the sprites for card images onto the array slots. Now these sprites can be accessed in the array, like any other object reference.

Type in how many array elements.

Drag sprite assets onto array elements.

Figure 5.8 The filled-in array of sprites

Incidentally, we used the `Random.Range()` method in chapter 3, so hopefully you recall that. The exact boundary values didn't matter there, but this time it's important to note that the minimum value is inclusive and may be returned, whereas the return value is always below the maximum.

Hit Play to run this new code. You'll see different images being applied to the revealed card each time you run the scene. The next step is to create a whole grid of cards, instead of only one.

5.3.3   Instantiating a grid of cards

`SceneController` already has a reference to the card object, so now you'll use the `Instantiate()` method (see the next listing) to clone the object numerous times, like spawning objects in chapter 3.

Listing 5.6   Cloning the card eight times and positioning in a grid

```
using UnityEngine;
using System.Collections;

public class SceneController : MonoBehaviour {
    public const int gridRows = 2;
    public const int gridCols = 4;
    public const float offsetX = 2f;
    public const float offsetY = 2.5f;

    [SerializeField] private MemoryCard originalCard;
```
┐ **Values for how many**
│ **grid spaces to make**
│ **and how far apart to**
┘ **place them**

```
[SerializeField] private Sprite[] images;

void Start() {
  Vector3 startPos = originalCard.transform.position;

  for (int i = 0; i < gridCols; i++) {
    for (int j = 0; j < gridRows; j++) {
      MemoryCard card;
      if (i == 0 && j == 0) {
        card = originalCard;
      } else {
        card = Instantiate(originalCard) as MemoryCard;
      }

      int id = Random.Range(0, images.Length);
      card.SetCard(id, images[id]);

      float posX = (offsetX * i) + startPos.x;
      float posY = -(offsetY * j) + startPos.y;
      card.transform.position = new Vector3(posX, posY, startPos.z);

    }
  }
}
```

Position of the first card; all other cards will be offset from here.

Nested loops to define both columns and rows of the grid

Container reference for either the original card or the copies

For 2D graphics, you only need to offset X and Y; keep Z the same.

Although this script is much longer than the previous listing, there's not a lot to explain because most of the additions are straightforward variable declarations and math. The oddest bit of this code is probably the if/else statement that begins if (i == 0 && j == 0). What that conditional does is either use the original card object for the first grid slot or clone the card object for all other grid slots. Because the original card already exists in the scene, if you copied the card at every iteration of the loop, you'd end up with one too many cards in the scene. The cards are then positioned by offsetting them according to the number of iterations through the loop.

> **TIP** Just as when moving 3D objects, 2D objects can be moved by manipulating transform.position to different points on the screen, and this position could be incremented repeatedly in Update(). But as you saw when moving the first-person player, collision detection isn't applied when adjusting transform.position directly. To move 2D objects with collision detection, assign Physics 2D components and then adjust rigidbody2D.velocity.

Run the code now and a grid of eight cards will be created (as depicted in figure 5.9). The last step in preparing the grid of cards is to organize them into pairs, instead of them being random.

Figure 5.9 The grid of eight cards, which are revealed when you click on them

5.3.4 Shuffling the cards

Instead of making every card random, we'll define an array of all the card IDs (numbers 0 through 3 twice, for a pair of each card) and then shuffle that array. We'll then use this array of card IDs when setting cards, rather than making each one random.

Listing 5.7 Placing cards from a shuffled list

```
...
void Start() {
    Vector3 startPos = originalCard.transform.position;

    int[] numbers = {0, 0, 1, 1, 2, 2, 3, 3};
    numbers = ShuffleArray(numbers);

    for (int i = 0; i < gridCols; i++) {
        for (int j = 0; j < gridRows; j++) {
            MemoryCard card;
            if (i == 0 && j == 0) {
                card = originalCard;
            } else {
                card = Instantiate(originalCard) as MemoryCard;
            }

            int index = j * gridCols + i;
            int id = numbers[index];
            card.SetCard(id, images[id]);

            float posX = (offsetX * i) + startPos.x;
            float posY = -(offsetY * j) + startPos.y;
            card.transform.position = new Vector3(posX, posY, startPos.z);
        }
    }
}
```

Much of this listing is context to show where the additions go.

Declare an integer array with a pair of IDs for all four card sprites.

Call a function that will shuffle the elements of the array.

Retrieve IDs from the shuffled list instead of random numbers.

```
private int[] ShuffleArray(int[] numbers) {
    int[] newArray = numbers.Clone() as int[];
    for (int i = 0; i < newArray.Length; i++ ) {
        int tmp = newArray[i];
        int r = Random.Range(i, newArray.Length);
        newArray[i] = newArray[r];
        newArray[r] = tmp;
    }
    return newArray;
}
...
```

An implementation of the Knuth shuffle algorithm

Now, when you hit Play, the grid of cards will be a shuffled assortment that reveals exactly two of each card image. The array of cards was run through the *Knuth* (also known as *Fisher-Yates*) shuffle algorithm, a simple yet effective way of shuffling the elements of an array. This algorithm loops through the array and swaps every element of the array with another randomly chosen array position.

You can click on all the cards to reveal them, but the game of Memory is supposed to proceed in pairs; a bit more code is needed.

5.4   *Making and scoring matches*

The last step in making a fully functional Memory game is checking for matches. Although we now have a grid of cards that are revealed when clicked, the various cards don't affect each other in any way. In the game of Memory, every time a pair of cards is revealed we should check to see if the revealed cards match.

This abstract logic—checking for matches and responding appropriately—requires that cards notify `SceneController` when they've been clicked. That requires the additions to SceneController.cs shown in the next listing.

Listing 5.8   `SceneController`, which must keep track of revealed cards

```
...
private MemoryCard _firstRevealed;
private MemoryCard _secondRevealed;

public bool canReveal {
    get {return _secondRevealed == null;}
}
...
public void CardRevealed(MemoryCard card) {
    // initially empty
}
...
```

Getter function that returns false if there's already a second card revealed

The `CardRevealed()` method will be filled in momentarily; we needed the empty scaffolding for now to refer to in `MemoryCard.cs` without any compiler errors. Note that there is a read-only getter again, this time used to determine whether another card can be revealed; the player can only reveal another card when there aren't already two cards revealed.

We also need to modify `MemoryCard.cs` to call the (currently empty) method in order to inform `SceneController` when a card is clicked. Modify the code in `Memory-Card.cs` according to this listing.

Listing 5.9 `MemoryCard.cs` modifications for revealing cards

```
...
public void OnMouseDown() {
    if (cardBack.activeSelf && controller.canReveal) {
        cardBack.SetActive(false);
        controller.CardRevealed(this);
    }
}

public void Unreveal() {
    cardBack.SetActive(true);
}
...
```

Check the controller's canReveal property to make sure only two cards are revealed at a time.

Notify the controller when this card is revealed.

A public method so that SceneController can hide the card again (by turning card_back back on)

If you were to put a debug statement inside `CardRevealed()` in order to test the communication between objects, you'd see the test message appear whenever you click a card. Let's first handle one revealed pair.

5.4.1 *Storing and comparing revealed cards*

The card object was passed into `CardRevealed()`, so let's start keeping track of the revealed cards.

Listing 5.10 Keeping track of revealed cards in `SceneController`

```
...
public void CardRevealed(MemoryCard card) {
    if (_firstRevealed == null) {
        _firstRevealed = card;
    } else {
        _secondRevealed = card;
        Debug.Log("Match? " + (_firstRevealed.id == _secondRevealed.id));
    }
}
...
```

Store card objects in one of the two card variables, depending on if the first variable is already occupied.

Compare the IDs of the two revealed cards.

The listing stores the revealed cards in one of the two card variables, depending on whether the first variable is already occupied. If the first variable is empty, then fill it; if it's already occupied, fill the second variable and check the card IDs for a match. The `Debug` statement prints either `true` or `false` in the console.

At the moment, the code doesn't respond to matches—it only checks for them. Now let's program the response.

5.4.2 *Hiding mismatched cards*

We'll use coroutines again because the reaction to mismatched cards should pause to allow the player to see the cards. Refer to chapter 3 for a full explanation of coroutines;

long story short, using a coroutine will allow us to pause before checking for a match. This listing shows more code for you to add to `SceneController`.

Listing 5.11 `SceneController`, scores match or hide missed matches

```
...
private int _score = 0;          ◄──── Add to the list near the top of SceneController
...
public void CardRevealed(MemoryCard card) {
  if (_firstRevealed == null) {
    _firstRevealed = card;
  } else {
    _secondRevealed = card;
    StartCoroutine(CheckMatch());
  }
}


private IEnumerator CheckMatch() {
  if (_firstRevealed.id == _secondRevealed.id) {
    _score++;
    Debug.Log("Score: " + _score);
  }
  else {
    yield return new WaitForSeconds(.5f);

    _firstRevealed.Unreveal();
    _secondRevealed.Unreveal();
  }

  _firstRevealed = null;
  _secondRevealed = null;
}
...
```

- Only changed line in this function—calls the coroutine when both cards are revealed
- Increment the score if the revealed cards have matching IDs.
- Unreveal the cards if they do not match.
- Clear out the variables whether or not a match was made.

First, add a `_score` value to track; then, launch a coroutine to `CheckMatch()` when a second card is revealed. In that coroutine there are two code paths, depending on whether the cards match. If they match, the coroutine doesn't pause; the `yield` command gets skipped over. If the cards don't match, the coroutine pauses for half a second before calling `Unreveal()` on both cards, hiding them again. Finally, whether or not a match was made, the variables for storing cards are both nulled out, paving the way for revealing more cards.

When you play the game, mismatched cards will display briefly before hiding again. There are debug messages when you score matches, but we want the score displayed as a label on the screen.

5.4.3 *Text display for the score*

Displaying information to the player is half of the reason for a UI in a game (the other half is receiving input from the player. UI buttons are discussed in the next section).

> **DEFINITION** *UI* stands for user interface. Another closely related term is *GUI* (graphical user interface, which refers to the visual part of the interface, such as text and buttons, and which is what a lot of people mean when they say UI.

Unity has multiple ways to create text displays. One way is to create a 3D text object in the scene. This is a special mesh component, so first create an empty object to attach this component to. From the GameObject menu, choose Create Empty, then click the Add Component button and choose Mesh > Text Mesh.

> **NOTE** 3D text might sound incompatible with a 2D game, but don't forget that this is technically a 3D scene that looks flat because it's being seen through an orthographic camera. That means we can put 3D objects into the 2D game if we want—they're displayed in a flat perspective.

> **TIP** While this explanation uses Unity's standard Text Mesh component, you should consider TextMesh Pro for your own projects. That is an improved text system that was developed externally and recently integrated into Unity.

Position this object at -4.75, 3.65, -10; that's 475 pixels to the left and 365 pixels up, putting it in the top-left corner, and nearer to the camera so that it'll appear on top of other game objects. In the Inspector, look for the Font setting toward the bottom; click the little circle button to bring up a file selector and then pick the Arial font that's available. Enter Score: as the Text setting. Correct positioning also requires Upper Left for the Anchor setting (this controls how letters expand out as they're typed), so change this if needed. By default, the text appears blurry, but that's easily fixed by adjusting the settings shown in figure 5.10.

Figure 5.10 Inspector settings for a text object to make the text sharp and clear

If you import a new TrueType font into the project you could use that instead, but for our purposes the default font is fine. Oddly enough, a bit of size adjustment is needed to make the default text sharp and clear. First, set the TextMesh component's Font Size setting to a very large value (I used 80). Now scale the object down to be very small (like .1, .1, 1). Increasing Font Size added a lot of pixels to the text displayed, and scaling the object compressed those pixels into a smaller space.

Manipulating this text object requires just a few adjustments in the scoring code.

Listing 5.12   Displaying the score on a text object

```
...
[SerializeField] private TextMesh scoreLabel;
...
private IEnumerator CheckMatch() {
  if (_firstRevealed.id == _secondRevealed.id) {
    _score++;
    scoreLabel.text = "Score: " + _score;     ◄─── Text displayed is a property
  }                                                  to set on text objects.
  ...
```

As you can see, `text` is a property of the object that you can set to a new string. Drag the text in the scene to the variable you just added to `SceneController`, and then hit Play. Now you should see the score displayed while you play the game and make matches. Huzzah, the game works!

5.5   *Restart button*

At this point, the Memory game is fully functional. You can play the game, and all the essential features are in place. But this playable core is still lacking the overarching functionality that players expect or need in a finished game. For example, right now, you can play the game only once; you need to quit and restart in order to play again. Let's add a control to the screen so that players can start the game over without having to quit.

This functionality breaks down into two tasks: create a UI button and reset the game when that button is clicked. Figure 5.11 shows what the game will look like with the Start button.

Figure 5.11   Complete Memory game screen, including the Start button

Neither task is specific to 2D games, by the way; all games need UI buttons, and all games need the ability to reset. We'll go over both topics to round out this chapter.

5.5.1 *Programming a UIButton component using SendMessage*

First, place the button sprite in the scene; drag it up from the Project view. Give it a position like 4.5, 3.25, -10; that will place the button in the top-right corner (that's 450 pixels to the right and 325 pixels up) and move it nearer to the camera so that it'll appear on top of other game objects. Because we want to be able to click on this object, give it a collider (just as with the card object, select Add Component > Physics 2D > Box Collider).

> **NOTE** As alluded to in the previous section, Unity provides multiple ways to create UI displays, including an advanced UI system introduced in later versions of Unity. For now, we'll build the single button out of standard display objects. A future chapter will teach you about the advanced UI functionality; the UI for both 2D and 3D games is ideally built with that system.

Now create a new script called UIButton.cs and assign it (shown next) to the button object.

> **Listing 5.13 Code to make a generic and reusable UI button**

```
using UnityEngine;
using System.Collections;

public class UIButton : MonoBehaviour {                    ← Reference a target object
  [SerializeField] private GameObject targetObject;           to inform about clicks.
  [SerializeField] private string targetMessage;
  public Color highlightColor = Color.cyan;

  public void OnMouseEnter() {
    SpriteRenderer sprite = GetComponent<SpriteRenderer>();
    if (sprite != null) {                                   ← Tint the button when the
      sprite.color = highlightColor;                          mouse hovers over it.
    }
  }
  public void OnMouseExit() {
    SpriteRenderer sprite = GetComponent<SpriteRenderer>();
    if (sprite != null) {
      sprite.color = Color.white;
    }
  }

  public void OnMouseDown() {                               ← The button's size pops
    transform.localScale = new Vector3(1.1f, 1.1f, 1.1f);    a bit when it's clicked.
  }
  public void OnMouseUp() {
    transform.localScale = Vector3.one;
    if (targetObject != null) {                            ← Send a message to the target
      targetObject.SendMessage(targetMessage);               object when the button is clicked.
    }
  }
}
```

The majority of this code happens inside a series of `OnMouseSomething` functions; like `Start()` and `Update()`, these are a series of functions automatically available to all script components in Unity. `MouseDown` was mentioned in section 5.2.2, but all these functions respond to mouse interactions if the object has a collider. `MouseEnter` and `MouseExit` are a pair of events used for hovering the mouse cursor over an object: `MouseEnter` is the moment when the mouse cursor first moves over an object, and `MouseExit` is the moment when the mouse cursor moves away. Similarly, `MouseDown` and `MouseUp` are a pair of events for clicking the mouse. `MouseDown` is the moment when the mouse button is physically pressed, and `MouseUp` is the moment when the mouse button is released.

You can see that this code tints the sprite when the mouse hovers over it and scales the sprite when it's clicked on. In both cases, you can see that the change (in color or scale) happens when the mouse interaction begins, and then the property returns to default (either white or scale 1) when the mouse interaction ends. For scaling, the code uses the standard transform component that all `GameObjects` have. For tint, though, the code uses the `SpriteRenderer` component that sprite objects have; the sprite is set to a color that's defined in Unity's editor through a public variable.

In addition to returning the scale to 1, `SendMessage()` is called when the mouse is released. `SendMessage()` calls the function of the given name in all components of that `GameObject`. Here, the target object for the message, as well as the message to send, are both defined by serialized variables. This way, the same `UIButton` component can be used for all sorts of buttons, with the target of different buttons set to different objects in the Inspector.

Normally, when doing OOP in a strongly typed language like C#, you need to know the type of a target object in order to communicate with that object (for example, to call a public method of the object, like calling `targetObject.SendMessage()` itself). But scripts for UI elements may have lots of different types of targets, so Unity provides the `SendMessage()` method to communicate specific messages with a target object even if you don't know exactly what type of object it is.

> **WARNING** Using `SendMessage()` is less efficient for the CPU than calling public methods on known types (that is, using `object.SendMessage("Method")` versus `component.Method()`), so only use `SendMessage()` when it's a big win in terms of making the code simpler to understand and work with. As a general rule of thumb, that will only be the case if there could be lots of different types of objects receiving the message. In situations like that, the inflexibility of inheritance or even interfaces will hinder the game development process and discourage experimentation.

With this code written, wire up the public variables in the button's Inspector. The highlight color can be set to whatever you'd like (although the default cyan looks pretty good on a blue button). Meanwhile, put the `SceneController` object in the target object slot, and then type `Restart` as the message.

If you play the game now, there's a Reset button in the top-right corner that changes color in response to the mouse, and it makes a slight visual pop when clicked on. But an error message will be emitted when you click the button; in the console, you'll see an error about there not being a receiver for the Restart message. That's because we haven't written a `Restart()` method in `SceneController`, so let's add that.

5.5.2 Calling LoadScene from SceneController

The `SendMessage()` from the button attempts to call `Restart()` in the `SceneController`, so let's add that now.

Listing 5.14 `SceneController` code that reloads the level

```
...
using UnityEngine.SceneManagement;      ◄─── Include SceneManagement code.
...
public void Restart() {
    SceneManager.LoadScene("Scene");    ◄─── The scene asset is loaded with this command.
}
...
```

You can see the one thing `Restart()` does is call `LoadScene()`. That command loads a saved scene asset (that is, the file created when you click Save Scene in Unity). Pass the method the name of the scene you want to load; in my case, the scene was saved with the name `Scene`, but if you used a different name, pass that to the method instead.

Hit Play to see what happens. Reveal a few cards and make a few matches; if you then click the Reset button, the game starts over, with all cards hidden and a score of 0. Great, just what we wanted!

As the name `LoadScene()` implies, this method can load different scenes. But what exactly happens when a scene loads, and why does this reset the game? What happens is that everything from the current level (all objects in the scene, and thus all scripts attached to those objects) is flushed from memory, and then everything from the new scene is loaded. Because the new scene, in this case, is the saved asset of the current scene, everything is flushed from memory and then reloaded from scratch.

> **TIP** You can mark specific objects to exclude from the default memory flush when a level is loaded. Unity provides the `DontDestroyOnLoad()` method to keep an object around in multiple scenes; you'll use this method on parts of the code architecture in later chapters.

Another game successfully completed! Well, completed is a relative term; you could always implement more features, but everything from the initial plan is done. Many of the concepts from this 2D game apply to 3D games as well, especially the checking of game state and loading levels. Time to switch gears yet again and move away from this Memory game and on to new projects.

Summary

- Displaying 2D graphics in Unity uses an orthographic camera.
- For pixel-perfect graphics, the camera size should be half the screen height.
- Clicking on sprites requires that you first assign 2D colliders to them.
- New images for sprites can be loaded programmatically.
- UI text can be made using 3D text objects.
- Loading levels resets the scene.

Creating a basic 2D platformer

This chapter covers

- Moving sprites around continuously
- Playing sprite-sheet animation
- 2D physics (collision, gravity)
- Camera control for side-scrolling games

Let's create a new game and continue learning about Unity's 2D functionality. Chapter 5 covered the fundamental concepts, so this chapter will build on those to create a more elaborate game. Specifically, you are going to build the core functionality of a 2D platform game. Also called a *platformer*, it's a common type of 2D action game, best known for classics like *Super Mario Brothers*: a character viewed from the side runs and jumps on platforms, and the view scrolls around to follow. Figure 6.1 shows what the end result will be.

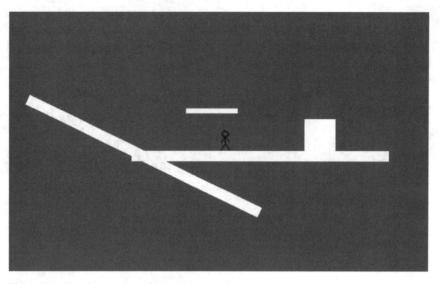

Figure 6.1   The final product of this chapter

This project will teach concepts like moving the player left and right, playing the sprite's animation, and adding the ability to jump. We'll also go over several special features common in platform games, like one-way floors and moving platforms. Going from this shell to a full game mostly means repeating those concepts over and over.

To get started, create a new project in 2D mode like in the last chapter: select New on Unity's opening window or New Project under the File menu, and select 2D in the window that appears. In the new project, create two folders, called Sprites and Scripts, to organize the various assets into. You could adjust the camera like in the last chapter, but for now just reduce Size to 4; this project doesn't require a perfect camera setup, although you'll need to adjust the size for a polished game that's ready for release.

> **TIP** The camera icon in the center of the screen can get in the way, so you can hide it from the Gizmos menu. Along the top of the Scene view is a label for Gizmos; click that for an alphabetical list, and next to Camera you can click the icon.

Now save the empty scene (and of course hit Save periodically while you work) to create the Scene asset in this project. Everything's empty at the moment, so the first step will be bringing in art assets.

6.1   Setting up the graphics

Before you can program the functionality of a 2D platform game, you need to import some images into the project (remember, images in a 2D game are referred to as *sprites* instead of *textures*) and then place those sprites into the scene. This game will be the shell of a 2D platform game, with a player-controlled character running around a basic and mostly empty scene, so all you need are a couple of sprites for the platforms and for the player. Let's go over each separately, because although the images in this example are simple, there are some nonobvious considerations involved.

6.1.1   *Placing the walls and floor*

Simply put, you need a single blank white image to use here. There is an image called blank.png included in the sample project for this chapter; download the sample and copy blank.png from there. Grab the PNG file from there, drag it into the Sprites folder of your new project, and make sure in the Inspector that Import Settings say it's a Sprite rather than a Texture (it should be automatic for a 2D project, but it's worth double-checking).

What you're doing now is essentially the same as the whiteboxing from chapter 4, but in 2D instead of 3D. Whiteboxing in 2D is done with sprites rather than meshes, but maintains the same activity of blocking out blank floors and walls for the player to move around.

To place the floor object, drag the blank sprite into the scene as shown in figure 6.2 (around position .15 -1.27 0), scale 50, 2, 1, and change its name to `Floor`. Then drag in another blank sprite, scale 6, 6, 1, place it on the floor off to the right (around 2 -.63 0), and name it `Block`.

Simple enough; now the floor and block are done. The other object you need is a character for the player.

Figure 6.2   Floor platform placement

6.1.2   *Importing sprite sheets*

The only other art asset you need is the player's sprite, so also copy stickman.png from the sample project. But unlike the blank image, this time it's a series of separate sprites assembled into one image. As shown in figure 6.3, the stickman image is the frames of two animations: standing idle and a walk cycle. We're not going into detail on how to animate, but suffice to say that *idle* and *cycle* are both common terms used by game developers. Idle refers to subtle movement while doing nothing, and cycle is an animation that loops continuously.

Figure 6.3   Stickman sprite
sheet—6 frames in a row

As explained in the previous chapter, an image file may be a bunch of sprite images packed together, rather than just a single sprite. Images like this are called *sprite sheets* when the multiple sprite images are frames of animation. In Unity, the sprite sheet will still appear in the Project view as a single asset, but if you click the arrow on the asset, it'll expand and show all the individual sprite images; figure 6.4 shows how that looks.

Figure 6.4   Slicing a sprite sheet into separate frames

Drag stickman.png into the Sprites folder to import the image, but this time change a lot of Import Settings in the Inspector. Select the sprite asset, set Sprite Mode to Multiple, then click Sprite Editor to open that window. Click Slice at the top-left of the window, set Type to Grid By Cell Size (shown in figure 6.4), use size 32, 64 (this is the size of each frame in the sprite sheet), and click Slice to see the frames split up. Now close the Sprite Editor window and click Apply to keep the changes.

The sprite asset is now split up, so click the arrow to expand the frames; drag one (probably the first) stickman sprite into the scene, place it standing on the middle of the floor, and name it Player. There, the player object is in the scene!

6.2   *Moving the player left and right*

Now that the graphics are set up, let's start programming the player's movement. First off, the player entity in the scene needs a couple of additional components for us to control. As mentioned briefly in previous chapters, the physics simulation in Unity acts on objects with the special Rigidbody component, and you want physics (collisions and gravity in particular) to act on the character. Meanwhile, the character also needs a Collider component to define its boundaries for collision detection. The difference between these components is subtle but important: the Collider defines the shape for physics to act on, and the Rigidbody tells the physics simulation what objects to act on.

> **NOTE** These components are kept separate (even though they are closely related) because many objects that don't need the physics simulation themselves *do* need to collide with other objects that *are* acted on by physics.

One other subtlety to be aware of is that Unity has a separate physics system for 2D games instead of 3D physics. Thus, in this chapter you'll be using components from the Physics 2D section instead of the regular Physics section of the list.

Select Player in the scene and then click Add Component in the Inspector; as shown in figure 6.5, choose Physics 2D > Rigidbody 2D in the menu. Now click Add Component again to add Physics 2D > Box Collider 2D. The Rigidbody needs a small amount of fine-tuning, so in the Inspector set Collision Detection as Continuous, Freeze Rotation Z (normally the physics simulation will attempt to rotate objects while moving them, but characters in games don't behave like normal objects), and Gravity Scale 0 (you'll reset this later, but for now you don't want gravity).

The player entity is now ready for the script that controls movement.

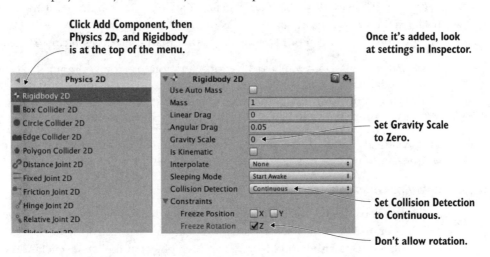

Figure 6.5 Add and adjust Rigidbody 2D component

6.2.1 *Writing keyboard controls*

To begin, you'll make the player move left and right; vertical movement is important also in a platformer, but you'll deal with that later. Create a C# script called `Plat-formerPlayer` in the Scripts folder, then drag that onto the Player object in the scene.

Open the script and write the code from this listing.

Listing 6.1 `PlatformerPlayer` **script to move with arrow keys**

```
using UnityEngine;
using System.Collections;

public class PlatformerPlayer : MonoBehaviour {
  public float speed = 250.0f;

  private Rigidbody2D _body;

  void Start() {
    _body = GetComponent<Rigidbody2D>();
  }

  void Update() {
    float deltaX = Input.GetAxis("Horizontal") * speed * Time.deltaTime;
    Vector2 movement = new Vector2(deltaX, _body.velocity.y);
    _body.velocity = movement;
  }
}
```

Need this other component
attached to this GameObject

Only set horizontal movement; preserve
pre-existing vertical movement.

After writing the code, hit Play and you can move the player using the arrow keys. The code is fairly similar to movement code in previous chapters, with the main difference being that it acts on Rigidbody2D instead of a Character Controller. Character Controller is for 3D, so for a 2D game you use a Rigidbody component. Note that the movement is applied to Rigidbody's `velocity`, rather than something like `position`.

> **TIP** By default, Unity applies a bit of acceleration to arrow key input. That can feel sluggish for a platformer, though; for snappier control, increase Sensitivity and Gravity of Horizontal input to 6. To find those settings, go to Edit > Project Settings > Input; it's a long list, but Horizontal is the first section.

This is already most of the way there for horizontal movement! You only need to address collision detection.

6.2.2   *Colliding with the walls*

As you've probably noticed, the player walks through the block right now. There are no colliders on the floor or block, so the player can move through them. To fix this, add Box Collider 2D to Floor and Block: select each object in the scene, click Add Component in the Inspector, and choose Physics 2D > Box Collider 2D.

And that's all you needed to do! Hit Play now, and the player won't be able to move through the block. As with moving the player in chapter 2, if you had adjusted the player's position directly then collision detection wouldn't work, but Unity's built-in collision detection can work if you apply the movement to the player's physics components. In other words, moving `Transform.position` would have ignored collision detection, so instead you manipulated `Rigidbody2D.velocity` in the movement script.

Adding colliders to more complex art could be slightly trickier, but frankly not much harder in that case. Even if the art is not exactly a rectangle, you may still want to use Box Colliders and roughly surround the shape of obstacles in the scene. Alternatively, there are a number of other collider shapes to try, including arbitrary custom Polygon shapes. Figure 6.6 illustrates how to work with Polygon colliders for oddly shaped objects.

Figure 6.6   Edit the shape of the Polygon collider with the Edit Collider button.

Anyway, collision detection is now working, so the next step is making the player animate along with its movement.

6.3   *Playing the sprite's animation*

When stickman.png was imported, it was split into multiple frames for animating. Now let's *play* that animation, so that the player isn't sliding around but appears to be walking.

6.3.1   *Explaining the Mecanim animation system*

As was mentioned briefly in chapter 4, the animation system in Unity is called *Mecanim.* It's designed so that you can visually set up a complex network of animations for a character, and then control those animations with a minimum of code. The system is most useful for 3D characters (thus, we'll cover it in more detail in future chapters), but is still useful for 2D characters too.

The heart of the animation system is composed of two different kinds of assets: anima*tion* clips and anima*tor* controllers (notice *animation* versus *animator*). Clips are the individual animation loops to play, whereas the controller is the network controlling when to play animations. This network is a *state machine* diagram, and the states in the diagram are different animations that could be playing. The controller shifts between states in reaction to conditions it is watching, and plays a different animation in each state.

Unity will create both kinds of assets automatically when you drag a 2D animation into the scene. That is, when you drag the frames of an animation into the scene, Unity will automatically create an animation clip and an animator controller using those frames. As depicted in figure 6.7, expand all the frames of the sprite asset, select frames 0-1, drag them into scene, and type the name stickman_idle in the confirmation window.

1. Select multiple frames and drag them into the Scene ...

2. ... to create animations automatically. (Delete the second controller and extra scene objects.)

3. After adding an Animator component to the Player, drag in the controller.

Figure 6.7   Steps to go from sprite sheet frames to Animator on player

In the Asset view, that created a clip named `stickman_idle` and a controller named `stickman_0`; rename the controller `stickman` with no suffix. Great, you created the character's idle animation! It also created an object called `stickman_0` in the scene, but you don't need that so delete it.

Now repeat the process for the walk animation. Select frames 2-5, drag them into scene, and name the animation `stickman_walk`. This time, delete both `stickman_2` in the scene and the controller in Assets; only one animator controller is needed to control both animation clips, so keep the first one and delete `stickman_2`, the newly created one.

To apply the controller to your player character, select Player in the scene and add component Miscellaneous > Animator. As shown in figure 6.7, drag the stickman controller into the controller slot in the Inspector. With the Player still selected, open Window > Animator (shown in figure 6.8).

Animations in the Animator window are displayed as blocks, referred to as *states*, and the controller switches between states when running. This particular controller already has the idle state in it, but you need to add a walking state; drag the `stickman_walk` animation clip from Assets into the Animator window.

By default, the idle animation will play too fast, so decrease idle speed to `.2`; select the idle animation state, and in the right-hand panel you'll see a speed setting. With that change, the animations are all set up for the next step.

Each of these blocks is an animation "state".

Click the Parameters tab.

Then click the + button to add a Float parameter called speed.

The Animator switches between states while running, playing the animation for that state.

Uncheck to allow transitions to cut off animations in the middle of playing.

Right-click a state to "Make Transition" and connect it to another state. Make sure to make transitions both to and from, since each transition is one-way.

Click the + button to add a condition for when to transition. In this case, it says to switch from idle to walk when speed is greater than 0.1.

Figure 6.8   Animator window, showing animation states and transitions

6.3.2   *Triggering animations from code*

Now that you've set up animation states in the Animator controller, you can switch between those states to play the different animations. As mentioned in the last section, a state machine switches states in reaction to conditions it is watching. In Unity's animation controllers, those conditions are referred to as *parameters*, so let's add one. Figure 6.8 pointed out the relevant controls: Select the Parameters tab and click the + button for a menu of different parameter types. Add a float parameter called *speed*.

Next, you need to switch between animation states based on that parameter. Right-click *idle* and select Make Transition; that'll start dragging out an arrow from the idle state. Click on *walk* to connect to that state, and because transitions are unidirectional, also right-click walk to transition back.

Now select the transition from idle (you can click on the arrows themselves), uncheck Has Exit Time, and click the + at the bottom to add a condition (again, shown in figure 6.8). Make the condition speed Greater than .2 so the states will transition in that condition. Now do it again for the walk-to-idle transition: Select the transition from walk, uncheck Has Exit Time, add a condition, make the condition speed Less than .2.

Finally, the movement script can manipulate the animator controller, as shown in this listing.

Listing 6.2   Trigger animations along with moving

```
...
private Animator _anim;                              Existing code to help show
...                                                  where to position new code
void Start() {
  _body = GetComponent<Rigidbody2D>();               Speed is greater than zero
  _anim = GetComponent<Animator>();                  even if velocity is negative.
}

void Update() {                                      Floats aren't always exact so
  ...                                                compare using Approximately().
  _anim.SetFloat("speed", Mathf.Abs(deltaX));
  if (!Mathf.Approximately(deltaX, 0)) {
    transform.localScale = new Vector3(Mathf.Sign(deltaX), 1, 1);
  }
}                                                    When moving, scale positive or
...                                                  negative I to face right or left.
```

Wow, that was barely any code for controlling the animations! Most of the work is handled by Mecanim, and only a small amount of code is needed to operate it. Play the game and move around to watch the player sprite animate. This game is really coming along, so on to the next step!

6.4   Adding the ability to jump

The player can move back and forth but isn't yet moving vertically. Vertical movement (both falling off ledges and jumping to higher platforms) is an important part of platform games, so let's implement that next.

6.4.1   Falling from gravity

Somewhat counter-intuitively, before you can make the player jump, it needs gravity to jump against. As you may recall, earlier you set Gravity Scale to 0 on the player's Rigidbody. That was so the player wouldn't fall due to gravity. Well, turn that back to 1 now: select the Player object in the scene, find Rigidbody in the Inspector, and then type 1 in Gravity Scale.

Gravity is now affecting the player, but (assuming you had added a Box Collider to the Floor object) the floor is holding them up. Walk off the sides of the floor to fall into oblivion. By default, gravity affects the player somewhat weakly, so you'll want to increase the magnitude of its effect. There is a global gravity setting for the physics simulation, and you can adjust that in the Edit menu. Specifically, go to Edit > Project Settings > Physics 2D. As shown in figure 6.9, at the top of the various controls and settings you should see Gravity Y; change that to -40.

Figure 6.9 Gravity intensity in Physics settings

There's one subtle issue you may have noticed: The falling player sticks to the side of the floor. To see this problem, walk off the edge of the platform and immediately press the other direction to move back toward the platform. Ugh, not good! Fortunately, Unity makes that easy to fix. Just add Physics 2D > Platform Effector 2D components to Block and Floor. This effector makes objects in the scene behave more like platforms in a platform game. Figure 6.10 points out two settings to adjust: Set Used By Effector on the Collider, and turn off Use One Way on the Effector (we'll use this latter setting for other platforms, but not now).

Figure 6.10 Collider and Effector settings in the Inspector

That takes care of the downward part of vertical movement, but you still need to take care of upward.

6.4.2   *Applying an upward impulse*

The next action you need is jumping. That is an upward jolt applied when the player hits the Jump button. Although your code directly changed the velocity for horizontal movement, you're going to leave vertical velocity alone so gravity can do its work. Instead, objects can be influenced by other forces besides gravity, so you'll add an upward force. Add this code to the movement script.

> **Listing 6.3   Jump when pressing the spacebar**

```
...
public float jumpForce = 12.0f;           | Existing code to help show
...                                        | where to position new code.
_body.velocity = movement;

                                           | Only add force when spacebar is pressed.
if (Input.GetKeyDown(KeyCode.Space)) {
  _body.AddForce(Vector2.up * jumpForce, ForceMode2D.Impulse);
}
...
```

The important line is the `AddForce()` command. The code adds an upward force to the Rigidbody, and does so in *impulse* mode; an impulse is a sudden jolt, as opposed to a continuously applied force. This code, then, applies a sudden upward jolt when the spacebar is pressed. Meanwhile, gravity continues to affect the jumping player, resulting in a nice arc when the player jumps.

You may have noticed one issue, however, so let's address that.

6.4.3   *Detecting the ground*

The jump control has one subtle problem: the player can jump in midair! If the player is already in midair (either because they jumped, or because they are falling), hitting the spacebar applies an upward force, but it shouldn't. Instead, the jump control should only work when the player is on the ground. You therefore need to detect when the player is on the ground.

> **Listing 6.4   Check if the player is on the ground**

```
...
private BoxCollider2D _box;
...                                        | Get this component to use the player's
_box = GetComponent<BoxCollider2D>();      | collider as area to check.
...
_body.velocity = movement;

Vector3 max = _box.bounds.max;
Vector3 min = _box.bounds.min;
Vector2 corner1 = new Vector2(max.x, min.y - .1f);     | Check below the
Vector2 corner2 = new Vector2(min.x, min.y - .2f);     | collider's min Y values.
Collider2D hit = Physics2D.OverlapArea(corner1, corner2);

bool grounded = false;
```

```
if (hit != null) {          ◄──────  If a collider was detected under the player ...
  grounded = true;
}
                                            ... add grounded to
                                            the jump condition.
if (grounded && Input.GetKeyDown(KeyCode.Space)) {  ◄──────
...
```

With this code in place, the player can no longer jump in midair. This addition to the script checks for colliders below the player, and takes that into account in the conditional statement for jumping. Specifically, the code first gets the bounds of the player's collision box, and then looks for overlapping colliders in an area of the same width just below the player. The result of that check is stored in the grounded variable and used in the conditional.

6.5 Additional features for a platform game

At this point, the most crucial aspects of the player's movement, walking and jumping, are implemented. Let's round out this platformer demo by adding new functionality to the environment around the player.

Designing levels using tilemaps

For our project, the floors and platforms are blank, white rectangles. A finished game should have nicer graphics, but an image the size of a level would be way too big for the computer to handle. The most common solution to this problem is to use *tilemaps*. In a nutshell, that's a technique for constructing a larger, combined image out of lots of small tiling images. This image shows an example of a tilemap.

The faint grid lines show tile boundaries; this grid isn't there in the actual map.

(image courtesy of mapeditor.org, using tiles from lpc.opengameart.org)

Note how the map is constructed out of small blocks that are repeated throughout the map. In that way, no single image is very large, but the entire screen can be covered with custom artwork. An official tilemap system for Unity is included in the latest versions. Alternatively, you could also use an external library like Tiled2Unity, a tilemap system that imports tilemaps created in Tiled, a very popular (and free) tilemap editor.

Here are websites with more information: http://mng.bz/318f and www.seanba.com/tiled2unity.

6.5.1   *Unusual floors: slopes and one-way platforms*

Right now, this demo has normal, level floors to stand on. Many interesting kinds of platforms are used in platform games, though, so let's implement a few other options. The first unusual floor you'll create is a slope: duplicate the Floor object, set the duplicate's rotation to 0, 0, -25, move it off to the left-hand side (around -3.47 -1.27 0), and name it Slope.

If you play now, the player already slides up and down correctly when moving, but it slowly slides down due to gravity when idle. To address this, let's turn off gravity for the player when the player is both (a) standing on the ground, and (b) idle. Fortunately, you already detect the ground, so that can be reused in the new code. Indeed, only a single new line is needed.

```
...
_body.gravityScale = grounded && deltaX == 0 ? 0 : 1;      Check both on ground
                                                           and not moving.
if (grounded && Input.GetKeyDown(KeyCode.Space)) {         Existing code to help show
...                                                         where to position new code
```

Listing 6.5   Turn off gravity when standing on the ground

With that adjustment to the movement code, your player character correctly navigates slopes. Next, one-way platforms are another sort of unusual floor common in platformers. I'm talking about platforms that you can jump through but still stand on; the player bonks their head against the bottom of normal, fully solid platforms.

Because they're fairly common in platform games, Unity provides functionality for one-way platforms. If you recall when you added the Platform Effector component earlier, there was a one-way setting that was turned off. Now turn that on! To create a new platform, duplicate the Floor object, scale the duplicate 10, 1, 1, place it above the floor around position -1.68 .11 0, and name the object Platform. Oh, and don't forget to turn on Use One Way in the Platform Effector component.

The player jumps through the platform from below, but stands on it when coming down from above. There's one possible issue to fix, shown in figure 6.11. Unity may display the platform sprite on top of the player (to see this more easily, test with Jump Force set to 7), but you probably want the player on top. You could adjust the player's Z like you did last chapter, but this time you'll adjust something else to show another option. Sprite renderers have a sorting order that can be used to control which sprites appear on top. Set Order in Layer to 1 in the Player's Sprite Renderer component.

That takes care of both sloped floors and one-way platforms. There's one more sort of unusual floor that I'm going to cover, but it is significantly more complex to implement.

The platform may overlap the player, but you want it the other way around.

Figure 6.11 Platform sprite overlapping the Player sprite

6.5.2 *Implementing moving platforms*

A third sort of unusual floor common in platform games is the moving platform. Implementing them requires both a new script to control the platform itself and changes in the player's movement script to handle moving platforms. You're going to write a script that takes two positions, start and finish, and makes the platform bounce between them. First, create a new C# script called MovingPlatform and write this code in it.

Listing 6.6 MovingPlatform script for floors that move back and forth

```
using UnityEngine;
using System.Collections;

public class MovingPlatform : MonoBehaviour {                  Position to move to
  public Vector3 finishPos = Vector3.zero;   ◄──────┘
  public float speed = 0.5f;

                                              How far along "track" between start and finish
  private Vector3 _startPos;
  private float _trackPercent = 0;   ◄──────
  private int _direction = 1;   ◄──────────────── Current movement direction

  void Start() {
    _startPos = transform.position;   ◄────── Placement in scene is position to move from
  }

  void Update() {
    _trackPercent += _direction * speed * Time.deltaTime;
    float x = (finishPos.x - _startPos.x) * _trackPercent + _startPos.x;
    float y = (finishPos.y - _startPos.y) * _trackPercent + _startPos.y;
    transform.position = new Vector3(x, y, _startPos.z);

    if ((_direction == 1 && _trackPercent > .9f) ||          Change direction at
      (_direction == -1 && _trackPercent < .1f)) {   ◄────── both start and end.
      _direction *= -1;
    }
  }
}
```

Drawing custom Gizmos

The majority of the code you'll write is for the running game, but Unity scripts can also affect Unity's *editor*. An often-overlooked feature of Unity is the ability to add new menus and windows. Your scripts can also draw custom helper images in the Scene view; such helper images are called *gizmos*.

You're already familiar with gizmos like the green boxes to display colliders. Those are built into Unity, but you can also draw your own gizmos in scripts. For example, it'd be useful to draw a line in the Scene view that shows the movement path of the platform, as shown here.

**Gizmos only show in the
Scene view, not the Game
view, to help with editing.**

**This line is a custom Gizmo
drawn to show the movement
of this platform.**

The code for drawing that line is very simple. Usually, when writing code that affects Unity's editing interface you need to add `using UnityEditor;` at the top (because most editor functions reside in that namespace), but in this case, you don't even need that. Add this method to the `MovingPlatform` script:

```
...
void OnDrawGizmos() {
  Gizmos.color = Color.red;
  Gizmos.DrawLine(transform.position, finishPos);
}
...
```

There're a few things to know about this code. One, it all happens in a method called `OnDrawGizmos()`. Like `Start` or `Update`, `OnDrawGizmos` is another method name Unity recognizes. Within the method, there are two lines of code: one sets the drawing color, and the other tells Unity to draw a line from the platform's position to the finish position.

Drag this script onto the platform object. Great, the platform moves left and right when you play the scene! Now you need to adjust the player's movement script in order to attach the player to the moving platform. Here are the changes to make.

Listing 6.7 Handling moving platforms in `PlatformerPlayer.cs`

```
...
  _body.AddForce(Vector2.up * jumpForce, ForceMode2D.Impulse);
}

MovingPlatform platform = null;
if (hit != null) {                                        ← Check if platform under
  platform = hit.GetComponent<MovingPlatform>();            player is moving platform.
}
if (platform != null) {                     ← Either attach to platform
  transform.parent = platform.transform;      or clear transform.parent.
} else {
  transform.parent = null;
}
                                            ← Existing code to help show
_anim.SetFloat("speed", Mathf.Abs(deltaX));   where to position new code
...
```

Now the player moves with the platform after jumping on it. It mostly comes down to attaching the player as a child of the platform; remember, when you set a parent object, the child object moves with the parent. Listing 6.7 uses `GetComponent()` to check if the ground detected is a moving platform. If so, it sets that platform as the player's parent; otherwise, the player is detached from any parent.

There's a big problem, though: the player inherits the platform's scale, resulting in weird scaling. That can be fixed by counter-scaling (scaling the player down to counteract the platform's scale up).

Listing 6.8 Correcting scaling of the player

```
...
  _anim.SetFloat("speed", Mathf.Abs(deltaX));

  Vector3 pScale = Vector3.one;   ← Default scale 1 if not on moving platform
  if (platform != null) {
    pScale = platform.transform.localScale;
  }
  if (deltaX != 0) {                              ← Replace existing
    transform.localScale = new Vector3(            scaling with new code.
    Mathf.Sign(deltaX) / pScale.x, 1/pScale.y, 1);
  }
}
...
```

The math for counter-scaling is pretty straightforward: set the player to 1 divided by the platform's scale. When the player's scale is then multiplied by the platform's scale, that leaves a scale of 1. The only tricky bit of this code is multiplying by the sign of the movement value; as you may recall from earlier, the player is flipped based on the movement direction.

And that's moving platforms fully implemented. This platformer demo needs only one final touch …

6.5.3   *Camera control*

Moving the camera is the final feature you'll add to this 2D platformer. Create a script called `FollowCam`, drag it onto the camera, and then write the following in it.

Listing 6.9   `FollowCam` script to move with the player

```
using UnityEngine;
using System.Collections;

public class FollowCam : MonoBehaviour {
  public Transform target;

  void LateUpdate() {
    transform.position = new Vector3(
    target.position.x, target.position.y, transform.position.z);
  }
}
```

Preserve Z position while changing X and Y.

With that code written, drag the Player object to the script's `target` slot in the Inspector. Play the scene and the camera moves around, keeping the player at the center of the screen. You can see the code applies the target object's position to the camera, and you set the player as the target object. Note that the method name is `LateUpdate` instead of `Update`; that's yet another name Unity recognizes. `LateUpdate` also executes every frame, but it happens after `Update` every frame.

It's slightly jarring that the camera moves *exactly* with the player at all times. The camera in most platformers has all kinds of subtle but complicated behavior, highlighting different parts of the level as the player moves around. In fact, camera control for platform games is a surprisingly deep topic; try searching for "platform game camera" and see all the results. In this case, though, you're just going to make the camera's movement smoother and less jarring; this listing makes that adjustment.

Listing 6.10   Smoothing the camera movement

```
...
public float smoothTime = 0.2f;

private Vector3 _velocity = Vector3.zero;
...
void LateUpdate() {
  Vector3 targetPosition = new Vector3(
  target.position.x, target.position.y, transform.position.z);

  transform.position = Vector3.SmoothDamp(transform.position,
  targetPosition, ref _velocity, smoothTime);
}
...
```

Preserve Z position while changing X and Y.

Smooth transition from current to target position

The main change is calling a function called `SmoothDamp`; the other changes (like adding `time` and `velocity` variables) are all to support that function. That's a function

Unity provides for making values smoothly transition to a new value. In this case, the values are the positions of the camera and target.

The camera moves smoothly with the player now. You implemented the player's movement, several different kinds of platforms, and now camera control. Looks like this chapter's project is finished!

Summary

- Sprite sheets are a common way to handle 2D animation.
- Characters in games don't behave like objects in the real world, so you must adjust their physics accordingly.
- Rigidbody objects can be controlled either by applying forces or by setting their velocity directly.
- Levels in 2D games are often constructed with tilemaps.
- A simple script can make the camera smoothly follow the player.

Putting a GUI onto a game

This chapter covers

- Comparing old (pre-Unity 4.6) and newer GUI systems
- Creating a canvas for the interface
- Positioning UI elements using anchor points
- Adding interactivity to the UI (buttons, sliders, and so on)
- Broadcasting and listening for events from the UI

In this chapter, you'll build a 2D interface display for a 3D game. So far, we've focused on the virtual scene itself while building a first-person demo. But every game needs abstract interaction and information displays in addition to the virtual scene the gameplay takes place in. This is true for all games, whether they're 2D or 3D, first-person shooters or puzzle games. So, while the techniques in this chapter will be used on a 3D game, they apply to 2D games as well.

These abstract interaction displays are referred to as the UI, or more specifically, the GUI. GUI refers to the visual part of the interface, such as text and buttons (see figure 7.1). Technically, the UI includes non-graphical controls, such as the keyboard or gamepad, but people tend to be referring to the graphical parts when they say "user interface."

Settings button: Part of the HUD displayed over the game view

Pop-up window displayed over the game view

A wall within the scene: This is the main game view.

Figure 7.1   The GUI (a heads-up display, or HUD) you'll create for a game

Although any software requires some sort of UI in order for the user of that software to control it, games often use their GUI in a slightly different way from other software. In a website, for example, the GUI basically *is* the website (in terms of visual representation). In a game, though, text and buttons are often an additional overlay on top of the game view, a kind of display called a heads-up display (HUD).

> **DEFINITION**   A *heads-up display* (*HUD*) superimposes graphics on top of the view of the world. The concept of a HUD originated with military jets—its purpose was so that pilots could see crucial information without having to look down. Similarly, a GUI superimposed on the game view is referred to as the HUD.

This chapter will show how to build the game's HUD using the latest UI tools in Unity. As you saw in chapter 5, Unity provides multiple ways to create UI displays. This chapter demonstrates the advanced UI system available with Unity 4.6 and later. I'll also discuss the previous UI system and the advantages of the newer system.

To learn about the UI tools in Unity, you'll build on top of the FPS project from chapter 3. The project in this chapter will involve these steps:

1. Planning the interface
2. Placing UI elements on the display
3. Programming interactions with the UI elements
4. Making the GUI respond to events in the scene
5. Making the scene respond to actions on the GUI

Copy the project from chapter 3 and open the copy to start working on this chapter. As usual, the art assets you need are in the sample download. With those files set up, you're ready to start building the game's UI.

NOTE This chapter is largely independent of the project you build on top of—it just adds a graphical interface on top of an existing game demo. All the examples in this chapter are built on top of the FPS created in chapter 3, and you could download that sample project, but you're free to use whatever game demo you'd like.

7.1   *Before you start writing code ...*

To start building the HUD, you first need to understand how the UI system works. Unity provides multiple approaches to building a game's HUD, so we need to go over how those systems work. Then we can briefly plan the UI and prepare the art assets that we'll need.

7.1.1   *Immediate mode GUI or advanced 2D interface?*

From its first version, Unity has come with an immediate mode GUI system.

> **DEFINITION** *Immediate mode* refers to explicitly issuing draw commands every frame, versus a system where you define all the visuals once and then for every frame the system knows what to draw without you having to tell it again. The latter approach is called *retained mode*.

The immediate mode system makes it easy to put a clickable button on the screen. Listing 7.1 shows the code to do that: simply attach this script to any object in the scene. For another example of immediate mode UI, recall the target cursor displayed in chapter 3. This GUI system is entirely based on code, with no work done in Unity's editor.

> **Listing 7.1   Example of a button using the immediate mode GUI**

```
using UnityEngine;                                      Function called every frame after
using System.Collections;                               everything else renders.

public class BasicUI : MonoBehaviour {
   void OnGUI() {
      if (GUI.Button(new Rect(10, 10, 40, 20), "Test")) {
         Debug.Log("Test button");
      }                              Parameters: position X, pos
   }                                 Y, width, height, text label
}
```

The core of the code in this listing is the OnGUI() method. Much like Start() and Update(), every MonoBehaviour automatically responds to OnGUI(). That function runs every frame after the 3D scene is rendered, providing a place to put GUI drawing commands. This code draws a button; note that the command for a button is executed every frame (that is, in immediate mode style). The button command is used in a conditional that responds when the button is clicked.

Because the immediate mode GUI makes it easy to get a few buttons onscreen with minimal effort, we'll sometimes use it for examples in future chapters. But default buttons are about the only thing easy to create with that system, so more recent versions of Unity now have a new interface system based on 2D graphics laid out in the editor. It takes a bit more effort to set up, but you'll probably want to use the newer interface system in finished games because it produces more polished results.

The newer UI system works in retained mode, so the graphics are laid out once and then drawn every frame without needing to be continually redefined. In this system, graphics for the UI are placed in Unity's editor. This provides two advantages over the immediate mode UI: (1) You can see what the UI looks like while placing UI elements, and (2) This system makes it straightforward to customize the UI with your own images.

To use this system, you're going to import images and then drag objects into the scene. Next, let's plan how this UI will look.

7.1.2 Planning the layout

The HUD for most games is a few different UI controls repeated over and over. That means this project doesn't need to be a terribly complex UI in order for you to learn how to build a game's UI. You're going to put a score display and a settings button in the corners of the screen (see figure 7.2) over the main game view. The settings button will bring up a pop-up window, and that window will have both a text field and a slider.

Figure 7.2   Planned GUI

For this example, those input controls will be used for setting the player's name and movement speed, but ultimately those UI elements could control any settings relevant to your game.

Well, that plan was pretty simple! The next step is bringing in the images that are needed.

7.1.3   Importing UI images

This UI requires some images to display for things like buttons. The UI is built from 2D images like the graphics in chapter 5, so you'll follow the same two steps:

1   Import images (if needed, set them to Sprite).
2   Drag the sprites into the scene.

To accomplish these steps, first drag the images into Project view to import them. Then, in the Inspector, change their Texture Type setting to Sprite (2D And UI).

> **WARNING**   The Texture Type setting defaults to Texture in 3D projects and to Sprite in 2D projects. If you want sprites in a 3D project, you need to adjust this setting manually.

Get all the necessary images from the sample download (see figure 7.3) and then import them into your project. Make sure all the imported assets are set to Sprite; you'll probably need to adjust Texture Type in the settings displayed after importing.

| Close | Enemy | Gear | Popup |

This image will be the close button on the pop-up.   This image will be the score display in the top-left corner.   This image will be the settings button in the top-right corner.   This image will be a scaled background of the pop-up.

Figure 7.3   Images that are needed for this chapter's project

These sprites comprise the buttons, score display, and pop-up that you'll create. Now that the images are imported, let's put these graphics onto the screen.

7.2   Setting up the GUI display

The art assets are the same kind of 2D sprites we used in chapter 5, but the use of those assets in the scene is a bit different. Unity provides special tools to make the images a HUD that's displayed over the 3D scene, rather than displaying the images as part of the scene. Some special tricks are used when positioning UI elements, because of the needs of a display that may change on different screens.

7.2.1   Creating a canvas for the interface

One of the most fundamental and nonobvious aspects of how the UI system works is that all images must be attached to a `Canvas` object.

> **TIP**   Canvas is a special kind of object that Unity renders as the UI for a game.

Open the GameObject menu to see the objects you can create; in the UI category, choose Canvas. A `Canvas` object will appear in the scene (it may be clearer to rename the object

HUD Canvas). This object represents the entire extent of the screen, and it's huge compared to the 3D scene because it scales one pixel of the screen to one unit in the scene.

> **WARNING** When you create a canvas object, an EventSystem object is automatically created, too. That object is required for UI interaction, but you can otherwise ignore it.

Switch to 2D view mode (refer to figure 7.4) and double-click the canvas in the Hierarchy in order to zoom out and view it fully. The 2D view mode is automatic when the entire project is 2D, but in a 3D project this toggle must be clicked to switch between the UI and the main scene. To return to viewing the 3D scene, toggle the 2D view mode off and then double-click the building to zoom in to that object.

2D view mode: Switch to this view when working in 2D, including the UI.

Canvas object displayed in the Scene view

It's scaled very large because 1 unit in the scene = 1 pixel on the UI.

The borders of the canvas scale to match the game's screen.

If you see the colored arrows of the manipulator, that means the Rect tool is NOT on. That button is in the top-left corner of Unity; you will see blue dots on every corner of a 2D object.

Figure 7.4   A blank canvas object in the Scene view

> **TIP** Don't forget this tip from chapter 4: Across the top of the Scene view's pane are buttons that control what's visible, so look there for the Effects button to turn off the skybox.

The canvas has a number of settings that you can adjust. The first is the Render Mode option. Leave this at the default setting (*Screen Space—Overlay*), but you should know what the three possible settings mean:

- *Screen Space—Overlay*—Renders the UI as 2D graphics on top of the camera view (this is the default setting).
- *Screen Space—Camera*—Also renders the UI on top of the camera view, but UI elements can rotate for perspective effects.
- *World Space*—Places the canvas object within the scene, as if the UI were part of the 3D scene.

The two modes besides the initial default can sometimes be useful for specific effects but are slightly more complicated.

The other important setting is Pixel Perfect. This setting causes the rendering to subtly adjust the position of images so that they're always perfectly crisp and sharp (as opposed to blurring them when positioned between pixels). Go ahead and select that check box. Now the HUD canvas is set up, but it's still blank and needs sprites.

7.2.2 Buttons, images, and text labels

The canvas object defines an area to display as the UI, but it still requires sprites to display. If you refer to the UI mock-up in figure 7.2, there's an image of the block/enemy in the top-left corner, text displaying the score next to that, and a gear-shaped button in the top-right corner. Accordingly, in the UI section of the GameObject menu, there are options to create an image, text, or button. Create one of each.

> **TIP** Just as with the text object used in chapter 5, you should consider Text-Mesh Pro for your own projects. That system was developed externally to improve Unity's text.

UI elements need to be a child of the canvas object in order to display correctly. Unity does this automatically, but remember that, as usual, you can drag objects around the Hierarchy view (see figure 7.5) to make parent-child linkages.

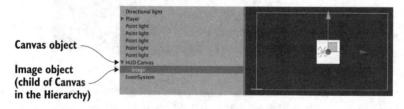

Canvas object

Image object (child of Canvas in the Hierarchy)

Figure 7.5   Canvas with an image linked in the Hierarchy view

Objects within the canvas can be parented together for positioning purposes, just like any other objects in the scene. For example, you may want to drag the text object onto the image so that the text will move with the image. Similarly, the default button object has a text object as its child; this button doesn't need a text label, so delete the text object.

Roughly position the UI elements into their corners. In the next section, we'll make the positions exact; for now, just drag the objects until they're pretty much in position. Click and drag the image object to the top-left of the canvas; the button goes in the top-right.

> **TIP** As noted in chapter 5, you use the Rect tool in 2D mode. I described it as a single manipulation tool that encompasses all three transforms: Move, Rotate, and Scale. These operations have to be separate tools in 3D but are combined in 2D because that's one less dimension to worry about. In 2D mode, this tool is selected automatically, or you can click the button in the top-left corner of Unity.

At the moment, the images are blank. If you select a UI object and look at the Inspector, you should see a Source Image slot near the top of the image component. As shown in figure 7.6, drag over sprites (remember, not textures!) from the Project view to assign images to the objects. Assign the enemy sprite to the image object, and the gear sprite to the button object (click Set Native Size after assigning sprites to properly size the image object).

1. Drag Sprite from Project view up to Source Image setting ...

2. ... and the image will appear on the UI element.

3. Click Set Native Size to resize the image correctly.

Figure 7.6   Assign 2D sprites to the Image property of UI elements.

That took care of the appearance of both the enemy image and the gear button. As for the text object, there are a bunch of settings in the Inspector. First, type a single number in the large Text box; this text will be overwritten later, but it's useful because it looks like a score display within the editor. The text is small, so increase the Font Size to 24 and make the style Bold. You also want to set this label to left horizontal alignment (see figure 7.7) and middle vertical alignment. For now, the remaining settings can be left at their default values.

The UI object displays text typed here.

Import a TrueType font to use that font; set it here.

These buttons adjust the horizontal and vertical alignment of the text.

Figure 7.7   Settings for a UI text object

NOTE Besides the Text box and alignment, the most common property to adjust is the font. You can import a TrueType font into Unity, and then put that font in the Inspector.

Now that sprites have been assigned to the UI images and the score text is set up, you can press Play to see the HUD on top of the 3D game. As shown in figure 7.8, the canvas displayed in Unity's editor shows the bounds of the screen, and UI elements are drawn onto the screen in those positions.

The Canvas displayed in the editor.

HUD overlays the main game scene when playing.

Figure 7.8   The GUI as seen in the editor (left) and when playing the game (right)

Great, you made a HUD with 2D images displayed over the 3D game! One more complex visual setting remains: positioning UI elements relative to the canvas.

7.2.3   Controlling the position of UI elements

All UI objects have an anchor, displayed in the editor as an X shape (see figure 7.9). An anchor is a flexible way of positioning objects on the UI.

Anchor point icon   **The image object**

Figure 7.9   The anchor point of an image object

> **DEFINITION**   The *anchor* of an object is the point where an object attaches to the canvas or screen. It determines what that object's position is measured relative to.

Positions are values like "50 pixels on the X-axis." But that leaves the question: 50 pixels from what? This is where anchors come in. The purpose of an anchor is that the object stays in place relative to the anchor point, whereas the anchor moves around relative to the canvas. The anchor is defined as something like "center of the screen," and then the anchor will stay centered while the screen changes size. Similarly, setting the anchor to the right-hand side of the screen will keep the object rooted to the right-hand side even if the screen changes size (for example, if the game is played on different monitors).

The easiest way to understand what I'm talking about is to see it in action. Select the image object and look over at the Inspector. Anchor settings (see figure 7.10) will appear right below the transform component. By default, UI elements have their anchor set to Center, but you want to set the anchor to Top Left for this image; figure 7.10 shows how to adjust that using the Anchor Presets.

Click the Anchor button (it looks like a target), to open the entire Anchor presets menu.

You can type in exact numbers for the anchor point, but usually the presets work best. For example, press this button to set a top-right anchor.

(Stretch presets affect the image size as well as position.)

Figure 7.10   How to adjust anchor settings

Change the gear button's anchor as well. Set it to Top Right for this object; click the top-right Anchor Preset. Now try scaling the window left and right: click and drag on the side of the Scene view. Thanks to the anchors, the UI objects will stay in their corners while the canvas changes size. As figure 7.11 shows, these UI elements are now rooted in place while the screen moves.

Drag the side of the Scene view to change the size of the screen.

The Canvas scales with it, and the images stay positioned at their anchors in the corners.

Figure 7.11   Anchors stay in place while the screen changes size.

TIP Anchor points can adjust scale as well as position. We're not going to explore that functionality in this chapter, but each corner of the image can be rooted to a different corner of the screen. In figure 7.11 the images didn't change size, but we could adjust the anchors so that when the screen changes size, the image stretches with it.

All of the visual setup is done, so it's time to program interactivity.

7.3   *Programming interactivity in the UI*

Before you can interact with the UI, you need to have a mouse cursor. If you recall, we adjusted `Cursor` settings in the `Start()` method of the `RayShooter` code. Those settings lock and hide the mouse cursor, a behavior that works for the controls in an FPS game but that interferes with using the UI. Remove those lines from `RayShooter.cs` so that you can click the HUD.

While you have `RayShooter.cs` open, you could also make sure not to shoot while interacting with the GUI. Here is the code for that.

> **Listing 7.2   Adding a GUI check to the code in `RayShooter.cs`**

```
using UnityEngine.EventSystems;      ◀─────  Include UI system code frameworks.
...
void Update() {                              ┌─  Italicized code was already in
    if (Input.GetMouseButtonDown(0) &&       │   script; shown for reference.
    !EventSystem.current.IsPointerOverGameObject()) {   ◀──  Check that GUI isn't being used.
        Vector3 point = new Vector3(
            camera.pixelWidth/2, camera.pixelHeight/2, 0);
        ...
```

Now you can play the game and click the button, although it doesn't do anything yet. You can watch the tinting of the button change as you mouse over it and click. This mouseover and click behavior is a default tint that can be changed for each button, but the default looks fine for now. You could speed up the default fading behavior; Fade Duration is a setting in the button component, so try decreasing that to .01 to see how the button changes.

TIP Sometimes, the default interaction controls of the UI also interfere with the game. Remember the `EventSystem` object that was created automatically along with the canvas? That object controls the UI interaction controls, and by default it uses the arrow keys to interact with the GUI. You may need to turn off the arrow keys to avoid interacting with the GUI by accident: to do this, deselect the Send Navigation Event check box in the settings for `EventSystem`.

But nothing else happens when you click the button because you haven't yet linked it up to any code. Let's take care of that next.

7.3.1 Programming an invisible UIController

In general, UI interaction is programmed with a standard series of steps that's the same for all UI elements:

1 Create a UI object in the scene (the button created in the previous section).
2 Write a script to call when the UI is operated.
3 Attach that script to an object in the scene.
4 Link UI elements (such as buttons) to the object with that script.

To follow these steps, first we need to create a controller object to link to the button. Create a script called UIController and drag that script onto the controller object in the scene.

> **Listing 7.3 UIController script used to program buttons**

```
using UnityEngine;
using UnityEngine.UI;          ◀──── Import UI code framework.
using System.Collections;

public class UIController : MonoBehaviour {        Reference Text object in
   [SerializeField] private Text scoreLabel;   ◀── scene to set text property.

   void Update() {
      scoreLabel.text = Time.realtimeSinceStartup.ToString();
   }

   public void OnOpenSettings() {  ◀──── Method called by Settings button
      Debug.Log("open settings");
   }
}
```

> **TIP** You might be wondering why we need separate objects for SceneController and UIController. Indeed, this scene is so simple that you could have one controller handling both the 3D scene and the UI. As the game gets more complex, though, it'll become increasingly useful for the 3D scene and the UI to be separate modules, communicating indirectly. This notion extends well beyond games to software in general: software engineers refer to this principle as *separation of concerns.*

Now drag objects to component slots in order to wire them up. Drag the score label (the text object we created before) to the UIController text slot. The code in UIController sets the text displayed on that label. Currently, the code displays a timer to test the text display; that will later be changed to the score.

Next, add an OnClick entry to the button to drag the controller object onto. Select the button to see its settings in the Inspector. Toward the bottom, you should see an OnClick panel; initially that panel is empty, but (as you can see in figure 7.12) you can click the + button to add an entry. Each entry defines a single function that gets called when that button is clicked; the listing has both a slot for an object and a menu for the function to call. Drag the `controller` object to the object slot, and then look for UIController in the menu; select `OnOpenSettings()` in that section.

On Click event panel near the bottom of settings

Drag an object in the scene to the object slot, then choose a function in the menu.

Press the + button to add an entry in the panel.

Figure 7.12 The `OnClick` panel toward the bottom of the button settings

---

Responding to other mouse events

`OnClick` is the only event that the button component exposes, but UI elements can respond to a number of different interactions. To go beyond the default interactions, use an `EventTrigger` component.

Add a new component to the `button` object and look for the Event section of the component's menu. Select EventTrigger from that menu. Although the button's `OnClick` only responded to a full click (the mouse button being pressed down and then released), let's try responding to the mouse button being pressed but not released. Perform the same steps as for `OnClick`, only responding to a different event. First add another method to `UIController`:

```
...
public void OnPointerDown() {
    Debug.Log("pointer down");
}
...
```

Now click Add New Event Type to add a new type to the `EventTrigger` component. Choose Pointer Down for the event. This will create an empty panel for that event, just like `OnClick` had. Click the + button to add an event listing, drag the `controller` object to this entry, and select `OnPointerDown()` in the menu. There you go!

Play the game and click the button to output debug messages in the console. Again, the code is currently random output in order to test the button's functionality. What we want to do is open a settings pop-up, so let's create that pop-up window next.

7.3.2   *Creating a pop-up window*

The UI has a button to open a pop-up window, but there's no pop-up yet. That will be a new image object, along with several controls (such as buttons and sliders) attached to that object. The first step is to create a new image, so choose GameObject > UI > Image. Just as before, the new image has a slot in the Inspector called Source Image. Drag a sprite to that slot to set this image. This time, use the sprite called popup.

Ordinarily, the sprite is stretched over the entire image object; this was how the score and gear images worked, and you clicked the Set Native Size button to resize the object to the size of the image. This behavior is the default for image objects, but the pop-up will do something different.

As you can see in figure 7.13, the image component has an Image Type setting. This setting defaults to Simple, which was the correct image type earlier. For the pop-up, though, set Image Type to Sliced.

Change the pop-up image from Simple to Sliced.

The Set Native Size button only applies to Simple and is replaced by a check box for Fill Center.

Figure 7.13   Settings for the image component, including Image Type

DEFINITION   A *sliced image* is split into nine sections that scale differently from one another. By scaling the edges of the image separately from the middle, you ensure that the image can scale to any size you want and it maintains its sharp, crisp edges. In other development tools, these kinds of images often have "9" somewhere in the name (such as 9-slice, 9-patch, scale-9) to indicate the 9 sections of the image.

After you switch to a sliced image, Unity may display an error in the component settings, complaining that the image doesn't have a border. That's because the popup sprite doesn't have the nine sections defined yet. To set that up, first select the popup sprite in the Project view. In the Inspector, you should see a Sprite Editor button (see figure 7.14); click that button and the Sprite Editor window will appear.

Click the Sprite Editor button ...

... to open a window and edit the sprite's borders.

Type in L R B T (left right bottom top) numbers to adjust the green border slices. For the pop-up sprite, set all borders to 12 pixels.

Figure 7.14   Sprite Editor button in the Inspector and a pop-up window

In the Sprite Editor, you can see green lines that indicate how the image will be sliced. Initially, the image won't have any border (that is, all of the Border settings are 0). Increase the border width of all four sides, which will result in the border shown in figure 7.14. Because all four sides (Left, Right, Bottom, and Top) have the border set to 12 pixels wide, the border lines will overlap into nine sections. Close the editor window and apply the changes.

Now that the sprite has the nine sections defined, the sliced image will work correctly (and the Image component settings will show Fill Center; make sure that setting is on). Click and drag the blue indicators in the corner of the image to scale it (switch to the Rect tool described in chapter 5 if you don't see any scale indicators). The border sections will maintain their size while the center portion scales.

Because the border sections maintain their size, a sliced image can be scaled to any size and still have crisp edges. This is perfect for UI elements—different windows may be different sizes but should still look the same. For this popup, enter a width of 250 and a height of 200 to make it look like figure 7.15 (also, center it on position 0, 0, 0).

Figure 7.15   Sliced image scaled to dimensions of the pop-up

TIP   How UI images stack on top of each other is determined by their order in the Hierarchy view. In the Hierarchy list, drag the pop-up object above other UI objects (always staying attached to the canvas, of course). Now move the pop-up around within the Scene view; you can see how images overlap the pop-up window. Finally, drag the pop-up to the bottom of the canvas hierarchy so that it will display on top of everything else.

The pop-up object is set up now, so write some code for it. Create a script called SettingsPopup and drag that script onto the pop-up object.

Listing 7.4 SettingsPopup script for the pop-up object

```
using UnityEngine;
using System.Collections;

public class SettingsPopup : MonoBehaviour {
   public void Open() {
      gameObject.SetActive(true);       ◄——— Turn the object on to open the window.
   }
   public void Close() {
      gameObject.SetActive(false);      ◄——— Deactivate this object to close the window.
   }
}
```

Next, open UIController.cs to make a few adjustments.

Listing 7.5 Adjusting UIController to handle the pop up

```
...
[SerializeField] private SettingsPopup settingsPopup;
void Start() {
   settingsPopup.Close();      ◄——— Close the pop-up when the game starts.
}
...
public void OnOpenSettings() {
   settingsPopup.Open();       ◄——— Replace the debug text with the pop-up's method.
}
...
```

This code adds a slot for the pop-up object, so drag the pop-up to UIController. The pop-up will be closed initially when you play the game, and it'll open when you click the settings button.

At the moment, there's no way to close it again, so add a close button to the pop-up. The steps are pretty much the same as for the button created earlier: choose Game-Object > UI> Button, position the new button in the top-right corner of the pop-up, drag the close sprite to this UI element's Source Image property, and then click Set Native Size to correctly resize the image. Unlike with the previous button, we want this text label, so select the text and type Close in the text field, and set Color to white. In the Hierarchy view, drag this button onto the pop-up object so that it will be a child of the pop-up window. And as a final touch of polish, adjust the button transition to a Fade Duration value of .01 and a darker Normal Color setting of 110, 110, 110, 255.

To make the button close the pop-up, it needs an OnClick entry; click the + button on the button's OnClick panel, drag the pop-up window into the object slot, and choose Close() from the function list. Now play the game and this button will close the pop-up window.

The pop-up window has been added to the HUD. The window is currently blank, though, so let's add some controls to it.

7.3.3   *Setting values using sliders and input fields*

Like the buttons we made earlier, adding controls to the settings pop-up involves two main steps. You create UI elements attached to the canvas and link those objects to a script. The input controls we need are a slider and a text field, and there will be a static text label to identify the slider. Choose GameObject > UI > Text to create the text object, GameObject > UI > InputField to create the text field, and GameObject > UI > Slider to create the slider object (see figure 7.16).

Input controls on the pop-up:

A text InputField

A numerical Slider

The close button is in the top corner, while a text label was placed just over the slider.

Figure 7.16   Input controls added to the pop-up window

Make all three objects children of the pop-up by dragging them in the Hierarchy view and then position them as indicated in the figure, lined up in the middle of the pop-up. Set the text to Speed so that it can be a label for the slider. The input field is for typing in text, and *Text* is shown in the box before the player types something else; set this value to Name. You can leave the options Content Type and Line Type at their defaults; if desired, you can use Content Type to restrict typing to things like only letters or only numbers, whereas you can use Line Type to switch from a single line to multiline text.

> **WARNING** You won't be able to click the slider if the text label covers it. Make sure the text object appears under the slider by placing it above the slider in the Hierarchy.

> **WARNING** You should probably leave the Input Field at the default size for this example, but if you do decide to shrink it then reduce only the Width, not the Height. If you set the Height to less than 30, that's too small for the text to appear.

As for the slider itself, several settings appear toward the bottom of the component inspector. Min Value is set to 0 by default; leave that. Max Value defaults to 1, but make it 2 for this example. Similarly, both Value and Whole Numbers can be left at their defaults; Value controls the starting value of the slider, and Whole Numbers constrains it to 0 1 2 rather than decimal values (a constraint we don't want).

And that wraps up all the objects. Now you need to write the code that the objects are linked to; add the methods shown in the following listing to SettingsPopup.cs.

Great! There are methods for the controls to use. Starting with the input field, in Settings, you'll see an End Edit panel; events listed here are triggered when the user finishes typing. Add an entry to this panel, drag the pop-up to the object slot, and choose OnSubmitName() in the function list.

Listing 7.6 `SettingsPopup` methods for the pop-up's input controls

```
...
public void OnSubmitName(string name) {          Triggers when the user types in the input field
    Debug.Log(name);
}
public void OnSpeedValue(float speed) {          Triggers when the user adjusts the slider
    Debug.Log("Speed: " + speed);
}
...
```

> **WARNING** Be sure to select the function in the End Edit panel's top section, Dynamic String, and not the bottom section, Static Parameters. The `OnSubmit-Name()` function appears in both sections, but selecting it under Static Parameters will send only a single string defined ahead of time; *dynamic string* refers to whatever value is typed in the input field.

Follow these same steps for the slider: look for the event panel toward the end of the component settings (in this case, the panel is OnValueChanged), click + to add an entry, drag in the settings pop-up, and choose `OnSpeedValue()` in the list of dynamic value functions.

Now both of the input controls are connected to code in the pop-up's script. Play the game, and watch the console while you move the slider or press Enter after typing input.

Saving settings between plays using PlayerPrefs

A few different methods are available for saving persistent data in Unity, and one of the simplest is called `PlayerPrefs`. Unity provides an abstracted way (that is, you don't worry about the details) to save small amounts of information that works on all platforms (with their differing filesystems). `PlayerPrefs` aren't too useful for large amounts of data (in future chapters, we'll use other methods to save the game's progress), but they're perfect for saving settings.

`PlayerPrefs` provides simple commands to get and set named values (it works a lot like a hash table or dictionary). For example, you can save the speed setting by adding the line `PlayerPrefs.SetFloat("speed", speed);` inside the `OnSpeedValue()` method of the SettingsPopup script. That method will save the float in a value called `speed`.

Similarly, you'll want to initialize the slider to the saved value. Add the following code to `SettingsPopup`:

```
using UnityEngine.UI;
...
[SerializeField] private Slider speedSlider;
void Start() {
    speedSlider.value = PlayerPrefs.GetFloat("speed", 1);
}
...
```

Note that the `get` command has both the value to get as well as a default value in case `speed` wasn't previously saved.

Although the controls generate debug output, they still don't affect the game. Making the HUD affect the game (and vice versa) is the topic of the final section of this chapter.

7.4 Updating the game by responding to events

Up to now, the HUD and main game have been ignoring each other, but they ought to be communicating back and forth. That could be accomplished via script references, as you've done for other sorts of inter-object communication, but that approach would have major downsides. In particular, doing so would tightly couple the scene and the HUD; you want to keep them fairly independent of each other so that you can freely edit the game without worrying that you've broken the HUD.

To alert the UI of actions in the scene, we're going to make use of a broadcast messenger system. Figure 7.17 illustrates how this event messaging system works: scripts can register to listen for an event, other code can broadcast an event, and listeners will be alerted about broadcast messages. Let's go over a messaging system to accomplish that.

Figure 7.17 Diagram of the broadcast event system we'll implement

TIP C# does have a built-in system for handling events, so you might wonder why we don't use that. Well, the built-in event system enforces targeted messages, whereas we want a broadcast messenger system. A targeted system requires the code to know exactly where messages originate from; broadcasts can originate from anywhere.

7.4.1 Integrating an event system

To alert the UI of actions in the scene, we're going to make use of a broadcast messenger system. Although Unity doesn't have this feature built in, you can download a good code library for this purpose. Among the resources listed in appendix D is the Unify community wiki; this is a repository of free code contributed by other developers. Their messenger system is great for providing a decoupled way of communicating events to the rest of the program. When some code broadcasts a message, that code doesn't need to know anything about the listeners, allowing for a great deal of flexibility in switching around or adding objects.

Create a script called `Messenger` and paste in the code from this page on Unity's wiki: http://wiki.unity3d.com/index.php/CSharpMessenger_Extended. Then, you also need to create a script called `GameEvent`.

Listing 7.7   `GameEvent` script to use with `Messenger`

```
public static class GameEvent {
    public const string ENEMY_HIT = "ENEMY_HIT";
    public const string SPEED_CHANGED = "SPEED_CHANGED";
}
```

The script in the listing defines a constant for a couple of event messages; the messages are more organized this way, and you don't have to remember and type the message string all over the place.

Now the event messenger system is ready to use, so let's start using it. First, we'll communicate from the scene to the HUD, and then we'll go in the other direction.

7.4.2   *Broadcasting and listening for events from the scene*

Up to now, the score display has displayed a timer as a test of the text display functionality. But we want to display a count of enemies hit, so let's modify the code in UIController. First, delete the entire `Update()` method, because that was the test code. When an enemy dies, it will emit an event, so the following listing makes `UIController` listen for that event:

Listing 7.8   Adding event listeners to `UIController`

```
...
private int _score;

void Awake() {
    Messenger.AddListener(GameEvent.ENEMY_HIT, OnEnemyHit);   ◄── Declare which method responds to the ENEMY_HIT event.
}
void OnDestroy() {
    Messenger.RemoveListener(GameEvent.ENEMY_HIT, OnEnemyHit);   ◄── When an object is destroyed, clean up the listener to avoid errors.
}

void Start() {
    _score = 0;
    scoreLabel.text = _score.ToString();   ◄── Initialize the score to 0.

    settingsPopup.Close();
}

private void OnEnemyHit() {   ── Increment the score in response to the event.
    _score += 1;
    scoreLabel.text = _score.ToString();
}
...
```

First notice the Awake() and OnDestroy() methods. Much like Start() and Update(), every MonoBehaviour automatically responds when the object awakens or is removed. A listener gets added and removed in Awake()/OnDestroy(). This listener is part of the broadcast messaging system, and it calls OnEnemyHit() when that message is received. OnEnemyHit() increments the score and then puts that value in the score display.

The event listeners are set up in the UI code, so now we need to broadcast that message whenever an enemy is hit. The code to respond to hits is in RayShooter.cs, so emit the message as shown here.

Listing 7.9   Broadcast event message from RayShooter

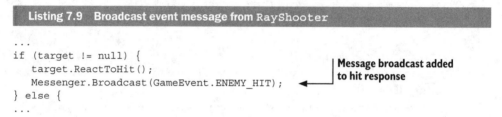

```
...
if (target != null) {
   target.ReactToHit();
   Messenger.Broadcast(GameEvent.ENEMY_HIT);     ◄─── Message broadcast added to hit response
} else {
...
```

Play the game after adding that message and watch the score display when you shoot an enemy. You should see the count going up every time you make a hit. That covers sending messages from the 3D game to the 2D interface, but we also want an example going in the other direction.

7.4.3   *Broadcasting and listening for events from the HUD*

In the previous section, an event was broadcast from the scene and received by the HUD. In a similar way, UI controls can broadcast a message that both players and enemies listen for. In this way, the settings pop-up can affect the settings of the game. Open WanderingAI.cs and add this code.

Listing 7.10   Event listener added to WanderingAI

```
...
public const float baseSpeed = 3.0f;     ◄─── Base speed that is adjusted by the speed setting
...
void Awake() {
   Messenger<float>.AddListener(GameEvent.SPEED_CHANGED, OnSpeedChanged);
}
void OnDestroy() {
   Messenger<float>.RemoveListener(GameEvent.SPEED_CHANGED, OnSpeedChanged);
}
...                                       ◄─── Method that was declared in listener for event SPEED_CHANGED
private void OnSpeedChanged(float value) {
   speed = baseSpeed * value;
}
...
```

Awake() and OnDestroy() add and remove, respectively, an event listener here, too, but the methods have a value this time. That value is used to set the speed of the wandering AI.

TIP The code in the previous section used a generic event, but this messaging system can pass a value along with the message. Supporting a value in the listener is as simple as adding a type definition; note the `<float>` added to the listener command.

Now make the same changes in `FPSInput.cs` to affect the speed of the player. The code in the next listing is almost the same as that in listing 7.10, except that the player has a different number for `baseSpeed`.

Listing 7.11   Event listener added to `FPSInput`

```
...
public const float baseSpeed = 6.0f;   ◄──── This value is changed from listing 7.10.
...
void Awake() {
    Messenger<float>.AddListener(GameEvent.SPEED_CHANGED, OnSpeedChanged);
}
void OnDestroy() {
    Messenger<float>.RemoveListener(GameEvent.SPEED_CHANGED, OnSpeedChanged);
}
...
private void OnSpeedChanged(float value) {
    speed = baseSpeed * value;
}
...
```

Finally, broadcast the speed values from `SettingsPopup` in response to the slider.

Listing 7.12   Broadcast message from `SettingsPopup`

Send slider value as `<float>` event.

```
public void OnSpeedValue(float speed) {
    Messenger<float>.Broadcast(GameEvent.SPEED_CHANGED, speed);
    ...
```

Now the enemy and player have their speed changed when you adjust the slider. Press Play and try it out!

> **Exercise: Changing the speed of spawned enemies**
>
> Currently, the speed value is only updated for enemies already in the scene and not for newly spawned enemies; new enemies aren't created at the correct speed setting. I'll leave it as an exercise for you to figure out how to set the speed on spawned enemies. Here's a hint: add a `SPEED_CHANGED` listener to `SceneController`, because that script is where enemies are spawned from.

You now know how to build a graphical interface using the new UI tools offered by Unity. This knowledge will come in handy in all future projects, even as we explore different game genres.

Summary

- Unity has both an immediate mode GUI system as well as a newer system based on 2D sprites.
- Using 2D sprites for a GUI requires that the scene have a canvas object.
- UI elements can be anchored to relative positions on the adjustable canvas.
- Set the Active property to turn UI elements on and off.
- A decoupled messaging system is a great way to broadcast events between the interface and the scene.

Creating a third-person 3D game: player movement and animation

This chapter covers

- Adding real-time shadows to the scene
- Making the camera orbit around its target
- Changing rotation smoothly using the Lerp algorithm
- Handling ground detection for jumping, ledges, and slopes
- Applying and controlling animation for a lifelike character

In this chapter, you'll create another 3D game, but this time you'll be working in a new game genre. In chapter 2, you built a movement demo for a first-person game. Now you're going to write another movement demo, but this time it'll involve third-person movement. The most important difference is the placement of the camera relative to the player: A player sees through their character's eyes in first-person view, and the camera is placed *outside* the character in third-person view. This view is probably familiar to you from adventure games, like the long-lived *Legend of Zelda* series, or the more recent *Uncharted* series of games. (Skip ahead to figure 8.3 if you want to see a comparison of first-person and third-person views.)

The project in this chapter is one of the more visually exciting prototypes we'll build in this book. Figure 8.1 shows how the scene will be constructed. Compare this with the diagram (figure 2.2) of the first-person scene we created in chapter 2.

1. Set up the walls, floor, and lights in the room. Simply import this from previous projects.

2. Import the character. Use a humanoid model this time, because in a third-person view, the player can see the character.

3. Turn on shadows for this scene. You can see the player now, so shadows are important.

4. Position the camera for this demo. The camera should be outside the character, looking down at it.

5. Write movement scripts for the camera and player. First write code to orbit the camera around the character, then write code to move the character around (including jumping!).

Figure 8.1   Roadmap for the third-person movement demo

You can see that the room construction is the same, and the use of scripts is much the same. But the look of the player, as well as the placement of the camera, are different in each case. Again, what defines this as a third-person view is that the camera is outside the player's character and looking inward at that character. You'll use a model that looks like a humanoid character (rather than a primitive capsule) because now players can actually see themselves.

Recall that two of the types of art assets discussed in chapter 4 were 3D models and animations. As mentioned in earlier chapters, the term *3D model* is almost a synonym for mesh object; the 3D model is the static shape defined by vertices and polygons (that is, mesh geometry). For a humanoid character, this mesh geometry is shaped into a head, arms, legs, and so forth (see figure 8.2).

Figure 8.2 Wireframe view of the model we'll use in this chapter

As usual, we'll focus on the last step in the roadmap: programming objects in the scene. Here's a recap of our plan of action:

1 Import a character model into the scene.
2 Implement camera controls to look at the character.
3 Write a script that enables the player to run around on the ground.
4 Add the ability to jump to the movement script.
5 Play animations on the model based on its movements.

Copy the project from chapter 2 to modify it, or create a new Unity project (be sure it's set to 3D, not the 2D project from chapter 5) and copy over the scene file from chapter 2's project; either way, also grab the scratch folder from this chapter's download to get the character model we'll use.

> **NOTE** You're going to build this chapter's project in the walled area from chapter 2. You'll keep the walls and lights but replace the player and all the scripts. If you need them, download the sample files from that chapter.

Assuming you're starting with the completed project from chapter 2 (the movement demo, not later projects), let's delete everything we don't need for this chapter. First, disconnect the camera from the player in the Hierarchy list (drag the camera object off the player object). Now delete the player object; if you hadn't disconnected the camera first then that would be deleted too, but what you want is to delete only the player capsule and leave the camera. Alternatively, if you already deleted the camera by accident, create a new camera object by selecting GameObject > Camera.

Delete all the scripts as well (which involves removing the script component from the camera and deleting the files in the Project view), leaving only the walls, floor, and lights.

8.1 Adjusting the camera view for third-person

Before you can write code to make the player move around, you need to put a character in the scene and set up the camera to look at that character. You'll import a faceless humanoid model to use as the player character, and then place the camera above at an angle to look down at the player obliquely. Figure 8.3 compares what the scene looks like in first-person view with what the scene will look like in third-person view (shown with a few large blocks, which you'll add in this chapter).

Figure 8.3   Side-by-side comparison of first-person and third-person views

You've prepared the scene already, so now you'll put a character model into the scene.

8.1.1 Importing a character to look at

The scratch folder for this chapter's download includes both the model and the texture; as you'll recall from chapter 4, FBX is the model and TGA is the texture. Import the FBX file into the project; either drag the file into the Project view, or right-click in the Project view and select Import New Asset. Then look in the Inspector to adjust import settings for the model. Later in the chapter you'll adjust imported animations, but for now you need to make only a couple of adjustments in the Model tab. First, change the Scale Factor value to 10 (to partially counteract the File Scale value of .01) so that the model will be the correct size.

A bit farther down, you'll find the Normals option (see figure 8.4). This setting controls how lighting and shading appear on the model, using a 3D math concept known as, well, *normals*.

Set the Scale Factor to partially
counteract File Scale. This determines
how big the model is in Unity, compared
to how big it was in the 3D art tool.

Select how to handle
Normals on the model.

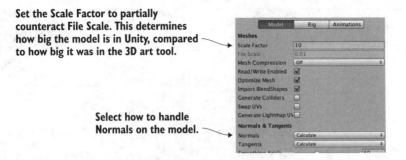

Figure 8.4   Import settings for the character model

> **DEFINITION**   *Normals* are direction vectors sticking out of polygons that tell the
> computer which direction the polygon is facing. This facing direction is used
> for lighting calculations.

The default setting for Normals is Import, which will use the normals defined in the
imported mesh geometry. But this particular model doesn't have correctly defined
normals and will react in odd ways to lights. Instead, change the setting to Calculate so
that Unity will calculate a vector for the facing direction of every polygon.

Once you've adjusted these two settings, click the Apply button in the Inspector.
Next, import the TGA file into the project and then assign this image as the texture in a
material. Select the player material in the Materials folder. Drag the texture image onto
the empty texture slot in the Inspector. Once the texture is applied, you won't see a
dramatic change in the model's color (this texture image is mostly white), but there are
shadows painted into the texture that'll improve the look of the model.

With the texture applied, drag the player model from the Project view up into the
scene. Position the character at 0, 1.1, 0 so that it'll be in the center of the room and
raised up to stand on the floor. We have a third-person character in the scene!

> **NOTE**   The imported character has his arms stuck straight out to each side, rather
> than the more natural arms-down pose. That's because animations haven't been
> applied yet; that arms-out position is referred to as the *T-pose* and the standard is
> for animated characters to default to a T-pose before they're animated.

8.1.2   Adding shadows to the scene

Before we move on, I want to explain a bit about the shadow being cast by the character. We take shadows for granted in the real world, but shadows aren't guaranteed in
the game's virtual world. Fortunately, Unity can handle this detail, and shadows are
turned on for the default light that comes with new scenes. Select the directional light
in your scene and then look in the Inspector for the Shadow Type option. That setting
(figure 8.5) is already on Soft Shadows for the default light, but notice the menu also
has a No Shadows option.

Figure 8.5   Before and after casting shadows from the directional light

That's all you need to do to set up shadows in this project, but there's a lot more you should know about shadows in games. Calculating the shadows in a scene is a particularly time-consuming part of computer graphics, so games often cut corners and fake things in various ways in order to achieve the visual look desired. The kind of shadow cast from the character is referred to as *real-time* shadow because the shadow is calculated while the game is running and moves around with moving objects. A perfectly realistic lighting setup would have all objects casting and receiving shadows in real time, but in order for the shadow calculations to run fast enough, real-time shadows are limited in how the shadows look or which lights can even cast shadows. Note that only the directional light is casting shadows in this scene.

Another common way of handling shadows in games is with a technique called *lightmapping.*

DEFINITION   *Lightmaps* are textures applied to the level geometry, with pictures of the shadows baked into the texture image.

DEFINITION   Drawing shadows onto a model's texture is referred to as *baking* the shadows.

Because these images are generated ahead of time (rather than while the game is running), they can be very elaborate and realistic. On the downside, because the shadows are generated ahead of time, they won't move. As such, lightmaps are great to use for static level geometry, but they aren't useful for dynamic objects like characters. Lightmaps are generated automatically rather than being painted by hand. The computer calculates how the lights in the scene will illuminate the level while subtle darkness builds up in corners. In Unity, the system for rendering lightmaps is called Enlighten, so you can look up that keyword in Unity's manual.

Whether or not to use real-time shadows or lightmaps isn't an all-or-nothing choice. You can set the Culling Mask property on a light so that real-time shadows are used only for certain objects, allowing you to use the higher-quality lightmaps for other objects in the scene. Similarly, though you almost always want the main character to cast shadows, sometimes you don't want the character to receive shadows; all mesh objects have settings to cast and receive shadows (see figure 8.6).

Shadows are projected
from this mesh.

This mesh darkens from
shadows projected onto it.

Figure 8.6   The Cast Shadows and Receive
Shadows settings in the Inspector

> **DEFINITION**   *Culling* is a general term for removing unwanted things. The word comes up a lot in computer graphics in many different contexts, but in this case *culling mask* is the set of objects you want to remove from shadow casting.

All right, now you understand the basics of how to apply shadows to your scenes. Lighting and shading a level can be a big topic in itself (books about level editing will often spend multiple chapters on lightmapping), but here we'll restrict ourselves to turning on real-time shadows on one light. And with that, let's turn our attention to the camera.

8.1.3   Orbiting the camera around the player character

In the first-person demo, the camera was linked to the player object in Hierarchy view so that they'd rotate together. In third-person movement, though, the player character will be facing different directions independently of the camera. Therefore, you don't want to drag the camera onto the player character in the Hierarchy view this time. Instead, the camera's code will move its position along with the character but will rotate independently of the character.

First, place the camera where you want it to be relative to the player; I went with position 0,3.5,-3.75 to put the camera above and behind the character (reset rotation to 0,0,0 if needed). Then create a script called OrbitCamera. Attach the script component to the camera and then drag the player character into the target slot of the script. Now you can play the scene to see the camera code in action.

Listing 8.1   Camera script for rotating around a target while looking at it

```
using UnityEngine;
using System.Collections;

public class OrbitCamera : MonoBehaviour {
    [SerializeField] private Transform target;          Serialized reference to the
                                                        object to orbit around
    public float rotSpeed = 1.5f;
```

```
private float _rotY;
private Vector3 _offset;

void Start() {
    _rotY = transform.eulerAngles.y;
    _offset = target.position - transform.position;
}

void LateUpdate() {
    float horInput = Input.GetAxis("Horizontal");
    if (horInput != 0) {
        _rotY += horInput * rotSpeed;
    } else {
        _rotY += Input.GetAxis("Mouse X") * rotSpeed * 3;
    }

    Quaternion rotation = Quaternion.Euler(0, _rotY, 0);
    transform.position = target.position - (rotation * _offset);
    transform.LookAt(target);
}
}
```

Store the starting position offset between the camera and the target.

Either rotate the camera slowly using arrow keys …

… or rotate quickly with the mouse.

Maintain the starting offset, shifted according to the camera's rotation.

No matter where the camera is relative to the target, always face the target.

As you're reading through the listing, note the serialized variable for `target`. The code needs to know which object to orbit the camera around, so this variable is serialized in order to appear within Unity's editor and have the player character linked to it. The next couple of variables are rotation values that are used in the same way as in the camera control code from chapter 2. And there's an `_offset` value declared; `_offset` is set within `Start()` to store the position difference between the camera and target. This way, the relative position of the camera can be maintained while the script runs. In other words, the camera will stay at the initial distance from the character regardless of which way it rotates. The remainder of the code is inside the `LateUpdate()` function.

> **TIP** Remember, `LateUpdate()` is another method provided by `MonoBehaviour` and it's very similar to `Update()`; it's a method run every frame. The difference, as the name implies, is that `LateUpdate()` is called on all objects after `Update()` has run on all objects. This way, you can ensure that the camera updates after the target has moved.

First, the code increments the rotation value based on input controls. This code looks at two different input controls—horizontal arrow keys and horizontal mouse movement—so a conditional is used to switch between them. The code checks if horizontal arrow keys are being pressed; if they are, then it uses that input, but if not, it checks the mouse. By checking the two inputs separately, the code can rotate at different speeds for each type of input.

Next, the code positions the camera based on the position of the target and the rotation value. The `transform.position` line is probably the biggest "aha!" in this code, because it provides crucial math that you haven't seen before. Multiplying a position vector by a quaternion (note that the rotation angle was converted to a quaternion using `Quaternion.Euler`) results in a position that's shifted over according to that rotation. This rotated position vector is then added as the offset from the character's position in order to calculate the position for the camera. Figure 8.7 illustrates the steps of the calculation and provides a detailed breakdown of this rather conceptually dense line of code.

Figure 8.7   The steps for calculating the camera's position

> **NOTE** The more mathematically astute among you may be thinking "Hmm, that transforming-between-coordinate-systems thing in chapter 2 . . . can't I do that here, too?" Yes, you could transform the offset position using a rotated coordinate system to get the rotated offset, but that'd require setting up the rotated coordinate system first, and it's more straightforward not to need that step.

Finally, the code uses the LookAt() method to point the camera at the target; this function points one object (not just cameras) at another object. The rotation value calculated previously was used to position the camera at the correct angle around the target, but in that step the camera was only positioned and not rotated. Thus, without the final LookAt line, the camera position would orbit around the character but wouldn't necessarily be looking at it. Go ahead and comment out that line to see what happens.

The camera has its script for orbiting around the player character; next up is code that moves the character around.

8.2   *Programming camera-relative movement controls*

Now that the character model is imported into Unity and you've written code to control the camera view, it's time to program controls for moving around the scene. Let's program camera-relative controls that'll move the character in various directions when arrow keys are pressed, as well as rotate the character to face those different directions.

What does "camera-relative" mean?

The whole notion of "camera-relative" is a bit nonobvious but very crucial to understand. This is similar to the local versus global distinction mentioned in previous chapters: "left" points in different directions when you mean "left of the local object" or "left of the entire world." In a similar way, when you "move the character to the left," do you mean toward the character's left, or the left-hand side of the screen?

The camera in a first-person game is placed inside the character and moves with it, so no distinction exists between the character's left and the camera's left. A third-person view places the camera outside the character, though, and thus the camera's left may be pointed in a different direction from the character's left. For example, they're literally opposite directions if the camera is looking at the front of the character. As such, you have to decide what you want to have happen in your specific game and controls setup.

Although games occasionally do it the other way, most third-person games make their controls camera-relative. When the player presses the left button, the character moves to the left of the screen, not the character's left. Over time and through experiments with trying out different control schemes, game designers have figured out that players find the controls more intuitive and easier to understand when "left" means "left-hand side of the screen" (which, not coincidentally, is also the player's left).

Implementing camera-relative controls involves two primary steps: first rotate the player character to face the direction of the controls, and then move the character forward. Let's write the code for these two steps next.

8.2.1   *Rotating the character to face movement direction*

First you'll write code to make the character face in the direction of the arrow keys. Create a C# script called `RelativeMovement` (see listing 8.2). Drag that script onto the player character, and then link the camera to the `target` property of the script component (just as you linked the character to the target of the camera script). Now the character will face different directions when you press the controls, facing directions relative to the camera, or stand still when you're not pressing any arrow keys (that is, when rotating using the mouse).

Listing 8.2   Rotating the character relative to the camera

```
using UnityEngine;
using System.Collections;

public class RelativeMovement : MonoBehaviour {
```

```
[SerializeField] private Transform target;        ◄──┐ This script needs a reference to
                                                      │ the object to move relative to.

void Update() {
    Vector3 movement = Vector3.zero;         ◄──┐ Start with vector (0, 0, 0) and add
                                                 │ movement components progressively.

    float horInput = Input.GetAxis("Horizontal");
    float vertInput = Input.GetAxis("Vertical");         ┌ Only handle movement while
    if (horInput != 0 || vertInput != 0) {      ◄────────┘ arrow keys are pressed.
        movement.x = horInput;
        movement.z = vertInput;
                                                 ┌ Keep the initial rotation to restore
                                                 │ after finishing with the target object.
        Quaternion tmp = target.rotation;   ◄────┘
        target.eulerAngles = new Vector3(0, target.eulerAngles.y, 0);
        movement = target.TransformDirection(movement);   ◄──┐
        target.rotation = tmp;                               │

        transform.rotation = Quaternion.LookRotation(movement);
    }
}
}
```

LookRotation()
calculates a quaternion
facing in that direction.

Transform movement direction from local to global coordinates.

The code in this listing starts the same way listing 8.1 did, with a serialized variable for target. Just as the previous script needed a reference to the object it'd orbit around, this script needs a reference to the object it'll move relative to. Then we get to the Update() function. The first line of the function declares a Vector3 value of 0, 0, 0. It's important to create a zeroed vector and fill in the values later rather than simply create a vector later with the movement values calculated, because the vertical and horizontal movement values will be calculated in different steps but they all need to be part of the same vector.

Next, check the input controls, just as you have in previous scripts. Here's where X and Z values are set in the movement vector, for horizontal movement around the scene. Remember that Input.GetAxis() returns 0 if no button is pressed, and it varies between 1 and –1 when those keys are being pressed; putting that value in the movement vector sets the movement to the positive or negative direction of that axis (the X-axis is left-right, and the Z-axis is forward-backward).

The next several lines are where the movement vector is adjusted to be camera-relative. Specifically, TransformDirection() is used to transform from local to global coordinates. This is the same thing we did with TransformDirection() in chapter 2, except this time you're transforming from the target's coordinate system instead of from the player's coordinate system. Meanwhile, the code just before and after the Transform-Direction() line is aligning the coordinate system for our needs: first store the target's rotation to restore later, and then adjust the rotation so that it's only around the Y-axis and not all three axes. Finally, perform the transformation and restore the target's rotation.

All of that code was for calculating the movement direction as a vector. The final line of code applies that movement direction to the character by converting the Vector3 into a Quaternion using Quaternion.LookRotation() and assigning that value. Try running the game now to see what happens!

Smoothly rotating (interpolating) by using Lerp

Currently, the character's rotation snaps instantly to different facings, but it'd look better if the character smoothly rotated to different facings. You can do so using a mathematical operation called *Lerp*. First add this variable to the script:

```
public float rotSpeed = 15.0f;
```

Then replace the existing `transform.rotation...` line at the end of listing 8.2 with the following code:

```
    ...
    Quaternion direction = Quaternion.LookRotation(movement);
    transform.rotation = Quaternion.Lerp(transform.rotation,
        direction, rotSpeed * Time.deltaTime);
  }
 }
}
```

Now, instead of snapping directly to the `LookRotation()` value, that value is used indirectly as the target direction to rotate toward. The `Quaternion.Lerp()` method smoothly rotates between the current and target rotations (with the third parameter controlling how quickly to rotate).

Incidentally, the term for smoothly changing between values is *interpolate*; you can interpolate between two of any kind of value, not just rotation values. Lerp is a quasi-acronym for "linear interpolation," and Unity provides Lerp methods for vectors and float values, too (to interpolate positions, colors, or anything else). Quaternions also have a closely related alternative method for interpolation called *Slerp* (for spherical linear interpolation). For slower turns, Slerp rotations may look better than Lerp.

Currently, the character is rotating in place without moving; in the next section, you'll add code for moving the character around.

> **NOTE**   Because sideways facing uses the same keyboard controls as orbiting the camera, the character will slowly rotate while the movement direction points sideways. This doubling up of the controls is desired behavior in this project.

8.2.2 *Moving forward in that direction*

As you'll recall from chapter 2, in order to move the player around the scene, you need to add a character controller component to the player object. Select the character and then choose Components > Physics > Character Controller. In the Inspector, you should slightly reduce the controller's radius to `.4`, but otherwise the default settings are all fine for this character model.

Here's what you need to add in the `RelativeMovement` script.

Listing 8.3   Adding code to change the player's position

```
using UnityEngine;
```

```
using System.Collections;

[RequireComponent(typeof(CharacterController))]      ◄─── The surrounding lines are
public class RelativeMovement : MonoBehaviour {           context for placing the
...                                                       RequireComponent() method.
public float moveSpeed = 6.0f;

private CharacterController _charController;          A pattern you've seen in previous
                                                     chapters, used for getting access
void Start() {                                            to other components.
    _charController = GetComponent<CharacterController>();  ◄───

}

void Update() {                                      Overwrite the existing X and Z
    ...                                              lines to apply movement speed.
    movement.x = horInput * moveSpeed;       ◄───
    movement.z = vertInput * moveSpeed;
    movement = Vector3.ClampMagnitude(movement, moveSpeed);
    ...

}                                            Always multiply movements by deltaTime
                                             to make them frame rate-independent.
    movement *= Time.deltaTime;       ◄───
    _charController.Move(movement);

}

}
```

Limit diagonal movement to the same speed as movement along an axis.

If you play the game now, you will see the character (stuck in a T-pose) moving around in the scene. Pretty much the entirety of this listing is code you've already seen, so I'll review everything briefly.

First, there's a RequireComponent() method at the top of the code. As explained in chapter 2, RequireComponent() will force Unity to make sure the GameObject has a component of the type passed into the command. This line is optional; you don't have to require it, but without this component the script will have errors.

Next there's a movement value declared, followed by getting this script a reference to the character controller. As you'll recall from previous chapters, GetComponent() returns other components attached to the given object, and if the object to search on isn't explicitly defined, then it's assumed to be this.gameObject.GetComponent() (that is, the same object as this script).

Movement values are assigned based on the input controls. This was in the previous listing, too; the change here is that you also account for the movement speed. Multiply both movement axes by the movement speed, and then use Vector3.ClampMagnitude() to limit the vector's magnitude to the movement speed; the clamp is needed because, otherwise, diagonal movement would have a greater magnitude than movement directly along an axis (picture the sides and hypotenuse of a right triangle).

Finally, at the end, you multiply the movement values by deltaTime in order to get frame rate–independent movement (recall that frame rate-independent means the character moves at the same speed on different computers with different frame rates). Pass the movement values to CharacterController.Move() to make the movement.

This handles all the horizontal movement; next, let's take care of vertical movement.

8.3   *Implementing the jump action*

In the previous section you wrote code to make the character run around on the ground. In the chapter introduction, I also mentioned making the character jump, so let's do that now. Most third-person games do have a control for jumping. And even if they don't, they almost always have vertical movement from the character falling off ledges. Our code will handle both jumping and falling. Specifically, this code will have gravity pulling the player down at all times, but occasionally an upward jolt will be applied when the player jumps.

Before you write this code, let's add a few raised platforms to the scene. There's currently nothing to jump on or fall off of! Create a couple more cube objects, and then modify their positions and scale to give the player platforms to jump on. In the sample project, I added two cubes and used these settings: Position 5, .75, 5 and Scale 4, 1.5, 4; Position 1, 1.5, 5.5 and Scale 4, 3, 4. Figure 8.8 shows the raised platforms.

Figure 8.8   A couple of raised platforms added to the sparse scene

8.3.1   *Applying vertical speed and acceleration*

As mentioned when you first started writing the `RelativeMovement` script in listing 8.2, the movement values are calculated in separate steps and added to the movement vector progressively. This listing adds vertical movement to the existing vector.

> **Listing 8.4   Adding vertical movement to the `RelativeMovement` script**

```
...
public float jumpSpeed = 15.0f;
public float gravity = -9.8f;
public float terminalVelocity = -10.0f;
public float minFall = -1.5f;

private float _vertSpeed;
...
void Start() {
    _vertSpeed = minFall;
    ...
}

    void Update() {
```

Initialize the vertical speed to the minimum falling speed at the start of the existing function.

```
    ...
    if (_charController.isGrounded) {
        if (Input.GetButtonDown("Jump")) {
            _vertSpeed = jumpSpeed;
        } else {
            _vertSpeed = minFall;
        }
    } else {
        _vertSpeed += gravity * 5 * Time.deltaTime;
        if (_vertSpeed < terminalVelocity) {
            _vertSpeed = terminalVelocity;
        }
    }
    movement.y = _vertSpeed;

    movement *= Time.deltaTime;
    _charController.Move(movement);
}
}
```

CharacterController has an isGrounded property to check if the controller is on the ground.

React to the Jump button while on the ground.

If not on the ground, then apply gravity until terminal velocity is reached.

The end of listing 8.3, so that you can see where this new code goes.

As usual, you start by adding a few new variables to the top of the script for various movement values, and initialize the values correctly. Then, you skip down to just after the big if statement for horizontal movement, where you'll add another big if statement for vertical movement. Specifically, the code will check if the character is on the ground, because the vertical speed will be adjusted differently depending on whether the character is on the ground. CharacterController includes isGrounded for checking whether the character is on the ground; this value is true if the bottom of the character controller collided with anything in the last frame.

If the character is on the ground, then the vertical speed value (the private _vert-Speed variable) should be reset to nothing. The character isn't falling while on the ground, so obviously its vertical speed is 0; if the character then steps off a ledge, you're going to get a nice, natural-looking motion because the falling speed will accelerate from nothing.

> **NOTE** Well, not *exactly* 0; you're setting the vertical speed to minFall, a slight downward movement, so that the character will always be pressing down against the ground while running around horizontally. There needs to be some downward force in order to run up and down on uneven terrain.

The exception to this grounded speed value is if the jump button is clicked. In that case, the vertical speed should be set to a high number. The if statement checks Get-ButtonDown(), a new input function that works much like GetAxis() does, returning the state of the indicated input control. And much like Horizontal and Vertical input axes, the exact key assigned to Jump is defined by going to Input settings under Edit > Project Settings (the default key assignment is Space—that is, the spacebar).

Getting back to the larger if condition, if the character is not on the ground, then the vertical speed should be constantly reduced by gravity. Note that this code doesn't simply set the speed value but rather decrements it; this way, it's not a constant speed but rather a downward acceleration, resulting in a realistic falling movement. Jumping will happen in a natural arc, as the character's upward speed gradually reduces to 0 and it starts falling instead.

Finally, the code makes sure the downward speed doesn't exceed terminal velocity. Note that the operator is less than and not greater than, because downward is a negative speed value. Then, after the big `if` statement, assign the calculated vertical speed to the Y-axis of the movement vector.

And that's all you need for realistic vertical movement! By applying a constant downward acceleration when the character isn't on the ground, and adjusting the speed appropriately when the character is on the ground, the code creates nice falling behavior. But this all depends on detecting the ground correctly, and there's a subtle glitch you need to fix.

8.3.2   *Modifying the ground detection to handle edges and slopes*

As explained in the previous section, the `isGrounded` property of `CharacterController` indicates whether the bottom of the character controller collided with anything in the last frame. Although this approach to detecting the ground works the majority of the time, you'll probably notice that the character seems to float in the air while stepping off edges. That's because the collision area of the character is a surrounding capsule (you can see it when you select the character object) and the bottom of this capsule will still be in contact with the ground when the player steps off the edge of the platform. Figure 8.9 illustrates the problem. This won't do at all!

... but the collision capsule around the character is still touching the platform edge. As a result, the player appears to be floating in the air.

The character has stepped completely off the platform ...

Figure 8.9   Diagram showing the character controller capsule touching the platform edge

Similarly, if the character stands on a slope, the current ground detection will cause problematic behavior. Try it now by creating a sloped block against the raised platforms. Create a new cube object and set its transform values to Position -1.5, 1.5, 5 Rotation 0, 0, -25 Scale 1, 4, 4.

If you jump onto the slope from the ground, you'll find that you can jump again from midway up the slope and thereby ascend to the top. That's because the slope touches the bottom of the capsule obliquely and the code currently considers any collision on the bottom to be solid footing. Again, this won't do; the character should slide back down, not have a solid footing to jump from.

NOTE Sliding back down is only desired on steep slopes. On shallow slopes, such as uneven ground, you want the player to run around unaffected. If you want one to test on, make a shallow ramp by creating a cube and set it to Position 5.25, .25, .25 Rotation 0, 90, 75 Scale 1, 6, 3.

All these problems have the same root cause: Checking for collisions on the bottom of the character isn't a great way of determining if the character is on the ground. Instead, let's use raycasting to detect the ground. In chapter 3, the AI used raycasting to detect obstacles in front of it; let's use the same approach to detect surfaces below the character. Cast a ray straight down from the player's position. If it registers a hit just below the character's feet, that means the player is standing on the ground.

This introduces a new situation to handle: when the raycast doesn't detect ground below the character but the character controller is colliding with the ground. As in figure 8.9, the capsule still collides with the platform while the character is walking off the edge. Figure 8.10 adds raycasting to the diagram in order to show what will happen now: the ray doesn't hit the platform, but the capsule does touch the edge. The code needs to handle this special situation.

... but the collision capsule around the character is still touching the platform edge. The code must handle this situation.

Raycasting straight down from the middle correctly detects that the character isn't standing on the ground ...

Figure 8.10   Diagram of raycasting downward while stepping off a ledge

In this case, the code should make the character slide off the ledge. The character will still fall (because it's not standing on the ground), but it'll also push away from the point of collision (because it needs to move the capsule away from the platform it's hitting). Thus, the code will detect collisions with the character controller and respond to those collisions by nudging away.

This listing adjusts the vertical movement with everything we just discussed.

Listing 8.5   Using raycasting to detect the ground

```
...
private ControllerColliderHit _contact;      ◄——— Needed to store collision data between functions
...
        bool hitGround = false;
        RaycastHit hit;                         ┌ Check if the player is falling.
        if (_vertSpeed < 0 &&        ◄—————————┘
            Physics.Raycast(transform.position, Vector3.down, out hit)) {
            float check =        ◄——┐
                                     │ Distance to check against (extend slightly
                                     └ beyond the bottom of the capsule)
```

```
                          (_charController.height + _charController.radius) / 1.9f;
                  hitGround = hit.distance <= check;
              }
                                                    Instead of using isGrounded,
                                                    check the raycasting result.
              if (hitGround) {
                  if (Input.GetButtonDown("Jump")) {
                      _vertSpeed = jumpSpeed;
                  } else {
                      _vertSpeed = minFall;
                  }
              } else {
                  _vertSpeed += gravity * 5 * Time.deltaTime;
                  if (_vertSpeed < terminalVelocity) {
                      _vertSpeed = terminalVelocity;
                  }
                                                          Raycasting didn't detect ground, but
                                                          the capsule is touching the ground.
                  if (_charController.isGrounded) {
                      if (Vector3.Dot(movement, _contact.normal) < 0) {
                          movement = _contact.normal * moveSpeed;
                      } else {
                          movement += _contact.normal * moveSpeed;
                      }
                                                                  Respond slightly
                  }                                               differently depending on
              }                                                   whether the character is
              movement.y = _vertSpeed;                            facing the contact point.

              movement *= Time.deltaTime;
              _charController.Move(movement);        Store the collision data in the
          }                                          callback when a collision is detected.

          void OnControllerColliderHit(ControllerColliderHit hit) {
              _contact = hit;
          }
      }
```

This listing contains much of the same code as the previous listing; the new code is interspersed throughout the existing movement script and this listing needed the existing code for context. The first line adds a new variable to the top of the Relative-Movement script. This variable is used to store data about collisions between functions.

The next several lines do raycasting. This code also goes below horizontal movement but before the if statement for vertical movement. The actual Physics.Raycast() call should be familiar from previous chapters, but the specific parameters are different this time. Although the position to cast a ray from is the same (the character's position), the direction will be down this time instead of forward. Then, you check how far away the raycast was when it hit something; if the distance of the hit is at the distance of the character's feet, then the character is standing on the ground, so set hitGround to true.

> **WARNING** It's a little nonobvious how the check distance is calculated, so let's go over that in detail. First, take the height of the character controller (which is the height without the rounded ends) and then add the rounded ends. Divide this value in half because the ray was cast from the middle of the character (that is, already halfway down) to get the distance to the bottom of the character. But

you really want to check a little beyond the bottom of the character to account for tiny inaccuracies in the raycasting, so divide by 1.9 instead of 2 to get a distance that's slightly too far.

Having done this raycasting, use `hitGround` instead of `isGrounded` in the `if` statement for vertical movement. Most of the vertical movement code will remain the same, but add code to handle when the character controller collides with the ground even though the player isn't over the ground (that is, when the player walks off the edge of the platform). There's a new `isGrounded` conditional added, but note that it's nested inside the `hitGround` conditional so that `isGrounded` is only checked when `hitGround` doesn't detect the ground.

The collision data includes a `normal` property (again, a normal vector says which way something is facing) that tells us the direction to move away from the point of collision. But one tricky thing is that you want the nudge away from the contact point to be handled differently depending on in which direction the player is already moving. When the previous horizontal movement is toward the platform, you want to replace that movement so that the character won't keep moving in the wrong direction; but when facing away from the edge, you want to add to the previous horizontal movement in order to keep the forward momentum away from the edge. The movement vector's facing relative to the point of collision can be determined using the dot product.

> **DEFINITION** The *dot product* is one kind of mathematical operation that can be done on two vectors. Long story short, the dot product of two vectors ranges between -1 and 1, with 1 meaning they point in exactly the same direction, and -1 when they point in exactly opposite directions. Don't confuse dot product and cross product; the cross product is a different but also commonly seen vector math operation.

`Vector3` includes a `Dot()` function to calculate the dot product of two given vectors. If you calculate the dot product between the movement vector and the collision normal, that will return a negative number when the two directions face away from each other and a positive number when the movement and the collision face the same direction.

The very end of listing 8.5 adds a new method to the script. In the previous code, you were checking the collision normal, but where did that information come from? It turns out that collisions with the character controller are reported through a callback function called `OnControllerColliderHit` that `MonoBehaviour` provides; in order to respond to the collision data anywhere else in the script, that data must be stored in an external variable. That's all the method is doing here: storing the collision data in `_contact` so that this data can be used within the `Update()` method.

Now the errors are corrected around platform edges and on slopes. Go ahead and play to test it out by stepping over edges and jumping onto the steep slope. This movement demo is almost complete. The character is moving around the scene correctly, so only one thing remains: animating the character out of the T-pose.

8.4   *Setting up animations on the player character*

Besides the more complex shape defined by mesh geometry, a humanoid character needs animations. In chapter 4, you learned that an animation is a packet of information that defines movement of the associated 3D object. The concrete example I gave was of a character walking around, and that situation is exactly what you're going to be doing now! The character is going to run around the scene, so you'll assign animations that make the arms and legs swing back and forth. Figure 8.11 shows what it'll look like when the character has an animation playing while it moves around the scene.

The character is now moving its arms and legs, instead of sliding around in a T-pose.

Figure 8.11   Character moving around with a run animation playing

A good analogy with which to understand 3D animation is to think about puppeteering: 3D models are the puppets, the animator is the puppeteer, and an animation is a recording of the puppet's movements. Animations can be created with a few different approaches; most character animation in modern games (certainly all the animations on this chapter's character) uses a technique called *skeletal animation.*

> **DEFINITION**   *Skeletal animation* is a kind of animation where a series of bones are set up inside the model, and then the bones are moved around during the animation. When a bone moves, the model's surface linked to that bone moves along with it.

As the name implies, skeletal animation makes the most intuitive sense when simulating the skeleton inside a character (figure 8.12 illustrates this), but the skeleton is an abstraction that's useful any time you want a model to bend and flex while still having a definite structure to how it moves (for example, a tentacle that waves around). Although the bones move rigidly, the model surface around the bones can bend and flex.

Achieving the result illustrated in figure 8.11 involves several steps: first, define animation clips in the imported file, then set up the controller to play those animation clips, and finally, incorporate that animation controller in your code. The animations on the character model will be played back according to the movement scripts you'll write.

Figure 8.12   Skeletal animation of a humanoid character

Of course, the very first thing you need to do, before any of those steps, is turn on the animation system. Select the player model in the Project view to see its Import settings in the Inspector. Select the Animations tab and make sure Import Animation is checked. Then go to the Rig tab and switch Animation Type from Generic to Humanoid (this is a humanoid character, naturally). Note that this last menu also has a Legacy setting; Generic and Humanoid are both settings within the umbrella term Mecanim.

Explaining Unity's Mecanim animation system

Unity has a sophisticated system for managing animations on models, called Mecanim. You were introduced to this animation system in chapter 6 with the caveat that we'd go into more detail later, so some of this chapter will be a review of previous explanations, now focusing on 3D animations instead of 2D.

The name Mecanim identifies the newer, more advanced animation system that was added to Unity as a replacement for the older animation system. The older system is still around, identified as Legacy animation, but it may be phased out in a future version of Unity, at which point Mecanim will simply be *the* animation system.

Although the animations you're going to use are all included in the same FBX file as our character model, one of the major advantages of Mecanim's approach is that you can apply animations from other FBX files to a character. For example, all of the human enemies can share a single set of animations. This has a number of advantages, including keeping all your data organized (models can go in one folder, whereas animations go in another folder) as well as saving time spent animating each separate character.

Click the Apply button at the bottom of the Inspector in order to lock these settings onto the imported model and then continue defining animation clips.

> **WARNING** You may notice a warning (not an error) in the console that says, "conversion warning: spine3 is between humanoid transforms." That specific warning isn't a cause for worry; it indicates that the skeleton in the imported model has extra bones beyond the skeleton that Mecanim expects.

8.4.1 Defining animation clips in the imported model

The first step in setting up animations for our character is defining the various animation clips that'll be played. If you think about a lifelike character, different movements can happen at different times: Sometimes the player is running around, sometimes the player is jumping on platforms, and sometimes the character is just standing there with its arms down. Each of these movements is a separate clip that can play individually.

Often, imported animations come as a single long clip that can be cut up into shorter individual animations. To split up the animation clips, first select the Animations tab in the Inspector. You'll see a Clips panel, shown in figure 8.13; this lists all the defined animation clips, which initially are one imported clip. You'll notice + and – buttons at the bottom of the list; you use these buttons to add and remove clips on the list. Ultimately, you need four clips for this character, so add and remove clips as necessary while you work.

Animation clips listed by name, along with the start and end frames → ← **+/– buttons** to add more clips to the list

Figure 8.13 The Clips list in Animation settings

When you select a clip, information about that clip (shown in figure 8.14) will appear in the area below the list. The top of this information area shows the name of this clip, and you can type in a new name. Name the first clip `idle`. Define Start and End frames for this animation clip; this allows you to slice a chunk out of the longer imported animation. For the idle animation, enter Start 3 and End 141. Next up are the Loop settings.

> **DEFINITION** *Loop* refers to a recording that plays over and over repeatedly. A looping animation clip is one that plays again from the start as soon as playback reaches the end.

The idle animation loops, so select both Loop Time and Loop Pose. Incidentally, the green indicator dot tells you when the pose at the beginning of the clip matches the pose at the end for correct looping; this indicator turns yellow when the poses are somewhat off, and it turns red when the start and end poses are completely different.

The name of the animation clip; type a new one here.

Set Start and End frames for this clip.

Turn on looping playback (including an option to blend together the start and end poses).

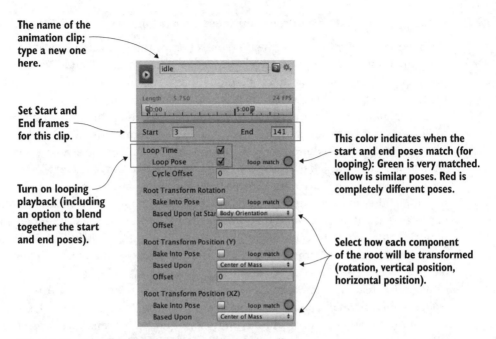

This color indicates when the start and end poses match (for looping): Green is very matched. Yellow is similar poses. Red is completely different poses.

Select how each component of the root will be transformed (rotation, vertical position, horizontal position).

Figure 8.14   Information about the selected animation clip

Below the Loop settings is a series of settings related to the root transform. The word *root* means the same thing for skeletal animation as it does for a hierarchy connected within Unity: the root object is the base object that everything else is connected to. Thus, the *animation root* can be thought of as the base of the character, and everything else moves relative to that base. There are a few different settings here for setting up that base, and you may want to experiment here when working with your own animations. For our purposes, though, the three menus should be set to Body Orientation, Center Of Mass, and Center Of Mass, in that order.

Now click Apply and you've added an idle animation clip to your character. Do the same for two more clips: walk starts at frame 144 and ends at 169, and run starts at 171 and ends at 190. All the other settings should be the same as for idle because they're also animation loops.

The fourth animation clip is jump, and the settings for that clip differ a bit. First, this isn't a loop but rather a still pose, so don't select Loop Time. Set the Start and End to 190.5 and 191; this is a single-frame pose, but Unity requires that Start and End be different. The animation preview below won't look quite right because of these tricky numbers, but this pose will look fine in the game.

Click Apply to confirm the new animation clips, and then move on to the next step: creating the animation controller.

8.4.2 Creating the animator controller for these animations

The next step is to create the animator controller for this character. This step allows us to set up animation states and create transitions between those states. Various animation clips are played during different animation states, and then our scripts will cause the controller to shift between animation states.

This might seem like an odd bit of indirection—putting the abstraction of a controller between our code and the actual playing of animations. You may be familiar with systems where you directly play animations from your code; indeed, the old Legacy animation system worked in exactly that way, with calls like Play("idle"). But this indirection enables us to share animations between models, rather than only being able to play animations that are internal to this model. In this chapter, we won't take advantage of this ability, but keep in mind that it can be helpful when you're working on a larger project. You can obtain your animations from several sources, including multiple animators, or you can buy individual animations from stores online (such as Unity's Asset Store).

Begin by creating a new animator controller asset (Assets > Create> Animator Controller—not Animation, a different sort of asset). In the Project view, you'll see an icon with a funny-looking network of lines on it (see figure 8.15); rename this asset player. Select the character in the scene and you'll notice this object has a component called Animator; any model that can be animated has this component, in addition to the Transform component and whatever else you've added. The Animator component has a Controller slot for you to link a specific animator controller, so drag and drop your new controller asset (and be sure to uncheck Root Motion).

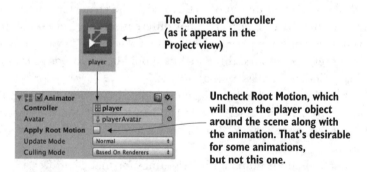

Figure 8.15 Animator controller and Animator component

The animator controller is a tree of connected nodes (hence the icon on that asset) that you can see and manipulate by opening the Animator view. This is another view, just like Scene or Project (shown in figure 8.16) except this view isn't open by default. Select Animator from the Window menu (be careful not to get confused with the Animation window; that's a separate selection from Animator). The node network displayed here is whichever animator controller is currently selected (or the animator controller on the selected character).

A series of number or Boolean values can be created here to control the animations. The currently active state transitions between states on the graph when these values change.

Each node on the graph is an animation state. The named animation clip plays when the controller is in that state.

(The orange node is the default animation state, before any transitions happen.)

The lines connecting nodes are transitions. Transitions have a direction for transitioning from A to B.

Figure 8.16   The Animator view with our completed animator controller

TIP   Remember that you can move tabs around in Unity and dock them wherever you like in order to organize the interface. I like to dock the Animator right next to the Scene and Game windows.

Initially, there are only two default nodes, for Entry and Any State. You're not going to use the Any State node. Instead, you'll drag in animation clips to create new nodes. In the Project view, click the arrow on the side of the model asset to expand that asset and see what it contains. Among the contents of this asset are the animation clips you defined (see figure 8.17), so drag those clips into the Animator view. Don't bother with the walking animation (that could be useful for other projects) and drag in idle, run, and jump.

Click the arrow to expand an asset and see its contents.

The imported model contains the various animation clips.

Figure 8.17   Expanded model asset in Project view

Right-click on the Idle node and select Set As Layer Default State. That node will turn orange while the other nodes stay gray; the default animation state is where the network of nodes starts before the game has made any changes. You'll need to link the nodes together with lines indicating transitions between animation states; right-click on a node and select Make Transition in order to start dragging out an arrow that you can click on another node to connect. Connect nodes in the pattern shown in figure 8.16 (be sure to make transitions in both directions for most nodes, but not from jump to run). These transition lines determine how the animation states connect to each other and control the changes from one state to another during the game.

The transitions rely on a set of controlling values, so let's create those parameters. In the top left of figure 8.16 is a tab called Parameters; click that to see a panel with a + button for adding parameters. Add a float called Speed and a Boolean called Jumping. Those values will be adjusted by our code, and they'll trigger transitions between animation states.

Click on the transition lines to see their settings in the Inspector (see figure 8.18).

Figure 8.18   Transition settings in the Inspector

Here's where you'll adjust how the animation states change when the parameters change. For example, click on the Idle-to-Run transition to adjust the conditions of that transition. Under Conditions, choose Speed, Greater, and 0.1. Turn off Has Exit Time (that would force playing the animation all the way through, as opposed to cutting short immediately when the transition happens). Then, click the arrow next to the Settings label in order to see that entire menu; other transitions should be able to interrupt this one, so change the Interruption Source menu from None to Current State. Repeat this for all the transitions in table 8.1.

Table 8.1 Conditions for all transitions in this animation controller

Transition	Condition	Interruption
Idle-to-Run	Speed greater than .1	Current State
Run-to-Idle	Speed less than .1	None
Idle-to-Jump	Jumping is true	None
Run-to-Jump	Jumping is true	None
Jump-to-Idle	Jumping is false	None

In addition to these menu-based settings, there's a complex visual interface, shown in figure 8.18, just above the Condition setting. This graph allows you to visually adjust the length in time of a transition. The default transition time looks fine for both transitions between Idle and Run, but all of the transitions to and from Jump should be shorter so that the character will snap faster to the jump animation. The shaded area of the graph indicates how long the transition takes; to see more detail, use Alt+left-click to pan across the graph and Alt+right-click to scale it (these are the same controls as navigating in the Scene view). Use the arrows on top of the shaded area to shrink it to under 4 milliseconds for all three Jump transitions.

Finally, you can perfect the animation network by selecting the animation nodes one at a time and adjusting the ordering of transitions. The Inspector will show a list of all transitions to and from that node; you can drag items in the list (their drag handles are the icon on the left-hand side) to reorder them. Make sure the Jump transition is on top for both the Idle and Run nodes so that the Jump transition has priority over the other transitions. While you're looking at these settings, you can also change the playback speed if the animation looks too slow (Run looks better at 1.5 speed).

The animation controller is set up, so now you can operate the animations from the movement script.

8.4.3 Writing code that operates the animator

Finally, you'll add methods to the RelativeMovement script. As explained earlier, most of the work of setting up animation states is done in the animation controller; only a small amount of code is needed to operate a rich and fluid animation system, shown here.

Listing 8.6 Code for setting values in the Animator component

```
...
private Animator _animator;
...                                            Added inside the Start() function
_animator = GetComponent<Animator>();
...
        _animator.SetFloat("Speed", movement.sqrMagnitude);

        if (hitGround) {                       Just below the entire if
            if (Input.GetButtonDown("Jump")) { statement for horizontal
                                               movement
```

```
            _vertSpeed = jumpSpeed;
        } else {
            _vertSpeed = minFall;
            _animator.SetBool("Jumping", false);
        }
    } else {
        _vertSpeed += gravity * 5 * Time.deltaTime;
        if (_vertSpeed < terminalVelocity) {
            _vertSpeed = terminalVelocity;
        }
        if (_contact != null ) {
            _animator.SetBool("Jumping", true);
        }

        if (_charController.isGrounded) {
            if (Vector3.Dot(movement, _contact.normal) < 0) {
                movement = _contact.normal * moveSpeed;
            } else {
                movement += _contact.normal * moveSpeed;
            }
        }
    }
}
...
```

Don't trigger this value right at the beginning of the level.

Again, much of this listing is repeated from previous listings; the animation code is a handful of lines interspersed throughout the existing movement script. Pick out the _animator lines in order to find additions to make in your code.

The script needs a reference to the Animator component, and then the code sets values (either floats or Booleans) on the animator. The only somewhat nonobvious bit of code is the condition (_contact != null) before setting the Jumping Boolean. That condition prevents the animator from playing the jump animation when the game starts. Even though the character is technically falling for a split second, there won't be any collision data until the character touches the ground for the first time.

And there you have it! Now we have a nice third-person movement demo, with camera-relative controls and character animation playing.

Summary

- Third-person view means the camera moves around the character instead of inside the character.
- Simulated shadows, like real-time shadows and lightmaps, improve the graphics.
- Controls can be relative to the camera instead of relative to the character.
- You can improve on Unity's ground detection by casting a ray downward.
- Sophisticated animation set up with Unity's animator controller results in lifelike characters.

Adding interactive devices and items within the game

9

This chapter covers

- Programming doors that the player can open

- Enabling physics simulations that scatter a stack of boxes

- Building collectible items that players store in their inventory

- Using code to manage game state, such as inventory data

- Equipping and using inventory items

Implementing functional items is the next topic we're going to focus on. Previous chapters covered a number of different elements of a complete game: movement, enemies, the UI, and so forth. But our projects have lacked anything to interact with other than enemies, nor have they had much in the way of game state. In this chapter, you'll learn how to create functional devices like doors. We'll also discuss collecting items, which involves both interacting with objects in the level and tracking game state. Games often have to track state like the player's current stats, progress through objectives, and so on. The player's inventory is an example of this sort of state, so you'll build a code architecture that can keep track of items collected by the

197

player. By the end of this chapter, you'll have built a dynamic space that really feels like a game!

We'll start by exploring devices (such as doors) that are operated with keypresses from the player. After that, you'll write code to detect when the player collides with objects in the level, enabling interactions like pushing objects around or collecting inventory items. Then you'll set up a robust MVC (Model-View-Controller) style code architecture to manage data for the collected inventory. Finally, you'll program interfaces to make use of the inventory for gameplay, such as requiring a key to open a door.

> **WARNING**   Previous chapters were relatively self-contained and didn't techni-
> cally require projects from earlier chapters, but this time some of the code list-
> ings make edits to scripts from chapter 8. If you skipped directly to this chapter,
> download the sample project for chapter 8 in order to build on that.

The example project will have these devices and items strewn about the level randomly. A polished game would have a lot of careful design behind the placement of items, but there's no need to carefully plan out a level that only tests functionality. Even so, though the placement of objects will be haphazard, the chapter opening bullets lay out the order in which we'll implement things.

As usual, the explanations build up the code step by step, but if you want to see all the finished code in one place, you can download the sample project.

9.1   Creating doors and other devices

Although levels in games mostly consist of static walls and scenery, they also usually incorporate a lot of functional devices as well. I'm talking about objects that the player can interact with and operate—things like lights that turn on or a fan that starts turning. The specific devices can vary a lot and are mostly limited only by your imagination, but almost all of them use the same sort of code to have the player activate the device. You'll implement a couple of examples in this chapter, and then you should be able to adapt this same code to work with all sorts of other devices.

9.1.1   Doors that open and close on a keypress

The first kind of device you'll program is a door that opens and closes, and you're going to start with operating the door by pressing a key. There are lots of different kinds of devices you could have in a game, and lots of different ways of operating those devices. We're eventually going to look at a couple of variations, but doors are the most common interactive devices found in games, and using items with a keypress is the most straightforward approach to start with.

The scene has a few spots where a gap exists between walls, so place a new object that blocks the gap. I created a new cube object and then set its transform to Position 2.5, 1.5, 17 and Scale 5, 3, .5, creating the door shown in figure 9.1.

Figure 9.1 Door object fit into a gap in the wall

Create a C# script, call it `DoorOpenDevice`, and put that script on the door object. This code will cause the object to operate as a door.

Listing 9.1 Script that opens and closes the door on command

```
using UnityEngine;
using System.Collections;

public class DoorOpenDevice : MonoBehaviour {
   [SerializeField] private Vector3 dPos;

   private bool _open;

   public void Operate() {
      if (_open) {
         Vector3 pos = transform.position - dPos;
         transform.position = pos;
      } else {
         Vector3 pos = transform.position + dPos;
         transform.position = pos;
      }
      _open = !_open;
   }
}
```

Position to offset to when the door opens

Boolean to keep track of the open state of the door

Open or close the door depending on the open state.

The first variable defines the offset that's applied when the door opens. The door will move this amount when it opens, and then it will subtract this amount when it closes. The second variable is a private Boolean for tracking whether the door is open or closed. In the `Operate()` method, the object's transform is set to a new position, adding or subtracting the offset depending on whether the door is already open; then _open is toggled on or off.

As with other serialized variables, dPos appears in the Inspector. But this is a Vector3 value, so instead of one input box there are three, all under the one variable name. Type in the relative position of the door when it opens; I decided to have the door slide down to open, so the offset was 0, -2.9, 0 (because the door object has a height of 3, moving down 2.9 leaves a tiny sliver of the door sticking up out of the floor).

> **NOTE**   The transform is applied instantly, but you may prefer seeing the move-ment when the door opens. As mentioned in chapter 3, you can use tweens to make objects move smoothly over time. The word *tween* means different things in different contexts, but in game programming it refers to code commands that cause objects to move around; appendix D mentions tweening systems for Unity.

Other code needs to call Operate() to make the door open and close (the single func-tion call handles both cases). You don't yet have that other script on the player; writing that is the next step.

9.1.2   Checking distance and facing before opening the door

Create a new script and name it DeviceOperator. This listing implements a control key that operates nearby devices.

Listing 9.2   Device control key for the player

```
using UnityEngine;
using System.Collections;

public class DeviceOperator : MonoBehaviour {
  public float radius = 1.5f;

  void Update() {
    if (Input.GetButtonDown("Fire3")) {
      Collider[] hitColliders =
          Physics.OverlapSphere(transform.position, radius);
      foreach (Collider hitCollider in hitColliders) {
        hitCollider.SendMessage("Operate",
          SendMessageOptions.DontRequireReceiver);
      }
    }
  }
}
```

How far away from the player to activate devices

Respond to the input button defined in Unity's input settings.

OverlapSphere() returns a list of nearby objects.

SendMessage() tries to call the named function, regardless of the target's type.

The majority of the script in this listing should look familiar, but a crucial new method is at the center of this code. First, establish a value for how far away to operate devices from. Then, in the Update() function, look for keyboard input; since the Jump key is already being used by the RelativeMovement script, this time you'll respond to Fire3 (which is defined in the project's input settings as the left Shift key).

Now we get to the crucial new method: OverlapSphere(). This method returns an array of all objects that are within a given distance of a given position. By passing in the position of the player and the radius variable, this detects all objects near the player. What you do with this list can vary (perhaps you set off a bomb and want to apply an explosive force), but in this situation you want to attempt to call `Operate()` on all nearby objects.

That method is called via `SendMessage()` instead of the typical dot notation, an approach you also saw with UI buttons in previous chapters. As was the case there, the reason to use `SendMessage()` is because you don't know the exact type of the target object, and that command works on all `GameObjects`. But this time you're going to pass the `DontRequireReceiver` option to the method. This is because most of the objects returned by `OverlapSphere()` won't have an `Operate()` method; normally, `SendMessage()` prints an error message if nothing in the object received the message, but in this case the error messages would be distracting because you already know most objects will ignore the message.

Once the code is written, you can attach this script to the player object. Now you can open and close the door by standing near it and pressing the key.

There's one little detail you can fix. Currently, it doesn't matter which way the player is facing, as long as the player is close enough. But you could also adjust the script to only operate devices the player is facing, so let's do that. Recall from chapter 8 that you can calculate the dot product for checking facing. That's a mathematical operation done on a pair of vectors that returns a range between -1 and 1, with 1 meaning they point in exactly the same direction and -1 when they point in exactly opposite directions. Here is the new code in the `DeviceOperator` script.

> **Listing 9.3   Adjusting `DeviceOperator` to only operate devices that player faces**

```
...
foreach (Collider hitCollider in hitColliders) {
   Vector3 direction = hitCollider.transform.position - transform.position;
   if (Vector3.Dot(transform.forward, direction) > .5f) {      ⬅
      hitCollider.SendMessage("Operate",
           SendMessageOptions.DontRequireReceiver);
   }
}
...
```

Only send the message when facing the right direction.

To use the dot product, you first determine the direction to check against. That would be the direction from the player to the object; make a direction vector by subtracting the position of the player from the position of the object. Then call `Vector3.Dot()` with both that direction vector and the forward direction of the player. When the dot product is close to 1 (specifically, this code checks whether it is greater than .5), that means the two vectors are close to pointing in the same direction.

With this adjustment made, the door won't open and close when the player faces away from it, even if the player is close. And this same approach to operating devices can be used with any sort of device. To demonstrate that flexibility, let's create another example device.

9.1.3   *Operating a color-changing monitor*

We've created a door that opens and closes, but that same device-operating logic can be used with any sort of device. You're going to create another device that's operated in the same way; this time, you'll create a color-changing display on the wall.

Create a new cube and place it so that one side is barely sticking out of the wall. For example, I went with Position 10.9, 1.5, -5. Now create a new script called Color-ChangeDevice and attach that script (listing 9.4) to the wall display. Now run up to the wall monitor and hit the same "operate" key as used with the door; you should see the display change color, as figure 9.2 illustrates.

Figure 9.2   Color-changing display embedded in the wall

Listing 9.4   Script for a device that changes color

The color is set in the material attached to the object.

Declare a method with the same name as the door script.

The numbers are RGB values that range from 0 to 1.

```
using UnityEngine;
using System.Collections;

public class ColorChangeDevice : MonoBehaviour {
    public void Operate() {
        Color random = new Color(Random.Range(0f,1f),
            Random.Range(0f,1f), Random.Range(0f,1f));
        GetComponent<Renderer>().material.color = random;
    }
}
```

To start with, declare the same function name as the door script used. Operate is the function name that the device operator script uses, so you need to use that name in order for it to be triggered. Inside this function, the code assigns a random color to the object's material (remember, color isn't an attribute of the object itself, but rather the object has a material and that material can have a color).

> **NOTE** Although the color is defined with Red, Blue, and Green components, as is standard in most computer graphics, the values in Unity's Color object vary between 0 and 1, instead of 0 and 255, as is common in most places (including Unity's color picker UI).

All right, so we've gone over one approach to interacting with devices in the game and have even implemented a couple of different devices to demonstrate. Another way of interacting with items is by bumping into them, so let's go over that next.

9.2 Interacting with objects by bumping into them

In the previous section, devices were operated by keyboard input from the player, but that's not the only way players can interact with items in the level. Another straightforward approach is to respond to collisions with the player. Unity handles most of that for you, by having collision detection and physics built into the game engine. Unity will detect collisions for you, but you still need to program the object to respond.

We'll go over three collision responses that are useful for games:

- Push away and fall over
- Trigger a device in the level
- Disappear on contact (for item pickups)

9.2.1 Colliding with physics-enabled obstacles

To start, you're going to create a pile of boxes and then cause the pile to collapse when the player runs into it. Although the physics calculations involved are complicated, Unity has all of that built in and will scatter the boxes in a realistic way.

By default, Unity doesn't use its physics simulation to move objects around. That can be enabled by adding a Rigidbody component to the object. This concept was first discussed in chapter 3, because the enemy's fireballs also needed a Rigidbody component. As I explained in that chapter, Unity's physics system will act only on objects that have a Rigidbody component. Look for Rigidbody by clicking Add Component and going to the Physics menu.

Create a new cube object and then add a Rigidbody component to it. Create several such cubes and position them in a neat stack. For example, in the sample download I created five boxes and stacked them into two tiers (see figure 9.3).

Each box has a
RigidBody component.
Their positions are:

-4.2 .5 -2.3
-4.2 .5 -1.2
-4.2 .5 -.1
-4.2 1.5 -1.9
-4.2 1.5 -.7

Figure 9.3 Stack of five boxes to collide with

The boxes are now ready to react to physics forces. To have the player apply a force to the boxes, make the small addition shown in the following listing to the Relative-Movement script (this is one of the scripts written in the previous chapter) that's on the player.

Listing 9.5   Adding physics force to the RelativeMovement script

```
...
public float pushForce = 3.0f;    ◄——— Amount of force to apply
...
void OnControllerColliderHit(ControllerColliderHit hit) {
    _contact = hit;                          Check if the collided
                                             object has a Rigidbody to
    Rigidbody body = hit.collider.attachedRigidbody;    receive physics forces.
    if (body != null && !body.isKinematic) {
        body.velocity = hit.moveDirection * pushForce;    Apply velocity to
    }                                                     the physics body.
}
...
```

There's not much to explain about this code: Whenever the player collides with something, check if the collided object has a Rigidbody component. If so, apply a velocity to that Rigidbody.

Play the game and then run into the pile of boxes; you should see them scatter around realistically. And that's all you had to do to activate physics simulation on a stack of boxes in the scene! Unity has physics simulation built in, so you didn't have to write much code. That simulation can cause objects to move around in response to collisions, but another possible response is firing trigger events, so let's use those trigger events to control the door.

9.2.2   *Operating the door with a trigger object*

Previously the door was operated by a keypress. This time it will open and close in response to the character colliding with another object in the scene. Create yet another door and place it in another wall gap (I duplicated the previous door and moved the new door to -2.5, 1.5, -17). Now create a new cube to use for the trigger object, and select the Is Trigger check box for the collider (this step was illustrated when making the fireball in chapter 3). In addition, set the trigger object to the Ignore Raycast layer; the top-right corner of the Inspector has a Layer menu. Finally, you should turn off shadows from this object (remember, this setting is under Mesh Renderer when you select the object).

> **WARNING**   These tiny steps are easy to miss but important: To use an object as a trigger, be sure to turn on Is Trigger. In the Inspector, look for the check box in the Collider component. Also, change the layer to Ignore Raycast so that the trigger object won't show up in raycasting.

NOTE When trigger objects were introduced in chapter 3, the object needed to have a Rigidbody component added. Rigidbody wasn't required for the trigger this time because the trigger would be responding to the player (versus colliding with a wall, the earlier situation). In order for triggers to work, either the trigger or the object entering the trigger needs to have Unity's physics system enabled; a Rigidbody component fulfills this requirement, but so does the player's Character Controller.

Position and scale the trigger object so that it both encompasses the door and surrounds an area around the door; I used Position `-2.5, 1.5, -17` (same as the door) and Scale `7.5, 3, 6`. Additionally, you may want to assign a semi-transparent material to the object so that you can visually distinguish trigger volumes from solid objects. Create a new material using the Assets menu, and select the new material in the Project view. Looking at the Inspector, the top setting is Rendering Mode (currently set to the default value of Opaque); select Transparent in this menu.

Now click its color swatch to bring up the Color Picker window. Pick green in the main part of the window, and lower the alpha using the bottom slider. Drag this material from Project onto the object; figure 9.4 shows the trigger with this material.

Box with a semitransparent material surrounding the door it triggers

Figure 9.4   Trigger volume surrounding the door it will trigger

DEFINITION *Triggers* are often referred to as volumes rather than objects in order to conceptually differentiate solid objects from objects you can move through.

Play the game now and you can freely move through the trigger volume; Unity still registers collisions with the object, but those collisions don't affect the player's movement anymore. To react to the collisions, you need to write code. Specifically, you want this trigger to control the door. Create a new script called `DeviceTrigger`.

Listing 9.6   Code for a trigger that controls a device

```
using UnityEngine;
using System.Collections;
```

```
public class DeviceTrigger : MonoBehaviour {
    [SerializeField] private GameObject[] targets;

    void OnTriggerEnter(Collider other) {
        foreach (GameObject target in targets) {
            target.SendMessage("Activate");
        }
    }

    void OnTriggerExit(Collider other) {
        foreach (GameObject target in targets) {
            target.SendMessage("Deactivate");
        }
    }
}
```

List of target objects that this trigger will activate

OnTriggerEnter() is called when another object enters the trigger volume ...

... whereas OnTriggerExit() is called when an object leaves the trigger volume.

This listing defines an array of target objects for the trigger; even though it'll only be a list of one most of the time, it's possible to have multiple devices controlled by a single trigger. Loop through the array of targets to send a message to all the targets. This loop happens inside the OnTriggerEnter() and OnTriggerExit() methods. These functions are called once when another object first enters and exits the trigger (as opposed to being called over and over while the object is inside the trigger volume).

Notice that the messages being sent are different than before; now you need to define the Activate() and Deactivate() functions on the door. Add the code in the next listing to the door script.

Listing 9.7   Adding activate and deactivate functions to the `DoorOpenDevice` script

```
...
public void Activate() {
    if (!_open) {
        Vector3 pos = transform.position + dPos;
        transform.position = pos;
        _open = true;
    }
}
public void Deactivate() {
    if (_open) {
        Vector3 pos = transform.position - dPos;
        transform.position = pos;
        _open = false;
    }
}
...
```

Only open the door if it isn't already open.

Only close the door if it isn't already closed.

The new Activate() and Deactivate() methods are much the same code as the Operate() method from earlier, except now there are separate functions to open and close the door instead of only one function that handles both cases.

With all the necessary code in place you can now use the trigger volume to open and close the door. Put the DeviceTrigger script on the trigger volume and then link the door to the targets property of that script; in the Inspector, first set the size of the array and then drag objects from the Hierarchy view over to slots in the targets array. Because you have only one door that you want to control with this trigger, type 1 in the array's Size field and then drag that door into the target slot.

With all of this done, play the game and watch what happens to the door when the player walks toward and away from it. It'll open and close automatically as the player enters and leaves the trigger volume.

That's another great way to put interactivity into levels! But this trigger volume approach doesn't only work with devices like doors; you can also use this approach to make collectible items.

Exercise: Trigger devices in 2D platformer

In this chapter, you've implemented triggers in a 3D game, but the logic is almost exactly the same to do this in a 2D game; you'd just be reacting to 2D colliders instead, using OnTrigger2D. As an exercise, go back to the 2D platform game from chapter 6 and implement trigger volumes and devices in that platformer.

9.2.3 *Collecting items scattered around the level*

Many games include items that can be picked up by the player. These items include equipment, health packs, and power-ups. The basic mechanism of colliding with items to pick them up is simple; most of the complicated stuff happens after items are picked up, but we'll get to that a bit later.

Create a sphere object and place it hovering at about waist height in an open area of the scene. Make the object small, like Scale .5, .5, .5, but otherwise prepare it like you did with the large trigger volume. Select the Is Trigger setting in the collider, set the object to the Ignore Raycast layer, and then create a new material to give the object a distinct color. Because the object doesn't cover much there's no need to make it semi-transparent, so don't turn down the alpha slider this time. Also, as mentioned in chapter 8, there are settings for removing the shadows cast from this object; whether or not to use the shadows is a judgment call, but for small pickup items like this I prefer to turn them off.

Now that the object in the scene is ready, create a new script to attach to that object. Call the script CollectibleItem.

Listing 9.8 Script that makes an item delete itself on contact with the player

```
using UnityEngine;
using System.Collections;

public class CollectibleItem : MonoBehaviour {        Type the name of this
    [SerializeField] private string itemName;    ◄──   item in the Inspector.

    void OnTriggerEnter(Collider other) {
        Debug.Log("Item collected: " + itemName);
        Destroy(this.gameObject);
    }
}
```

This script is extremely short and simple. Give the item a `name` value so that there can be different items in the scene. `OnTriggerEnter()` destroys itself. There's also a debug message being printed to the console; eventually it will be replaced with useful code.

> **WARNING** Be sure to call `Destroy` on `this.gameObject` and not `this`! Don't get confused between the two; `this` only refers to this script component, whereas `this.gameObject` refers to the object the script is attached to.

Back in Unity, the variable you added to the code should become visible in the Inspector. Type in a name to identify this item; I went with `energy` for my first item. Then duplicate the item a few times and change the name of the copies; I also created `ore`, `health`, and `key` (these names must be exact because they'll be used in code later on). Also create separate materials for each item in order to give them distinct colors: I did light blue energy, dark gray ore, pink health, and yellow key.

> **TIP** Rather than a name, like we've done here, items in more complex games often have an identifier used to look up further data. For example, one item might be assigned ID 301, and ID 301 correlates to a certain display name, image, description, and so forth.

Now make prefabs of the items so that you can clone them throughout the level. In chapter 3, I explained that dragging an object from the Hierarchy view down to the Project view will turn that object into a prefab; do that for all four items.

> **NOTE** The object's name will turn blue in the Hierarchy list; blue names indicate objects that are instances of a prefab. Right-click a prefab instance to pick Select Prefab and select the prefab that the object is an instance of.

Drag out instances of the prefabs and place the items in open areas of the level; even drag out multiple copies of the same item to test with. Play the game and run into items to collect them. That's pretty neat, but at the moment nothing happens when you collect an item. You're going to start keeping track of the items collected; to do that, you need to set up the inventory code structure.

9.3   *Managing inventory data and game state*

Now that you've programmed the features of collecting items, you need background data managers (similar to web coding patterns) for the game's inventory. The code you'll write will be similar to the MVC architectures behind many web applications. Their advantage is in decoupling data storage from the objects that are displayed onscreen, allowing for easier experimentation and iterative development. Even when the data and/or displays are complex, changes in one part of the application don't affect other parts of the application.

That said, such structures vary a lot between different games, because not every game has the same data-management needs.

For example, a role-playing game will have high data-management needs, so you probably want to implement something like an MVC architecture. A puzzle game, though, has little data to manage, so building a complex decoupled structure of data managers would be overkill. Instead, the game state can be tracked in the scene-specific controller objects (indeed, that's how we handled game state in previous chapters).

In this project, you need to manage the player's inventory. Let's set up the code structure needed for that.

9.3.1 Setting up player and inventory managers

The general idea here is to split up all the data management into separate, well-defined modules that each manage their own area of responsibility. You're going to create separate modules to maintain player state in `PlayerManager` (things like the player's health) and maintain the inventory list in `InventoryManager`. These data managers will behave like the Model in MVC; the Controller is an invisible object in most scenes (it wasn't needed here, but recall `SceneController` in previous chapters), and the rest of the scene is analogous to the View.

There will be a higher-level *manager-of-managers* that keeps track of all the separate modules. Besides keeping a list of all the managers, this higher-level manager will control the lifecycle of the various managers, in particular initializing them at the start. All the other scripts in the game will be able to access these centralized modules by going through the main manager. Specifically, other code can use a number of static properties in the main manager in order to connect with the specific module desired.

Design patterns for accessing centralized shared modules

Over the years, a variety of design patterns have emerged to solve the problem of connecting parts of a program to centralized modules that are shared throughout the program. For example, the Singleton pattern was enshrined in the original "Gang of Four" book about design patterns.

But that pattern has fallen out of favor with many software engineers, so they use alternative patterns like service locator and dependency injection. In my code, I use a compromise between the simplicity of static variables and the flexibility of a service locator.

This design leaves the code simple to use while also allowing for swapping in different modules. For example, requesting `InventoryManager` using a singleton will always refer to the exact same class, and thus will tightly couple your code to that class; conversely, requesting `Inventory` from a service locator leaves the option to return either `InventoryManager` or `DifferentInventoryManager`. Sometimes it's handy to be able to switch between slightly different versions of the same module (deploying the game on different platforms, for example).

In order for the main manager to reference other modules in a consistent way, these modules must all inherit properties from a common base. You're going to do that with an interface; many programming languages (including C#) allow you to define a sort of blueprint that other classes need to follow. Both `PlayerManager` and `InventoryManager` will implement a common interface (called `IGameManager` in this case) and then the main `Managers` object can treat both `PlayerManager` and `InventoryManager` as type `IGameManager`. Figure 9.5 illustrates the setup I'm describing.

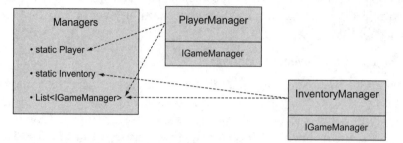

Figure 9.5   Diagram of the various modules and how they're related

Incidentally, whereas all of the code architecture I've been talking about consists of invisible modules that exist in the background, Unity still requires scripts to be linked to objects in the scene in order to run that code. As you've done with the scene-specific controllers in previous projects, you're going to create an empty `GameObject` to link these data managers to.

9.3.2   Programming the game managers

All right, so that explained all the concepts behind what you'll do; it's time to write the code. To start, create a new script called `IGameManager`.

Listing 9.9   Base interface that the data managers will implement

```
public interface IGameManager {
    ManagerStatus status {get;}      ◀──── This is an enum you need to define.

    void Startup();
}
```

Hmm, there's barely any code in this file. Note that it doesn't even inherit from `MonoBehaviour`; an interface doesn't do anything on its own and exists only to impose structure on other classes. This interface declares one property (a variable that has a getter function) and one method; both need to be implemented in any class that implements this interface. The `status` property tells the rest of the code whether this module has completed its initialization. The purpose of `Startup()` is to handle the initialization of the manager, so initialization tasks happen there and the function sets the manager's status.

Notice that the property is of type `ManagerStatus`; that's an enum you haven't written yet, so create the `ManagerStatus.cs` script.

Listing 9.10   `ManagerStatus`: possible states for `IGameManager` status

```
public enum ManagerStatus {
```

```
    Shutdown,
    Initializing,
    Started
}
```

This is another file with barely any code in it. This time you're listing the different possible states that managers can be in, thereby enforcing that the `status` property will always be one of these listed values.

Now that `IGameManager` is written, you can implement it in other scripts. Listings 9.11 and 9.12 contain code for `InventoryManager` and `PlayerManager`.

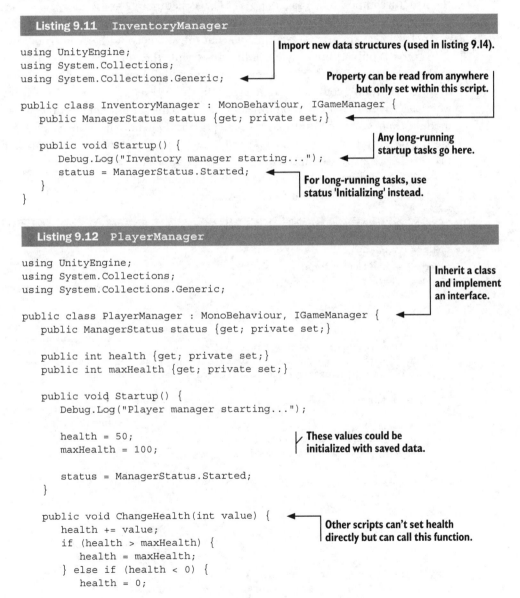

Listing 9.11 `InventoryManager`

```
using UnityEngine;                                    Import new data structures (used in listing 9.14).
using System.Collections;
using System.Collections.Generic;                      Property can be read from anywhere
                                                       but only set within this script.
public class InventoryManager : MonoBehaviour, IGameManager {
    public ManagerStatus status {get; private set;}

                                                      Any long-running
    public void Startup() {                           startup tasks go here.
        Debug.Log("Inventory manager starting...");
        status = ManagerStatus.Started;              For long-running tasks, use
    }                                                status 'Initializing' instead.
}
```

Listing 9.12 `PlayerManager`

```
using UnityEngine;
using System.Collections;                              Inherit a class
using System.Collections.Generic;                      and implement
                                                       an interface.
public class PlayerManager : MonoBehaviour, IGameManager {
    public ManagerStatus status {get; private set;}

    public int health {get; private set;}
    public int maxHealth {get; private set;}

    public void Startup() {
        Debug.Log("Player manager starting...");

        health = 50;                    These values could be
        maxHealth = 100;                initialized with saved data.

        status = ManagerStatus.Started;
    }

    public void ChangeHealth(int value) {      Other scripts can't set health
        health += value;                       directly but can call this function.
        if (health > maxHealth) {
            health = maxHealth;
        } else if (health < 0) {
            health = 0;
```

```
        }

        Debug.Log("Health: " + health + "/" + maxHealth);
    }
}
```

For now, InventoryManager is a shell that will be filled in later, whereas PlayerManager has all the functionality needed for this project. These managers both inherit from the MonoBehaviour class and implement the IGameManager interface. That means the managers gain all the functionality of MonoBehaviour while also needing to implement the structure imposed by IGameManager. The structure in IGameManager was one property and one method, so the managers define those two things.

The status property was defined so that the status could be read from anywhere (the getter is public) but only set within this script (the setter is private). The method in the interface is Startup(), so both managers define that function. In both managers, initialization completes right away (InventoryManager doesn't do anything yet, whereas PlayerManager sets a couple of values), so the status is set to Started. But data modules may have long-running tasks as part of their initialization (such as loading saved data), in which case Startup() will launch those tasks and set the manager's status to Initializing. Change status to Started after those tasks complete.

Great! We're finally ready to tie everything together with a main manager-of-managers. Create one more script and call it Managers.

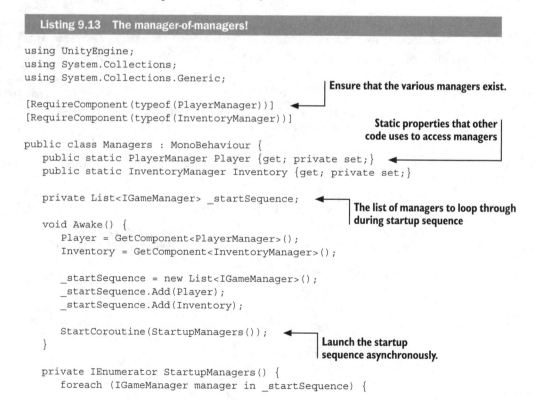

Listing 9.13   The manager-of-managers!

```
using UnityEngine;
using System.Collections;
using System.Collections.Generic;
                                                    Ensure that the various managers exist.
[RequireComponent(typeof(PlayerManager))]
[RequireComponent(typeof(InventoryManager))]
                                                    Static properties that other
                                                    code uses to access managers
public class Managers : MonoBehaviour {
    public static PlayerManager Player {get; private set;}
    public static InventoryManager Inventory {get; private set;}

    private List<IGameManager> _startSequence;
                                                    The list of managers to loop through
                                                    during startup sequence
    void Awake() {
        Player = GetComponent<PlayerManager>();
        Inventory = GetComponent<InventoryManager>();

        _startSequence = new List<IGameManager>();
        _startSequence.Add(Player);
        _startSequence.Add(Inventory);

        StartCoroutine(StartupManagers());
                                                    Launch the startup
    }                                               sequence asynchronously.

    private IEnumerator StartupManagers() {
        foreach (IGameManager manager in _startSequence) {
```

```
        manager.Startup();
    }

    yield return null;

    int numModules = _startSequence.Count;
    int numReady = 0;
                                                    Keep looping until all
                                                    managers are started.
    while (numReady < numModules) {  ◄─┐
        int lastReady = numReady;
        numReady = 0;

        foreach (IGameManager manager in _startSequence) {
            if (manager.status == ManagerStatus.Started) {
                numReady++;
            }
        }

        if (numReady > lastReady)
            Debug.Log("Progress: " + numReady + "/" + numModules);
        yield return null;                    ◄─┐  Pause for one frame
    }                                            │  before checking again.

    Debug.Log("All managers started up");
    }
}
```

The most important parts of this pattern are the static properties at the top. Those enable other scripts to use syntax like `Managers.Player` or `Managers.Inventory` to access the various modules. Those properties are initially empty, but they're filled immediately when the code runs in the `Awake()` method.

> **TIP** Like `Start()` and `Update()`, `Awake` is another method automatically provided by `MonoBehaviour`. It's similar to `Start()`, running once when the code first starts running. But in Unity's code-execution sequence, `Awake()` is even sooner than `Start()`, allowing for initialization tasks that absolutely must run before any other code modules.

The `Awake()` method also lists the startup sequence, and then launches the coroutine to start all the managers. Specifically, the function creates a `List` object and then uses `List.Add()` to add the managers.

> **DEFINITION** `List` is a collection data structure provided by C#. List objects are similar to arrays: they're declared with a specific type and store a series of entries in sequence. But a `List` can change size after being created, whereas arrays are created at a static size that can't change later.

Because all the managers implement `IGameManager`, this code can list them all as that type and can call the `Startup()` method defined in each. The startup sequence is run as a coroutine so that it will run asynchronously, with other parts of the game proceeding too (for example, a progress bar animated on a startup screen).

The startup function first loops through the entire list of managers and calls `Startup()` on each one. Then it enters a loop that keeps checking whether the managers have started up and won't proceed until they all have. Once all the managers are started, the startup function finally alerts us to this fact before finally completing.

> **TIP**   The managers you wrote earlier have such simple initialization that there's no waiting, but in general this coroutine-based startup sequence can elegantly handle long-running asynchronous startup tasks like loading saved data.

Now all of the code structure has been written. Go back to Unity and create a new empty `GameObject`; as usual with these sorts of empty code objects, position it at 0, 0, 0 and give the object a descriptive name like Game Managers. Attach the `Managers`, `PlayerManager`, and `InventoryManager` script components to this new object.

When you play the game now, there should be no visible change in the scene, but in the console, you should see a series of messages logging the progress of the startup sequence. Assuming the managers are starting up correctly, it's time to start programming the inventory manager.

9.3.3 *Storing inventory in a collection object: List vs. Dictionary*

The list of items collected could also be stored as a `List` object. This listing adds a `List` of items to `InventoryManager`.

> **Listing 9.14   Adding items to `InventoryManager`**

```
...
private List<string> _items;

public void Startup() {
    Debug.Log("Inventory manager starting...");

    _items = new List<string>();      ◄──── Initialize the empty item list.

    status = ManagerStatus.Started;
}

private void DisplayItems() {
    string itemDisplay = "Items: ";
    foreach (string item in _items) {
        itemDisplay += item + " ";
    }
    Debug.Log(itemDisplay);
}

public void AddItem(string name) {
    _items.Add(name);

    DisplayItems();
}
...
```

Print console message of the current inventory.

Other scripts can't manipulate the item list directly but can call this.

Two key additions were made to InventoryManager: you added a List object to store items in and you added a public method, AddItem(), that other code can call. This function adds the item to the list and then prints the list to the console. Now let's make a slight adjustment in the CollectibleItem script to call the new AddItem() method.

Listing 9.15 Using the new InventoryManager in CollectibleItem

```
...
void OnTriggerEnter(Collider other) {
    Managers.Inventory.AddItem(itemName);
    Destroy(this.gameObject);
}
...
```

Now when you run around collecting items, you should see your inventory growing in the console messages. This is pretty cool, but it does expose one limitation of List data structures: as you collect multiples of the same type of item (such as collecting a second Health item), you'll see both copies listed, instead of aggregating all items of the same type (refer to figure 9.6). Depending on your game, you may want the inventory to track each item separately, but in most games the inventory should aggregate multiple copies of the same item. It's possible to accomplish this using List, but it's done more naturally and efficiently using Dictionary instead.

Items: energy health ore health energy ore key
UnityEngine.Debug:Log(Object)

Figure 9.6 Console message with multiples of the same item listed multiple times

DEFINITION Dictionary is another collection data structure provided by C#. Entries in the dictionary are accessed by an identifier (or key) rather than by their position in the list. This is similar to a hash table but more flexible, because the keys can be literally any type (for example, "Return the entry for this GameObject").

Change the code in InventoryManager to use Dictionary instead of List. Replace everything from listing 9.14 with the code from this listing.

Listing 9.16 Dictionary of items in InventoryManager

```
...
private Dictionary<string, int> _items;    ◄── Dictionary is declared with two
                                               types: the key and the value.
public void Startup() {
    Debug.Log("Inventory manager starting...");

    _items = new Dictionary<string, int>();

    status = ManagerStatus.Started;
}

private void DisplayItems() {
    string itemDisplay = "Items: ";
```

```
    foreach (KeyValuePair<string, int> item in _items) {
        itemDisplay += item.Key + "(" + item.Value + ") ";
    }
    Debug.Log(itemDisplay);
}

public void AddItem(string name) {                Check for existing entries
    if (_items.ContainsKey(name)) {        ◄━━━━  before entering new data.
        _items[name] += 1;
    } else {
        _items[name] = 1;
    }

    DisplayItems();
}
...
```

Overall this code looks the same as before, but a few tricky differences exist. If you aren't already familiar with `Dictionary` data structures, note that it was declared with two types. Whereas `List` was declared with only one type (the type of values that'll be listed), a `Dictionary` declares both the type of key (that is, what the identifiers will be) and the type of value.

A bit more logic exists in the `AddItem()` method. Whereas before every item was appended to the `List`, now you need to check if the `Dictionary` already contains that item; that's what the `ContainsKey()` method is for. If it's a new entry, then you'll start the count at 1, but if the entry already exists, then increment the stored value.

Play with the new code and you'll see the inventory messages have an aggregated count of each item (refer to figure 9.7).

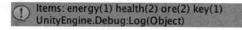
Items: energy(1) health(2) ore(2) key(1)
UnityEngine.Debug:Log(Object)

Figure 9.7   Console message with multiples of the same item aggregated

Whew, finally, collected items are managed in the player's inventory! This probably seems like a lot of code to handle a relatively simple problem, and if this were the entire purpose then, yeah, it would be over-engineered. The point of this elaborate code architecture, though, is to keep all the data in separate flexible modules, a useful pattern once the game gets more complex. For example, now you can write UI displays and the separate parts of the code will be much easier to handle.

9.4   *Inventory UI for using and equipping items*

The collection of items in your inventory can be used in multiple ways within the game, but all of those uses first rely on some sort of inventory UI so that players can see their collected items. Then, once the inventory is being shown to the player, you can program interactivity into the UI by enabling players to click on their items. Again, you'll program a couple of specific examples (equipping a key and consuming health packs), and then you should be able to adapt this code to work with other types of items.

NOTE As mentioned in chapter 7, Unity has both an older immediate mode GUI and a newer sprite-based UI system. We'll use the immediate mode GUI in this chapter because that system is faster to implement and requires less setup; less setup is great for practice exercises. The sprite-based UI system is more polished, though, and for an actual game you'd want a more polished interface.

9.4.1 Displaying inventory items in the UI

To show the items in a UI display, you first need to add a couple more methods to InventoryManager. Right now, the item list is private and only accessible within the manager; in order to display the list, that information must have public methods for accessing the data. Add two methods shown in the following listing to InventoryManager.

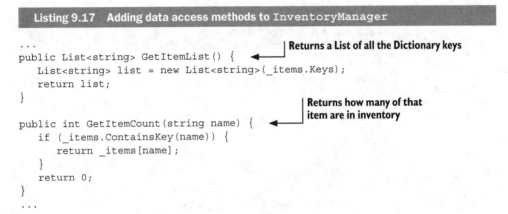

Listing 9.17 Adding data access methods to `InventoryManager`

```
...
public List<string> GetItemList() {          ◄──  Returns a List of all the Dictionary keys
    List<string> list = new List<string>(_items.Keys);
    return list;
}

public int GetItemCount(string name) {       ◄──  Returns how many of that
    if (_items.ContainsKey(name)) {                item are in inventory
        return _items[name];
    }
    return 0;
}
...
```

The GetItemList() method returns a list of items in the inventory. You might be thinking, "Wait a minute, didn't we just spend lots of effort to convert the inventory away from a List?" The difference now is that each type of item will appear only once in the list. If the inventory contains two health packs, for example, the word health will still appear only once in the list. That's because the List was created from the keys in the Dictionary, not from every individual item.

The GetItemCount() method returns a count of how many of a given item are in the inventory. For example, call GetItemCount("health") to ask "How many health packs are in the inventory?" This way, the UI can display a number of each item along with displaying each item.

With these methods added to InventoryManager, you can create the UI display. Let's display all the items in a horizontal row across the top of the screen. The items will be displayed using icons, so you need to import those images into the project. Unity handles assets in a special way if those assets are in a folder called Resources.

TIP Assets placed into the Resources folder can be loaded in code using the Resources.Load() method Otherwise, assets can only be placed in scenes through Unity's editor.

Figure 9.8 shows the four icon images, along with the directory structure showing where to put those images. Create a folder called `Resources` and then create a folder called `Icons` inside it.

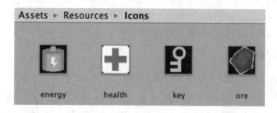

Figure 9.8   Image assets for equipment icons placed inside the Resources folder

The icons are all set up, so create a new empty `GameObject` named `Controller` and then assign it a new script called `BasicUI`.

Listing 9.18   `BasicUI` displays the inventory

```
using UnityEngine;
using System.Collections;
using System.Collections.Generic;

public class BasicUI : MonoBehaviour {
    void OnGUI() {
        int posX = 10;
        int posY = 10;
        int width = 100;
        int height = 30;
        int buffer = 10;

        List<string> itemList = Managers.Inventory.GetItemList();
        if (itemList.Count == 0) {
            GUI.Box(new Rect(posX, posY, width, height), "No Items");
        }
        foreach (string item in itemList) {
            int count = Managers.Inventory.GetItemCount(item);
            Texture2D image = Resources.Load<Texture2D>("Icons/"+item);
            GUI.Box(new Rect(posX, posY, width, height),
                    new GUIContent("(" + count + ")", image));
            posX += width+buffer;
        }
    }
}
```

> Display a message if the inventory is empty.

> Method loads assets from the Resources folder.

> Shift sideways each time through the loop.

This listing displays the collected items in a horizontal row (see figure 9.9) along with displaying the number collected. As mentioned in chapter 3, every `MonoBehaviour` automatically responds to an `OnGUI()` method. That function runs every frame right after the 3D scene is rendered.

Figure 9.9   UI display of the inventory

Inside `OnGUI()`, first define a bunch of values for positioning UI elements. These values are incremented when you loop through all the items in order to position UI elements in a row. The specific UI element drawn is `GUI.Box`; those are non-interactive displays that show text and images inside boxes.

The `Resources.Load()` method is used to load assets from the Resources folder. This method is a handy way to load assets by name; notice that the name of the item is passed as a parameter. You have to specify a type to load; otherwise, the return value for that method is a generic object.

The UI shows us what items have been collected. Now you can use the items.

9.4.2   *Equipping a key to use on locked doors*

Let's go over a couple of examples of using inventory items so that you can extrapolate out to any type of item you want. The first example involves equipping a key required to open the door.

At the moment, the `DeviceTrigger` script doesn't pay attention to your items (because that script was written before the inventory code). This listing shows how to adjust that script.

Listing 9.19   Requiring a key in `DeviceTrigger`

```
...
public bool requireKey;

void OnTriggerEnter(Collider other) {
```

```
    if (requireKey && Managers.Inventory.equippedItem != "key") {
        return;
    }
...
```

As you can see, all that's needed is a new public variable in the script and a condition that looks for an equipped key. The `requireKey` Boolean appears as a check box in the Inspector so that you can require a key from some triggers but not others. The condition at the beginning of `OnTriggerEnter()` checks for an equipped key in `InventoryManager`; that requires that you add the code from the next listing to `InventoryManager`.

Listing 9.20   Equipping code for `InventoryManager`

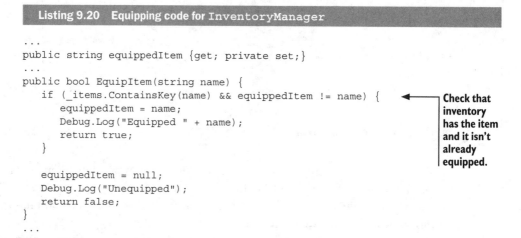

```
...
public string equippedItem {get; private set;}
...
public bool EquipItem(string name) {
    if (_items.ContainsKey(name) && equippedItem != name) {      Check that
        equippedItem = name;                                     inventory
        Debug.Log("Equipped " + name);                           has the item
        return true;                                             and it isn't
    }                                                            already
                                                                 equipped.
    equippedItem = null;
    Debug.Log("Unequipped");
    return false;
}
...
```

At the top, add the `equippedItem` property that gets checked by other code. Then add the public `EquipItem()` method to allow other code to change which item is equipped. That method equips an item if it isn't already equipped, or *unequips* if that item is already equipped.

Finally, in order for the player to equip an item, add that functionality to the UI. This listing will add a row of buttons for that purpose.

Listing 9.21   Equip functionality added to `BasicUI`

```
...
    foreach (string item in itemList) {        Italicized code was already in the script,
                                               shown here for reference.
        int count = Managers.Inventory.GetItemCount(item);
        GUI.Box(new Rect(posX, posY, width, height), item +
                "(" + count + ")");
        posX += width+buffer;
    }

    string equipped = Managers.Inventory.equippedItem;
    if (equipped != null) {                     Display the currently equipped item.
      posX = Screen.width - (width+buffer);
```

```
            Texture2D image = Resources.Load("Icons/"+equipped) as Texture2D;
            GUI.Box(new Rect(posX, posY, width, height),
                    new GUIContent("Equipped", image));
        }


        posX = 10;
        posY += height+buffer;

        foreach (string item in itemList) {
            if (GUI.Button(new Rect(posX, posY, width, height),
                    "Equip "+item)) {
                Managers.Inventory.EquipItem(item);
            }
            posX += width+buffer;
        }
    }
}
```

Loop through all items to make buttons (annotation pointing to `foreach` loop)

Run the contained code if the button is clicked. (annotation pointing to `Managers.Inventory.EquipItem(item);`)

GUI.Box() is used again to display the equipped item. But that element is non-interactive, so the row of Equip buttons is drawn using GUI.Button() instead. That method creates a button that executes the code inside the if statement when clicked.

With all the necessary code in place, select the requireKey option in DeviceTrigger and then play the game. Try running into the trigger volume before equipping a key; nothing happens. Now collect a key and click the button to equip it; running into the trigger volume opens the door.

Just for fun, you could put a key at Position -11, 5, -14 to add a simple gameplay challenge to see if you can figure out how to reach the key. Whether or not you try that, let's move on to using health packs.

9.4.3 *Restoring the player's health by consuming health packs*

Using items to restore the player's health is another generally useful example. That requires two code changes: a new method in InventoryManager and a new button in the UI (see listings 9.22 and 9.23, respectively).

Listing 9.22 New method in `InventoryManager`

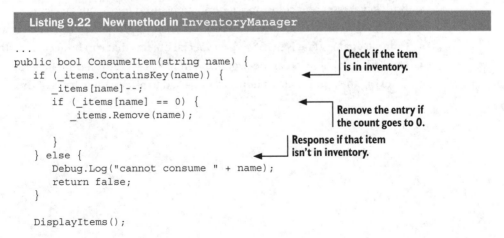

```
...
public bool ConsumeItem(string name) {
    if (_items.ContainsKey(name)) {
        _items[name]--;
        if (_items[name] == 0) {
            _items.Remove(name);

        }
    } else {
        Debug.Log("cannot consume " + name);
        return false;
    }

    DisplayItems();
```

Check if the item is in inventory. (annotation pointing to `if (_items.ContainsKey(name)) {`)

Remove the entry if the count goes to 0. (annotation pointing to `_items.Remove(name);`)

Response if that item isn't in inventory. (annotation pointing to `} else {`)

```
   return true;
}
...
```

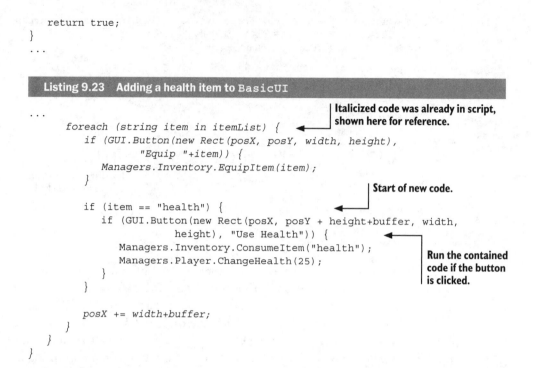

Listing 9.23   Adding a health item to `BasicUI`

```
...
    foreach (string item in itemList) {
        if (GUI.Button(new Rect(posX, posY, width, height),
                "Equip "+item)) {
            Managers.Inventory.EquipItem(item);
        }

        if (item == "health") {
            if (GUI.Button(new Rect(posX, posY + height+buffer, width,
                    height), "Use Health")) {
                Managers.Inventory.ConsumeItem("health");
                Managers.Player.ChangeHealth(25);
            }
        }

        posX += width+buffer;
    }
}
}
```

Italicized code was already in script, shown here for reference.

Start of new code.

Run the contained code if the button is clicked.

The new `ConsumeItem()` method is pretty much the reverse of `AddItem()`; it checks for an item in the inventory and decrements if the item is found. It has responses to a couple of tricky cases, such as if the item count decrements to 0. The UI code calls this new inventory method, and it calls the `ChangeHealth()` method that `PlayerManager` has had from the beginning.

If you collect some health items and then use them, you'll see health messages appear in the console. And there you go—multiple examples of how to use inventory items!

Summary

- Both keypresses and collision triggers can be used to operate devices.
- Objects with physics enabled can respond to collision forces or trigger volumes.
- Complex game state is managed via special objects that can be accessed globally.
- Collections of objects can be organized in `List` or `Dictionary` data structures.
- Tracking the equip state of items can be used to affect other parts of the game.

part 3

Strong finish

Y ou know a fair amount about Unity by now. You know how to program the player's controls, how to create enemies that wander around, and how to add interactive devices to the game. You even know how to build a game using both 2D and 3D graphics! That's *almost* everything you need to know in order to develop a complete game, but not quite. You still need to learn about a few final tasks like putting audio in the game, and you need to understand how to put together all the disparate pieces we've been working with.

This is the home stretch, with just four chapters left!

Connecting your game to the internet

This chapter covers

- Generating dynamic visuals for the sky
- Downloading data using web requests in coroutines
- Parsing common data formats like XML and JSON
- Displaying images downloaded from the internet
- Sending data to a web server

In this chapter, you'll learn how to send and receive data over a network. The projects built in previous chapters represented a variety of game genres, but all have been isolated to the player's machine. As you know, connecting to the internet and exchanging data is increasingly important for games in all genres. Many games exist almost entirely over the internet, with constant connection to a community of other players; games of this sort are referred to as MMOs (massively multiplayer online) and are most widely known through MMORPGs (MMO role-playing games). Even when a game doesn't require such constant connectivity, modern video games usually incorporate features like reporting scores to a global list of high scores, or record analytics to help improve the game. Unity provides support for such networking, so we'll be going over those features.

Unity supports multiple approaches to network communication, since different approaches are better suited to different needs. But, this chapter will mostly cover the most general sort of internet communication: issuing HTTP requests.

What are HTTP requests?

I assume most readers know what HTTP requests are, but here's a quick primer just in case: HTTP is a communication protocol for sending requests to and receiving responses from web servers. When you click a link on a web page, your browser (the client) sends out a request to a specific address, and then that server responds with the new page. HTTP requests can be set to a variety of methods, in particular either GET or POST, to retrieve or to send data.

HTTP requests are reliable, and that's why the majority of the internet is built around them. The requests themselves, as well as the infrastructure for handling such requests, are designed to be robust and handle a wide range of failures in the network.

As a good comparison, imagine how a modern single-page web application works (as opposed to old-school web development based on web pages generated server-side). In an online game built around HTTP requests, the project developed in Unity is essentially a thick client that communicates with the server in an Ajax style. The familiarity of this approach can be misleading for experienced web developers. Video games often have much more stringent performance requirements than web applications, and these differences can affect design decisions.

> **WARNING**   Time scales can be vastly different between web apps and videogames. Half a second can seem like a short wait for updating a website, but pausing even just a fraction of that time can be excruciating in the middle of a high-intensity action game. The concept of *fast* is definitely relative to the situation.

Online games usually connect to a server specifically intended for that game; for learning purposes, however, we'll connect to some freely available internet data sources, including both weather data and images we can download. The last section of this chapter requires you to set up a custom web server; that section is optional because of that requirement, although I'll explain an easy way to do it with open source software.

The plan for this chapter is to go over multiple uses of HTTP requests so that you can learn how they work within Unity:

1 Set up an outdoor scene (in particular, build a sky that can react to the weather data).
2 Write code to request weather data from the internet.
3 Parse the response and then modify the scene based on the data.

    4 Download and display an image from the internet.

    5 Post data to your own server (in this case, a log of what the weather was).

The actual game that you'll use for this chapter's project matters little. Everything in this chapter will add new scripts to an existing project and won't modify any of the existing code. For the sample code, I used the movement demo from chapter 2, mostly so that we can see the sky in first-person view when it gets modified. The project for this chapter isn't directly tied into the gameplay, but obviously for most games you create you would want the networking tied to the gameplay (for example, spawning enemies based on responses from the server).

    On to the first step!

10.1 Creating an outdoor scene

Because we're going to be downloading weather data, we'll first set up an outdoor area where the weather will be visible. The trickiest part of that will be the sky, but first, let's take a moment to apply outdoors-looking textures on the level geometry.

    Just as in chapter 4, I obtained a couple of images from www.textures.com/ to apply to the walls and floor of the level. Remember to change the size of the downloaded images to a power of 2, such as 256 x 256. Then import the images into the Unity project, create materials, and assign the images to the materials (that is, drag an image into the texture slot of the material). Drag the materials onto the walls or floor in the scene, and increase tiling in the material (try numbers like 8 or 9 in one or both directions) so that the image won't be stretched in an ugly way.

    Once the ground and walls are taken care of, it's time to address the sky.

10.1.1 Generating sky visuals using a skybox

Start by importing the skybox images as you did in chapter 4: go to www.93i.de/ to download skybox images. This time, get the images for the DarkStormy set in addition to TropicalSunnyDay (the sky will be more complex in this project). Import these textures into the Project view, and (as explained in chapter 4) set their Wrap Mode to Clamp.

    Now create a new material to use for this skybox. At the top of the settings for this material, click the Shader menu in order to see the drop-down list with all the available shaders. Move down to the Skybox section and choose 6-Sided in that submenu. With this shader active, the material now has six texture slots (instead of only the small Albedo texture slot that the standard shader had).

    Drag the SunnyDay skybox images to the texture slots of the new material. The names of the images correspond to the texture slot to assign them to (top, front, and so on). Once all six textures are linked, you can use this new material as the skybox for the scene.

    Assign this skybox material in the Lighting window (Window > Lighting > Settings). Assign the material for your skybox to the Skybox slot at the top of the window (either drag the material over or click the little circle button next to the slot). Press Play and you should see something like figure 10.1.

Figure 10.1   Scene with background pictures of the sky

Great, now you have an outdoors scene! A skybox is an elegant way to create the illusion of a vast atmosphere surrounding the player. But the skybox shader built into Unity does have one significant limitation: the images can never change, resulting in a sky that appears completely static. We'll address that limitation by creating a new custom shader.

10.1.2   Setting up an atmosphere that's controlled by code

The images in the TropicalSunnyDay set look great for a sunny day, but what if we want to transition between sunny and overcast weather? This will require a second set of sky images (some pictures of a cloudy sky), so we need a new shader for the skybox.

As explained in chapter 4, a shader is a short program with instructions for how to render the image. This implies that you can program new shaders, and that is in fact the case. We're going to create a new shader that takes two sets of skybox images and transitions between them. Fortunately, a shader for this purpose already exists in the Unify Community wiki's collection of scripts: http://wiki.unity3d.com/index.php?title=SkyboxBlended.

In Unity, create a new shader script: Go to the Create menu just like when you create a new C# script, but select a Standard Surface Shader instead. Name the asset `Skybox-Blended` and then double-click the shader to open the script. Copy the code from that wiki page (the default one, not the fog shader) and paste it into the shader script. The top line says `Shader "Skybox/Blended"`, which tells Unity to add the new shader into the shader list under the Skybox category (the same category as the regular skybox).

> **NOTE** We're not going to go over all the details of the shader program right now. Shader programming is a pretty advanced computer graphics topic, thus outside the scope of this book. You may want to look that up after you've finished this book; if so, start here: http://docs.unity3d.com/Manual/Shaders Overview.html.

Now you can set your material to the Skybox Blended shader. There are 12 texture slots, in 2 sets of 6 images. Assign TropicalSunnyDay images to the first six textures just as before; for the remaining textures, use the DarkStormy set of skybox images.

This new shader also added a Blend slider near the top of the settings. The Blend value controls how much of each set of skybox images you want to display; when you adjust the slider from one side to the other, the skybox transitions from sunny to overcast. You can test by adjusting the slider and playing the game, but manually adjusting the sky isn't terribly helpful while the game is running, so let's write code to transition the sky.

Create an empty object in the scene and name it `Controller`. Create a new script and name it `WeatherController`. Drag that script onto the empty object, and then write this listing in that script.

Listing 10.1 `WeatherController` script transitioning from sunny to overcast

```
using UnityEngine;
using System.Collections;

public class WeatherController : MonoBehaviour {          Reference the material in Project
    [SerializeField] private Material sky;                view, not only objects in the scene.
    [SerializeField] private Light sun;

    private float _fullIntensity;

    private float _cloudValue = 0f;
                                                          Initial intensity of the light is
    void Start() {                                        considered "full" intensity.
        _fullIntensity = sun.intensity;
    }

    void Update() {                                       Increment the value every frame
        SetOvercast(_cloudValue);                         for a continuous transition.
        _cloudValue += .005f;
    }
                                                          Adjust both the material's Blend
                                                          value and the light's intensity.
    private void SetOvercast(float value) {
        sky.SetFloat("_Blend", value);
        sun.intensity = _fullIntensity - (_fullIntensity * value);
    }
}
```

I'll point out a number of things in this code, but the key new method is `SetFloat()`, which appears almost at the bottom. Everything up to that point should be fairly familiar, but that one is new. The method sets a number value on the material. The first parameter to that method defines *which* value specifically. In this case, the material has a property called `Blend` (note that material properties in code start with an underscore).

As for the rest of the code, a few variables are defined, including both the material and a light. For the material, you want to reference the blended skybox material we just created, but what's with the light? That's so that the scene will also darken when transitioning from sunny to overcast; as the Blend value increases, we'll turn down the light. The directional light in the scene acts as the main light and provides illumination everywhere; drag that light into the Inspector.

> **NOTE** The advanced lighting system in Unity takes the skybox into account in order to achieve realistic results. But, this lighting approach won't work right with a changing skybox, so you may want to freeze the lighting setup. In the Lighting window, you can turn off the Auto generate check box at the bottom; now it will only update when you click the button. Set the Blend of the skybox to the middle for an average look, and then click the button next to the Auto check box to manually bake lightmaps (lighting information was saved in a new folder that's named after the scene).

When the script starts, it initializes the intensity of the light. The script will store the starting value and consider that to be the full intensity. This full intensity will be used later in the script when dimming the light.

Then the code increments a value every frame and uses that value to adjust the sky. Specifically, it calls SetOvercast() every frame, and that function encapsulates the multiple adjustments made to the scene. I've already explained what SetFloat() is doing so we won't go over that again, and the last line adjusts the intensity of the light.

Now play the scene to watch the code running. You'll see what figure 10.2 depicts: over a couple of seconds, you'll see the scene transition from a sunny day to dark and overcast.

Sunny before transition   Overcast after transition

Figure 10.2   Before and after: scene transition from sunny to overcast

> **WARNING** One unexpected quirk about Unity is that the Blend change on the material is permanent. Unity resets objects in the scene when the game stops running, but assets that were linked directly from the Project view (such as the skybox material) are changed permanently. This only happens within Unity's editor (changes don't carry over between plays after the game is deployed outside the editor), thus resulting in frustrating bugs if you forget about it.

It's pretty cool watching the scene transition from sunny to overcast. But this was all just a setup for the actual goal: having the weather in the game sync up to real-world weather conditions. For that, we need to start downloading weather data from the internet.

10.2   *Downloading weather data from an internet service*

Now that we have the outdoors scene set up, we can write code that will download weather data and modify the scene based on that data. This task will provide a good example of retrieving data using HTTP requests. There are many web services for weather data; there's an extensive list at www.programmableweb.com/. I chose Open-WeatherMap; the code examples use their API (application programming interface, a way to access their service using code commands instead of a graphical interface) located at http://openweathermap.org/api.

> **DEFINITION**   A *web service* or *web API* is a server connected to the internet that returns data upon request. There's no technical difference between a web API and a website; a website is a web service that happens to return the data for a web page, and browsers interpret HTML data as a visible document.

> **NOTE**   Web services often require you to register, even for free service. For example, if you go to the API page for OpenWeatherMap, it has instructions for obtaining an API key, a value you will paste into requests.

The code you'll write will be structured around the same `Managers` architecture from chapter 9. This time, you'll have a `WeatherManager` class that gets initialized from the central manager-of-managers. `WeatherManager` will be in charge of retrieving and storing weather data, but to do so it'll need the ability to communicate with the internet.

To accomplish that, you'll create a utility class called `NetworkService`. `NetworkService` will handle the details of connecting to the internet and making HTTP requests. `WeatherManager` can then tell `NetworkService` to make those requests and pass back the response. Figure 10.3 shows how this code structure will operate.

Figure 10.3   Diagram showing how the networking code will be structured

For this to work, obviously `WeatherManager` will need to have access to the `Network-Service` object. You're going to address this by creating the object in Managers and then injecting the `NetworkService` object into the various managers when they're initialized. In this way, not only will `WeatherManager` have a reference to the `NetworkSer-vice`, but so will any other managers you create later.

To start bringing over the `Managers` code architecture from chapter 9, first copy over `ManagerStatus` and `IGameManager` (remember that `IGameManager` is the interface that all managers must implement, whereas `ManagerStatus` is an enum that `IGameManager` uses). You'll need to modify `IGameManager` slightly to accommodate the new `Network-Service` class, so create a new script called `NetworkService` (delete `:MonoBehaviour` and otherwise leave it empty for now; you'll fill it in later) and then adjust `IGameManager`.

Listing 10.2   Adjusting `IGameManager` to include `NetworkService`

```
public interface IGameManager {
   ManagerStatus status {get;}

   void Startup(NetworkService service);     ◄─────  Startup function now takes one
}                                                    parameter: the injected object.
```

Next let's create `WeatherManager` to implement this slightly adjusted interface. Create a new C# script.

Listing 10.3   Initial script for `WeatherManager`

```
using UnityEngine;
using System.Collections;
using System.Collections.Generic;

public class WeatherManager : MonoBehaviour, IGameManager {
   public ManagerStatus status {get; private set;}

   // Add cloud value here (listing 10.8)
   private NetworkService _network;

   public void Startup(NetworkService service) {
      Debug.Log("Weather manager starting...");

      _network = service;                    ◄─────  Store the injected
                                                     NetworkService object.
      status = ManagerStatus.Started;
   }
}
```

This initial pass at `WeatherManager` doesn't really do anything. For now, it's the minimum amount that `IGameManager` requires that the class implements: Declare the `status` property from the interface, as well as implement the `Startup()` function. You'll fill in this empty framework over the next few sections. Finally, copy over `Managers` from chapter 9 and adjust it to start up `WeatherManager`.

Listing 10.4   `Managers.cs` adjusted to initialize `WeatherManager`

```
using UnityEngine;
using System.Collections;
using System.Collections.Generic;
                                              Require the new manager
                                              instead of player and inventory.
[RequireComponent(typeof(WeatherManager))]    ◄─────
```

```
public class Managers : MonoBehaviour {
    public static WeatherManager Weather {get; private set;}

    private List<IGameManager> _startSequence;

    void Awake() {
        Weather = GetComponent<WeatherManager>();

        _startSequence = new List<IGameManager>();
        _startSequence.Add(Weather);

        StartCoroutine(StartupManagers());
    }

    private IEnumerator StartupManagers() {
        NetworkService network = new NetworkService();

        foreach (IGameManager manager in _startSequence) {
            manager.Startup(network);
        }

        yield return null;

        int numModules = _startSequence.Count;
        int numReady = 0;

        while (numReady < numModules) {
            int lastReady = numReady;
            numReady = 0;

            foreach (IGameManager manager in _startSequence) {
                if (manager.status == ManagerStatus.Started) {
                    numReady++;
                }
            }

            if (numReady > lastReady)
                Debug.Log("Progress: " + numReady + "/" + numModules);

            yield return null;
        }

        Debug.Log("All managers started up");
    }
}
```

Instantiate NetworkService to inject in all managers ← `NetworkService network = new NetworkService();`

Pass the network service to managers during startup ← `manager.Startup(network);`

And that's everything needed codewise for the Managers code architecture. As you have in previous chapters, create the game managers object in the scene and then attach both Managers and WeatherManager to the empty object. Even though the manager isn't doing anything yet, you can see startup messages in the console when it's set up correctly.

Whew, there were quite a few boilerplate things to get out of the way! Now we can get on with writing the networking code.

10.2.1 *Requesting HTTP data using coroutines*

NetworkService is currently an empty script, so you can write code in it to make HTTP requests. The primary class you need to know about is UnityWebRequest. Unity provides the UnityWebRequest class to communicate with the internet. Instantiating a request object using a URL will send a request to that URL.

Coroutines can work with the UnityWebRequest class to wait for the request to complete. Coroutines were introduced in chapter 3, where we used them to pause code for a set period of time. Recall the explanation given there: Coroutines are special functions that seemingly run in the background of a program, in a repeated cycle of running partway and then returning to the rest of the program. When used along with the Start-Coroutine() method, the yield keyword causes the coroutine to temporarily pause, handing back the program flow and picking up again from that point in the next frame.

In chapter 3, the coroutines yielded at WaitForSeconds(), an object that caused the function to pause for a specific number of seconds. Yielding a coroutine when sending a request will pause the function until that network request completes. The program flow here is similar to making asynchronous Ajax calls in a web application: First you send a request, then you continue with the rest of the program, and after some time you receive a response.

THAT WAS THE THEORY; NOW LET'S WRITE THE CODE

All right, let's implement this stuff in our code. First open the NetworkService script and replace the default template with the contents of this listing.

> **Listing 10.5 Making HTTP requests in NetworkService**

```
using UnityEngine;
using UnityEngine.Networking;
using System.Collections;
using System;

public class NetworkService {                              URL to send
   private const string xmlApi =                           request to
"http://api.openweathermap.org/data/2.5/                                Create
     weather?q=Chicago,us&mode=xml&APPID=<your api key>";       UnityWebRequest
                                                             object in GET mode.
   private IEnumerator CallAPI(string url, Action<string> callback) {
     using (UnityWebRequest request = UnityWebRequest.Get(url)) {

        yield return request.Send();                       Pause while downloading.

        if (request.isNetworkError) {
          Debug.LogError("network problem: " + request.error);    Check for
        } else if (request.responseCode !=                        errors in the
            (long)System.Net.HttpStatusCode.OK) {                 response.
          Debug.LogError("response error: " + request.responseCode);
        } else {
          callback(request.downloadHandler.text);          Delegate can be called just
        }                                                  like the original function.
     }
```

```
    }

    public IEnumerator GetWeatherXML(Action<string> callback) {
        return CallAPI(xmlApi, callback);
    }
}
```

Yield cascades through coroutine methods that call each other

WARNING The Action type is contained in the System namespace; notice the additional using statement at the top of the script. Don't forget this detail in your scripts!

Remember the code design explained earlier: WeatherManager will tell NetworkService to go fetch data. All this code doesn't actually run yet; you're setting up code that will be called by WeatherManager a bit later. To explore this code listing, let's start at the bottom and work our way up.

WRITING COROUTINE METHODS THAT CASCADE THROUGH EACH OTHER

GetWeatherXML() is the coroutine method that outside code can use to tell NetworkService to make an HTTP request. Notice that this function has IEnumerator for its return type; methods used in coroutines must have IEnumerator declared as the return type.

It might look odd at first that GetWeatherXML() doesn't have a yield statement. Coroutines are paused by the yield statement, which implies that every coroutine must yield somewhere. It turns out that the yielding can cascade through multiple methods. If the initial coroutine method itself calls another method, and that other method yields part of the way through, then the coroutine will pause inside that second method and resume there. Thus, the yield statement in CallAPI() pauses the coroutine that was started in GetWeatherXML(); figure 10.4 shows this code flow.

Figure 10.4 Diagram showing how the network coroutine works

The next potential head-scratcher is the callback parameter of type Action.

UNDERSTANDING HOW THE CALLBACK WORKS

When the coroutine is started, the method is called with a parameter called callback, and callback has the Action type. But what is an Action?

DEFINITION   The Action type is a delegate (C# has a few approaches to delegates, but this one is the simplest). Delegates are references to some other method/function. They allow you to store the function (or rather, a pointer to the function) in a variable and to pass that function as a parameter to another function.

If you're unfamiliar with the concept of delegates, realize that they enable you to pass around functions just as you do numbers and strings. Without delegates, you can't pass around functions to call later—you can only directly call the function immediately. With delegates, you can tell code about other methods to call later. This is useful for many purposes, especially for implementing callback functions.

DEFINITION   A *callback* is a function used to communicate back to the calling object. Object A could tell Object B about one of the methods in A. B could later call A's method to communicate back to A.

In this case, for example, the callback is used to communicate the response data back after waiting for the HTTP request to complete. In CallAPI(), the code first makes an HTTP request, then yields until that request completes, and finally uses callback() to send back the response.

Note the <> syntax used with the Action keyword; the type written in the angle brackets declares the parameters required to fit this Action. In other words, the function this Action points to must take parameters matching the declared type. In this case, the parameter is a single string, so the callback method must have a signature like this:

```
MethodName(string value)
```

The concept of a callback may make more sense after you've seen it in action, which you will in listing 10.6; this initial explanation is so that you'll recognize what's going on when you see that additional code.

The rest of listing 10.5 is pretty straightforward. The request object is created inside a using statement so that the object's memory will be cleaned up once done. The conditional checks for errors in the HTTP response. There are two kinds of errors: the request could've failed due to a bad internet connection or the response returned could have an error code. A const value is declared with the URL to make the request to. (Incidentally, you should replace <your api key> at the end with your OpenWeatherMap API key.)

MAKING USE OF THE NETWORKING CODE

That wraps up the code in NetworkService. Now let's use NetworkService in WeatherManager.

> **Listing 10.6   Adjusting WeatherManager to use NetworkService**

```
...
public void Startup(NetworkService service) {
    Debug.Log("Weather manager starting...");

    _network = service;
    StartCoroutine(_network.GetWeatherXML(OnXMLDataLoaded));
```

Start loading data from the internet.

```
    status = ManagerStatus.Initializing;          Instead of Started, make
}                                                  the status Initializing.

public void OnXMLDataLoaded(string data) {         Callback method once
    Debug.Log(data);                               the data is loaded

    status = ManagerStatus.Started;
}
...
```

Three primary changes are made to the code in this manager: starting a coroutine to download data from the internet, setting a different startup status, and defining a callback method to receive the response.

Starting the coroutine is simple. Most of the complexity behind coroutines was handled in `NetworkService`, so calling `StartCoroutine()` is all you need to do here. Then you set a different startup status, because the manager isn't finished initializing; it needs to receive data from the internet before startup is complete.

> **WARNING** Always start networking methods using `StartCoroutine()`; don't just call the function normally. This can be easy to forget because creating request objects outside of a coroutine doesn't generate any sort of compiler error.

When you call the `StartCoroutine()` method, you need to invoke the method. That is, actually type the parentheses—()—and don't only provide the name of the function. In this case, the coroutine method needs a callback function as its one parameter, so let's define that function. We'll use `OnXMLDataLoaded()` for the callback; notice that this method has a string parameter, which fits the `Action<string>` declaration from `NetworkService`. The callback function doesn't do a lot right now; the debug line simply prints the received data to the console to verify that the data was received correctly. Then the last line of the function changes the startup status of the manager to say that it's completely started up.

Click Play to run the code. Assuming you have a solid internet connection, you should see a bunch of data appear in the console. This data is simply a long string, but the string is formatted in a specific way that we can make use of.

10.2.2 Parsing XML

Data that exists as a long string usually has individual bits of information embedded within the string. You extract those bits of information by parsing the string.

> **DEFINITION** *Parsing* means analyzing a chunk of data and dividing it up into separate pieces of information.

In order to parse the string, it needs to be formatted in a way that allows you (or rather, the parser code) to identify separate pieces. There are a couple of standard formats commonly used to transfer data over the internet; the most common standard format is *XML*.

DEFINITION   *XML* stands for Extensible Markup Language. It's a set of rules for encoding documents in a structured way, similar to HTML web pages.

Fortunately, Unity (or rather Mono, the code framework built into Unity) provides functionality for parsing XML. The weather data we requested is formatted in XML, so we're going to add code to `WeatherManager` to parse the response and extract the cloudiness. Put the URL into a web browser in order to see the code; there's a lot there, but we're only interested in the node that contains something like `<clouds value="40" name="scattered clouds"/>`.

In addition to adding code to parse XML, we're going to make use of the same messenger system we did in chapter 7. That's because once the weather data is downloaded and parsed, we still need to inform the scene about that. Create a script called `Messenger` and paste the code from this page on the Unify wiki: http://wiki.unity3d.com/index.php/CSharpMessenger_Extended.

Then you need to create a script called `GameEvent`. As explained in chapter 7, this messenger system is great for providing a decoupled way of communicating events to the rest of the program.

Listing 10.7   `GameEvent` **code**

```
public static class GameEvent {
    public const string WEATHER_UPDATED = "WEATHER_UPDATED";
}
```

Once the messenger system is in place, adjust `WeatherManager`.

Listing 10.8   **Parsing XML in** `WeatherManager`

```
...
using System;
using System.Xml;
...
public float cloudValue {get; private set;}
...
public void OnXMLDataLoaded(string data) {
    XmlDocument doc = new XmlDocument();
    doc.LoadXml(data);
    XmlNode root = doc.DocumentElement;

    XmlNode node = root.SelectSingleNode("clouds");
    string value = node.Attributes["value"].Value;
    cloudValue = Convert.ToInt32(value) / 100f;
    Debug.Log("Value: " + cloudValue);

    Messenger.Broadcast(GameEvent.WEATHER_UPDATED);

    status = ManagerStatus.Started;
}
...
```

Be sure to add needed using statements.

Cloudiness is modified internally but read-only elsewhere.

Parse XML into a searchable structure.

Pull out a single node from the data.

Convert the value to a 0-1 float.

Broadcast message to inform the other scripts.

You can see that the most important changes were made inside `OnXMLDataLoaded()`. Previously, this method simply logged the data to the console to verify that data was coming through correctly. This listing adds a lot of code to parse the XML.

First create a new empty XML document; this is an empty container that you can fill with a parsed XML structure. The next line parses the data string into a structure contained by the XML document. Then we start at the root of the XML tree so that everything can search up the tree in subsequent code.

At this point, you can search for nodes within the XML structure in order to pull out individual bits of information. In this case, `<clouds>` is the only node we're interested in. First find that node in the XML document, and then extract the `value` attribute from that node. This data defines the cloud value as a 0-100 integer, but we're going to need it as a 0-1 float in order to adjust the scene later. Converting that is a simple bit of math added to the code.

Finally, after extracting out the cloudiness value from the full data, broadcast a message that the weather data has been updated. Currently, nothing is listening for that message, but the broadcaster doesn't need to know anything about listeners (indeed, that's the entire point of a decoupled messenger system). Later, we'll add a listener to the scene.

Great—we've written code to parse XML data! But before we move on to applying this value to the visible scene, I want to go over another option for data transfer.

10.2.3 Parsing JSON

Before continuing to the next step in the project, let's explore an alternative format for transferring data. XML is one common format for data transferred over the internet; another common one is *JSON*.

> **DEFINITION** *JSON* stands for JavaScript Object Notation. Similar in purpose to XML, JSON was designed to be a lightweight alternative. Although the syntax for JSON was originally derived from JavaScript, the format is not language-specific and is readily used with a variety of programming languages.

Unlike XML, Mono doesn't come with a parser for this format. Fortunately, there are a number of good JSON parsers available. Two simple options are MiniJSON (https://gist .github.com/darktable/1411710) and SimpleJSON (http://wiki.unity3d.com/index .php/SimpleJSON).

For this example, we'll use MiniJSON. Create a script called `MiniJSON` and paste in that code. Now you can use this library to parse JSON data. We've been getting XML from the OpenWeatherMap API, but as it happens, they can also send the same data formatted as JSON. To do that, modify `NetworkService` to request JSON.

> **Listing 10.9 Making `NetworkService` request JSON instead of XML**

```
...
private const string jsonApi =      ◄─── The URL is slightly different this time.
"http://api.openweathermap.org/data/2.5/weather?q=Chicago,us&APPID=<your api
    key>";
...
```

```
public IEnumerator GetWeatherJSON(Action<string> callback) {
    return CallAPI(jsonApi, callback);
}
...
```

This is pretty much the same as the code to download XML data, except that the URL is slightly different. The data returned from this request has the same values, but it's formatted differently. This time we're looking for a chunk like "clouds":{"all":40}.

There wasn't a ton of additional code required this time. That's because we set up the code for requests into nicely parceled separate functions, so every subsequent HTTP request will be easy to add. Nice! Now let's modify WeatherManager to request JSON data instead of XML.

Listing 10.10   Modifying WeatherManager to request JSON

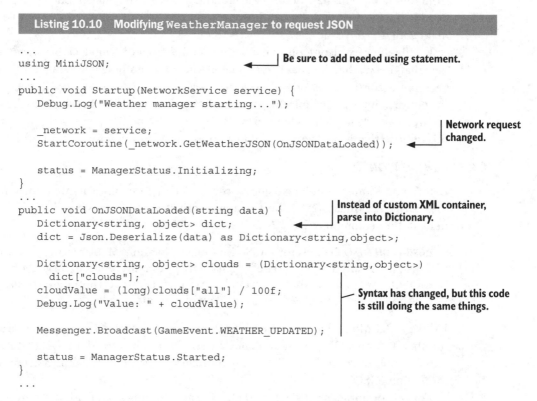

```
...
using MiniJSON;                              ◄——| Be sure to add needed using statement.
...
public void Startup(NetworkService service) {
    Debug.Log("Weather manager starting...");

    _network = service;                                              | Network request
    StartCoroutine(_network.GetWeatherJSON(OnJSONDataLoaded)); ◄——| changed.

    status = ManagerStatus.Initializing;
}
...
public void OnJSONDataLoaded(string data) {              | Instead of custom XML container,
    Dictionary<string, object> dict;        ◄——| parse into Dictionary.
    dict = Json.Deserialize(data) as Dictionary<string,object>;

    Dictionary<string, object> clouds = (Dictionary<string,object>)
        dict["clouds"];
    cloudValue = (long)clouds["all"] / 100f;           | Syntax has changed, but this code
    Debug.Log("Value: " + cloudValue);                 | is still doing the same things.

    Messenger.Broadcast(GameEvent.WEATHER_UPDATED);

    status = ManagerStatus.Started;
}
...
```

As you can see, the code for working with JSON looks similar to the code for XML. The only real difference is that this JSON parser works with a standard Dictionary instead of a custom document container like XML did. There's a command to *deserialize*, and that may be an unfamiliar word.

DEFINITION   *Deserialize* means pretty much the same thing as parse. This is the reverse of *serialize*, which means to encode a batch of data into a form that can be transferred and stored, such as a JSON string.

Aside from the different syntax, all the steps are the very same. Extract the value from the data chunk (for some reason the value is called `all` this time, but that's just a quirk of the API) and do some simple math to convert the value to a 0-1 float.

With that done, it's time to apply the value to the visible scene.

10.2.4 *Affecting the scene based on weather data*

Regardless of exactly how the data is formatted, once the cloudiness value is extracted from the response data, we can use that value in the `SetOvercast()` method of `WeatherController`. Whether XML or JSON, the data string ultimately gets parsed into a series of words and numbers. The `SetOvercast()` method takes a number as a parameter. In section 9.1.2 we used a number incremented every frame, but we could just as easily use the number returned by the weather API.

This shows the full `WeatherController` script again, after modifications.

> **Listing 10.11** `WeatherController` that reacts to downloaded weather data

```
using UnityEngine;
using System.Collections;

public class WeatherController : MonoBehaviour {
    [SerializeField] private Material sky;
    [SerializeField] private Light sun;

    private float _fullIntensity;

    void Awake() {                                          Add/Remove event listeners.
        Messenger.AddListener(GameEvent.WEATHER_UPDATED, OnWeatherUpdated);
    }
    void OnDestroy() {
        Messenger.RemoveListener(GameEvent.WEATHER_UPDATED, OnWeatherUpdated);
    }

    void Start() {
        _fullIntensity = sun.intensity;
    }

    private void OnWeatherUpdated() {                        Use the cloudiness value
        SetOvercast(Managers.Weather.cloudValue);           from WeatherManager.
    }

    private void SetOvercast(float value) {
        sky.SetFloat("_Blend", value);
        sun.intensity = _fullIntensity - (_fullIntensity * value);
    }
}
```

Notice that the changes aren't only additions; several bits of test code got removed. Specifically, we removed the local cloudiness value that was incremented every frame; we don't need that anymore, because we'll use the value from `WeatherManager`.

A listener gets added and removed in `Awake()`/`OnDestroy()` (these are the functions of `MonoBehaviour` called when the object awakes or is removed). This listener is part of the broadcast messaging system, and it calls `OnWeatherUpdated()` when that message is received. `OnWeatherUpdated()` retrieves the cloudiness value from `Weather-Manager` and calls `SetOvercast()` using that value. In this way, the appearance of the scene is controlled by downloaded weather data.

Run the scene now and you'll see the sky update according to the cloudiness in the weather data. You may see it take time to request the weather; in a real game, you'd probably want to hide the scene behind a loading screen until the sky updates.

Game networking beyond HTTP

HTTP requests are robust and reliable, but the latency between making a request and receiving a response can be too slow for many games. HTTP requests are therefore a good way of sending relatively slow-paced messages to a server (such as moves in a turn-based game, or submission of high scores for any game), but something like a multiplayer FPS would need a different approach to networking.

These approaches involve various communication technologies, as well as techniques to compensate for lag. For example, Unity provides a high-level API, built on top of a lower-level transport layer, for multiplayer games.

The cutting edge for networked action games is a complex topic that goes beyond the scope of this book. You can look up more information on your own, starting here: http://docs.unity3d.com/Manual/UNetOverview.html.

Now that you know how to get numerical and string data from the internet, let's do the same thing with an image.

10.3 Adding a networked billboard

Although the responses from a web API are almost always text strings formatted in XML or JSON, many other sorts of data are transferred over the internet. Besides text data, the most common kind of data requested is images. The `UnityWebRequest` object can be used to download images, too.

You're going to learn about this task by creating a billboard that displays an image downloaded from the internet. You need to code two steps: downloading an image to display, and applying that image to the billboard object. As a third step, you'll improve the code so that the image will be stored to use on multiple billboards.

10.3.1 Loading images from the internet

First let's write the code to download an image. You're going to download some public domain landscape photography (see figure 10.5) to test with. The downloaded image won't be visible on the billboard yet; I'll show you a script to display the image in the next section, but before that, let's get the code in place that will retrieve the image.

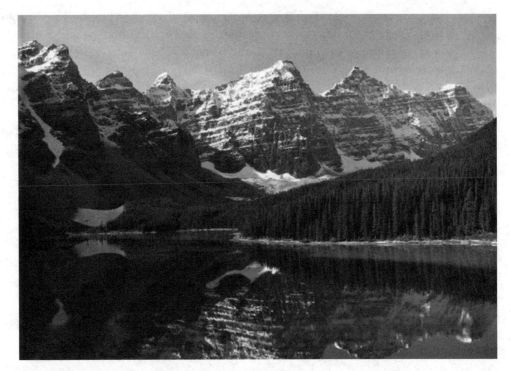

Figure 10.5   Image of Moraine Lake in Banff National Park, Canada

The code architecture for downloading an image looks much the same as the architecture for downloading data. A new manager module (called ImagesManager) will be in charge of downloaded images to be displayed. Once again, the details of connecting to the internet and sending HTTP requests will be handled in NetworkService, and ImagesManager will call upon NetworkService to download images for it.

The first addition to code is in NetworkService. This listing adds image downloading to that script.

Listing 10.12   Downloading an image in NetworkService

```
...
private const string webImage =          ◄──┤ Put this const up near the top with the other URLs.
"http://upload.wikimedia.org/wikipedia/commons/c/c5/Moraine_Lake_17092005.
    jpg";                                This callback takes a Texture2D instead of a string.
...
public IEnumerator DownloadImage(Action<Texture2D> callback) {  ◄──
    UnityWebRequest request = UnityWebRequestTexture.GetTexture(webImage);
    yield return request.Send();
    callback(DownloadHandlerTexture.GetContent(request));       ◄──────
}
...                                                  Retrieve downloaded image using
                                                      the DownloadHandler utility.
```

The code that downloads an image looks almost identical to the code for downloading data. The primary difference is the type of callback method; note that the callback takes a Texture2D this time instead of a string. That's because you're sending back the relevant response: you downloaded a string of data previously—now you're downloading an image. This listing contains code for the new ImagesManager. Create a new script and enter that code.

Listing 10.13 Creating `ImagesManager` to retrieve and store images

```
using UnityEngine;
using System.Collections;
using System.Collections.Generic;
using System;

public class ImagesManager : MonoBehaviour, IGameManager {
   public ManagerStatus status {get; private set;}

   private NetworkService _network;

   private Texture2D _webImage;          ◄──── Variable to store downloaded image

   public void Startup(NetworkService service) {
      Debug.Log("Images manager starting...");

      _network = service;

      status = ManagerStatus.Started;
   }
                                                          Check if the image is
                                                          already stored.
   public void GetWebImage(Action<Texture2D> callback) {
      if (_webImage == null) {
         StartCoroutine(_network.DownloadImage(callback));
      }
      else {                                         Invoke callback right away (don't
         callback(_webImage);                        download) if there's a stored image.
      }
   }
}
```

The most interesting part of this code is GetWebImage(); everything else in this script consists of standard properties and methods that implement the manager interface. When GetWebImage() is called, it'll return (via a callback function) the web image. First, it'll check if _webImage already has a stored image. If not, it'll invoke the network call to download the image. If _webImage already has a stored image, GetWebImage() will send back the stored image (rather than downloading the image anew).

> **NOTE** Currently, the downloaded image is never being stored, which means _webImage will always be empty. Code that specifies what to do when _webImage is *not* empty is already in place, so you'll adjust the code to store that image in the following sections. This adjustment is in a separate section because it involves some tricky code wizardry.

Of course, just like all manager modules, `ImagesManager` needs to be added to `Managers` and this listing details the additions to `Managers.cs`.

Listing 10.14   Adding the new manager to `Managers.cs`

```
...
[RequireComponent(typeof(ImagesManager))]
...
public static ImagesManager Images {get; private set;}
...
void Awake() {
    Weather = GetComponent<WeatherManager>();
    Images = GetComponent<ImagesManager>();

    _startSequence = new List<IGameManager>();
    _startSequence.Add(Weather);
    _startSequence.Add(Images);

    StartCoroutine(StartupManagers());
}
...
```

Unlike how we set up `WeatherManager`, `GetWebImage()` in `ImagesManager` isn't called automatically on startup. Instead, the code waits until invoked; that'll happen in the next section.

10.3.2   *Displaying images on the billboard*

The `ImagesManager` you just wrote doesn't do anything until it's called upon, so now we'll create a billboard object that will call methods in `ImagesManager`. First create a new cube and then place it in the middle of the scene, at something like Position 0 1.5 -5 and Scale 5 3 .5 (see figure 10.6).

Billboard without image   Billboard with downloaded image

Figure 10.6   The billboard object, before and after displaying the downloaded image

You're going to create a device that operates just like the color-changing monitor in chapter 9. Copy the `DeviceOperator` script and put it on the player. As you may recall, that script will operate nearby devices when the Fire3 button is pressed (which is defined in the project's input settings as the left Shift key). Also create a script for the billboard device called `WebLoadingBillboard`, put that script on the billboard object, and enter this code.

Listing 10.15   `WebLoadingBillboard` device script

```
using UnityEngine;
using System.Collections;

public class WebLoadingBillboard : MonoBehaviour {
   public void Operate() {
      Managers.Images.GetWebImage(OnWebImage);
   }

   private void OnWebImage(Texture2D image) {
      GetComponent<Renderer>().material.mainTexture = image;
   }
}
```

Call the method in ImagesManager.

Downloaded image is applied to the material in the callback.

This code does two primary things: It calls `ImagesManager.GetWebImage()` when the device is operated, and it applies the image from the callback function. Textures are applied to materials, so you can change the texture in the material that's on the billboard. Figure 10.6 shows what the billboard will look like after you play the game.

AssetBundles: How to download other kinds of assets

Downloading an image is fairly straightforward using `UnityWebRequest`, but what about other kinds of assets, like mesh objects and prefabs? `UnityWebRequest` has properties for text and images, but other assets are a bit more complicated.

Unity can download any kind of asset through a mechanism called AssetBundles. Long story short, you first package some assets into a bundle, and then Unity can extract the assets after downloading the bundle. The details of both creating and downloading AssetBundles are beyond the scope of this book; if you want to learn more, start by reading these sections of Unity's manual https://docs.unity3d.com/Manual/AssetBundlesIntro.html and https://docs.unity3d.com/Manual/UnityWebRequest-DownloadingAssetBundle.html.

Great, the downloaded image is displayed on the billboard! But this code could be optimized further to work with multiple billboards. Let's tackle that optimization next.

10.3.3 *Caching the downloaded image for reuse*

As noted in section 9.3.1, `ImagesManager` doesn't yet store the downloaded image. That means the image will be downloaded over and over for multiple billboards. This is inefficient, because it'll be the same image each time. To address this, we're going to adjust `ImagesManager` to cache images that have been downloaded.

> **DEFINITION**   *Cache* means to keep stored locally. The most common (but not only!) context involves images downloaded from the internet.

The key is to provide a callback function in `ImagesManager` that first saves the image, and then calls the callback from `WebLoadingBillboard`. This is tricky to do (as opposed to the current code that directly uses the callback from `WebLoadingBillboard`) because the code doesn't know ahead of time what the callback from `WebLoadingBillboard` will be. Put another way, there's no way to write a method in `ImagesManager` that calls a specific method in `WebLoadingBillboard` because we don't yet know what that specific method will be. The way around this conundrum is to use *lambda functions*.

> **DEFINITION** A *lambda function* (also called an *anonymous function*) is a function that doesn't have a name. These functions are usually created on the fly inside other functions.

Lambda functions are a tricky code feature supported in a number of programming languages, including C#. By using a lambda function for the callback in `ImagesManager`, the code can create the callback function on the fly using the method passed in from `WebLoadingBillboard`. You don't need to know the method to call ahead of time, because this lambda function doesn't exist ahead of time! This listing shows how to do this voodoo in `ImagesManager`.

> **Listing 10.16 Lambda function for callback in `ImagesManager`**

```
...
using System;
...
public void GetWebImage(Action<Texture2D> callback) {
    if (_webImage == null) {
        StartCoroutine(_network.DownloadImage((Texture2D image) => {
            _webImage = image;           ◄─────    Store downloaded image
            callback(_webImage);         ◄─────
        }));                                        Callback is used in lambda
    }                                               function instead of sent directly
    else {                                          to NetworkService.
        callback(_webImage);
    }
}
...
```

The main change was in the function passed to `NetworkService.DownloadImage()`. Previously, the code was passing through the same callback method from `WebLoadingBillboard`. After the change, though, the callback sent to `NetworkService` was a separate lambda function declared on the spot that called the method from `WebLoadingBillboard`. Take note of the syntax to declare a lambda method: `() => {}`.

Making the callback a separate function made it possible to do more than call the method in `WebLoadingBillboard`; specifically, the lambda function also stores a local copy of the downloaded image. Thus, `GetWebImage()` only has to download the image the first time; all subsequent calls will use the locally stored image.

Because this optimization applies to subsequent calls, the effect will be noticeable only on multiple billboards. Let's duplicate the billboard object so that there will be a second billboard in the scene. Select the billboard object, click Duplicate (look under the Edit menu or right-click), and move the duplicate over (for example, change the X position to 18).

Now play the game and watch what happens. When you operate the first billboard, there will be a noticeable pause while the image downloads from the internet. But when you then walk over to the second billboard, the image will appear immediately because it has already been downloaded.

This is an important optimization for downloading images (there's a reason web browsers cache images by default). There's one more major networking task remaining to go over: sending data back to the server.

10.4   *Posting data to a web server*

We've gone over multiple examples of downloading data, but we still need to see an example of *sending* data. This last section does require you to have a server to send requests to, so this section is optional. But it's easy to download open source software to set up a server to test on.

I recommend XAMPP for a test server. Go to www.apachefriends.org to download XAMPP. Once that's installed and the server is running, you can access XAMPP's htdocs folder with the address http://localhost/ just like you would a server on the internet. Once you have XAMPP up and running, create a folder called uia in htdocs; that's where you'll put the server-side script.

Whether you use XAMPP or your own existing web server, the actual task will be to post weather data to the server when the player reaches a checkpoint in the scene. This checkpoint will be a trigger volume, just like the door trigger in chapter 9. You need to create a new cube object, position the object off to one side of the scene, set the collider to Trigger, and apply a semitransparent material like you did in the previous chapter (remember, set the material's Rendering Mode). Figure 10.7 shows the checkpoint object with a green semitransparent material applied.

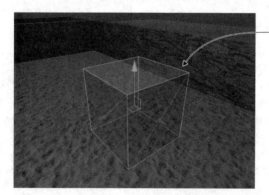

Trigger volume: Box with a semitransparent material

Figure 10.7   The checkpoint object that triggers data sending

Now that the trigger object is in the scene, let's write the code that it invokes.

10.4.1 *Tracking current weather: sending post requests*

The code that's invoked by the checkpoint object will cascade through several scripts. As with the code for downloading data, the code for sending data will involve WeatherManager telling NetworkService to make the request, and NetworkService handles the details of HTTP communication. This shows the adjustments you need to make to NetworkService.

Listing 10.17 Adjusting NetworkService **to post data**

Address of the server-side script; change this if needed.

```
...
private const string localApi = "http://localhost/uia/api.php";   ◄
...
private IEnumerator CallAPI(string url, WWWForm form, Action<string>
    callback) {                        ◄── Added arguments to CallAPI() parameters
  using (UnityWebRequest request = (form == null) ?
    UnityWebRequest.Get(url) : UnityWebRequest.Post(url, form)) {   ◄

    yield return request.Send();        Either POST using
                                        WWWForm or GET without

    if (request.isError) {
       Debug.LogError("network problem: " + request.error);
    } else if (request.responseCode != (long)System.Net.HttpStatusCode.OK)
  {
       Debug.LogError("response error: " + request.responseCode);
    } else {
       callback(request.downloadHandler.text);
    }
  }
}

public IEnumerator GetWeatherXML(Action<string> callback) {     Calls modified because
  return CallAPI(xmlApi, null, callback);                       of changed parameters
}
public IEnumerator GetWeatherJSON(Action<string> callback) {
  return CallAPI(jsonApi, null, callback);
}

public IEnumerator LogWeather(string name, float cloudValue, Action<string>
    callback) {
  WWWForm form = new WWWForm();                 ◄── Define a form with values to send.
  form.AddField("message", name);
  form.AddField("cloud_value", cloudValue.ToString());
  form.AddField("timestamp", DateTime.UtcNow.Ticks.ToString());   ◄

  return CallAPI(localApi, form, callback);     Send timestamp along
}                                               with the cloudiness.
...
```

First, notice that CallAPI() has a new parameter. This is a WWWForm object, a series of values to send along with the HTTP request. There's a condition in the code that uses the presence of a WWWForm object to alter the request created. Normally we want to send a GET request, but WWWForm will change it to a POST request to send data. All the

other changes in the code react to that central change (for example, modifying the
GetWeather() code because of the CallAPI() parameters).

This is what you need to add in WeatherManager.

Listing 10.18   Adding code to `WeatherManager` that sends data

```
...
public void LogWeather(string name) {
   StartCoroutine(_network.LogWeather(name, cloudValue, OnLogged));
}
private void OnLogged(string response) {
   Debug.Log(response);
}
...
```

Finally, make use of that code by adding a checkpoint script to the trigger volume in
the scene. Create a script called CheckpointTrigger, put that script on the trigger volume, and enter the contents of the next listing.

Listing 10.19   `CheckpointTrigger` script for the trigger volume

```
using UnityEngine;
using System.Collections;

public class CheckpointTrigger : MonoBehaviour {
   public string identifier;

   private bool _triggered;              ◄─── Track if the checkpoint has already been triggered.

   void OnTriggerEnter(Collider other) {
      if (_triggered) {return;}

      Managers.Weather.LogWeather(identifier);    ◄─── Call to send data.
      _triggered = true;
   }
}
```

An Identifier slot will appear in the Inspector; name it something like checkpoint1.
Run the code and data will be sent when you enter the checkpoint. The response will
indicate an error, though, because there's no script on the server to receive the request.
That's the last step in this section.

10.4.2   *Server-side code in PHP*

The server needs to have a script to receive data sent from the game. Coding server
scripts is beyond the scope of this book, so we won't go into detail here. We'll just whip
up a PHP script, because that's the easiest approach. Create a text file in htdocs (or
wherever your web server is located) and name it api.php (listing 10.20).

Listing 10.20 Server script written in PHP that receives our data

```php
<?php

$message = $_POST['message'];                              ◄─── Extract post data into variables.
$cloudiness = $_POST['cloud_value'];
$timestamp = $_POST['timestamp'];
$combined = $message." cloudiness=".$cloudiness." time=".$timestamp."\n";

                                                           Define the filename to write to.
$filename = "data.txt";                          ◄───
file_put_contents($filename, $combined, FILE_APPEND | LOCK_EX);   ◄───  Write
                                                                        the file.
echo "Logged";

?>
```

Note that this script writes received data into data.txt, so you also need to put a text file with that name on the server. Once api.php is in place, you'll see weather logs appear in data.txt when triggering checkpoints in the game. Great!

Summary

- Skybox is designed for sky visuals that render behind everything else.
- Unity provides UnityWebRequest to download data.
- Common data formats like XML and JSON can be parsed easily.
- Materials can display images downloaded from the internet.
- UnityWebRequest can also post data to a web server.

Playing audio: sound effects and music

11

This chapter covers

- Importing and playing audio clips for various sound effects

- Using 2D sounds for the UI and 3D sounds in the scene

- Modulating the volume of all sounds when they play

- Playing background music while the game is being played

- Fading in and out between different background tunes

Although graphics get most of the attention when it comes to content in video games, audio is crucial, too. Most games play background music and have sound effects. Accordingly, Unity has audio functionality so that you can put sound effects and music into your games. Unity can import and play a variety of audio file formats, adjust the volume of sounds, and even handle sounds playing from a specific position within the scene.

NOTE Audio is handled the same way for both 2D and 3D games. Although the sample project in this chapter is a 3D game, everything we'll do applies to 2D games as well.

This chapter starts off looking at sound effects rather than music. Sound effects are short clips that play along with actions in the game (such as a gunshot that plays when the player fires), whereas the sound clips for music are longer (often running into minutes) and playback isn't directly tied to events in the game. Ultimately, both boil down to the same kind of audio files and playback code, but the simple fact that the sound files for music are usually much larger than the short clips used for sound effects (indeed, files for music are often the largest files in the game!) merits covering them in a separate section.

The complete roadmap for this chapter will be to take a game without sound and do the following:

1 Import audio files for sound effects.
2 Play sound effects for the enemy and for shooting.
3 Program an audio manager to control volume.
4 Optimize the loading of music.
5 Control music volume separately from sound effects, including cross-fading tracks.

NOTE This chapter is largely independent of the project you build; it simply adds audio capabilities on top of an existing game demo. All of the examples in this chapter are built on top of the FPS created in chapter 3, and you could download that sample project, but you're free to use whatever game demo you'd like.

Once you have an existing game demo copied to use for this chapter, you can tackle the first step: importing sound effects.

11.1 Importing sound effects

Before you can play any sounds, you obviously need to import the sound files into your Unity project. First, you'll collect sound clips in the desired file format, and then you'll bring the files into Unity and adjust them for your purposes.

11.1.1 Supported file formats

Much as you saw with art assets in chapter 4, Unity supports a variety of audio formats with different pros and cons. Table 11.1 lists the audio file formats that Unity supports.

Table 11.1   Audio file formats supported by Unity

File type	Pros and cons
WAV	Default audio format on Windows. Uncompressed sound file.
AIF	Default audio format on Mac. Uncompressed sound file.
MP3	Compressed sound file; sacrifices a bit of quality for much smaller files.
OGG	Compressed sound file; sacrifices a bit of quality for much smaller files.
MOD	Music tracker file format. A specialized kind of efficient digital music.
XM	Music tracker file format. A specialized kind of efficient digital music.

The primary consideration differentiating audio files is the compression applied. Compression reduces a file's size but accomplishes that by throwing out a bit of information from the file. Audio compression is clever about only throwing out the least important information so that the compressed sound still sounds good. Nevertheless, it results in a small amount of loss of quality, so you should choose uncompressed audio when the sound clip is short and thus wouldn't be a large file. Longer sound clips (especially music) should use compressed audio, because the audio clip would be prohibitively large otherwise.

Unity adds a small wrinkle to this decision, though.

TIP Although music should be compressed in the final game, Unity can compress the audio after you've imported the file. When developing a game in Unity, you usually want to use uncompressed file formats even for lengthy music, as opposed to importing compressed audio.

How digital audio works

In general, audio files store the waveform that'll be created in the speakers when the sound plays. Sound is a series of waves that travel through the air, and different sounds are made with different sizes and frequencies of sound waves. Audio files record these waves by sampling them repeatedly at short time intervals and saving the state of the wave at each sample.

Recordings that sample waves more frequently get a more accurate recording of them changing over time—the gaps between changes are smaller. But more frequent samples mean more data to save, resulting in a larger file. Compressed sound files reduce the file size through a number of tricks, including tossing out data at sound frequencies that aren't noticeable to listeners.

Music trackers are a special type of sequencer software used to create music. Whereas traditional audio files store the raw waveform for the sound, sequencers store something more akin to sheet music: the tracker file is a sequence of notes, with information like intensity and pitch stored with each note. These "notes" consist of little waveforms, but the total amount of data stored is reduced because the same note is used repeatedly throughout the sequence. Music composed this way can be efficient, but this is a fairly specialized sort of audio.

Because Unity will compress the audio after it's been imported, you should always choose either WAV or AIF file format. You'll probably need to adjust the import settings differently for short sound effects and longer music (in particular, to tell Unity when to apply compression), but the original files should always be uncompressed.

There are various ways to create sound files (appendix B mentions tools like Audacity which can record sounds from a microphone), but for our purposes we'll download sounds from one of the many free sound websites. We're going to use a number of clips downloaded from www.freesound.org/ and get the clips in WAV file format.

> **WARNING** "Free" sounds are offered under a variety of licensing schemes, so always make sure that you're allowed to use the sound clip in the way you intend. For example, many free sounds are for noncommercial use only.

The sample project uses the following public domain sound effects (of course, you can choose to download your own sounds; look for a 0 license listed on the side):

- "thump" by hy96
- "ding" by Daphne_in_Wonderland
- "swish bamboo pole" by ra_gun
- "fireplace" by leosalom

Once you have the sound files to use in your game, the next step is to import the sounds into Unity.

11.1.2 Importing audio files

After gathering some audio files, you need to bring them into Unity. Just as you did with art assets in chapter 4, you have to import audio assets into the project before they can be used in the game.

The mechanics of importing files are simple and are the same as with other assets: drag the files from their location on the computer to the Project view within Unity (create a folder called Sound FX to drag the files into). Well, that was easy! But just like other assets, there are import settings (shown in figure 11.1) to adjust in the Inspector.

Leave Force To Mono unchecked. That refers to mono versus stereo sound; often, sounds are recorded in stereo, where there are actually two waveforms in the file, one each for the left and right ears/speakers. To save on file size, you might want to halve the audio information so that the same waveform is sent to both speakers rather than separate waves sent to the left and right speakers. (There's also a Normalize setting, which only applies when mono is on, so it's greyed out when mono is off.)

Below Force To Mono, there are check boxes for Load In Background and Preload Audio Data. The preload setting relates to balancing playback performance and memory usage; preloading audio will consume memory while the sound waits to be used but will avoid having to wait to load. Thus, you don't want to preload long audio clips, but turn it on for short sound effects like this. Loading audio in the background of the program will allow the program to keep running while the audio is loading; this is generally a good idea for long music clips so that the program doesn't freeze. But this means the audio won't start playing right away; usually you want to keep this setting off for short sound clips to ensure that they load completely before they play. Because the imported clips are short sound effects, you should leave Load In Background unchecked.

Ready the sound by loading it ahead of time and/or behind the scenes while other code is running?

Should stereo sounds be converted to mono?

Select different platforms to apply settings; select Default to apply to all platforms.

Data format to store the (possibly compressed) audio in. Choose PCM or Vorbis.

Load all at once or stream this audio?

Figure 11.1   Import settings for audio files

Finally, the most important settings are Load Type and Compression Format. Compression Format controls the formatting of the audio data that's stored. As discussed in the previous section, music should be compressed, so choose Vorbis (it's the name of a compressed audio format) in that case. Short sound clips don't need to be compressed, so choose PCM (Pulse Code Modulation, the technical term for the raw, sampled sound wave) for these clips. The third setting, ADPCM, is a variation on PCM and occasionally results in slightly better sound quality.

Load Type controls how the data from the file will be loaded by the computer. Because computers have limited memory and audio files can be large, sometimes you want the audio to play while it's streaming into memory, saving the computer from needing to have the entire file loaded. But there's a bit of computing overhead when streaming audio like this, so audio plays fastest when it's loaded into memory first. Even then, you can choose whether the loaded audio data will be in compressed form or will be decompressed for faster playback. Because these sound clips are short, they don't need to stream and can be set to Decompress On Load.

The last setting is Sample Rate; leave that at Preserve Sample Rate so Unity won't change the samples in the imported file. At this point, the sound effects are all imported and ready to use.

11.2 Playing sound effects

Now that you have some sound files added to the project, you naturally want to play the sounds. The code for triggering sound effects isn't terribly hard to understand, but the audio system in Unity does have a number of parts that must work in concert.

11.2.1 Explaining what's involved: Audio Clip vs. Source vs. Listener

Although you might expect playing a sound to be simply a matter of telling Unity which clip to play, it turns out that you must define three different parts in order to play sounds in Unity: `AudioClip`, `AudioSource`, and `AudioListener`. The reason for breaking the sound system into multiple components has to do with Unity's support for 3D sounds: The different components tell Unity positional information that it uses for manipulating 3D sounds.

> **2D vs. 3D sound**
>
> Sounds in games can be either 2D or 3D. 2D sounds are what you're already familiar with: standard audio that plays normally. The moniker "2D sound" mostly means "not 3D sound."
>
> 3D sounds are specific to 3D simulations and may not already be familiar to you; these are sounds that have a specific location within the simulation. Their volume and pitch are influenced by the movement of the listener. A sound effect triggered in the distance will sound very faint, for example.
>
> Unity supports both kinds of audio, and you decide if an audio source should play audio as 2D sounds or 3D sounds. Things like music should be 2D sounds, but using 3D sounds for most sound effects will create immersive audio in the scene.

As an analogy, imagine a room in the real world. The room has a stereo playing a CD. If a man comes into the room, he hears it clearly. When he leaves the room, he hears it less clearly, and eventually not at all. Similarly, if we move the stereo around the room, he'll hear the music changing volume as it moves. As figure 11.2 illustrates, in this analogy the CD is an `AudioClip`, the stereo is an `AudioSource`, and the man is the `AudioListener`.

Figure 11.2 Diagram of the three things you control in Unity's audio system

The first of the three different parts is an *audio clip*. That refers to the sound file that we imported in the last section. This raw waveform data is the foundation for everything else the audio system does, but audio clips don't do anything by themselves.

The next kind of object is an *audio source*. This is the object that plays audio clips. This is an abstraction over what the audio system is actually doing, but it's a useful abstraction that makes 3D sounds easier to understand. A 3D sound played from a specific audio source is located at the position of that audio source; 2D sounds must also be played from an audio source, but the location doesn't matter.

The third kind of object involved in Unity's audio system is an *audio listener*. As the name implies, this is the object that hears sounds projected from the audio sources. This is another abstraction on top of what the audio system is doing (obviously the actual listener is the player of the game!), but—much like how the position of the audio source gives the position that the sound is projected from—the position of the audio listener gives the position that the sound is heard from.

Advanced sound control using Audio Mixers

Audio Mixers were added in Unity 5. Rather than playing audio clips directly, audio mixers enable you to process audio signals and apply various effects to your clips. Learn more about AudioMixer in Unity's documentation. You can watch this tutorial video, for example: http://mng.bz/Mlp3.

Although both audio clips and `AudioSource` components have to be assigned, an `AudioListener` component is already on the default camera when you create a new scene. Typically, you want 3D sounds to react to the position of the viewer.

11.2.2 Assigning a looping sound

All right, now let's set our first sound in Unity! The audio clips were already imported, and the default camera has an `AudioListener` component, so we only need to assign an `AudioSource` component. We're going to put a crackling fire sound on the Enemy prefab, the enemy character that wanders around.

> **NOTE**   Because the enemy will sound like it's on fire, you might want to give it a particle system so that it looks like it's on fire. You can copy over the particle system created in chapter 4 by making the particle object into a prefab and then choosing Export Package from the Asset menu. Alternatively, you could redo the steps from chapter 4 here to create a new particle object from scratch (drag the Enemy prefab into the scene to edit it and then choose GameObject > Apply Changes To Prefab).

Usually, you need to drag a prefab into the scene in order to edit it, but you can edit the prefab asset directly when you're just adding a component onto the object. Select the Enemy prefab so that its properties appear in the Inspector. Now add a new component; choose Audio > Audio Source. An `AudioSource` component will appear in the Inspector.

Tell the audio source what sound clip to play. Drag an audio file from the Project view up to the Audio Clip slot in the Inspector; we're going to use the "fireplace" sound effect for this example (refer to figure 11.3).

Figure 11.3 Settings for the `AudioSource` component

Skip down a bit in the settings and select both Play On Awake and Looping (of course, make sure that Mute isn't checked). Play On Awake tells the audio source to begin playing as soon as the scene starts (in the next section, you'll learn how to trigger sounds manually while the scene is running). Looping tells the audio source to keep playing continuously, repeating the audio clip when playback is over.

You want this audio source to project 3D sounds. As explained earlier, 3D sounds have a distinct position within the scene. That aspect of the audio source is adjusted using the Spatial Blend setting. That setting is a slider between 2D and 3D; set it to 3D for this audio source.

Now play the game and make sure your speakers are turned on. You can hear a crackling fire coming from the enemy, and the sound becomes faint if you move away because you used a 3D audio source.

11.2.3 *Triggering sound effects from code*

Setting the `AudioSource` component to play automatically is handy for some looping sounds, but for the majority of sound effects you'll want to trigger the sound with code commands. That approach still requires an `AudioSource` component, but now the audio source will only play sound clips when told to by the program, instead of automatically all the time.

Add an `AudioSource` component to the player object (not the camera object). You don't have to link in a specific audio clip because the audio clips will be defined in code. You can turn off Play On Awake because sounds from this source will be triggered in code. Also, adjust Spatial Blend to 3D because this sound is located in the scene.

Now make the additions shown in the next listing to `RayShooter`, the script that handles shooting.

Listing 11.1 Sound effects added in the `RayShooter` script

```
...
[SerializeField] private AudioSource soundSource;
[SerializeField] private AudioClip hitWallSound;       References the two sound
[SerializeField] private AudioClip hitEnemySound;      files you want to play
...
                        If target is not null, the player has hit an enemy, so ...
if (target != null) {
    target.ReactToHit();                          ... call PlayOneShot() to play
    soundSource.PlayOneShot(hitEnemySound);       the Hit An Enemy sound, or ...
} else {
    StartCoroutine(SphereIndicator(hit.point));   ... call PlayOneShot() to play the Hit
    soundSource.PlayOneShot(hitWallSound);        A Wall sound if the player missed.
}
...
```

The new code includes several serialized variables at the top of the script. Drag the player object (the object with an `AudioSource` component) to the `soundSource` slot in the Inspector. Then drag the audio clips to play onto the sound slots; "swish" is for hitting the wall and "ding" is for hitting the enemy.

The other two lines added are `PlayOneShot()` methods. That method causes an audio source to play a given audio clip. Add those methods inside the `target` conditional in order to play sounds when different objects are hit.

> **NOTE** You could set the clip in the `AudioSource` and call `Play()` to play the clip. Multiple sounds would cut each other off, though, so we used `PlayOneShot()` instead. Replace `PlayOneShot()` with this code and shoot a bunch rapidly to see (er, hear) the problem:
>
> ```
> soundSource.clip=hitEnemySound; soundSource.Play();
> ```

All right, play the game and shoot around. You now have several different sound effects in the game. These same basic steps can be used to add all sorts of sound effects. A robust sound system in a game requires a lot more than a bunch of disconnected sounds, though; at a minimum, all games should offer volume control. You'll implement that control next through a central audio module.

11.3 *Audio control interface*

Continuing the code architecture established in previous chapters, you're going to create an `AudioManager`. Recall that the `Managers` object has a master list of the various code modules used by the game, such as a manager for the player's inventory. This time, you'll create an audio manager to stick into the list. This central audio module will allow you to modulate the volume of audio in the game and even mute it. Initially, you'll only worry about sound effects, but in later sections you'll extend the `AudioManager` to handle music as well.

11.3.1 Setting up the central AudioManager

The first step in setting up AudioManager is to put in place the Managers code framework. From the chapter 10 project, copy over IGameManager, ManagerStatus, and NetworkService; we won't change them. (Remember that IGameManager is the interface that all managers must implement, whereas ManagerStatus is an enum that IGameManager uses. NetworkService provides calls to the internet and won't be used in this chapter.)

> **NOTE** Unity will probably issue a warning because NetworkService is assigned but not used. You can ignore Unity's warning; we want to enable the code framework to access the internet, even though we don't use that functionality in this chapter.

Also copy over the Managers file, which will be adjusted for the new AudioManager. Leave it be for now (or comment out the erroneous sections if the sight of compiler errors drives you crazy!). Create a new script called AudioManager that the Managers code can refer to.

Listing 11.2 Skeleton code for `AudioManager`

```
using UnityEngine;
using System.Collections;
using System.Collections.Generic;

public class AudioManager : MonoBehaviour, IGameManager {
   public ManagerStatus status {get; private set;}

   private NetworkService _network;

   // Add volume controls here (listing 11.4)

   public void Startup(NetworkService service) {
      Debug.Log("Audio manager starting...");

      _network = service;

      // Initialize music sources here (listing 11.11)      ← Any long-running
                                                              startup tasks go here

      status = ManagerStatus.Started;      ← Set status to Initializing if there are
   }                                          long-running startup tasks.
}
```

This initial code looks like managers from previous chapters; this is the minimum amount that IGameManager requires the class to implement. The Managers script can now be adjusted with the new manager.

Listing 11.3 Managers script adjusted with `AudioManager`

```
using UnityEngine;
using System.Collections;
```

```
using System.Collections.Generic;

[RequireComponent(typeof(AudioManager))]

public class Managers : MonoBehaviour {
    public static AudioManager Audio {get; private set;}

    private List<IGameManager> _startSequence;

    void Awake() {
        Audio = GetComponent<AudioManager>();
```

Only list **AudioManager** in this project, instead of **PlayerManager**, and so on.

```
        _startSequence = new List<IGameManager>();
        _startSequence.Add(Audio);

        StartCoroutine(StartupManagers());
    }

    private IEnumerator StartupManagers() {
        NetworkService network = new NetworkService();

        foreach (IGameManager manager in _startSequence) {
            manager.Startup(network);
        }

        yield return null;

        int numModules = _startSequence.Count;
        int numReady = 0;

        while (numReady < numModules) {
            int lastReady = numReady;
            numReady = 0;

            foreach (IGameManager manager in _startSequence) {
                if (manager.status == ManagerStatus.Started) {
                    numReady++;
                }
            }

            if (numReady > lastReady)
                Debug.Log("Progress: " + numReady + "/" + numModules);

            yield return null;
        }

        Debug.Log("All managers started up");
    }
}
```

As you have in previous chapters, create the Game Managers object in the scene and then attach both Managers and AudioManager to the empty object. Playing the game will show the managers' startup messages in the console, but the audio manager doesn't do anything yet.

11.3.2 *Volume control UI*

With the bare-bones `AudioManager` set up, it's time to give it volume control function-ality. These volume control methods will then be used by UI displays in order to mute the sound effects or adjust the volume.

You'll use the new UI tools that were the focus of chapter 7. Specifically, you're going to create a pop-up window with a button and a slider to control volume settings (see figure 11.4). I'll list the steps involved without going into detail; if you need a refresher, refer to chapter 7:

1. Import popup.png as a sprite (set Texture Type to Sprite).
2. In Sprite Editor, set a 12-pixel border on all sides (remember to apply changes).
3. Create a canvas in the scene (GameObject > UI > Canvas).
4. Turn on the Pixel Perfect setting for the canvas.
5. (Optional) Name the object `HUD Canvas` and switch to 2D view mode.
6. Create an image connected to that canvas (GameObject > UI > Image).
7. Name the new object `Settings Popup`.
8. Assign the `popup` sprite to the image's Source Image.
9. Set Image Type to Sliced and turn on Fill Center.
10. Position the pop-up image at 0, 0 to center it.
11. Scale the pop-up to 250 width and 150 height.
12. Create a button (GameObject > UI > Button).
13. Parent the button to the pop-up (drag it in the Hierarchy).
14. Position the button at 0, 40.
15. Expand the button's hierarchy in order to select its text label.
16. Change the text to say `Toggle Sound`.
17. Create a slider (GameObject > UI > Slider).
18. Parent the slider to the pop-up and position it at 0, 15.
19. Set the slider's Value (at the bottom of the Inspector) to 1.

Figure 11.4   UI display for mute and volume control

Those were all the steps to create the settings pop-up! Now that the pop-up has been created, let's write code that it'll work with. This will involve both a script on the pop-up object itself, as well as the volume control functionality that the pop-up script calls. First, adjust the code in AudioManager according to this listing.

Listing 11.4   Volume control added to AudioManager

```
...
public float soundVolume {                    Property with getter and setter for volume
   get {return AudioListener.volume;}
   set {AudioListener.volume = value;}        Implement the getter/setter
}                                              using AudioListener.

public bool soundMute {                        Add a similar property to mute.
   get {return AudioListener.pause;}
   set {AudioListener.pause = value;}
}
                                               Italicized code was already in
                                               script, shown here for reference.
public void Startup(NetworkService service) {
   Debug.Log("Audio manager starting...");

   _network = service;
                                               Initialize the value (0 to 1
   soundVolume = 1f;                           range; 1 is full volume).

   status = ManagerStatus.Started;
}
...
```

Properties for soundVolume and soundMute were added to AudioManager. For both properties, the get and set functions were implemented using global values on Audio-Listener. The AudioListener class can modulate the volume of all sounds received by all AudioListener instances. Setting AudioManager's soundVolume property has the same effect as setting the volume on AudioListener. The advantage here is encapsulation: everything having to do with audio is being handled in a single manager, without code outside the manager needing to know the details of the implementation.

With those methods added to AudioManager, you can now write a script for the pop-up. Create a script called SettingsPopup and add the contents of this listing.

Listing 11.5   SettingsPopup script with controls for adjusting the volume

```
using UnityEngine;
using System.Collections;

public class SettingsPopup : MonoBehaviour {        Button will toggle the mute
                                                    property of AudioManager.
   public void OnSoundToggle() {
      Managers.Audio.soundMute = !Managers.Audio.soundMute;
   }

   public void OnSoundValue(float volume) {         Slider will adjust the volume
      Managers.Audio.soundVolume = volume;          property of AudioManager.
   }
}
```

This script has two methods that affect the properties of AudioManager: OnSoundToggle() sets the soundMute property, and OnSoundValue() sets the soundVolume property. As usual, link in the SettingsPopup script by dragging it onto the Settings Popup object in the UI.

Then, in order to call the functions from the button and slider, link the pop-up object to interaction events in those controls. In the Inspector for the button, look for the panel labeled OnClick. Click the + button to add a new entry to this event. Drag Settings Popup to the object slot in the new entry and then look for SettingsPopup in the menu; select OnSoundToggle() to make the button call that function.

The method used to link the function applies to the slider as well. First look for the interaction event in a panel of the slider's settings; in this case, the panel is called OnValueChanged. Click the + button to add a new entry and then drag Settings Popup to the object slot. In the function menu, find the SettingsPopup script and then choose OnSoundValue() under Dynamic Float.

> **WARNING** Remember to choose the function under Dynamic Float and not Static Parameter! Although the method appears in both sections of the list, in the latter case it will only receive a single value typed in ahead of time.

The settings controls are now working, but there's one more script we need to address —the pop-up is currently always covering up the screen. A simple fix is to make the pop-up only open when you press the M key. Create a new script called UIController, link that script to the Controller object in the scene, and write this code.

Listing 11.6 `UIController` that toggles the settings pop-up

```
using UnityEngine;
using System.Collections;

public class UIController : MonoBehaviour {          References pop-up
    [SerializeField] private SettingsPopup popup;    object in scene

    void Start() {                                   Initializes hidden pop-up
        popup.gameObject.SetActive(false);
    }

    void Update() {                                  Toggles pop-up with the M key
        if (Input.GetKeyDown(KeyCode.M)) {
            bool isShowing = popup.gameObject.activeSelf;
            popup.gameObject.SetActive(!isShowing);

            if (isShowing) {
                Cursor.lockState = CursorLockMode.Locked;
                Cursor.visible = false;              Also toggles
            } else {                                 cursor along with
                Cursor.lockState = CursorLockMode.None;    pop-up
                Cursor.visible = true;
            }
        }
    }
}
```

To wire up this object reference, drag the settings pop-up to the slot on this script. Play now and try changing the slider (remember to activate the UI by pressing the M key) while shooting around to hear the sound effects; you'll hear the sound effects change volume according to the slider.

11.3.3 *Playing UI sounds*

You're going to make another addition to `AudioManager` now to allow the UI to play sounds when buttons are clicked. This task is more involved than it seems at first, owing to Unity's need for an `AudioSource`. When sound effects were issued from objects in the scene, it was fairly obvious where to attach the `AudioSource`. But UI sound effects aren't part of the scene, so you'll set up a special `AudioSource` for `AudioManager` to use when there isn't any other audio source.

Create a new empty `GameObject` and parent it to the main `Game Managers` object; this new object is going to have an `AudioSource` used by `AudioManager`, so call the new object `Audio`. Add an `AudioSource` component to this object (leave the Spatial Blend setting at 2D this time, because the UI doesn't have a specific position in the scene) and then add this code to use this source in `AudioManager`.

Listing 11.7   **Play sound effects in** `AudioManager`

```
...
[SerializeField] private AudioSource soundSource;
...
public void PlaySound(AudioClip clip) {
    soundSource.PlayOneShot(clip);
}
...
```

Variable slot in the Inspector to reference the new audio source

Play sounds that don't have any other source.

A new variable slot will appear in the Inspector; drag the `Audio` object onto this slot. Now add the UI sound effect to the pop-up script.

Listing 11.8   **Adding sound effects to** `SettingsPopup`

```
...
[SerializeField] private AudioClip sound;
...
public void OnSoundToggle() {
    Managers.Audio.soundMute = !Managers.Audio.soundMute;
    Managers.Audio.PlaySound(sound);
}
...
```

Inspector slot to reference the sound clip

Play the sound effect when the button is pressed.

Drag the UI sound effect onto the variable slot; I used the 2D sound "thump." When you press the UI button, that sound effect plays at the same time (when the sound isn't muted, of course!). Even though the UI doesn't have an audio source itself, `AudioManager` has an audio source that plays the sound effect.

Great, we've set up all our sound effects! Now let's turn our attention to music.

11.4 *Background music*

You're going to add background music to the game, and you'll do that by adding music to `AudioManager`. As explained in the chapter introduction, music clips aren't fundamentally different from sound effects. The way digital audio functions through waveforms is the same, and the commands for playing the audio are largely the same. The main difference is the length of the audio, but that difference cascades out into a number of consequences.

For starters, music tracks tend to consume a large amount of memory on the computer, and that memory consumption must be optimized. You must watch out for two areas of memory issues: having the music loaded into memory before it's needed, and consuming too much memory when loaded.

Optimizing *when* music loads is done using the `Resources.Load()` command introduced in chapter 9. As you learned, this command allows you to load assets by name; though that's certainly one handy feature, that's not the only reason to load assets from the Resources folder. Another key consideration is delaying loading: normally Unity loads all assets in a scene as soon as the scene loads, but assets from Resources aren't loaded until the code manually fetches them. In this case, we want to *lazy-load* the audio clips for music. Otherwise, the music could consume a lot of memory even when it isn't being used.

> **DEFINITION** *Lazy-loading* is when a file isn't loaded ahead of time but rather is delayed until it's needed. Typically, data responds faster (for example, the sound plays immediately) if it's loaded in advance of use, but lazy-loading can save a lot of memory when responsiveness doesn't matter as much.

The second memory consideration is dealt with by streaming music off the disc. As explained in section 11.1.2, streaming the audio saves the computer from ever needing to have the entire file loaded at once. The style of loading was a setting in the Inspector of the imported audio clip.

Ultimately, there are several steps to go through for playing background music, including steps to cover these memory optimizations.

11.4.1 *Playing music loops*

The process of playing music involves the same series of steps as UI sound effects did (background music is also 2D sound without a source within the scene), so we're going to go through all those steps again:

1 Import audio clips.
2 Set up an `AudioSource` for `AudioManager` to use.
3 Write code to play the audio clips in `AudioManager`.
4 Add music controls to the UI.

Each step will be modified slightly to work with music instead of sound effects. Let's look at the first step.

STEP 1: IMPORT AUDIO CLIPS

Obtain some music by downloading or recording tracks. For the sample project, I went to www.freesound.org/ and downloaded the following public domain music loops:

- "loop" by Xythe/Ville Nousiainen
- "Intro Synth" by noirenex

Drag the files into Unity to import them and then adjust their import settings in the Inspector. As explained earlier, audio clips for music generally have different settings than audio clips for sound effects. First, the audio format should be set to Vorbis, for compressed audio. Remember, compressed audio will have a significantly smaller file size. Compression also degrades the audio quality slightly, but that slight degradation is an acceptable trade-off for long music clips; set Quality to 50% in the slider that appears.

The next import setting to adjust is Load Type. Again, music should stream from the disc rather than being loaded completely. Choose Streaming from the Load Type menu. Similarly, turn on Load In Background so that the game won't pause or slow down while music is loading.

Even after you adjust all the import settings, the asset files must be moved to the correct location in order to load correctly. Remember that the `Resources.Load()` command requires the assets to be in the Resources folder. Create a new folder called Resources, create a folder within that called Music, and drag the audio files into the Music folder (see figure 11.5).

Figure 11.5   Music audio clips placed inside the Resources folder

That took care of step number 1.

STEP 2: SET UP AN AUDIOSOURCE FOR AUDIOMANAGER TO USE

Step 2 is to create a new `AudioSource` for music playback. Create another empty `Game-Object`, name this object `Music 1` (instead of `Music` because we'll add `Music 2` later in the chapter), and parent it to the Audio object.

Add an `AudioSource` component to `Music 1` and then adjust the settings in the component. Deselect Play On Awake but turn on the Loop option this time; whereas sound effects usually only play once, music plays over and over in a loop. Leave the Spatial Blend setting at 2D, because music doesn't have any specific position in the scene.

You may want to reduce the Priority value, too. For sound effects, this value didn't matter, so we left the value at the default `128`. But for music you probably want to lower this value, so I set the music source to 60. This value tells Unity which sounds are most important when layering multiple sounds; somewhat counterintuitively, lower values are higher priority. When too many sounds are playing simultaneously, the audio system will start discarding sounds; by making music higher priority than sound effects, you ensure the music will keep playing when too many sound effects trigger at the same time.

STEP 3: WRITE CODE TO PLAY THE AUDIO CLIPS IN AUDIOMANAGER

The Music audio source has been set up, so add the next code shown to AudioManager.

Listing 11.9   Playing music in AudioManager

```
...
[SerializeField] private AudioSource music1Source;

[SerializeField] private string introBGMusic;        Write music names in these strings.
[SerializeField] private string levelBGMusic;
...
public void PlayIntroMusic() {                        Load intro music from Resources.
   PlayMusic(Resources.Load("Music/"+introBGMusic) as AudioClip);
}
public void PlayLevelMusic() {                        Load main music from Resources.
   PlayMusic(Resources.Load("Music/"+levelBGMusic) as AudioClip);
}

private void PlayMusic(AudioClip clip) {              Play music by setting AudioSource.clip.
   music1Source.clip = clip;
   music1Source.Play();
}

public void StopMusic() {
   music1Source.Stop();
}
...
```

As usual, the new serialized variables will be visible in the Inspector when you select the Game Managers object. Drag Music 1 into the audio source slot. Then type in the names of the music files in the two string variables: intro-synth and loop.

The remainder of the added code calls commands for loading and playing music (or, in the last added method, stopping the music). The Resources.Load() command loads the named asset from the Resources folder (taking into account that the files are placed in the Music subfolder within Resources). A generic object is returned by that command, but the object can be converted to a more specific type (in this case, an AudioClip) using the as keyword.

The loaded audio clip is then passed into the PlayMusic() method. This function sets the clip in the AudioSource and then calls Play(). As I explained earlier, sound effects are better implemented using PlayOneShot(), but setting the clip in the Audio-Source is a more robust approach for music, allowing you to stop or pause the playing music.

STEP 4: ADD MUSIC CONTROLS TO THE UI

The new music playback methods in AudioManager won't do anything unless they're called from elsewhere. Let's add more buttons to the audio UI that will play different music when pressed. Here are the steps again enumerated with little explanation (refer to chapter 7 if needed):

1 Change the pop-up's width to 350 (to fit more buttons).
2 Create a new UI button and parent it to the pop-up.
3 Set the button's width to 100 and position to 0, -20.
4 Expand the button's hierarchy to select the text label and set that to Level Music.
5 Repeat these steps twice more to create two additional buttons.
6 Position one at -105, -20 and the other at 105, -20 (so they appear on either side).
7 Change the first text label to Intro Music and the last text label to No Music.

Now the pop-up has three buttons for playing different music. Write a method in SettingsPopup that will be linked to each button.

Listing 11.10 Adding music controls to SettingsPopup

```
...
public void OnPlayMusic(int selector) {        ◄──── This method gets a number
    Managers.Audio.PlaySound(sound);                 parameter from the button.

    switch (selector) {                        ◄──── Call a different music function in
    case 1:                                          AudioManager for each button.
        Managers.Audio.PlayIntroMusic();
        break;
    case 2:
        Managers.Audio.PlayLevelMusic();
        break;
    default:
        Managers.Audio.StopMusic();
        break;
    }
}
...
```

Note that the function takes an int parameter this time; normally button methods don't have a parameter and are simply triggered by the button. In this case, we need to distinguish between the three buttons, so the buttons will each send a different number.

Go through the typical steps to connect a button to this code: add an entry to the OnClick panel in the Inspector, drag the pop-up to the object slot, and choose the appropriate function from the menu. This time, there will be a text box for typing in a number, because OnPlayMusic() takes a number for a parameter. Type 1 for Intro Music, 2 for Level Music, and anything else for No Music (I went with 0). The switch statement in OnMusic() plays intro music or level music, depending on the number, or stops the music as a default if the number isn't 1 or 2.

When you press the music buttons while the game is playing, you'll hear the music. Great! The code is loading the audio clips from the Resources folder. Music plays efficiently, although there are still two bits of polish we'll add: separate music volume control and cross-fading when changing the music.

11.4.2 *Controlling music volume separately*

The game already has volume control, and currently that affects the music, too. Most games have separate volume controls for sound effects and music, though, so let's tackle that now.

The first step is to tell the music `AudioSource` to ignore the settings on `AudioListener`. We want volume and mute on the global `AudioListener` to continue to affect all sound effects, but we don't want this volume to apply to music. Listing 11.10 includes code to tell the music source to ignore the volume on `AudioListener`. The code in the following listing also adds volume control and mute for music, so add it to `AudioManager`.

> **Listing 11.11   Controlling music volume separately in `AudioManager`**

```
...
private float _musicVolume;          ◄———  Private variable that won't be accessed
public float musicVolume {                 directly, only through the property's getter.
   get {
      return _musicVolume;
   }
   set {
      _musicVolume = value;
                                                        Adjust volume of the
      if (music1Source != null) {          ◄———       AudioSource directly.
         music1Source.volume = _musicVolume;
      }
   }
}
...
public bool musicMute {
   get {
      if (music1Source != null) {
         return music1Source.mute;
      }
      return false;                  ◄———  Default value in case the
   }                                        AudioSource is missing
   set {
      if (music1Source != null) {
         music1Source.mute = value;
      }
   }
}
                                                    Italicized code was already in
}                                                   script, shown here for reference.
public void Startup(NetworkService service) {   ◄———
   Debug.Log("Audio manager starting...");

   _network = service;
```

```
music1Source.ignoreListenerVolume = true;        These properties tell the AudioSource to
music1Source.ignoreListenerPause = true;          ignore the AudioListener volume.

soundVolume = 1f;
musicVolume = 1f;

status = ManagerStatus.Started;                    Italicized code was already in script,
}                                                   shown here for reference.
...
```

The key to this code is realizing you can adjust the volume of an `AudioSource` directly, even though that audio source is ignoring the global volume defined in `AudioListener`. There are properties for both volume and mute that manipulate the individual music source.

The `Startup()` method initializes the music source with both `ignoreListenerVolume` and `ignoreListenerPause` turned on. As the names suggest, those properties cause the audio source to ignore the global volume setting on `AudioListener`.

You can click Play now to verify that the music is no longer affected by the existing volume control. Let's add a second UI control for the music volume; start by adjusting `SettingsPopup`.

> **Listing 11.12 Music volume controls in `SettingsPopup`**

```
...
public void OnMusicToggle() {
    Managers.Audio.musicMute = !Managers.Audio.musicMute;      Repeat the mute
    Managers.Audio.PlaySound(sound);                            control, only use
}                                                               musicMute instead.

public void OnMusicValue(float volume) {
    Managers.Audio.musicVolume = volume;                       Repeat the volume control, only
}                                                               use musicVolume instead.
...
```

There's not a lot to explain about this code—it's mostly repeating the sound volume controls. Obviously the `AudioManager` properties used have changed from `soundMute`/ `soundVolume` to `musicMute`/`musicVolume`.

In the editor, create a button and slider, as you did before. Here are those steps again:

1 Change the pop-up's height to 225 (to fit more controls).
2 Create a UI button.
3 Parent the button to the pop-up.
4 Position the button at 0, -60.
5 Expand the button's hierarchy in order to select its text label.
6 Change the text to `Toggle Music`.
7 Create a slider (from the same UI menu).
8 Parent the slider to the pop-up and position it at 0, -85.
9 Set the slider's Value (at the bottom of the Inspector) to 1.

Link these UI controls to the code in `SettingsPopup`. Find the `OnClick/OnValue-Changed` panel in the UI element's settings, click the + button to add an entry, drag the pop-up object to the object slot, and select the function from the menu. The functions you need to pick are `OnMusicToggle()` and `OnMusicValue()` from the Dynamic Float section of the menu.

Run this code and you'll see that the controls affect sound effects and music separately. This is getting pretty sophisticated, but there's one more bit of polish remaining: cross-fade between music tracks.

11.4.3 Fading between songs

As a final bit of polish, let's make `AudioManager` fade in and out between different background tunes. Currently, the switch between different music tracks is pretty jarring, with the sound suddenly cutting off and changing to the new track. We can smooth out that transition by having the volume of the previous track quickly dwindle away while the volume quickly rises from 0 on the new track. This is a simple but clever bit of code that combines both the volume control methods you just saw, along with a coroutine to change the volume incrementally over time.

Listing 11.13 adds a lot of bits to `AudioManager`, but most revolve around a simple concept: Now that we'll have two separate audio sources, play separate music tracks on separate audio sources, and incrementally increase the volume of one source while simultaneously decreasing the volume of the other. (As usual, italicized code was already in the script and is shown here for reference.)

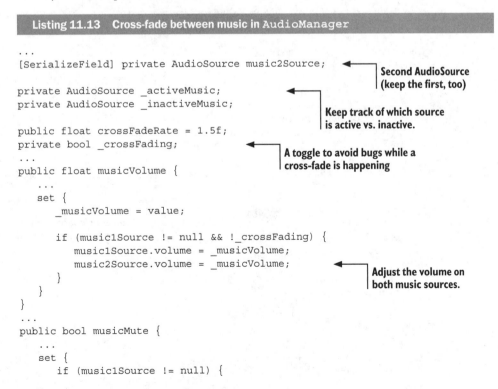

Listing 11.13 Cross-fade between music in `AudioManager`

```
...
[SerializeField] private AudioSource music2Source;          Second AudioSource
                                                            (keep the first, too)
private AudioSource _activeMusic;
private AudioSource _inactiveMusic;
                                                    Keep track of which source
                                                    is active vs. inactive.
public float crossFadeRate = 1.5f;
private bool _crossFading;                           A toggle to avoid bugs while a
...                                                  cross-fade is happening
public float musicVolume {
    ...
    set {
        _musicVolume = value;

        if (music1Source != null && !_crossFading) {
            music1Source.volume = _musicVolume;
            music2Source.volume = _musicVolume;      Adjust the volume on
        }                                            both music sources.
    }
}
...
public bool musicMute {
    ...
    set {
        if (music1Source != null) {
```

```
            music1Source.mute = value;
            music2Source.mute = value;
        }
    }
}

public void Startup(NetworkService service) {
    Debug.Log("Audio manager starting...");

    _network = service;

    music1Source.ignoreListenerVolume = true;
    music2Source.ignoreListenerVolume = true;
    music1Source.ignoreListenerPause = true;
    music2Source.ignoreListenerPause = true;

    soundVolume = 1f;
    musicVolume = 1f;
```

◄── **Initialize one as the active AudioSource.**

```
    _activeMusic = music1Source;
    _inactiveMusic = music2Source;

    status = ManagerStatus.Started;
}
...
private void PlayMusic(AudioClip clip) {
    if (_crossFading) {return;}
    StartCoroutine(CrossFadeMusic(clip));
}
```

◄── **Call a coroutine when changing music.**

```
private IEnumerator CrossFadeMusic(AudioClip clip) {
    _crossFading = true;

    _inactiveMusic.clip = clip;
    _inactiveMusic.volume = 0;
    _inactiveMusic.Play();

    float scaledRate = crossFadeRate * _musicVolume;
    while (_activeMusic.volume > 0) {
        _activeMusic.volume -= scaledRate * Time.deltaTime;
        _inactiveMusic.volume += scaledRate * Time.deltaTime;

        yield return null;
    }
```

◄─── **Yield statement pauses for one frame**

```
    AudioSource temp = _activeMusic;
```

◄── **Temporary variable to use while swapping _active and _inactive**

```
    _activeMusic = _inactiveMusic;
    _activeMusic.volume = _musicVolume;

    _inactiveMusic = temp;
    _inactiveMusic.Stop();

    _crossFading = false;
}

public void StopMusic() {
    _activeMusic.Stop();
```

```
    _inactiveMusic.Stop();
}
...
```

The first addition is a variable for the second music source. While keeping the first AudioSource object, duplicate that object (make sure the settings are the same—select Loop) and then drag the new object into this Inspector slot. The code also defines the AudioSource variables active and inactive, but those are private variables used within the code and not exposed in the Inspector. Specifically, those variables define which of the two audio sources is considered active or inactive at any given time.

The code now calls a coroutine when playing new music. This coroutine sets the new music playing on one AudioSource while the old music keeps playing on the old audio source. Then, the coroutine incrementally increases the volume of the new music while incrementally decreasing the volume of the old music. Once the cross-fading is complete (that is, the volumes have completely exchanged places), the function swaps which audio source is considered active and inactive.

Great! We've completed the background music for our game's audio system.

FMOD: a tool for game audio

The audio system in Unity is powered by FMOD, a popular audio programming library. The library is available at www.fmod.org/, but it's already integrated into Unity. Unity has many features of FMOD integrated, although it lacks the library's most advanced features (you can visit the website to learn about those features).

Such advanced audio features are offered through FMOD Studio (a plug-in that adds more functionality to Unity), but the examples in this chapter stuck to the functionality built into Unity. That core functionality comprises the most important features for a game's audio system. Most game developers have their audio needs served quite well by this core functionality, but the plug-in is useful for those wishing to get even more intricate with their game's audio.

Summary

- Sound effects should be uncompressed audio and music should be compressed, but use the WAV format for both because Unity applies compression to imported audio.
- Audio clips can be 2D sounds that always play the same, or 3D sounds that react to the listener's position.
- The volume of sound effects is easily adjusted globally using Unity's AudioListener.
- You can set the volume on individual audio sources that play music.
- You can fade background music in and out by setting the volume on individual audio sources.

Putting the parts together
into a complete game

This chapter covers

- Assembling objects and code from other projects
- Programming point-and-click controls
- Upgrading the UI from the old to a new system
- Loading new levels in response to objectives
- Setting up win/loss conditions
- Saving and loading the player's progress

The project in this chapter will tie together everything from previous chapters. Most chapters have been pretty self-contained, and there hasn't been an end-to-end look at the entire game. I'll walk you through pulling together pieces that have been introduced separately so that you know how to build a complete game out of all the pieces. I'll also discuss the encompassing structure of the game, including switching levels and ending the game (displaying "Game Over" when you die, and "Success" when you reach the exit). And I'll show you how to save the game, because saving the player's progress becomes increasingly important as the game grows in size.

WARNING   Much of this chapter will use tasks that were explained in detail in previous chapters, so I'll move through the steps quickly. If certain steps confuse you, refer to the relevant chapter (for example, chapter 7 about the UI) for a more detailed explanation.

This chapter's project is a demo of an action RPG. In this sort of game, the camera is placed high and looks down sharply (see figure 12.1), and the character is controlled by clicking the mouse where you want to go; you may be familiar with the game *Diablo*, which is an action RPG like this. I'm switching to yet another game genre so that we can squeeze in one more genre before the end of the book!

Figure 12.1   Screenshot of the top-down viewpoint

In full, the project in this chapter will be the biggest game yet. It'll feature:

- A top-down view with point-and-click movement
- The ability to click devices to operate them
- Scattered items you can collect
- Inventory that's displayed in a UI window
- Enemies wandering around the level
- The ability to save the game and restore your progress
- Three levels that must be completed in sequence

Whew, that's a lot to pack in; good thing this is almost the last chapter!

12.1   *Building an action RPG by repurposing projects*

We'll develop the action RPG demo by building on the project from chapter 9. Copy that project's folder and open the copy in Unity to start working. Or, if you skipped directly to this chapter, download the sample project for chapter 9 in order to build on that.

The reason we're building on the chapter 9 project is that it's the closest to our goal for this chapter and thus will require the least modification (compared to other projects). Ultimately, we'll pull together assets from several chapters, so technically it's not that different than if we started with one of those projects and pulled in assets from chapter 9.

Here's a recap of what's in the project from chapter 9:

- A character with an animation controller already set up
- A third-person camera that follows the character around
- A level with floors, walls, and ramps
- Lights and shadows all placed
- Operable devices, including a color-changing monitor
- Collectible inventory items
- Backend managers code framework

This hefty list of features covers quite a bit of the action in the RPG demo already, but there's a bit more that we'll either need to modify or add.

12.1.1 Assembling assets and code from multiple projects

The first two modifications will be to update the managers framework and to bring in computer-controlled enemies. For the former task, recall that updates to the framework were made in chapter 10, which means those updates aren't in the project from chapter 9. For the latter task, recall that you programmed an enemy in chapter 3.

UPDATING THE MANAGERS FRAMEWORK

Updating the managers is a fairly simple task, so let's get that out of the way first. The `IGameManager` interface was modified in chapter 10.

Listing 12.1 Adjusted `IGameManager`

```
public interface IGameManager {
    ManagerStatus status {get;}

    void Startup(NetworkService service);
}
```

The code in this listing adds a reference to `NetworkService`, so also be sure to copy over that additional script; drag the file from its location in the chapter 10 project (remember, a Unity project is a folder on your disc, so get the file from there), and drop it in the new project. Now modify `Managers.cs` to work with the changed interface.

Listing 12.2 Changing a bit of code in the `Managers` script

```
...
private IEnumerator StartupManagers() {
    NetworkService network = new NetworkService();        ◄────┐  The adjustments are at the
                                                                │  beginning of this method.
    foreach (IGameManager manager in _startSequence) {
        manager.Startup(network);
    }
    ...
```

Finally, adjust both `InventoryManager` and `PlayerManager` to reflect the changed interface. The next listing shows the modified code from `InventoryManager`; `PlayerManager` needs the same code modifications but with different names.

> **Listing 12.3 Adjusting `InventoryManager` to reflect `IGameManager`**

```
...
private NetworkService _network;

public void Startup(NetworkService service) {       ⟵  Same adjustments in both
    Debug.Log("Inventory manager starting...");          managers, but change names

    _network = service;

    _items = new Dictionary<string, int>();
    ...
```

Once all the minor code changes are in, everything should still act as before. This update should work invisibly, and the game will still work the same. That adjustment was easy, but the next one will be harder.

BRING OVER THE AI ENEMY

Besides the `NetworkServices` adjustments from chapter 10, you also need the AI enemy from chapter 3. Implementing enemy characters involved a bunch of scripts and art assets, so you need to import all those assets.

First, copy over these scripts (remember, `WanderingAI` and `ReactiveTarget` were behaviors for the AI enemy, `Fireball` was the projectile fired, the enemy attacks the `PlayerCharacter` component, and `SceneController` handles spawning enemies):

- `PlayerCharacter.cs`
- `SceneController.cs`
- `WanderingAI.cs`
- `ReactiveTarget.cs`
- `Fireball.cs`

Similarly, get the Flame material, Fireball prefab, and Enemy prefab by dragging those files in. If you got the enemy from chapter 11 instead of 3, you may also need the added fire particle material.

After copying over all the required assets, the links between assets will probably be broken, so you'll need to relink everything in order to get them to work. In particular, check the scripts on all prefabs because they probably disconnected. For example, the Enemy prefab has two missing scripts in the Inspector, so click the circle button (indicated in figure 12.2) to choose `WanderingAI` and `ReactiveTarget` from the list of scripts. Similarly, check the Fireball prefab and relink that script if needed. Once you're through with the scripts, check the links to materials and textures.

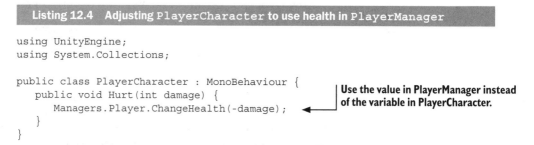

Click the circle button that's just to the right of the script slot.

Figure 12.2   Linking a script to a component

Now add `SceneController.cs` to the controller object and drag the Enemy prefab onto that component's Enemy slot in the Inspector. You may need to drag the Fireball prefab onto the Enemy's script component (select the Enemy prefab and look at `WanderingAI` in the Inspector). Also attach `PlayerCharacter.cs` to the player object so that enemies will attack the player.

Play the game and you'll see the enemy wandering around. The enemy shoots fireballs at the player, although it won't do much damage; select the Fireball prefab and set its Damage value to 10.

> **NOTE** Currently, the enemy isn't particularly good at tracking down and hitting the player. In this case, I'd start by giving the enemy a wider field of vision (using the dot product approach from chapter 9). Ultimately, you'll spend a lot of time polishing a game, and that includes iterating on the behavior of enemies. Polishing a game to make it more fun, though crucial for a game to be released, isn't something you'll do in this book.

The other issue is that when you wrote this code in chapter 3, the player's health was an ad hoc thing for testing. Now the game has a `PlayerManager`, so modify `PlayerCharacter` according to the next listing in order to work with health in that manager.

Listing 12.4   Adjusting `PlayerCharacter` to use health in `PlayerManager`

```
using UnityEngine;
using System.Collections;

public class PlayerCharacter : MonoBehaviour {
    public void Hurt(int damage) {
        Managers.Player.ChangeHealth(-damage);      ◄─── Use the value in PlayerManager instead
    }                                                     of the variable in PlayerCharacter.
}
```

At this point, you have a game demo with pieces assembled from multiple previous projects. An enemy character has been added to the scene, making the game more threatening. But the controls and viewpoint are still from the third-person movement demo, so let's implement point-and-click controls for an action RPG.

12.1.2 *Programming point-and-click controls: movement and devices*

This demo needs a top-down view and mouse control of the player's movement (refer to figure 12.1). Currently, the camera responds to the mouse, whereas the player responds to the keyboard (that is, what was programmed in chapter 8), which is the reverse of what you want in this chapter. In addition, you'll modify the color-changing monitor so that devices are operated by clicking them. In both cases, the existing code isn't terribly far from what you need; you'll make adjustments to both the movement and device scripts.

TOP-DOWN VIEW OF THE SCENE

First, you'll raise the camera to 8 Y to position it for an overhead view. You'll also adjust `OrbitCamera` to remove mouse controls from the camera and only use arrow keys.

Listing 12.5 **Adjusting `OrbitCamera` to remove mouse controls**

```
...
void LateUpdate() {
    _rotY -= Input.GetAxis("Horizontal") * rotSpeed;        Reverse the direction
    Quaternion rotation = Quaternion.Euler(0, _rotY, 0);    from before.
    transform.position = target.position - (rotation * _offset);
    transform.LookAt(target);
}
...
```

The camera's Near/Far clipping planes

While you're adjusting the camera, I want to point out the Near/Far clipping planes. These settings never came up before because the defaults are fine, but you may need to adjust these in a future project.

Select the camera in the scene and look for the Clipping Planes section in the Inspector; both Near and Far are numbers you'll type here. These values define near and far boundaries within which meshes are rendered; polygons closer than the Near clipping plane or farther than the Far clipping plane aren't drawn.

You want the Near/Far clipping planes as close together as possible while still being far enough apart to render everything in your scene. When those planes are too far apart (Near is too close or Far is too far), the rendering algorithm can no longer tell which polygons are closer. This results in a characteristic rendering error called *z-fighting* (as in the Z-axis for depth) where polygons flicker on top of each other.

With the camera raised even higher, the view when you play the game will be top-down. At the moment, though, the movement controls still use the keyboard, so let's write a script for point-and-click movement.

WRITING THE MOVEMENT CODE

The general idea for this code (illustrated in figure 12.3) will be to automatically move the player toward its target position. This position is set by clicking in the scene. In this way, the code that moves the player isn't directly reacting to the mouse, but the player's movement is being controlled indirectly by clicking.

Every frame, the following sequence of steps is run:

1. Check for mouse clicks; set target position.

2. Always rotate to face the target position.

3. Move forward (which will be toward the target).

Figure 12.3 Diagram of how point-and-click controls work

NOTE This movement algorithm is useful for AI characters as well. Rather than using mouse clicks, the target position could be on a path that the character follows.

To implement this, create a new script called `PointClickMovement` and replace the `RelativeMovement` component on the player. Start coding `PointClickMovement` by pasting in the entirety of `RelativeMovement` (because you still want most of that script for handling falling and animations). Then, adjust the code according to this listing.

> **Listing 12.6 New movement code in `PointClickMovement` script**

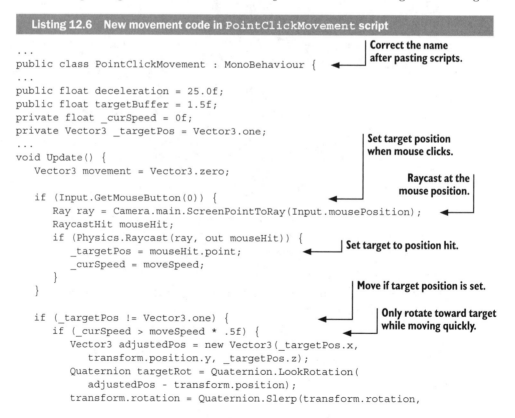

```
...
public class PointClickMovement : MonoBehaviour {          ◄── Correct the name
...                                                            after pasting scripts.
public float deceleration = 25.0f;
public float targetBuffer = 1.5f;
private float _curSpeed = 0f;
private Vector3 _targetPos = Vector3.one;
...                                                        Set target position
void Update() {                                            when mouse clicks.
    Vector3 movement = Vector3.zero;
                                                              Raycast at the
    if (Input.GetMouseButton(0)) {                           mouse position.
        Ray ray = Camera.main.ScreenPointToRay(Input.mousePosition);  ◄──
        RaycastHit mouseHit;
        if (Physics.Raycast(ray, out mouseHit)) {
            _targetPos = mouseHit.point;           ◄── Set target to position hit.
            _curSpeed = moveSpeed;
        }
    }                                                      Move if target position is set.

    if (_targetPos != Vector3.one) {               ◄──     Only rotate toward target
        if (_curSpeed > moveSpeed * .5f) {         ◄──     while moving quickly.
            Vector3 adjustedPos = new Vector3(_targetPos.x,
                transform.position.y, _targetPos.z);
            Quaternion targetRot = Quaternion.LookRotation(
                adjustedPos - transform.position);
            transform.rotation = Quaternion.Slerp(transform.rotation,
```

```
            targetRot, rotSpeed * Time.deltaTime);
    }

    movement = _curSpeed * Vector3.forward;
    movement = transform.TransformDirection(movement);

    if (Vector3.Distance(_targetPos, transform.position) < targetBuffer) {
        _curSpeed -= deceleration * Time.deltaTime;          ◄──┐  Decelerate to 0
        if (_curSpeed <= 0) {                                    │  when close to target
            _targetPos = Vector3.one;
        }
    }
}
_animator.SetFloat("Speed", movement.sqrMagnitude);     ◄──┐  Everything stays the
...                                                         │  same from here down
```

Almost everything at the beginning of the Update() method was gutted, because that
code was handling keyboard movement. Notice that this new code has two main if
statements: one that runs when the mouse clicks, and one that runs when a target is set.

When the mouse clicks, set the target according to where the mouse clicked. Here's
yet another great use for raycasting: to determine which point in the scene is under the
mouse cursor. The target position is set to where the mouse hits.

As for the second conditional, first rotate to face the target. Quaternion.Slerp()
rotates smoothly to face the target, rather than immediately snapping to that rotation;
also lock rotation while slowing down (otherwise the player can rotate oddly when at
the target) by only rotating over half-speed. Then, transform the forward direction
from the player's local coordinates to global coordinates (in order to move forward).
Finally, check the distance between the player and the target: If the player has almost
reached the target, decrement the movement speed and eventually end the movement
by removing the target position.

Exercise: Turn off jump control

Currently, this script still has the jump control from RelativeMovement. The player still
jumps when the spacebar is pressed, but there shouldn't be a jump button with point-
and-click movement. Here's a hint: adjust the code inside the 'if (hitGround)' conditional branch.

This takes care of moving the player using mouse controls. Play the game to test it out.
Next, let's make devices operate when clicked.

OPERATING DEVICES USING THE MOUSE

In chapter 9 (and here, until we adjust the code), devices were operated by pressing a
button. Instead, they should operate when clicked. To do this, you'll first create a base
script that all devices will inherit from; the base script will have the mouse control, and
devices will inherit that. Create a new script called BaseDevice and write the code
shown in listing 12.7.

Listing 12.7   `BaseDevice` script that operates when clicked

```
using UnityEngine;
using System.Collections;

public class BaseDevice : MonoBehaviour {
   public float radius = 3.5f;

   void OnMouseDown() {                              Function that runs when clicked
      Transform player = GameObject.FindWithTag("Player").transform;
      if (Vector3.Distance(player.position, transform.position) < radius) {
         Vector3 direction = transform.position - player.position;
         if (Vector3.Dot(player.forward, direction) > .5f) {
            Operate();
         }                                            Call Operate() if player is nearby and facing.
      }
   }
                                                     virtual marks a method that
   public virtual void Operate() {                   inheritance can override.
      // behavior of the specific device
   }
}
```

Most of this code happens inside `OnMouseDown` because `MonoBehaviour` calls that method when the object is clicked. First, it checks the distance to the player, and then it uses the dot product to see if the player is facing the device. `Operate()` is an empty shell to be filled in by devices that inherit this script.

> **NOTE**   This code looks in the scene for an object with the `Player` tag, so assign this tag to the player object. Tag is a drop-down menu at the top of the Inspector; you can define custom tags as well, but several tags are defined by default, including `Player`. Select the player object to edit it, and then select the `Player` tag.

Now that `BaseDevice` is programmed, you can modify `ColorChangeDevice` to inherit from that script. This is the new code.

Listing 12.8   Adjusting `ColorChangeDevice` to inherit from `BaseDevice`

```
using UnityEngine;                                   Inherit BaseDevice instead
using System.Collections;                            of MonoBehaviour.

public class ColorChangeDevice : BaseDevice {
   public override void Operate() {                  Override this method
      Color random = new Color(Random.Range(0f,1f),  from the base class.
         Random.Range(0f,1f), Random.Range(0f,1f));
      GetComponent<Renderer>().material.color = random;
   }
}
```

Because this script inherits from `BaseDevice` instead of `MonoBehaviour`, it gets the mouse control functionality. Then it overrides the empty `Operate()` method to program the color-changing behavior.

Now it will operate when you click it. Also remove the player's `DeviceOperator` script component, because that script operates devices using the control key.

This new device input brings up an issue with the movement controls: currently, the movement target is set any time the mouse clicks, but you don't want to set the movement target when clicking devices. You can fix this issue by using layers; similar to how a tag was set on the player, objects can be set to different layers and the code can check for that. Adjust `PointClickMovement` to check for the object's layer.

Listing 12.9 Adjusting mouse click code in `PointClickMovement`

```
...
Ray ray = Camera.main.ScreenPointToRay(Input.mousePosition);
RaycastHit mouseHit;
if (Physics.Raycast(ray, out mouseHit)) {
   GameObject hitObject = mouseHit.transform.gameObject;        ⎬ Added code; the rest
   if (hitObject.layer == LayerMask.NameToLayer("Ground")) {    ⎬ is reference.
    _targetPos = mouseHit.point;
    _curSpeed = moveSpeed;
   }
}
...
```

This listing adds a conditional inside the mouse click code to see if the clicked object is on the Ground layer. Layers (like Tags) is a drop-down menu at the top of the Inspector; click it to see the options. Also, like tags, several layers are already defined by default. You want to create a new layer, so choose Edit Layers in the menu. Type `Ground` in an empty layer slot (probably slot 8; `NameToLayer()` in the code converts names into layer numbers so that you can say the name instead of the number).

Now that the Ground layer has been added to the menu, set ground objects to the Ground layer—that means the floor of the building, along with the ramps and platforms that the player can walk on. Select those objects, and then select Ground in the Layers menu.

Play the game and you won't move when clicking the color-changing monitor. Great, the point-and-click controls are complete! One more thing to bring into this project from previous projects is the UI.

12.1.3 *Replacing the old GUI with a new interface*

Chapter 9 used Unity's old immediate-mode GUI because that approach was simpler to code. But the UI from chapter 9 doesn't look as nice as the one from chapter 7, so let's bring over that interface system. The newer UI is more visually polished than the old GUI; figure 12.4 shows the interface you're going to create.

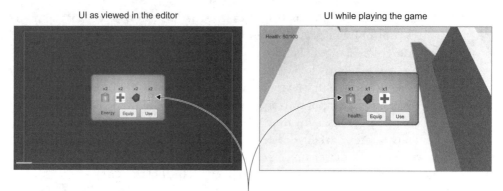

There are four sets of text labels and icons set up in the editor, but during play they can change appearance or be hidden depending on your inventory.

Figure 12.4   The UI for this chapter's project

First, you'll set up the UI graphics. Once the UI images are all in the scene, you can attach scripts to the UI objects. I'll list the steps involved without going into detail; if you need a refresher, refer to chapter 7:

1 Import popup.png as a sprite (choose Texture Type).
2 In the Sprite Editor, set a 12-pixel border on all sides (remember to apply changes).
3 Create a canvas in the scene (GameObject > UI > Canvas).
4 Choose the Pixel Perfect setting of the canvas.
5 Optional: name the object HUD Canvas and switch to 2D view mode.
6 Create a Text object connected to that canvas (GameObject > UI > Text).
7 Set the Text object's anchor to top-left and position 100, -40.
8 Type Health: as the text on the label.
9 Create an image connected to that canvas (GameObject > UI > Image).
10 Name the new object Inventory Popup.
11 Assign the pop-up sprite to the image's Source Image.
12 Set Image Type to Sliced and select Fill Center.
13 Position the pop-up image at 0, 0 and scale the pop-up to 250 for width and 150 for height.

NOTE Recall how to switch between viewing the 3D scene and the 2D interface: toggle 2D view mode and double-click either the Canvas or the Building to zoom in on that object.

Now you have the Health label in the corner and the large blue pop-up window in the center. Let's program these parts first before getting deeper into the UI functionality.

The interface code will use the same Messenger system from chapter 7, so copy over the Messenger script. Then create a GameEvent script.

Listing 12.10 `GameEvent` **script to use with this Messenger system**

```
public static class GameEvent {
   public const string HEALTH_UPDATED = "HEALTH_UPDATED";
}
```

For now, only one event is defined; over the course of this chapter you'll add a few more events. Broadcast this event from PlayerManager.cs.

Listing 12.11   Broadcasting the health event from `PlayerManager.cs`

```
...
public void ChangeHealth(int value) {
   health += value;
   if (health > maxHealth) {
      health = maxHealth;
   } else if (health < 0) {
      health = 0;
   }

   Messenger.Broadcast(GameEvent.HEALTH_UPDATED);       ◄── Add a line to the end
}                                                            of this function
...
```

The event is broadcast every time ChangeHealth() finishes to tell the rest of the program that the health has changed. You want to adjust the health label in response to this event, so create a UIController script.

Listing 12.12   The script `UIController`**, which handles the interface**

```
using UnityEngine;
using UnityEngine.UI;
using System.Collections;

public class UIController : MonoBehaviour {                   ◄── Reference UI object in scene
   [SerializeField] private Text healthLabel;
   [SerializeField] private InventoryPopup popup;

   void Awake() {       ◄── Set listener for health update event
      Messenger.AddListener(GameEvent.HEALTH_UPDATED, OnHealthUpdated);
   }
   void OnDestroy() {
      Messenger.RemoveListener(GameEvent.HEALTH_UPDATED, OnHealthUpdated);
   }

   void Start() {
      OnHealthUpdated();       ◄── Call function manually at startup

      popup.gameObject.SetActive(false);       ◄── Initialize pop-up to be hidden
   }
```

```
void Update() {
    if (Input.GetKeyDown(KeyCode.M)) {          ◀━━━┃ Toggle pop-up with M key
        bool isShowing = popup.gameObject.activeSelf;
        popup.gameObject.SetActive(!isShowing);
        popup.Refresh();
    }
}
                                        ┃ Event listener calls function
                                        ┃ to update health label
private void OnHealthUpdated() {    ◀━━━┛
    string message = "Health: " + Managers.Player.health + "/" + Managers.
    Player.maxHealth;
    healthLabel.text = message;
}
}
```

Attach this new script to the `Controller` object and remove `BasicUI`. Also, create an `InventoryPopup` script (add an empty public `Refresh()` method for now; the rest will be filled in later) and attach it to the pop-up window (the `Image` object). Now you can drag the pop-up to the reference slot in the Controller component and also link the health label to the Controller.

The health label changes when you get hurt or use health packs, and pressing the M key toggles the pop-up window. One last detail to adjust is that clicking the pop-up window currently causes the player to move; as with devices, you don't want to set the target position when the UI has been clicked. Make the adjustment to `PointClickMovement`.

Listing 12.13   Checking the UI in `PointClickMovement`

```
using UnityEngine.EventSystems;
...
void Update() {
   Vector3 movement = Vector3.zero;
   if (Input.GetMouseButton(0) && !EventSystem.current.
     IsPointerOverGameObject()) {
   ...
```

Note that the conditional checks whether or not the mouse is on the UI. That completes the overall structure of the interface, so now let's deal with the inventory pop-up specifically.

IMPLEMENTING THE INVENTORY POP-UP

The pop-up window is currently blank, but it should display the player's inventory (depicted in figure 12.5). These steps will create the UI objects:

1   Create four images and parent them to the pop-up (that is, drag objects in the Hierarchy).

2   Create four text labels and parent them to the pop-up.

3   Position all the images at 0 Y and X values -75, -25, 25, and 75.

4 Text objects

4 Image objects

1 Text object   **2 Button objects**

Figure 12.5   Diagram of the inventory UI

4 Position the text labels at 50 Y and X values -75, -25, 25, and 75.

5 Set the text (not the anchor!) to Center alignment, Bottom vertical align, and Height 60.

6 In Resources, set all inventory icons as Sprite (instead of Textures).

7 Drag these sprites to the Source Image slot of the Image objects (also set Native Size).

8 Enter x2 for all the text labels.

9 Add another text label and two buttons, all parented to the pop-up.

10 Position this text label at -120, -55 and set Right alignment.

11 Type Energy: for the text on this label

12 Set both buttons to Width 60, then Position at -50 Y and X values 0 or 70.

13 Type Equip on one button and Use on the other.

These are the visual elements for the inventory pop-up; next is the code. Write the contents of the following into the InventoryPopup script.

Listing 12.14   Full script for `InventoryPopup`

```
using UnityEngine;
using UnityEngine.UI;
using UnityEngine.EventSystems;
using System.Collections;
using System.Collections.Generic;

public class InventoryPopup : MonoBehaviour {
    [SerializeField] private Image[] itemIcons;        │ Arrays to reference four
    [SerializeField] private Text[] itemLabels;        │ images and text labels

    [SerializeField] private Text curItemLabel;
    [SerializeField] private Button equipButton;
    [SerializeField] private Button useButton;
```

```
private string _curItem;

public void Refresh() {
   List<string> itemList = Managers.Inventory.GetItemList();

   int len = itemIcons.Length;
   for (int i = 0; i < len; i++) {                    Check inventory list while
      if (i < itemList.Count) {                       looping through all UI images.
         itemIcons[i].gameObject.SetActive(true);
         itemLabels[i].gameObject.SetActive(true);

         string item = itemList[i];
                                                       Load sprite from Resources.
         Sprite sprite = Resources.Load<Sprite>("Icons/"+item);
         itemIcons[i].sprite = sprite;
         itemIcons[i].SetNativeSize();        ◄─── Resize image to native size of the sprite.

         int count = Managers.Inventory.GetItemCount(item);
         string message = "x" + count;
         if (item == Managers.Inventory.equippedItem) {
            message = "Equipped\n" + message;  ◄───
         }                                             Label may say "Equipped" in
         itemLabels[i].text = message;                 addition to item count.

         EventTrigger.Entry entry = new EventTrigger.Entry();   Enable clicking
         entry.eventID = EventTriggerType.PointerClick;  ◄──    on icons.
         entry.callback.AddListener((BaseEventData data) => {
            OnItem(item);   ◄───
         });                        Lambda function to trigger
                                    differently for each item

         EventTrigger trigger = itemIcons[i].GetComponent<EventTrigger>();
         trigger.triggers.Clear();  ◄───┐
         trigger.triggers.Add(entry);  ◄┴─ Clear listener to refresh from clean slate.
      }                                 └── Add this listener function to EventTrigger.
      else {
         itemIcons[i].gameObject.SetActive(false);    Hide this image/text if
         itemLabels[i].gameObject.SetActive(false);   no item to display.
      }
   }

   if (!itemList.Contains(_curItem)) {
      _curItem = null;
   }                                                 Hide buttons if no item selected.
   if (_curItem == null) {                    ◄───
      curItemLabel.gameObject.SetActive(false);
      equipButton.gameObject.SetActive(false);
      useButton.gameObject.SetActive(false);
   }
   else {                                         Display currently selected item.
      curItemLabel.gameObject.SetActive(true);
      equipButton.gameObject.SetActive(true);
      if (_curItem == "health") {            ◄─── Use button only for health item.
```

```
                useButton.gameObject.SetActive(true);
            } else {
                useButton.gameObject.SetActive(false);
            }

            curItemLabel.text = _curItem+":";
        }
    }

    public void OnItem(string item) {          ◄─────┐ Function called by mouse click listener
        _curItem = item;
        Refresh();                                    ◄───┐ Refresh inventory display after making changes.
    }

    public void OnEquip() {
        Managers.Inventory.EquipItem(_curItem);
        Refresh();
    }

    public void OnUse() {
        Managers.Inventory.ConsumeItem(_curItem);
        if (_curItem == "health") {
            Managers.Player.ChangeHealth(25);
        }
        Refresh();
    }
}
```

Whew, that was a long script! With this programmed, it's time to link everything in the interface. The script component now has the various object references, including the two arrays; expand both arrays and set to a length of 4 (see figure 12.6). Drag the four images to the icons array, and drag the four text labels to the labels array.

An array defined by the script component. Expand the array by clicking the arrow.

Set the length of the array.

Drag Image objects to these slots.

Figure 12.6   Arrays displayed in the Inspector

NOTE   If you aren't sure which object is linked where (they all look the same), click the slot in the Inspector to see that object highlighted in the Hierarchy view.

Similarly, slots in the component reference the text label and buttons at the bottom of the pop-up. After linking those objects, you'll add OnClick listeners for both buttons.

Link these events to the pop-up object, and choose either OnEquip() or OnUse() as appropriate.

Finally, add an EventTrigger component to all four of the item images. The InventoryPopup script modifies this component on each icon, so they better have this component! You'll find EventTrigger under Add Component > Event. (It may be more convenient to copy/paste the component by clicking the little gear button in the top corner of the component, select Copy Component from one object, and then Paste As New on the other.) Add this component but don't assign event listeners, because that's done in the InventoryPopup code.

That completes the inventory UI! Play the game to watch the inventory pop-up respond when you collect items and click buttons. We're now finished assembling parts from previous projects; next I'll explain how to build a more expansive game from this beginning.

12.2 *Developing the overarching game structure*

Now that you have a functioning action RPG demo, we're going to build the overarching structure of this game. By that I mean the overall flow of the game through multiple levels and progressing through the game by beating levels. What we got from chapter 9's project was a single level, but the roadmap for this chapter specified three levels.

Doing this will involve decoupling the scene even further from the Managers backend, so you'll broadcast messages about the managers (just as PlayerManager broadcasts health updates). Create a new script called StartupEvent (listing 12.15); define these events in a separate script because these events go with the reusable Managers system, whereas GameEvent is specific to the game.

> **Listing 12.15   The StartupEvent script**

```
public static class StartupEvent {
    public const string MANAGERS_STARTED = "MANAGERS_STARTED";
    public const string MANAGERS_PROGRESS = "MANAGERS_PROGRESS";
}
```

Now it's time to start adjusting Managers, including broadcasting these new events!

12.2.1 *Controlling mission flow and multiple levels*

Currently the project has only one scene, and the Game Managers object is in that scene. The problem with that is that every scene will have its own set of game managers, whereas you want a single set of game managers shared by all scenes. To do that, you'll create a separate Startup scene that initializes the managers and then shares that object with the other scenes of the game.

We're also going to need a new manager to handle progress through the game. Create a new script called MissionManager.

Listing 12.16   Creating `MissionManager`

```
using UnityEngine;
using UnityEngine.SceneManagement;
using System.Collections;
using System.Collections.Generic;

public class MissionManager : MonoBehaviour, IGameManager {
   public ManagerStatus status {get; private set;}

   public int curLevel {get; private set;}
   public int maxLevel {get; private set;}

   private NetworkService _network;

   public void Startup(NetworkService service) {
      Debug.Log("Mission manager starting...");

      _network = service;

      curLevel = 0;
      maxLevel = 1;

      status = ManagerStatus.Started;
   }

   public void GoToNext() {
      if (curLevel < maxLevel) {              ◄———| Check if last level reached.
         curLevel++;
         string name = "Level" + curLevel;
         Debug.Log("Loading " + name);
         SceneManager.LoadScene(name);        ◄———| Unity's command to load a scene
      } else {
         Debug.Log("Last level");
      }
   }
}
```

For the most part, there's nothing unusual going on in this listing, but note the Load-Scene() method near the end; although I mentioned that method before (in chapter 5), it wasn't important until now. That's Unity's method for loading a scene file; in chapter 5 you used it to reload the one scene in the game, but you can load any scene by passing in the name of the scene file.

Attach this script to the Game Managers object in the scene. Also add the new component to the Managers script.

Listing 12.17   Adding a new component to the `Managers` script

```
...
[RequireComponent(typeof(MissionManager))]

public class Managers : MonoBehaviour {
   public static PlayerManager Player {get; private set;}
```

```
public static InventoryManager Inventory {get; private set;}
public static MissionManager Mission {get; private set;}
...
void Awake() {
    DontDestroyOnLoad(gameObject);

    Player = GetComponent<PlayerManager>();
    Inventory = GetComponent<InventoryManager>();
    Mission = GetComponent<MissionManager>();

    _startSequence = new List<IGameManager>();
    _startSequence.Add(Player);
    _startSequence.Add(Inventory);
    _startSequence.Add(Mission);

    StartCoroutine(StartupManagers());
}

private IEnumerator StartupManagers() {
    ...
    if (numReady > lastReady) {
        Debug.Log("Progress: " + numReady + "/" + numModules);
        Messenger<int, int>.Broadcast(
            StartupEvent.MANAGERS_PROGRESS, numReady, numModules);
    }

    yield return null;
}

    Debug.Log("All managers started up");
    Messenger.Broadcast(StartupEvent.MANAGERS_STARTED);
}
...
```

Unity's command to persist an object between scenes ← (points to `DontDestroyOnLoad(gameObject);`)

Startup event broadcast with data related to the event. → (points to `StartupEvent.MANAGERS_PROGRESS, numReady, numModules`)

Startup event broadcast without parameters. ← (points to `Messenger.Broadcast(StartupEvent.MANAGERS_STARTED);`)

Most of this code should already be familiar to you (adding `MissionManager` is like adding other managers), but there are two new parts. One is the event that sends two integer values; you saw both generic valueless events and messages with a single number before, but you can send an arbitrary number of values with the same syntax.

The other new bit of code is the `DontDestroyOnLoad()` method. It's a method provided by Unity for persisting an object between scenes. Normally, all objects in a scene are purged when a new scene loads, but by using `DontDestroyOnLoad()` on an object, you ensure that that object will still be there in the new scene.

SEPARATE SCENES FOR STARTUP AND LEVEL

Because the `Game Managers` object will persist in all scenes, you must separate the managers from individual levels of the game. In Project view, duplicate the scene file (Edit > Duplicate) and then rename the two files appropriately: one `Startup` and the other `Level1`. Open `Level1` and delete the `Game Managers` object (it'll be provided by Startup). Open Startup and delete everything other than `Game Managers`, `Controller`, Main Camera, `HUD Canvas`, and `EventSystem`. Adjust the camera by removing the `OrbitCamera` component, and changing the `Clear Flags` menu from `Skybox` to `Solid`

Color. Remove the script components on `Controller`, and delete the UI objects (health label and `InventoryPopup`) parented to the `Canvas`.

The UI is currently empty, so create a new slider (see figure 12.7) and then turn off its Interactable setting. The `Controller` object also has no script components anymore, so create a new `StartupController` script (listing 12.18) and attach that to the `Controller` object.

Remaining objects:
Game Managers
Controller
HUD Canvas
EventSystem

The non-interactive slider

Figure 12.7   The Startup scene with everything unnecessary removed

---

Listing 12.18   The new `StartupController` script

```
using UnityEngine;
using UnityEngine.UI;
using System.Collections;

public class StartupController : MonoBehaviour {
   [SerializeField] private Slider progressBar;

   void Awake() {
      Messenger<int, int>.AddListener(StartupEvent.MANAGERS_PROGRESS,
         OnManagersProgress);
      Messenger.AddListener(StartupEvent.MANAGERS_STARTED,
         OnManagersStarted);
   }
   void OnDestroy() {
      Messenger<int, int>.RemoveListener(StartupEvent.MANAGERS_PROGRESS,
         OnManagersProgress);
      Messenger.RemoveListener(StartupEvent.MANAGERS_STARTED,
         OnManagersStarted);
   }

   private void OnManagersProgress(int numReady, int numModules) {
      float progress = (float)numReady / numModules;
      progressBar.value = progress;               ◄─── Update the slider to
   }                                                   show loading progress.

   private void OnManagersStarted() {
      Managers.Mission.GoToNext();                ◄─── Load the next scene once
   }                                                   managers have started.
}
```

Next, link the `Slider` object to the slot in the Inspector. One last thing to do in preparation is add the two scenes to Build Settings. Building the app will be the topic of the next chapter, so for now choose File > Build Settings to see and adjust the list of scenes. Click the Add Current button to add a scene to the list (load both scenes and do this for each).

> **NOTE**   You need to add the scenes to Build Settings so that they can be loaded. If you don't, Unity won't know what scenes are available. You didn't need to do this in chapter 5 because you weren't actually switching levels—you were reloading the current scene.

Now you can launch the game by clicking Play from the Startup scene. The `Game Managers` object will be shared in both scenes.

> **WARNING**   Because the managers are loaded in the Startup scene, you always need to launch the game from that scene. You could remember to always open that scene before clicking Play, but there's a script on the Unity wiki that will automatically switch to a set scene when you click Play: http://wiki.unity3d .com/index.php/SceneAutoLoader.

> **TIP**   By default, the lighting system regenerates the lightmaps when the level is loaded. But this only works while you are editing the level; lightmaps won't be generated when loading levels while the game is running. As you did in chapter 10, you can turn off Auto lighting in the lighting window (Window > Lighting) and then click the button to manually bake lightmaps (remember, don't touch the lighting folder that's created).

This structural change handles the sharing of game managers between different scenes, but you still don't have any success or failure conditions within the level.

12.2.2   *Completing a level by reaching the exit*

To handle level completion, you'll put an object in the scene for the player to touch, and that object will inform `MissionManager` when the player reaches the objective. This will involve the UI responding to a message about level completion, so add another `GameEvent`.

Listing 12.19   Level Complete added to `GameEvent.cs`

```
public static class GameEvent {
    public const string HEALTH_UPDATED = "HEALTH_UPDATED";
    public const string LEVEL_COMPLETE = "LEVEL_COMPLETE";
}
```

Now add a new method to `MissionManager` in order to keep track of mission objectives and broadcast the new event message.

Listing 12.20   Objective method in `MissionManager`

```
...
public void ReachObjective() {
    // could have logic to handle multiple objectives
    Messenger.Broadcast(GameEvent.LEVEL_COMPLETE);
}
...
```

Adjust the `UIController` script to respond to that event.

Listing 12.21   New event listener in `UIController`

```
...
[SerializeField] private Text levelEnding;
...
void Awake() {
    Messenger.AddListener(GameEvent.HEALTH_UPDATED, OnHealthUpdated);
    Messenger.AddListener(GameEvent.LEVEL_COMPLETE, OnLevelComplete);
}
void OnDestroy() {
    Messenger.RemoveListener(GameEvent.HEALTH_UPDATED, OnHealthUpdated);
    Messenger.RemoveListener(GameEvent.LEVEL_COMPLETE, OnLevelComplete);
}
...
void Start() {
    OnHealthUpdated();

    levelEnding.gameObject.SetActive(false);
    popup.gameObject.SetActive(false);
}
...
private void OnLevelComplete() {
    StartCoroutine(CompleteLevel());
}
private IEnumerator CompleteLevel() {
    levelEnding.gameObject.SetActive(true);
    levelEnding.text = "Level Complete!";

    yield return new WaitForSeconds(2);          ◄─────┐  Show message for two seconds
                                                        │  and then go to next level.
    Managers.Mission.GoToNext();
}
...
```

You'll notice that this listing has a reference to a text label. Open the `Level1` scene to edit it, and create a new UI text object. This label will be a level completion message that appears in the middle of the screen. Set this text to Width 240, Height 60, Center for both Align and Vertical-align, and Font Size 22. Type `Level Complete!` in the text area and then link this text object to the `levelEnding` reference of UIController.

Finally, we'll create an object that the player touches to complete the level (figure 12.8 shows what the objective looks like). This will be similar to collectible items: it needs a material and a script, and you'll make the entire thing a prefab.

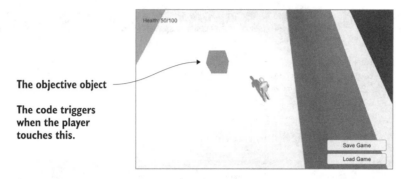

The objective object —

The code triggers when the player touches this.

Figure 12.8   Objective object that the player touches to complete the level

Create a cube object at Position 18, 1, 0. Select the Is Trigger option of the Box Collider, turn off both Cast and Receive Shadows in Mesh Renderer, and set the object to the Ignore Raycast layer. Create a new material called `objective`; make it bright green and set the shader to Unlit > Color for a flat, bright look.

Next, create the `ObjectiveTrigger` script and attach that script to the objective object.

Listing 12.22   Code for `ObjectiveTrigger` to put on objective objects

```
using UnityEngine;
using System.Collections;

public class ObjectiveTrigger : MonoBehaviour {
    void OnTriggerEnter(Collider other) {
        Managers.Mission.ReachObjective();
    }
}
```

Call the new objective method in MissionManager.

Drag this object from the Hierarchy into Project view to turn it into a prefab; in future levels, you could put the prefab in the scene. Now play the game and go reach the objective. The completion message shows when you beat the level.

Next, let's have a failure message to show when you lose.

12.2.3   *Losing the level when caught by enemies*

The failure condition will be when the player runs out of health (because of the enemy attacking). First, add another `GameEvent`:

```
public const string LEVEL_FAILED = "LEVEL_FAILED";
```

Now adjust `PlayerManager` to broadcast this message when the player's health drops to 0.

Listing 12.23   Broadcast Level Failed from `PlayerManager`

```
...
public void Startup(NetworkService service) {
    Debug.Log("Player manager starting...");
```

```
    _network = service;

    UpdateData(50, 100);

    status = ManagerStatus.Started;
}

public void UpdateData(int health, int maxHealth) {
    this.health = health;
    this.maxHealth = maxHealth;
}

public void ChangeHealth(int value) {
    health += value;
    if (health > maxHealth) {
        health = maxHealth;
    } else if (health < 0) {
        health = 0;
    }

    if (health == 0) {
        Messenger.Broadcast(GameEvent.LEVEL_FAILED);
    }
    Messenger.Broadcast(GameEvent.HEALTH_UPDATED);
}

public void Respawn() {
    UpdateData(50, 100);
}
...
```

⟵ **Call the update method instead of setting variables directly.**

⟵ **Reset the player to the initial state.**

Add a method to `MissionManager` for restarting the level.

Listing 12.24 `MissionManager`, which can restart the current level

```
...
public void RestartCurrent() {
    string name = "Level" + curLevel;
    Debug.Log("Loading " + name);
    SceneManager.LoadScene(name);
}
...
```

With that in place, add another event listener to `UIController`.

Listing 12.25 Responding to Level Failed in `UIController`

```
...
Messenger.AddListener(GameEvent.LEVEL_FAILED, OnLevelFailed);
...
Messenger.RemoveListener(GameEvent.LEVEL_FAILED, OnLevelFailed);
...
private void OnLevelFailed() {
    StartCoroutine(FailLevel());
}
```

```
private IEnumerator FailLevel() {
    levelEnding.gameObject.SetActive(true);
    levelEnding.text = "Level Failed";

    yield return new WaitForSeconds(2);

    Managers.Player.Respawn();
    Managers.Mission.RestartCurrent();
}
...
```

Reuse the same text label, but set a different message.

Restart the current level after a 2-second pause.

Play the game and let the enemy shoot you several times; the level failure message will appear. Great job—the player can now complete and fail levels! Building off that, the game must keep track of the player's progress.

12.3   *Handling the player's progression through the game*

Right now, the individual level operates independently, without any relation to the overall game. You'll add two things that will make progress through the game feel more complete: saving the player's progress and detecting when the game (not just the level) is complete.

12.3.1   *Saving and loading the player's progress*

Saving and loading the game is an important part of most games. Unity and Mono provide I/O functionality that you can use for this purpose. Before you can start using that, though, you must add UpdateData() for both MissionManager and Inventory-Manager. That method will work like it does in PlayerManager and will enable code outside the manager to update data within the manager. Listing 12.26 and listing 12.27 show the changed managers.

> **Listing 12.26**   UpdateData() method in MissionManager

```
...
public void Startup(NetworkService service) {
    Debug.Log("Mission manager starting...");

    _network = service;

    UpdateData(0, 1);                            Modify this line using the new method.

    status = ManagerStatus.Started;
}

public void UpdateData(int curLevel, int maxLevel) {
    this.curLevel = curLevel;
    this.maxLevel = maxLevel;
}
...
```

Listing 12.27 `UpdateData()` **method in** `InventoryManager`

```
...
public void Startup(NetworkService service) {
    Debug.Log("Inventory manager starting...");

    _network = service;

    UpdateData(new Dictionary<string, int>());        ◄──── Initialize an empty list.

    status = ManagerStatus.Started;
}

public void UpdateData(Dictionary<string, int> items) {
    _items = items;
}
                                                        Need getter in order for save
public Dictionary<string, int> GetData() {        ◄──── game code to access the data.
    return _items;
}
...
```

Now that the various managers all have `UpdateData()` methods, the data can be saved from a new code module. Saving the data will involve a procedure referred to as *serializing* the data.

> **DEFINITION**　*Serialize* means to encode a batch of data into a form that can be stored.

You'll save the game as binary data, but note that C# is also fully capable of saving text files. For example, the JSON strings you worked with in chapter 10 were data serialized as text. Previous chapters used `PlayerPrefs` but in this project, you're going to save a local file; `PlayerPrefs` are only intended to save a handful of values, like settings, not an entire game. Create the `DataManager` script (listing 12.28).

> **WARNING**　You can't directly access the filesystem in a web game. This is a security feature of web browsers. To save data for web games, you may need to write a plugin as described in the next chapter, or post the data to your server.

Listing 12.28 **New script for** `DataManager`

```
using UnityEngine;
using System.Collections;
using System.Collections.Generic;
using System.Runtime.Serialization.Formatters.Binary;
using System.IO;

public class DataManager : MonoBehaviour, IGameManager {
    public ManagerStatus status {get; private set;}

    private string _filename;
```

```
    private NetworkService _network;

    public void Startup(NetworkService service) {
       Debug.Log("Data manager starting...");

        _network = service;

        _filename = Path.Combine(
             Application.persistentDataPath, "game.dat");

        status = ManagerStatus.Started;
    }

    public void SaveGameState() {
       Dictionary<string, object> gamestate =
          new Dictionary<string, object>();
       gamestate.Add("inventory", Managers.Inventory.GetData());
       gamestate.Add("health", Managers.Player.health);
       gamestate.Add("maxHealth", Managers.Player.maxHealth);
       gamestate.Add("curLevel", Managers.Mission.curLevel);
       gamestate.Add("maxLevel", Managers.Mission.maxLevel);

       FileStream stream = File.Create(_filename);
       BinaryFormatter formatter = new BinaryFormatter();
       formatter.Serialize(stream, gamestate);
       stream.Close();
    }

    public void LoadGameState() {
       if (!File.Exists(_filename)) {
          Debug.Log("No saved game");
          return;
       }

       Dictionary<string, object> gamestate;

       BinaryFormatter formatter = new BinaryFormatter();
       FileStream stream = File.Open(_filename, FileMode.Open);
       gamestate = formatter.Deserialize(stream) as Dictionary<string,
       object>;
       stream.Close();

       Managers.Inventory.UpdateData((Dictionary<string, int>)
       gamestate["inventory"]);
       Managers.Player.UpdateData((int)gamestate["health"], (int)
       gamestate["maxHealth"]);
       Managers.Mission.UpdateData((int)gamestate["curLevel"], (int)
       gamestate["maxLevel"]);
       Managers.Mission.RestartCurrent();
    }
}
```

Construct full path to the game.dat file.

Dictionary that will be serialized

Create a file at the file path.

Serialize the Dictionary as contents of the created file.

Only continue to load if the file exists.

Dictionary to put loaded data in

Update managers with deserialized data.

During Startup(), the full file path is constructed using Application.persistent-DataPath, a location Unity provides to store data in. The exact file path differs on different platforms, but Unity abstracts it behind this static variable (incidentally, this path includes both Company Name and Product Name from Player Settings, so adjust those if needed). The `File.Create()` method will create a binary file; call `File.CreateText()` if you want a text file.

> **WARNING** When constructing file paths, the path separator is different on different computer platforms. C# has `Path.DirectorySeparatorChar` to account for this.

Open the Startup scene to find `Game Managers`. Add the `DataManager` script component to the `Game Managers` object, and then add the new manager to the `Managers` script.

Listing 12.29 Adding `DataManager` to `Managers.cs`

```
...
[RequireComponent(typeof(DataManager))]
...
public static DataManager Data {get; private set;}
...
void Awake() {
   DontDestroyOnLoad(gameObject);

   Data = GetComponent<DataManager>();
   Player = GetComponent<PlayerManager>();
   Inventory = GetComponent<InventoryManager>();
   Mission = GetComponent<MissionManager>();

   _startSequence = new List<IGameManager>();        ◄─── Managers start in this order.
   _startSequence.Add(Player);
   _startSequence.Add(Inventory);
   _startSequence.Add(Mission);
   _startSequence.Add(Data);

   StartCoroutine(StartupManagers());
}
...
```

> **WARNING** Because `DataManager` uses other managers (in order to update them), you should make sure that the other managers appear earlier in the startup sequence.

Finally, in `Level1`, add buttons to use functions in `DataManager` (figure 12.9 shows the buttons). Create two buttons parented to the HUD Canvas (not in the Inventory pop-up). Call them (set the attached text objects) `Save Game` and `Load Game`, set Anchor to bottom-right, and position them at `-100,65` and `-100,30`.

Figure 12.9   Save and Load buttons on the bottom right of the screen

These buttons will link to functions in `UIController`, so write those methods.

Listing 12.30   Save and Load methods in `UIController`

```
...
public void SaveGame() {
   Managers.Data.SaveGameState();
}

public void LoadGame() {
   Managers.Data.LoadGameState();
}
...
```

Link these functions to `OnClick` listeners in the buttons (add a listing in the `OnClick` setting, drag in the `UIController` object, and select functions from the menu). Now play the game, pick up a few items, use a health pack to increase your health, and then save the game. Restart the game and check your inventory to verify that it's empty. Click Load; you now have the health and items you had when you saved the game!

12.3.2   *Beating the game by completing three levels*

As implied by our saving of the player's progress, this game can have multiple levels, not just the one level you've been testing. To properly handle multiple levels, the game must detect not only the completion of a single level, but also the completion of the entire game. First, add yet another `GameEvent`:

```
public const string GAME_COMPLETE = "GAME_COMPLETE";
```

Now modify `MissionManager` to broadcast that message after the last level.

Listing 12.31   Broadcasting Game Complete from `MissionManager`

```
...
public void GoToNext() {
   ...
   } else {
      Debug.Log("Last level");
```

```
        Messenger.Broadcast(GameEvent.GAME_COMPLETE);
    }
}
```

Respond to that message in `UIController`.

Listing 12.32   Adding an event listener to `UIController`

```
...
Messenger.AddListener(GameEvent.GAME_COMPLETE, OnGameComplete);
...
Messenger.RemoveListener(GameEvent.GAME_COMPLETE, OnGameComplete);
...
private void OnGameComplete() {
    levelEnding.gameObject.SetActive(true);
    levelEnding.text = "You Finished the Game!";
}
...
```

Try completing the level to see what happens: move the player to the level objective to complete the level as before. You'll first see the Level Complete message, but after a couple of seconds it'll change to a message about completing the game.

ADDING MORE LEVELS

At this point, you can add an arbitrary number of additional levels, and `MissionManager` will watch for the last level. The final thing you'll do in this chapter is add a few more levels to the project in order to demonstrate the game progressing through multiple levels.

Duplicate the `Level1` scene file twice (Unity should automatically increment the numbers to `Level2` and `Level3`) and add the new levels to Build Settings (so that they can be loaded during gameplay; remember to generate the lighting). Modify each scene so that you can tell the difference between levels; feel free to rearrange most of the scene, but there are several essential game elements that you must keep: the player object that's tagged Player, the floor object set to the Ground layer, and the objective object, Controller, HUD Canvas, and `EventSystem`.

You also need to adjust `MissionManager` to load the new levels. Change `maxLevel` to 3 by changing the `UpdateData(0, 1)` call to `UpdateData(0, 3)`. Now play the game and you'll start on `Level1` initially; reach the level objective and you'll move on to the next level! Incidentally, you can also save on a later level to see that the game will restore that progress.

Exercise: Integrating audio into the full game

Chapter 11 was all about implementing audio in Unity. I didn't explain how to integrate that into this chapter's project, but at this point you should understand how. I encourage you to practice your skills by integrating the audio functionality from the previous chapter into this chapter's project. Here's a hint: change the key to toggle the audio settings pop up so that it doesn't interfere with the inventory pop up.

You now know how to create a full game with multiple levels. The obvious next task is the final chapter: getting your game into the hands of players.

Summary

- Unity makes it easy to repurpose assets and code from a project in a different game genre.
- Another great use for raycasting is to determine where in the scene the player is clicking.
- Unity has simple methods for both loading levels and persisting certain objects between levels.
- You progress through levels in response to various events within the game.
- You can use the I/O methods that come with C# to store data at `Application`
  `.persistentDataPath`.

Deploying your game to players' devices

This chapter covers

- Building an application package for various platforms
- Assigning build settings, such as the app icon or name
- Interacting with the web page for web games
- Developing plug-ins for apps on mobile platforms

Throughout this book, you've learned how to program various games within Unity, but the crucial last step has been missing so far: deploying those games to players. Until a game is playable outside the Unity editor, it's of little interest to anyone other than the developer. Unity shines at this last step, with the ability to build applications for a huge variety of gaming platforms. This final chapter will go over how to build games for these various platforms.

When I speak of "building" for a platform, I'm referring to generating an application package that will run on that platform. On each platform (Windows, iOS, and so on) the exact form of a built application differs, but once the executable has been generated, that app package can be played without Unity and can be distributed to players. A single Unity project can be deployed to any platform without needing to be redone for each one.

This "build once, deploy anywhere" capability applies to the vast majority of the features in your games, but not to everything. I would estimate that 95% of the code written in Unity (for example, almost everything we've done so far in this book) is platform-agnostic and will work just as well across all platforms. But there are a few specific tasks that differ for different platforms, so we'll go over those platform-specific areas of development.

Unity is capable of building apps for the following platforms:

- Windows PC
- Mac OS X
- Linux
- WebGL
- iOS
- Android
- Windows Phone
- Tizen
- Oculus Rift
- Steam VR/Vive
- Daydream
- HoloLens

In addition, by contacting the platform owners for access, Unity can even build apps for

- XBox One
- PlayStation 4
- PS Vita
- Switch
- 3DS

Whew, that full list is really long! Frankly, that's almost comically long, and way more than the supported platforms of almost any other game development tool out there. This chapter will focus on the first six platforms listed, because those platforms are of primary interest to the majority of people exploring Unity, but keep in mind how many options are available to you.

To see all these platforms, open the Build Settings window. That's the window you used in the previous chapter to add scenes to be loaded; to access it, choose File > Build Settings. In chapter 12, you only cared about the list at the top, but now you want to pay attention to the buttons at the bottom (see figure 13.1). You'll notice a lot of space taken up by the list of platforms; the currently active platform is indicated with the Unity icon. Select platforms in this list and then click the Switch Platform button.

NOTE When installing Unity, the installer asks which export modules you want, and you can only build the selected modules. If you later want to install a module you hadn't selected initially, in the Build Settings window, there's a button to add it.

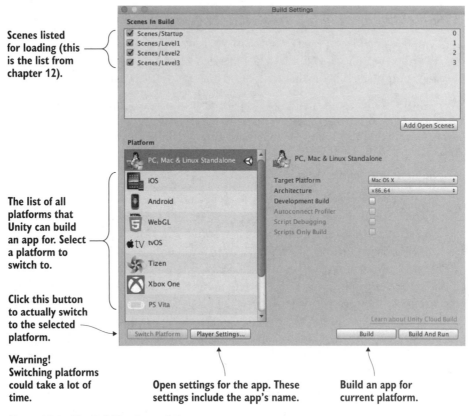

Scenes listed for loading (this is the list from chapter 12).

The list of all platforms that Unity can build an app for. Select a platform to switch to.

Click this button to actually switch to the selected platform.

Warning! Switching platforms could take a lot of time.

Open settings for the app. These settings include the app's name.

Build an app for current platform.

Figure 13.1   The Build Settings window

WARNING When in a big project, switching platforms often takes quite a bit of time to complete; make sure you're ready to wait. This is because Unity recompresses all assets (such as textures) in an optimal way for each platform.

Also across the bottom of this window are the Player Settings and Build buttons. Click Player Settings to view settings for the app in the Inspector, such as the name and icon for the app. Clicking Build launches the build process.

TIP Build And Run does the same thing as Build, plus it automatically runs the built application. I usually want to do that part manually, so I rarely use Build And Run.

When you click Build, the first thing that comes up is a file selector so that you can tell Unity where to generate the app package. Once you select a file location, the build process starts. Unity creates an executable app package for the currently active platform. Let's go over the build process for the most popular platforms: desktop, web, and mobile.

13.1   *Start by building for the desktop: Windows, Mac, and Linux*

The simplest place to start when first learning to build Unity games is by deploying to desktop computers—Windows PC, Mac OS X, or Linux. Because Unity runs on desktop computers, that means you'll build an app for the computer you're already using.

> **NOTE**   Open up any project to work with in this section. Seriously, any Unity project will work. In fact, I strongly suggest using a different project in every section to drive home the fact that Unity can build any project to any platform!

13.1.1 *Building the application*

First choose File > Build Settings to open the Build Settings window. By default, the current platform will be set to PC, Mac, and Linux, but if that isn't current, select the correct platform from the list and click Switch Platform.

On the right-hand side of the window, you'll notice the Target Platform menu. This menu lets you choose between Windows PC, Mac OS X, and Linux. All three are treated as one platform in the list on the left-hand side, but these are very different platforms, so choose the correct one.

Once you've chosen your desktop platform, click Build. A file dialog pops up, allowing you to choose where the built application will go. Then the build process starts; this could take a while for a big project, but the build process should be fast for the tiny demos you've been making.

Custom post-build script

Although the basic build process works fine in most situations, you may want a series of steps to be taken (such as moving help files into the same directory as the application) every time you build your game. You can easily automate such tasks by programming them in a script that will execute after the build process completes.

First, create a new folder in the Project view and name that folder Editor; any scripts that affect Unity's editor (and that includes the build process) must go in the Editor folder. Create a new script named TestPostBuild in that folder and write the following code in it:

```
using UnityEngine;
using UnityEditor;
using UnityEditor.Callbacks;

public static class TestPostBuild {
```

```
    [PostProcessBuild]
    public static void OnPostprocessBuild(BuildTarget target, string
pathToBuiltProject) {
        Debug.Log("build location: " + pathToBuiltProject);
    }
}
```

The `[PostProcessBuild]` directive tells the script to run the function that's immediately after it. That function will receive the location of the built app; you could then use that location with the various filesystem commands provided by C#.

The application will appear in the location you chose; double-click it to run it, like any other program. Congrats, that was easy! Building applications is a snap, but the process can be customized in a number of ways; let's look at how to adjust the build.

TIP Quit fullscreen games with Alt+F4 on Windows or Cmd+Q on Mac. Finished games should have a button that calls `Application.Quit()`.

13.1.2 *Adjusting Player Settings: setting the game's name and icon*

Go back to the Build Settings window, but this time click Player Settings instead of Build. A huge list of settings will appear in the Inspector (see figure 13.2); these settings control a number of aspects of the built application.

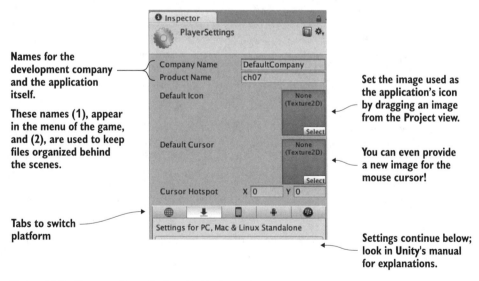

Figure 13.2 Player settings displayed in the Inspector

Because of the large number of settings, you'll probably want to look them up in Unity's manual; the relevant doc page is http://docs.unity3d.com/Manual/class-PlayerSettings.html.

The first three settings at the top are easiest to understand: Company Name, Product Name, and Default Icon. Type in values for the first two. Company Name is the name for your development studio, and Product Name is the name of this specific game. Then drag an image from the Project view (import an image into the project if needed) to set that image as the icon; when the app is built, this image will appear as the application's icon.

Supporting Virtual Reality (VR)

Unity has special support built-in for VR hardware like Oculus and Vive, but VR isn't technically considered a separate platform when building the application. Instead, VR support is a setting that can be toggled within relevant build platforms, such as desktop VR or Android. Go to the correct tab in Player Settings (note the platform buttons just under the top section) and then expand the section Other Settings. Listed there is a toggle for Virtual Reality Supported; turn that on when developing VR!

Setting for VR Support

Customizing the icon and name of the application is important for giving it a finished appearance. Another useful way of customizing the behavior of built applications is with platform-dependent code.

13.1.3   *Platform-dependent compilation*

By default, all the code you write will run the same way on all platforms. But Unity provides a number of compiler directives (known as *platform defines*) that cause different code to run on different platforms. You'll find the full list of platform defines on this page of the manual: http://docs.unity3d.com/Manual/PlatformDependentCompilation.html.

As that page indicates, there are directives for every platform that Unity supports, allowing you to run separate code on every platform. Usually, the majority of your code doesn't have to be inside platform directives, but occasionally small bits of the code need to run differently on different platforms. Some code assemblies only exist on one platform, so you need to have platform compiler directives around those commands. The following listing shows how to write such code.

Listing 13.1 `PlatformTest` **script showing how to write platform-dependent code**

```
using UnityEngine;
using System.Collections;

public class PlatformTest : MonoBehaviour {
    void OnGUI() {
#if UNITY_EDITOR              ◄──┐  This section only runs within the editor
        GUI.Label(new Rect(10, 10, 200, 20), "Running in Editor");
#elif UNITY_STANDALONE                                                    ◄──┐
        GUI.Label(new Rect(10, 10, 200, 20), "Running on Desktop");          │
#else                                                                        │
        GUI.Label(new Rect(10, 10, 200, 20), "Running on other platform");   │
#endif                               Only in desktop/standalone applications │
    }
}
```

Create a script called `PlatformTest` and write the code from this listing in it. Attach that script to an object in the scene (any object will do for testing), and a small message will appear in the top-left of the screen. When you play the game within Unity's editor, the message will say "Running in the Editor," but if you build the game and run the built application, the message will say "Running on Desktop." Different code is being run in each case!

For this test, you used the platform define that treats all desktop platforms as one, but as indicated on that doc page, separate platform defines are available for Windows, Mac, and Linux. In fact, there are platform defines for all the platforms supported by Unity so that you can run different code on each. Let's move on to the next important platform: the web.

Quality settings

The built application is also affected by project settings located under the Edit menu. In particular, the visual quality of the final app can be tuned there. Go to Project Settings in the Edit menu and then choose Quality from the drop-down menu.

Quality settings appear in the Inspector, and the most important settings are the grid of check marks at the top. The different platforms that Unity can target are listed as icons across the top, and the possible quality settings are listed along the side. The boxes are checked for quality settings available for that platform, and the check box is highlighted green for the setting being used. Most of the time, these settings default to Fastest (which is the lowest quality) but you can change to Fantastic quality if things look bad; if you click the down arrow underneath a platform's column, a pop-up menu will appear.

It seems a bit redundant that this UI has both check boxes and the Default menu, but there you have it. Different platforms often have different graphical capabilities, so Unity allows you to set different quality levels for different build targets (such as highest quality on desktop and lower quality on mobile).

The green highlights indicate the current quality setting for each platform.

Click the down arrow in the Default row to change the quality setting. Select from the menu that appears.

Grid of quality settings in the Inspector

13.2 *Building for the web*

Although desktop platforms are the most basic targets to build for, another important platform for Unity games is deployment to the web. This refers to games that run within a web browser and can thus be played over the internet.

13.2.1 *Unity Player vs. HTML5/WebGL*

Previously, Unity had to deploy web builds in a form that played within a custom browser plug-in. This had long been necessary because 3D graphics weren't built into web browsers. In the last several years, though, a standard has emerged for 3D graphics on the web called *WebGL*. Technically, WebGL is separate from HTML5, although the two terms are related and are often used interchangeably.

For version 5, Unity added WebGL to the build platforms list, and a few versions later the browser plug-in was dropped, making WebGL the sole avenue for doing web builds. In part, these changes in Unity's web build were being driven by strategic decisions made within Unity (the company). But these changes were also being driven by pushes from browser makers, who are moving away from custom plug-ins and embracing HTML5/WebGL as the way to do interactive web applications, including games.

13.2.2 *Building the game embedded in a web page*

Open a different project (again, this is to emphasize how any project will work) and open the Build Settings window. Switch the platform to WebGL and then click the Build button. A file selector will come up; type in the name WebTest for this application, and change to a safe location if necessary (that is, a location not within the Unity project).

The build process will now create a folder containing an index.html web page, as well as subfolders with all the game's code and other assets. Open this web page and the game should be embedded in the middle of the otherwise blank page.

There's nothing particularly special about this page; it's just an example to test your game with. It's possible to customize the code on that page, or even provide your own web page (discussed later). One of the most important customizations to make is enabling communication between Unity and the browser, so let's go over that next.

13.2.3 *Communicating with JavaScript in the browser*

A Unity web game can communicate with the browser (or rather with JavaScript running in the browser), and these messages can go in both directions: from Unity to the browser, and from the browser to Unity. To send messages to the browser, you write JavaScript code into a code library, and then Unity has special commands to use functions in that library.

Meanwhile, for messages from the browser, JavaScript in the browser identifies an object by name and then Unity passes the message to the named object in the scene. Thus, you must have an object in the scene that will receive communications from the browser.

To demonstrate these tasks, create a new script in Unity called WebTestObject. Also create an empty object in the active scene called JSListener (the object in the scene must have that exact name, because that's the name used by the JavaScript code in listing 13.4). Attach the new script to that object, and then write in the code from this listing.

Listing 13.2 WebTestObject script for testing communication with the browser

```
using UnityEngine;
using System.Runtime.InteropServices;

public class WebTestObject : MonoBehaviour {
    private string _message;

    [DllImport("__Internal")]          ⟵  Import function from JS library.
    private static extern void ShowAlert(string msg);

    void Start() {
        _message = "No message yet";
    }
```

```
    void Update() {
        if (Input.GetMouseButtonDown(0)) {        ◄──────┤ On mouse click, call imported function.
            ShowAlert("Hello out there!");
        }
    }

    void OnGUI() {                                              ┌─ Display message in
        GUI.Label(new Rect(10, 10, 200, 20), _message);  ◄──────┤ top left of screen.
    }
                                                           ┌─ Function for the
    public void RespondToBrowser(string message) {  ◄──────┤ browser to call
        _message = message;
    }
}
```

The main new bit is the DLLImport command. That imports a function from the JavaScript library to use in C# code. That obviously implies you *have* a JavaScript library, so write that next. First create the special folder to contain it: create a folder called Plugins, and within that create a folder called WebGL. Now put a file called WebTest that has the extension jslib (so WebTest.jslib) in the WebGL folder; the simplest way is to create a text file outside Unity, rename it, and then drag the file in. Unity will recognize that file as a JavaScript library, so write this code in it.

Listing 13.3 WebTest JavaScript library

```
var TestLib = {

    ShowAlert: function(msg) {        ◄──────┤ The function imported and called from C#
        window.alert(Pointer_stringify(msg));
    },

}
mergeInto(LibraryManager.library, TestLib);
```

The jslib file contains both a JavaScript object containing functions and the command to merge the custom object into Unity's library manager. Note that the function written includes Pointer_stringify() besides standard JavaScript commands; when passing a string from Unity it's turned into a numeric identifier, so Unity provides that function to look up the string pointed to.

Now build for web again to see the new code in action. The WebTestObject in Unity calls a function in the JavaScript code when you click within the Unity game part of the web page; try clicking a few times and you'll see an alert box appear in the browser!

NOTE Unity also has Application.ExternalEval() for running code in the browser; ExternalEval runs arbitrary snippets of JavaScript, rather than calling defined functions. This method is deprecated and should be avoided, but sometimes its simplicity is useful, like reloading the page with just:

```
Application.ExternalEval("location.reload();")
```

All right, you have tested communication from the Unity game to JavaScript in the web page, but the web page can also send a message back to Unity, so let's do that too. This will involve new code and buttons on the page; fortunately, Unity provides an easy way to customize the web page. Specifically, Unity fills in a web page *template* when it builds to WebGL, and you can choose a custom template instead of the default one.

The default templates can be found in the Unity installation folder, under Editor\ Data\PlaybackEngines\WebGLSupport\BuildTools\WebGLTemplates on Windows. On a Mac they can be found at /PlaybackEngines/WebGLSupport/BuildTools/WebGL-Templates. Open a template page in a text editor and you'll see that a template is largely standard HTML and JavaScript, plus some special tags that Unity replaces with generated information. Although it's best for you to leave Unity's built-in templates alone, they (especially the *minimal* one) make a good base on which to build your own. You'll copy the minimal template web page into the custom template you make.

In Unity, create a folder called WebGLTemplates (no space); that's where custom templates go. Now create a folder within it named WebTest; that folder is for your new template. Put an index.html file in here (you can copy in the web page from the minimal template), open that in a text editor, and write this code in it.

> **Listing 13.4 WebGL template to enable browser–Unity communication**

```
<!doctype html>
<html lang="en-us">
<head>
<title>Unity WebGL Player | %UNITY_WEB_NAME%</title>
<style>
body { background-color: #333; }          ◄─── Making the page dark instead of white
</style>

<script src="%UNITY_WEBGL_LOADER_URL%"></script>
<script>
var gameInstance = UnityLoader.instantiate("gameContainer", "%UNITY_WEBGL_
    BUILD_URL%");
                                           SendMessage() points to
function SendToUnity() {                    named object in Unity
   gameInstance.SendMessage("JSListener",  ◄───
      "RespondToBrowser", "Hello from the browser!");
}
</script>
</head>

<body>
<div id="gameContainer" style="width: %UNITY_WIDTH%px; height: %UNITY_
    HEIGHT%px; margin: auto"></div>
<br><input type="button" value="Send" onclick="SendToUnity();" />  ◄───
</body>                                     Button that calls the JavaScript function
</html>
```

If you copied the minimal template, you'll see that listing 13.4 is simply a few lines added there. The two important additions are a function in the header script and an input button added at the bottom; the added style changes the color of the page to make it easier to see the embedded game. The button's HTML tag links to a JavaScript function, and that function calls SendMessage() on the Unity instance. This method calls a function on a named object within Unity; the first parameter is the name of the object, the second parameter is the name of the method, and the third parameter is a string to pass in while calling the method.

You've made your custom template, but you still have to tell Unity to use this template instead of the default. Open the Player Settings again (remember, click Player Settings in the Build Settings window) and find WebGL Template in the web settings (shown in figure 13.3). You'll see that Default is currently selected, but WebTest (the template folder you created) is also on the list; click that one instead.

Figure 13.3   WebGL Template setting

With the custom template selected, build to WebGL again. Open the generated web page and this time there's a button at the bottom of the page. Click the button and you'll see the changed message displayed in Unity!

That wraps up browser communication for web builds. There's one more platform (or rather, set of platforms) to discuss building apps for: mobile.

13.3   *Building for mobile: iOS and Android*

Mobile apps are another important build target for Unity. My gut impression (totally unscientific) is that most commercial games created using Unity are mobile games.

> **DEFINITION**   *Mobile* is a category of handheld computing devices. The designation started with smartphones but now includes tablets. The two most widely used mobile computing platforms are iOS (from Apple) and Android (from Google).

Setting up the build process for mobile apps is more complicated than either desktop or web builds, so this is an optional section—optional as in only read through it without actually following the steps; I'll still write as if you're working along, but you'd have to buy a developer license for iOS and install all the developer tools for Android.

> **WARNING**   Mobile devices are undergoing so much innovation that the exact build process is likely to be slightly different by the time you read this. The high-level concepts are probably still true, but you should look at up-to-date documentation online for an exact rundown of the commands to execute and buttons to push. For starters, here are the doc pages from Apple (http://mng.bz/z1VP) and Google (http://developer.android.com/tools/building/index.html).

> ## Touch input
>
> Input on mobile devices works differently than on desktop or the web. Mobile input is done by touching the screen, rather than with the mouse and keyboard. Unity has input functionality for handling touches, including code like `Input.touchCount` and `Input.GetTouch()`.
>
> You may want to use these commands to write platform-specific code on mobile devices. Handling input that way can be a hassle, though, so a number of code frameworks are available to streamline the use of touch input. For example, search on Unity's Asset Store for Fingers or Lean Touch.

All right, with those caveats out of the way, I'll explain the overall build process for both iOS and Android. Keep in mind that these platforms occasionally change the details of the build process.

13.3.1 Setting up the build tools

Mobile devices are all separate from the computer you're developing on, and that separateness makes the process of building and deploying to devices slightly more complex. You'll need to set up a variety of specialized tools before you can click Build.

SETTING UP IOS BUILD TOOLS

At a high level, the process of deploying a Unity game on iOS requires first building an Xcode project from Unity and then building the Xcode project into an IPA (an iOS application package) using Xcode. Unity can't build the final IPA directly because all iOS apps have to go through Apple's build tools. That means you need to install Xcode (Apple's programming IDE), including the iOS SDK.

> **WARNING** That means you have to be working on a Mac—Xcode only runs on OS X. Developing a game within Unity can be done on either Windows or Mac, but building the iOS app must be done on a Mac.

Get Xcode from Apple's website, in the developer section: https://developer.apple.com/xcode/.

> **NOTE** You need membership in the Apple Developer Program in order to sell your iOS game on the App Store. Apple's developer program costs $99/year; enroll at https://developer.apple.com/programs/.

Once Xcode is installed, go back to Unity and switch to iOS. You need to adjust the Player settings for the iOS app (remember, open Build Settings and click Player Settings). You should already be on the iOS tab of the Player settings, but click the iPhone icon tab if needed. Scroll down to Other Settings and then look for Identification. Bundle Identifier needs to be adjusted so that Apple will correctly identify the app.

> **NOTE** iOS calls it Bundle Identifier and Android calls it Package Name, but naming otherwise works the same way on both platforms. The identifier should follow the same convention as that for any code package: all lowercase in the form `com.companyname.productname`.

Another important setting that applies to both iOS and Android is Version (this is the version number of the app). Most of the settings beyond that are platform-specific; for example, iOS added an additional build number, separate from the main version number. There's also a setting for Scripting Backend; Mono was always used in the past, but the newer IL2CPP backend can support platform updates, like 64-bit binaries.

Now click Build in Unity. Select the location for the built files, and that'll generate an Xcode project in that location. The Xcode project that results can be modified directly if you want (some simple modifications could be part of the postbuild script). Regardless, open the Xcode project; the built folder has many files, but double-click the .xcodeproj file (it has an icon of a blueprint). Xcode will open with this project loaded; Unity already took care of most of the settings needed in the project, but you do need to adjust the provisioning profiles being used.

iOS provisioning profiles

Of all the aspects of iOS development, provisioning profiles change the most frequently and are the most unusual. In short, these are files used for identification and authorization. Apple tightly controls what apps can run on what devices; apps submitted to Apple for approval use special provisioning profiles that allow them to work through the App Store, whereas apps in development use provisioning profiles that are specific to registered devices.

You'll need to add both your iPhone's UDID (an ID specific to your device) and the app's ID (the Bundle Identifier in Unity) to a control panel at iOS Dev Center, Apple's website for iOS developers. For a complete explanation of this process, visit https://developer.apple.com/support/code-signing/.

| iOS Dev Center | Mac Dev Center | Safari Dev Center |

Hi, **Joseph Hocking** | My Profile | Sign out

iOS Developer Program

Certificates, Identifiers & Profiles   ❯

Apple Developer Forums   ❯

Developer Support Center   ❯

Click here to add devices, app IDs, and generate provisioning profiles.

Where to manage provisioning profiles in iOS Dev Center

Make sure Scheme Destination at the top is set to iOS Device and not the simulator (Unity projects only work on device, not simulator, and some necessary build options are grayed out if this is wrong). Xcode will attempt to set up the signing profiles automatically, but if necessary this can be adjusted manually. Select your app in the project list on the left-hand side of Xcode. Several tabs relevant to the selected project will appear; go to Build Settings and scroll down to Code Signing to set the provisioning profiles (see figure 13.4).

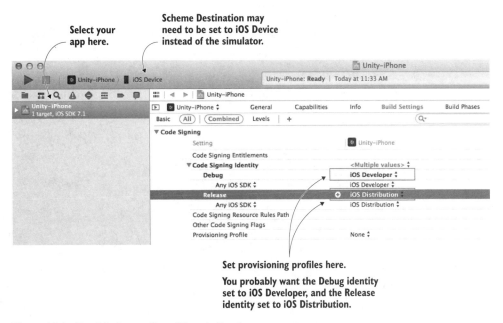

Figure 13.4   Provisioning profile settings in Xcode

Once the provisioning profiles are set, you're ready to build the app. From the Product menu, choose either Run or Archive. There are a lot of options in the Product menu, including the tantalizingly named Build, but for our purposes the two options that are useful are either Run or Archive. Build generates executable files but doesn't bundle them for iOS, whereas this is what Run and Archive do:

- Run will test the application on an iPhone connected to the computer with a USB cable.
- Archive will create an application package that can be sent to other registered devices (what Apple refers to as *ad hoc distribution*).

Archive doesn't create the app package directly but rather creates a bundle in an intermediate stage between the raw code files and an IPA. The created archive will be listed in Xcode's Organizer window; in that window, select the generated archive and click Export on the right-hand side. After you click Export, you'll be asked if you want to distribute the app on the store or ad hoc.

If you choose ad hoc distribution, you'll end up with an IPA file that can be sent to testers. You could send the file directly for them to install through iTunes, but it's more convenient to use TestFlight (https://developer.apple.com/testflight/) to handle distributing and installing test builds.

SETTING UP ANDROID BUILD TOOLS

Unlike iOS apps, Unity can generate the APK (an Android application package) directly. This requires pointing Unity to the Android SDK, which includes the necessary compiler. Download the Android SDK from the Android website, then choose this file location in Unity's preferences (see figure 13.5). You can download the SDK here: http://developer.android.com/sdk/index.html.

> **TIP** Although you only need the command-line SDK for basic building, you probably want to download Android Studio instead. We'll use that tool later in this chapter.

Figure 13.5 Unity preference setting to point to Android SDK

After setting the Android SDK in Unity's preferences, you need to specify the app's identifier just as you did for iOS. You'll find Package Name in Player Settings; set it to com.companyname.productname (as explained in section 13.3.1). Then click Build to start the process. As with all builds, it'll first ask where to save the file. Then it'll create an APK file in that location.

Now that you have the app package, you must install it on a device. You can get the APK file onto an Android phone by downloading the file from the web or by transferring the file via a USB cable connected to your computer (an approach referred to as *sideloading*). The details of how to transfer files onto your phone vary for every device, but once there it can be installed using a file manager app. I don't know why file managers aren't built into Android, but you can install one for free from the Play Store. Navigate to your APK file within the file manager and then install the app.

As you can see, the basic build process for Android is a lot simpler than the build process for iOS. Unfortunately, the process of customizing the build and implementing plug-ins is more complicated than with iOS; you'll learn how in the final section. But before that, let's talk about texture compression.

13.3.2 *Texture compression*

Assets can eat up a lot of memory, and this especially includes textures. To reduce their file size, you can compress assets in various ways, with pros and cons to each method. Because of these pros and cons, you may need to adjust how Unity compresses textures.

It's essential to manage texture compression on mobile devices, but technically, textures are often compressed on other platforms, too. But you don't have to pay as much attention to compression on other platforms for various reasons, the chief one being that the platform is more technologically mature. On mobile devices, you need to pay closer attention to texture compression because the devices are touchier about this detail.

Unity automatically compresses textures for you; in most development tools you need to compress images yourself, but in Unity you generally import uncompressed images, and then it applies image compression in the import settings for the image (see figure 13.6).

Texture compression works the same for both Default (3D textures) and Sprite.

Override default settings to change compression on this image.

Click the Android icon to see settings for this platform.

Select compression formats from the Format menu.

Figure 13.6   Texture compression settings in the Inspector

The compression settings are different on different platforms, so Unity recompresses images when you switch platforms. Initially, the settings are default values, and you may need to adjust them for specific images and specific platforms. In particular, image compression is trickier on Android. This is mostly due to the fragmentation of Android devices: because all iOS devices use pretty much the same video hardware, iOS apps can have texture compression optimized for their graphics chips (the GPU). Android apps don't enjoy the same uniformity of hardware, so their texture compression has to aim for the lowest common denominator.

To be more specific, all iOS devices use PowerVR GPUs; thus, iOS apps can use the optimized PVR texture compression. Some Android devices also use PowerVR chips, but they just as frequently use Adreno chips from Qualcomm, Mali GPUs from ARM, or other options. As a result, Android apps generally rely on Ericsson Texture Compression (ETC), a compression algorithm supported by all Android devices. Unity defaults to ETC2 (the more advanced second version) for textures on Android.

This default works fairly well most of the time, but if you need to adjust compression on a texture, adjust the settings shown in figure 13.6. Click the Android icon tab to override the default settings for that platform, and then use the Format menu (confusingly, *not* the Compression menu) to pick specific compressions formats. In particular, you may find that certain key images need to be uncompressed; although their file size will be much larger, the image quality will be better. As long as you compress the majority of textures and only choose uncompressed on a case-by-case basis, the increased file size probably won't be too bad.

With that discussion out of the way, the final topic for mobile development is developing native plug-ins.

13.3.3 Developing plug-ins

Unity has a huge amount of functionality built-in, but that functionality is mostly limited to features common across all platforms. Taking advantage of platform-specific toolkits (such as Play Game Services on Android) often requires add-on plug-ins for Unity.

> **TIP** A variety of premade mobile plug-ins are available for iOS- and Android-specific features; appendix D lists a few places to get mobile plug-ins. These plug-ins operate in the manner described here, except that the plug-in code is already written for you.

The process of communicating with mobile plug-ins is similar to the process of communicating with the browser. On the Unity side of things, there are special commands that call functions within the plug-in. On the plug-in's side, the plug-in can use Send-Message() to send a message to an object in Unity's scene. The exact code looks different on different platforms, but the general idea is always the same.

> **WARNING** Just as with the initial build process, the process for developing mobile plug-ins tends to change frequently—not the Unity end of the process, but the native code part. I'll cover things at a high level, but you should look for up-to-date documentation online.

Plug-ins for both platforms are put in the same place within Unity. If needed, create a folder in the Project view called Plugins; then, inside Plugins create a folder each for Android and iOS. Once they're put into Unity, plug-in files also have settings for what platforms they apply to. Normally, Unity figures this out automatically (iOS plug-ins are set to iOS, Android plug-ins are set to Android, and so on), but if necessary, look for these settings in the Inspector.

iOS PLUG-INS

The plug-in is really just some native code that gets called by Unity. First, create a script in Unity to handle the native code; call this script `TestPlugin` (see the next listing).

Listing 13.4 `TestPlugin` **script that calls iOS native code from Unity**

```
using UnityEngine;
using System;
using System.Collections;
using System.Runtime.InteropServices;

public class TestPlugin : MonoBehaviour {
    private static TestPlugin _instance;

    public static void Initialize() {                    Object is created in this static function, so
        if (_instance != null) {                          you don't have to create it in the editor.
            Debug.Log("TestPlugin instance was found. Already initialized");
            return;
        }
        Debug.Log("TestPlugin instance not found. Initializing...");

        GameObject owner = new GameObject("TestPlugin_instance");
        _instance = owner.AddComponent<TestPlugin>();
        DontDestroyOnLoad(_instance);
    }                                                Tag that identifies section of code; tag
                                                     doesn't do anything by itself.
    #region iOS
    [DllImport("__Internal")]
    private static extern float _TestNumber();        Refer to function in the iOS code.

    [DllImport("__Internal")]
    private static extern string _TestString(string test);
    #endregion iOS

    public static float TestNumber() {
        float val = 0f;
        if (Application.platform == RuntimePlatform.IPhonePlayer)
            val = _TestNumber();
        return val;                                  Call this if platform is IPhonePlayer.
    }

    public static string TestString(string test) {
        string val = "";
        if (Application.platform == RuntimePlatform.IPhonePlayer)
            val = _TestString(test);
        return val;
    }
}
```

First, note that the static `Initialize()` function creates a permanent object in the scene so that you don't have to do it manually in the editor. You haven't previously seen code to create an object from scratch because it's a lot simpler to use a prefab in most cases, but in this case, it's cleaner to create the object in code (so that you can use the plug-in script without editing the scene).

The main wizardry going on here involves the DLLImport and static extern commands. Those commands tell Unity to link up to functions in the native code you provide, then you can use those referenced functions in this script's methods (with a check to make sure the code is running on iPhone/iOS).

Next, you'll use these plug-in functions to test them. Create a new script called MobileTestObject, create an empty object in the scene, and then attach the script to the object.

> **Listing 13.5   Using the plug-in from MobileTestObject**

```
using UnityEngine;
using System.Collections;

public class MobileTestObject : MonoBehaviour {
    private string _message;

    void Awake() {
        TestPlugin.Initialize();              ◄──────  Initialize the plug-in at the beginning.
    }

    // Use this for initialization
    void Start() {
        _message = "START: " + TestPlugin.TestString("ThIs Is A tEsT");
    }

    // Update is called once per frame
    void Update() {

        // Make sure the user touched the screen
        if (Input.touchCount==0){return;}

        Touch touch = Input.GetTouch(0);       ◄──────  Respond to touch input.
        if (touch.phase == TouchPhase.Began) {
            _message = "TOUCH: " + TestPlugin.TestNumber();
        }
    }
                                                        Display a message in the
    void OnGUI() {                                      corner of the screen.
        GUI.Label(new Rect(10, 10, 200, 20), _message);  ◄──────
    }
}
```

The script in this listing initializes the plug-in object and then calls plug-in methods in response to touch input. Once this is running on the device, you'll see the test message in the corner change whenever you tap the screen.

The final thing left to do is to write the native code that TestPlugin references. Code on iOS devices is written using Objective C and/or C, so you need both a .h header file and a .mm implementation file. As described earlier, they need to go in the Plugins/iOS/ folder in the Project view. Create TestPlugin.h and TestPlugin.mm there; in the .h file, write this code.

Listing 13.6   TestPlugin.h header for iOS code

```
#import <Foundation/Foundation.h>

@interface TestObject : NSObject {
NSString* status;
}

@end
```

Look for an explanation about iOS programming to understand what this header is doing; explaining iOS programming is beyond this book. Write the code from this listing in the .mm file.

Listing 13.7   TestPlugin.mm implementation

```
#import "TestPlugin.h"

@implementation TestObject
@end

NSString* CreateNSString (const char* string)
{
if (string)
return [NSString stringWithUTF8String: string];
else
return [NSString stringWithUTF8String: ""];
}

char* MakeStringCopy (const char* string)
{
if (string == NULL)
return NULL;

char* res = (char*)malloc(strlen(string) + 1);
strcpy(res, string);
return res;
}

extern "C" {
    const char* _TestString(const char* string) {
        NSString* oldString = CreateNSString(string);
        NSString* newString = [oldString uppercaseString];
        return MakeStringCopy([newString UTF8String]);
    }

    float _TestNumber() {
        return (arc4random() % 100)/100.0f;
    }
}
```

Again, a detailed explanation of this code is a bit beyond this book. Note that many of the string functions are there to convert between how Unity represents string data and what the native code uses.

TIP This sample communicates in only one direction, from Unity to the plug-in. But the native code could also communicate to Unity by using the UnitySendMessage() method. You can send a message to a named object in the scene; during initialization, the plug-in created TestPlugin_instance to send messages to.

With the native code in place, you can build the iOS app and test it on a device. Tap the screen to watch the numbers displayed. Very cool! That's how to make an iOS plug-in, so let's look at Android, too.

ANDROID PLUG-INS

To create an Android plug-in, the Unity side of things is almost exactly the same. You don't need to change MobileTestObject at all. Make the additions shown here in TestPlugin.

> **Listing 13.8   Modifying TestPlugin to use the Android plug-in**

```
...
    #region iOS
    [DllImport("__Internal")]
    private static extern float _TestNumber();

    [DllImport("__Internal")]
    private static extern string _TestString(string test);
    #endregion iOS

#if UNITY_ANDROID
    private static Exception _pluginError;
    private static AndroidJavaClass _pluginClass;          ⟍ AndroidJNI
    private static AndroidJavaClass GetPluginClass() {        functionality
        if (_pluginClass == null && _pluginError == null) {  provided by Unity.
            AndroidJNI.AttachCurrentThread();
            try {
                _pluginClass = new AndroidJavaClass("com.testcompany.testplugin.
    TestPlugin");                            ◄━━━
            } catch (Exception e) {
                _pluginError = e;                   Name of the class you programmed;
            }                                       change this name as needed.
        }
        return _pluginClass;
    }

    private static AndroidJavaObject _unityActivity;
    private static AndroidJavaObject GetUnityActivity() {
        if (_unityActivity == null) {
            AndroidJavaClass unityPlayer = new AndroidJavaClass("com.unity3d.
    player.UnityPlayer");                       ◄━━┓ Unity creates an activity
            _unityActivity = unityPlayer.                for the Android app.
    GetStatic<AndroidJavaObject>("currentActivity");
        }
        return _unityActivity;
    }
#endif

    public static float TestNumber() {
```

```
        float val = 0f;
        if (Application.platform == RuntimePlatform.IPhonePlayer)
            val = _TestNumber();
#if UNITY_ANDROID
        if (!Application.isEditor && _pluginError == null)
            val = GetPluginClass().CallStatic<int>("getNumber");
#endif
        return val;
    }

    public static string TestString(string test) {
        string val = "";
        if (Application.platform == RuntimePlatform.IPhonePlayer)
            val = _TestString(test);
#if UNITY_ANDROID
        if (!Application.isEditor && _pluginError == null)
            val = GetPluginClass().CallStatic<string>("getString", test);
#endif
        return val;
    }
}
```

Call to functions in plugin .jar

You'll notice most of the additions happen inside UNITY_ANDROID platform defines; as explained earlier in the chapter, these compiler directives cause code to apply only to certain platforms and are omitted on other platforms. Whereas the iOS code wasn't doing anything that would break on other platforms (it won't do anything, but it won't cause errors, either), the code for Android plug-ins will only compile when Unity is set to the Android platform.

In particular, note the calls to AndroidJNI. That's the system within Unity for connecting to native Android. The other possibly confusing word that appears is Activity; in Android apps, an activity is an app process. The Unity game is an activity of the Android app, so the plug-in code needs access to that activity to pass it around when needed.

Finally, you need the native Android code. Whereas iOS code is written in languages like Objective C and C, Android is programmed in Java. But you can't simply provide the raw Java code for the plug-in; the plug-in must be a JAR packaged from the Java code. Here, again, the details of Android programming are out of scope for an introduction to Unity, but we'll go over the basics briefly. First off, you should install Android Studio if you didn't do so as part of downloading the Android SDK.

Figure 13.7 illustrates the steps to set up a plug-in project in Android Studio. First, select Start a New Project. In the configuration window that appears, name it Test-PluginProj; for this test it doesn't matter what the company domain is, but take note of the project location because you'll need to find it later. Click Next to proceed; for now, Minimum SDK doesn't matter, but select Add No Activity (since this is a plug-in, not a standalone Android app).

Once you click Finish, there will be a brief wait while the new project is set up. Once the editor view appears, select File > New > New Module to add a library. Choose Java Library in the configuration window, name it test-plugin, click Edit to change the Java package name to com.testcompany.testplugin, and finally, class name TestPlugin. Now open the Project view (it's a button along the left-hand edge), expand test-plugin, and double-click the TestPlugin class to open it.

Start Android Studio and then start New Project.

App name TestPluginProj; other settings don't matter for now.

Select No Activity because this is just a library, not a full app.

None of these settings matter for a library, so hit Next.

File > New > New Module to add library to the project.

Open the Project view either using the View menu or just click this side button.

Select Java Library for this module.

Library name test-plugin, class TestPlugin, and click Edit here to set company.

Finally, open the TestPlugin class to write library code.

Figure 13.7   Setting up Android Studio to build a plug-in

TestPlugin is currently empty, so write the plug-in functions in it. Listing 13.9 shows the Java code for the plug-in.

Listing 13.9 TestPlugin.java that compiles into a JAR

```java
package com.testcompany.testplugin;

public class TestPlugin {
    private static int number = 0;

    public static int getNumber() {
        number++;
        return number;
    }

    public static String getString(String message) {
        return message.toLowerCase();
    }
}
```

All right, now you can package this code into a JAR. In the top menu, select Build > Build APK; despite the name, this will also build the library, and you can ignore the apk itself. Once the build is complete, go to project on your computer and find test-plugin.jar in /test-plugin/build/libs/. Drag the JAR into Unity's Android plug-ins folder to import it.

Android's manifest and resources folder

It wasn't required for this simple test plug-in, but Android plug-ins often must edit the manifest file. All Android apps are controlled by a main configuration file called Android-Manifest.xml; Unity creates a basic manifest file if you don't provide one, but you could provide one manually by putting it in Plugins/Android/ alongside the plug-in JAR.

When an Android app is built, Unity puts the generated manifest file in the Temp folder at StagingArea/AndroidManifest.xml; copy that file to manually edit it (the downloaded code includes a sample manifest file).

Similarly, there's a folder called res where you can put resources like custom icons; you could create res in the Android plug-ins folder.

With the JAR file in Plugins/Android, build the game and install on a device, and the message will change whenever you tap the screen. Also, like the iOS plug-in, an Android plug-in could use `UnityPlayer.UnitySendMessage()` to communicate with the object in the scene (the Java code would need to import Unity's Android Player library/JAR).

I know I glossed over a lot in developing Android libraries, but that's because the process is both too complicated and changes frequently. If you become advanced enough to develop plug-ins for your Android games, you're going to have to look up documentation on Android's developer website.

CONGRATULATIONS, YOU'VE REACHED THE END!

Congratulations, you now know the steps for deploying a Unity game to mobile devices. The basic build process for all platforms is simple (just a single button), but customizing the app on various platforms can get complicated. Now you're ready to get out there and build your own games!

Summary

- Unity can build executable applications for a huge variety of platforms, including desktop computers, mobile devices, and websites.
- A host of settings can be applied to builds, including details like the icon for the app and the name that appears.
- Web games can interact with the web page they're embedded in, allowing for all kinds of interesting web apps.
- Unity supports custom plug-ins in order to extend its functionality.

afterword

At this point, you know everything you need to know to build a complete game using Unity—everything from a programming standpoint, that is; a top-notch game needs fantastic art and sound, too. But success as a game developer involves a lot more than technical skills. Let's face it—learning Unity isn't your end goal. Your goal is to create successful games, and Unity is just a tool (granted, a very good tool) to get you to that goal.

Beyond the technical skills to implement everything in the game, you need an additional intangible attribute: grit. I'm talking about the doggedness and confidence to keep working on a challenging project and see it through to the end; what I sometimes refer to as "finishing ability." There's only one way to build up your finishing ability, and that's to complete lots of projects. That seems like a catch-22 (to gain the ability to complete projects, you first need to complete a lot of projects), but the key point to recognize is that small projects are way easier to complete than large projects.

Therefore, the path forward is to first build a lot of small projects—because those are easy to complete—and work up to larger projects. Many new game developers make the mistake of tackling a project that's too large for two main reasons: they want to copy their favorite (big) game, and everyone underestimates how much work it takes to make a game. The project seemingly starts off fine but quickly gets bogged down in too many challenges, and eventually the developer gets dejected and quits.

Instead, someone new to game development should start small. Start with projects so small that they seem trivial. The projects in this book are the sort of "small, almost to the point of trivial" projects that you should start with. If you've done all the projects in this book, then you've already gotten a lot of these starter projects out of the way. Try something bigger for your next project, but be wary of making too big a jump. You'll build up your skills and confidence, so you can get a little more ambitious each time.

You'll hear this same advice almost any time you ask how to start developing games. For example, Unity asked the web series *Extra Credits* (a great series about game development) make some videos about starting in game dev, and you'll find them at http://mng.bz/X9ec.

Game design

The entire *Extra Credits* series goes way beyond this handful of videos sponsored by Unity. It covers a lot of ground but mostly focuses on the discipline of game design.

> **DEFINITION** *Game design* is the process of defining a game by creating its goals, rules, and challenges. It is not to be confused with *visual design*, which is designing appearance, not function. This is a common mistake because the average person is most familiar with "design" in the context of "graphic design."

> **DEFINITION** One of the most central parts of game design is crafting game *mechanics*—the individual actions (or systems of actions) within a game. The mechanics in a game are often set up by its rules, whereas the challenges in a game generally come from applying the mechanics to specific situations. For example, walking around the game is a mechanic; a maze is a kind of challenge based on that mechanic.

Thinking about game design can be tricky for newcomers to game development. The most successful (and satisfying to create!) games are built with interesting and innovative game mechanics. Conversely, worrying too much about the design of your first game can distract you from other aspects of game development, like learning how to program it. You're better off starting out by aping the design of existing games. (Remember, I'm only talking about *starting out*; cloning existing games is great for initial practice, but eventually you'll have enough skills and experience to branch out further.)

That said, any successful game developer should be curious about game design. There are lots of ways to learn more about game design—you already know about the *Extra Credits* videos, but here are some other websites:

- www.gamasutra.com—Offers jobs, games updates, good news/bad news about games; everything you want/need to know about the art and business of making games.
- www.lostgarden.com—Readable thoughtful essays on game design theory, art, and the business of design (quoted from its home page).
- http://sloperama.com—Click School-a-rama for the game biz advice page

There are also a number of great books on the subject, such as the following:

- *Game Design Workshop*, Third Edition, by Tracy Fullerton (A K Peters/CRC Press, 2014)

- *A Theory of Fun for Game Design*, Second Edition, by Raph Koster (O'Reilly Media, 2013)
- *The Art of Game Design*, Second Edition, by Jesse Schell (A K Peters/CRC Press, 2014)

Marketing your game

In the *Extra Credits* videos, the fourth video is about marketing your game. Sometimes game developers put off thinking about marketing. They only want to think about building the game and not marketing it, but that attitude will probably result in a failed game. The best game in the world still won't be successful if nobody knows about it!

The word *marketing* often evokes thoughts of ads, and if you have the budget, then running ads for your game is certainly one way to market it. But there are lots of low-cost or even free ways to get the word out about your game. Specifics tend to change over time, but overall strategies mentioned in that video include tweeting about your game (or posting on social media in general, not just Twitter) and creating a trailer video to share on YouTube with reviewers, bloggers, and so on. Be persistent and get creative!

Now go and create some great games. Unity is an excellent tool for doing just that, and you've learned how to use it. Good luck on your journey!

appendix A
Scene navigation and keyboard shortcuts

Operating Unity is done through mouse and keyboard, but it isn't obvious to a newcomer *how* the mouse and keyboard are used in Unity. In particular, the most basic sort of mouse and keyboard input is navigating around the scene and looking around the 3D objects. Unity also has a number of keyboard commands for commonly used operations.

I'll explain the input controls here, but there are also a couple of web pages you could refer to (these are the relevant pages in Unity's online manual): http://docs .unity3d.com/Documentation/Manual/SceneViewNavigation.html and http:// docs.unity3d.com/Documentation/Manual/UnityHotkeys.html.

A.1 Scene navigation using the mouse

Scene navigation is primarily done with three main navigation maneuvers: Move, Orbit, and Zoom. The three movements involve clicking and dragging while holding down a combination of Alt (or Option on the Mac) and Control. The exact controls vary for one-, two-, and three-button mice; table A.1 lists all the controls.

Table A.1 Scene navigation controls for various kinds of mice

Navigation action	Three-button mouse	Two-button mouse	One-button mouse
Move	Middle button click/drag	Alt+Command+left-click/drag	Alt+Command+click/drag
Orbit	Hold Alt+left-click/drag	Alt+left-click/drag	Alt+click/drag
Zoom	Hold Alt+right-click/drag	Alt+right-click/drag	Alt+Ctrl+click/drag

NOTE Although Unity can be used with one- or two-button mice, I highly recommend getting a three-button mouse (and yes, a three-button mouse works fine on Mac OS X).

Besides the navigation maneuvers done using the mouse, there are also some view controls based on the keyboard. If you hold down the right button on the mouse, the WASD keys on the keyboard can be used to walk around in the manner common to most first-person games. Hold Shift during any other control to move faster. But most important, if you press F while an object is selected, the view will pan and zoom to focus on that object. If you get lost while navigating your scene, a common "escape hatch" is to select an object listed in the Hierarchy and then press F.

A.2 *Commonly used keyboard shortcuts*

Unity has a number of keyboard commands to quickly access important functions. The most important keyboard shortcuts are W, E, R, and T: those buttons activate the transform tools Translate, Rotate, and Scale (refer to chapter 1 if you don't recall what the transform tools do), as well as the 2D Rect tool. Because those keys are right next to each other, it's common to leave your left hand on those keys while your right hand operates the mouse.

In addition to the transform tools, there are a number of keyboard shortcuts; table A.2 lists many useful keyboard shortcuts in Unity.

Table A.2   Useful keyboard shortcuts

Keystroke	Function
W	Translate (move the selected object)
E	Rotate (rotate the selected object)
R	Scale (resize the selected object)
T	Rect tool (manipulate 2D objects)
F	Focus view on the selected object
V	Snap to vertices
Ctrl/Command+Shift+N	New GameObject
Ctrl/Command+P	Play game
Ctrl/Command+R	Refresh project
Ctrl/ Command+1	Set current window to Scene view
Ctrl/Command+2	Set to Game view
Ctrl/Command+3	Set to Inspector view
Ctrl/Command+4	Set to Hierarchy view
Ctrl/Command+5	Set to Project view
Ctrl/Command+6	Set to Animation view

Unity responds to a number of other keyboard shortcuts as well, but they get increasingly obscure the further down the list we get.

appendix B
External tools used
alongside Unity

Developing a game using Unity relies on a variety of external software tools for taking care of various tasks. In chapter 1, we discussed one external tool; MonoDevelop is technically a separate application, even though it's bundled along with Unity. In a similar manner, developers rely on an array of external tools to do work not internal to Unity.

This isn't to say that Unity is lacking capabilities that it ought to have. Rather, the game development process is so complex and multifaceted that any well-designed piece of software with a clear focus and clean separation of concerns will inevitably limit itself to being good at a limited subset of the process. In this case, Unity concentrates on being the glue and the engine that brings together all the content of a game and makes it function. Creating all that content is done with other tools; let's take a look at several categories of software that could be useful to you.

B.1 Programming tools

We've already looked at MonoDevelop, the most significant programming tool used alongside Unity. But there are other programming tools to be aware of, as you'll see in this section.

B.1.1 Visual Studio

As mentioned in chapter 1, although Unity comes with MonoDevelop and you can use that IDE on both Windows and Mac, on Windows you could also choose to use Visual Studio. Recently, Microsoft acquired SyntaxTree, a company that has been improving the integration of Visual Studio (http://unityvs.com/).

B.1.2 Xcode

Xcode is the programming environment provided by Apple (in particular an IDE, but also including SDKs for Apple platforms). Although you'd still be doing the vast majority of the work within Unity, you need to use Xcode to deploy a game to iOS. That work often involves debugging or profiling your app using the tools in Xcode (https://developer.apple.com/xcode/).

B.1.3 Android SDK

Similar to how you need to install Xcode in order to deploy to iOS, you need to download the Android SDK in order to deploy to Android. Unlike when building an iOS game, you don't need to fire up any development tools outside of Unity—you simply have to set preferences in Unity that point to the Android SDK: http://developer.android.com/sdk/index.html.

B.1.4 SVN, Git, or Mercurial

Any decent-sized software development project will involve a lot of complex revisions to code files, so programmers have developed a class of software called VCS (version control system) to handle this problem. Three of the most popular systems are Subversion (also known as SVN) (http://subversion.apache.org/), Git (http://git-scm.com/), and Mercurial (https://www.mercurial-scm.org). If you don't already use a VCS, I highly recommend starting to use one. Unity fills the project folder with temp files and workspace settings, but the only two folders that need to be in version control are Assets (make sure your version control is picking up the meta files generated by Unity) and Project Settings.

B.2 3D art applications

Although Unity is perfectly capable of handling 2D graphics (chapters 5 and 6 focus on 2D graphics), it originated as a 3D game engine and continues to have strong 3D graphics features. Many 3D artists work with at least one of the software packages described in this section.

B.2.1 Maya

Maya (www.autodesk.com/products/autodesk-maya/overview) is a 3D art and animation package with deep roots in moviemaking. Maya's feature set covers almost every task that comes up for 3D artists, from crafting beautiful cinematic animations to making efficient game-ready models. 3D animation done in Maya (such as a character walking) can be exported over to Unity.

B.2.2 3ds Max

Another widely used 3D art and animation package, 3ds Max (www.autodesk.com/products/autodesk-3ds-max/overview), offers an almost identical feature set and is quite comparable in workflow to Maya. 3ds Max runs only on Windows (whereas other tools, including Maya, are cross-platform), but it's used just as often in the game industry.

B.2.3   Blender

Though not as commonly used in the game industry as either 3ds Max or Maya, Blender (www.blender.org/) is comparable to those other applications. Blender also covers almost all 3D art tasks and, best of all, Blender is open source. Given that it's available for free on all platforms, Blender is the only 3D art application that's assumed to be available by this book.

B.2.4   SketchUp

This is a very simple-to-use modeling tool, especially well-suited for buildings and architectural elements. Unlike the previous tools, SketchUp (www.sketchup.com) does not cover all or even most 3D art tasks; instead, it focuses on making it easy to model buildings and other simple shapes. This tool is useful in game development for white-boxing and level editing.

B.3   2D image editors

2D images are crucial to all games, be they displayed directly for 2D games or as textures on the surface of 3D models. Several 2D graphics tools come up often in game development, as you'll see in this section.

B.3.1   Photoshop

Photoshop (www.photoshop.com) is easily the most widely used 2D image application there is. The tools in Photoshop can be used to touch up existing images, apply image filters, or even paint pictures from scratch. Photoshop supports dozens of different file formats, including all image formats used in Unity.

B.3.2   GIMP

An acronym standing for GNU Image Manipulation Program, GIMP (www.gimp.org/) is the best-known open source 2D graphics application. GIMP trails Photoshop in both features and usability, but it's still a useful image editor, and you can't beat the price!

B.3.3   TexturePacker

Whereas the previously mentioned tools are all used beyond the field of game development, TexturePacker is only useful for game development. But it's very good at the task it was designed for: assembling sprite sheets to use in 2D games. If you're developing a 2D game, then you probably want to try out TexturePacker (www.codeandweb.com/texturepacker).

B.3.4 *Aseprite, Pyxel Edit*

Pixel art is one of the most recognizable 2D gaming art styles, and these are good pixel art tools. Photoshop can technically be used for pixel art as well, but it's not focused on that task. Furthermore, the animation features are more front-and-center at Aseprite (www.aseprite.org/) and Pyxel Edit (www.pyxeledit.com).

B.4 *Audio software*

A dizzying array of audio production tools is available, including both sound editors (which work with raw waveforms) and sequencers (which compose music using a sequence of notes). To give a taste of the audio software available, this section looks at two major sound-editing tools (other examples beyond this list include Logic, Ableton, and Reason).

B.4.1 *Pro Tools*

Pro Tools audio software (www.avid.com/US/products/family/Pro-Tools) boasts many useful features and is considered the industry standard by countless music producers and audio engineers. It's frequently used for all sorts of professional audio work, including game development.

B.4.2 *Audacity*

Although nowhere near as useful for professional audio work, Audacity (http://audacity.sourceforge.net/) is a handy sound editor for small-scale audio work, like preparing short sound files to use as sound effects in a game. This is a popular choice for those looking for open source sound editing software.

appendix C
Modeling a bench in Blender

In chapters 2 and 4, we looked at creating levels with large flat walls and floors. But what about more detailed objects? What if you want, say, interesting furniture in the room? You can accomplish that by building 3D models in external 3D art apps. Recall the definition from the introduction to chapter 4: 3D models are the mesh objects in the game (that is, the 3D shapes). In this appendix, I'll show you how to create a mesh object of a simple bench (figure C.1).

Figure C.1   Diagram of the simple bench
you're going to model.

Although appendix B lists a number of 3D art tools, we'll use Blender for this exercise because it's open source and thus accessible to all readers. You'll create a mesh object in Blender and export that to an art asset that works with Unity.

> **TIP** Modeling is a huge topic, but we'll cover only a handful of modeling functions that will allow you to create the bench. If you want to keep learning more about modeling after this chapter, look at some of the many books and tutorials on the subject (to start with, look at the learning resources at www.blender.org).

WARNING I used Blender 2.67, so the explanations and screenshots come from that version of the software. Newer versions of Blender are released frequently, and there may be slight changes to the placement of buttons or names of commands.

C.1 *Building the mesh geometry*

Launch Blender; the initial default screen looks like figure C.2, with a cube in the middle of the scene. Use the middle mouse button to manipulate the camera view: click and drag to tumble, Shift with click-drag to pan, and Control with click-drag to zoom.

The default camera (delete this)   **A default cube**   **The default light (delete this)**

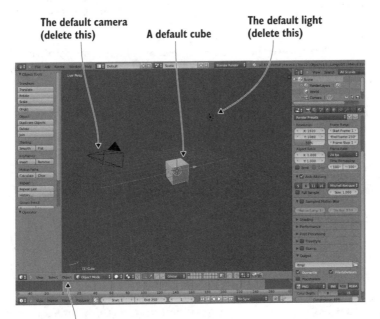

The toolbar (settings for this viewport)

Figure C.2   The initial default screen in Blender

Blender starts out in Object mode, which, as the name implies, is when you manipulate entire objects, moving them around the scene. To edit a single object in detail, you must switch to Edit mode; figure C.3 shows the menu you use (Edit appears in this menu only when an object is selected, and Blender starts out with the object selected). Similarly, when you first switch to Edit mode, Blender is set to Vertex Selection mode, but there are buttons (refer to figure C.4) that let you switch between Vertex, Edge, and Face Selection modes. The various selection modes allow you to select different mesh elements.

Switch to Edit mode
instead of Object mode.

The editing mode menu

Figure C.3   Menu for switching
from Object to Edit mode

DEFINITION   *Mesh elements* are the vertices, edges, and faces that comprise the geometry of the mesh—in other words, the individual corner points, the lines connecting the points, and the shapes filled in between connected lines.

Transform tool:
translate, rotate,
scale

Selection mode:
vertex, edge,
or face

Toggle:
select back
of object, too

Figure C.4   Controls along the bottom of the viewport

Fundamental mouse and keyboard shortcuts in Blender

Also depicted in figure C.4 are the transform tools. As in Unity, the transforms are Translate, Rotate, and Scale. The first button toggles the Transform Gizmo (the arrows in the scene) on and off; I recommend leaving that gizmo on, because otherwise you can only access the transform tools via keyboard shortcuts. The keyboard shortcuts in Blender are often unexpected, as is the mouse functionality.

For example, though the use of the middle mouse button to manipulate the camera makes intuitive sense, selecting elements in the scene is done with the right mouse button (in most applications, the left mouse button selects things). Even weirder, a box selection is done by pressing B and then left-clicking-and-dragging. You add to the selection (as opposed to replacing the selection) by holding Shift while clicking elements, and you clear the selection by pressing A.

These are the basic controls for using Blender, so now we'll see some functions for editing the model. To start, scale the cube into a long, thin plank. Select every vertex of the model (be sure to also select vertices on the side of the object facing away) and then switch to the Scale tool. Click-drag the blue arrow for the Z-axis to scale down vertically, and then click-drag the green arrow for Y to scale out sideways (see figure C.5).

Blue arrow of the Transform Gizmo

Long, thin plank that will be top of bench

(1) Cube

Edit Mode   Global

Figure C.5   Mesh scaled into a long, thin plank

Switch to Face Selection mode (use the button indicated in figure C.4) and select both small ends of the plank. Now click on the Mesh menu at the bottom of the viewport and select Extrude Individual (see figure C.6). As you move the mouse you'll see additional sections added to the ends of the plank; move them out slightly and then left-click to confirm. This additional section is only the width of the bench legs, giving you a little additional geometry to work with.

Select the thin polygons on either end of the bench, then choose Extrude Individual in the Mesh menu.

Only move the mouse out slightly in order to extrude small end sections.

Figure C.6   In the Mesh menu, use Extrude Individual to pull out extra sections.

DEFINITION   *Extrude* is when you push out new geometry with a cross-section in the shape of the selected faces. The two different extrude commands define what to do when multiple elements are selected: Extrude Individual treats each element as a separate piece to extrude, whereas Extrude Region treats the entire selection as a single piece.

Now look at the bottom of the plank and select the two thin faces on each end. Use the Extrude Individual command again to pull down legs for the bench (refer to figure C.7).

Select thin faces underneath and Extrude them down to make legs.

Figure C.7   Select the thin faces underneath the bench and pull down legs.

The shape is complete! But before you export the model over to Unity, you want to take care of texturing the model.

C.2   *Texture-mapping the model*

3D models can have 2D images (referred to as *textures*) displayed on their surface. How exactly the 2D images relate to the 3D surface is straightforward for a large flat surface like a wall: simply stretch the image across the flat surface. But what about an oddly shaped surface, like the sides of the bench? This is where it becomes important to understand the concept of *texture coordinates*.

Texture coordinates define how parts of the texture relate to parts of the mesh. These coordinates assign mesh elements to areas of the texture. Think about it like wrapping paper (see figure C.8); the 3D model is the box being wrapped, the texture is the wrapping paper, and the texture coordinates represent where on the wrapping paper each side of the box will go. The texture coordinates define points and shapes on the 2D image; those shapes correlate to polygons on the mesh, and that part of the image appears on that part of the mesh.

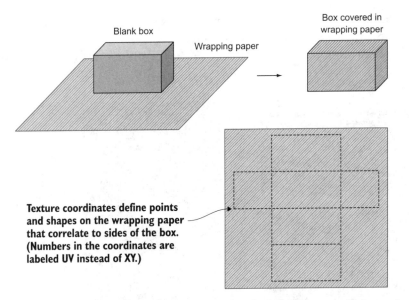

Box covered in
wrapping paper

Blank box

Wrapping paper

**Texture coordinates define points
and shapes on the wrapping paper
that correlate to sides of the box.
(Numbers in the coordinates are
labeled UV instead of XY.)**

Figure C.8   Wrapping paper makes a good analogy for how texture coordinates work.

TIP Another name for texture coordinates is *UV coordinates*. This name comes
from the fact that texture coordinates are defined using the letters U and V,
like coordinates on the 3D model are defined using X, Y, and Z.

The technical term for correlating part of one thing to part of another is *mapping*—
hence the term *texture mapping* for the process of creating texture coordinates. Coming
from the wrapping paper analogy, another name for the process is *unwrapping*. And
then there are terms created by mashing up the other terminology, like *UV unwrapping*;
there are a lot of essentially synonymous terms surrounding texture mapping, so try
not to get confused.

Traditionally, the process of texture mapping has been wickedly complicated, but
fortunately, Blender provides tools to make the process fairly simple. First you define
seams on the model; if you think further about wrapping around a box (or better yet,
think about the other direction, unfolding a box) you'll realize that not every part of
a 3D shape can remain seamless when unfolded into two dimensions. There will have
to be seams in the 3D form where the sides come apart. Blender enables you to select
edges and declare them as seams.

Switch to Edge Selection mode (see the buttons in figure C.4) and select the
edges along the outside of the bottom of the bench. Now select Mesh > Edges > Mark
Seam (see figure C.9). This tells Blender to separate the bottom of the bench for the

purposes of texture mapping. Do the same thing for the sides of the bench, but don't separate the sides entirely. Instead, only seam edges running up the legs of the bench; this way, the sides will remain connected to the bench while spreading out like wings.

Figure C.9   Seam edges along the bottom of the bench and along the legs

Once all the seams are marked, run the Texture Unwrap command. First, select the entire mesh (don't forget the side of the object facing away). Next, choose Mesh > UV Unwrap > Unwrap to create the texture coordinates. But you can't see the texture coordinates in this view; Blender defaults to a 3D view of the scene. To see the texture coordinates, you must switch from 3D View to UV Editor, using the Viewports menu located on the far left of the toolbar (not the word *View* but the little icon; see figure C.10).

Now you can see the texture coordinates. You can see the polygons of the bench laid out flat, separated, and unfolded according to the seams you marked. To paint a texture, you have to see these UV coordinates in your image-editing program. Referring again to figure C.10, under the UVs menu, choose Export UV Layout; save the image as bench.png (this name will also be used later when importing into Unity).

Export UV Layout menu

Texture coordinates displayed as points of the flattened-out bench.

Figure C.10 Switch from 3D View to UV Editor, where the texture coordinates are displayed.

Open this image in your image editor and paint colors for the various parts of your texture. Painting different colors for different UVs will put different colors on those faces. For example, figure C.11 shows darker blue where the bottom of the bench was unfolded on the top of the UV layout, and red was painted on the sides of the bench. Now the image can be brought back into Blender to texture the model; select Image > Open Image.

UV Editor after choosing Open in the Image menu

Exported UV layout

Texture image painted

Figure C.11 Paint colors over the exported UVs and then bring the texture into Blender.

At this point, you can return to the 3D view (using the same menu you used to switch to UV Editor). You still can't see the texture on the model, but that only requires a couple more steps. You need to delete the default light and then turn on textures in the viewport (see figure C.12).

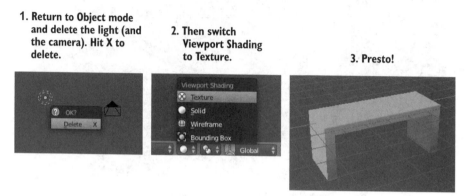

1. Return to Object mode and delete the light (and the camera). Hit X to delete.

2. Then switch Viewport Shading to Texture.

3. Presto!

Figure C.12   Delete the default light and view the texture on the model.

To delete the light, first switch back to Object mode in order to select it (using the same menu you used to switch to Edit mode). Press X to delete a selected object; delete the camera while you're at it. Finally, go to the Viewport Shading menu to switch to Texture. Now you can see the finished bench, with texture applied!

Save the model now. Blender will save the file with the .blend extension, using the native file format for Blender. Work in the native file format so that all the features of Blender will be preserved correctly, but later you'll have to export the model to a different file format to import it into Unity. Note that the texture image isn't saved in the model file; what's saved is a reference to the image, but you still need the image file that's being referenced.

appendix D
Online learning resources

This book is designed to be a complete introduction to game development in Unity, but there's much more to learn beyond this introduction. You'll find lots of great resources online that you can use to go further after finishing this book.

D.1 Additional tutorials

Many sites that provide directed information on a variety of topics within Unity exist. Several of these are even provided officially by the company behind Unity.

UNITY MANUAL

This is the comprehensive user manual provided by Unity. Not only is it useful for looking up information, but the list of topics is useful by itself for providing a full idea of what Unity is capable of. You can find the manual at http://docs.unity3d .com/Documentation/Manual/index.html.

SCRIPT REFERENCE

Unity programmers end up reading the script reference more than any other (at least, I do!). The user manual covers the capabilities of the engine and use of the editor, but the script reference is a thorough reference to Unity's entire API. Every Unity command is listed here at http://docs.unity3d.com/Documentation/ ScriptReference/index.html.

UNITY LEARN TUTORIALS

Unity's official website includes several comprehensive tutorials, found in the *Learn* section. Most importantly, the tutorials are all videos. This may be good or bad depending on your perspective; if you are someone who likes to watch video tutorials, then https://unity3d.com/learn/tutorials is a good site to check out.

CATLIKE CODING

Rather than walking learners through a complete game, Catlike Coding offers a grab-bag of useful and interesting topics. The topics aren't even necessarily about game development specifically, but are a great way to build up programming skills in Unity. The tutorials can be found at catlikecoding.com/unity/tutorials/.

GAME DEVELOPMENT AT STACKEXCHANGE

StackExchange is another great information site with a different format from the previous ones listed. Rather than a series of self-contained tutorials, StackExchange presents a mostly text QA that encourages searching. StackExchange has sections about a huge array of topics; https://gamedev.stackexchange.com/ is the area of the site focused on game development. For what it's worth, I look for Unity information there almost as often as I use the script reference.

MAYA LT GUIDE

As described in appendix B, external art applications are a crucial part of creating visually stunning games. Many resources that teach about Maya, 3ds Max, Blender, or any of the other 3D art applications are available. Appendix C offers a tutorial about Blender. One online guide about using Maya LT (a game development–oriented and less expensive version of Maya) is steamcommunity.com/sharedfiles/filedetails/?id=242847724.

D.2   *Code libraries*

Although the previously listed resources provide tutorials and/or learning information about Unity, the sites in this section provide code that can be used in your projects. Libraries and plug-ins are another kind of resource that can be useful for new developers, both for using directly but also for learning from (by reading their code).

UNIFY COMMUNITY WIKI

The Unity wiki (called Unify) is a central database of code contributions from many developers, and the scripts hosted there cover a wide range of functionality. Throughout this book, I sometimes directed you to specific scripts hosted here (the messenger system, for example). You can find many more useful scripts at wiki.unity3d.com/index.php/Scripts.

DOTWEEN, LEANTWEEN, ITWEEN

As mentioned briefly in chapter 3, a kind of motion effect commonly used in games is referred to as a *tween*. This is a type of movement where a single code command can set an object moving to a target over a certain amount of time. Tweening functionality can be added using libraries like dotween.demigiant.com/, https://github.com/dented-pixel/LeanTween, and www.itween.pixelplacement.com/.

POST-PROCESSING STACK

The post-processing stack is an easy way to add a bunch of visual effects like depth of field and motion blur to your games. Many of these effects had previously been provided separately in Unity, but now they've been integrated into one über effect. This component is available on the Asset Store or can be downloaded from https://github .com/Unity-Technologies/PostProcessing.

PRIME[31]

Unity provides deployment to mobile platforms like iOS and Android, but the plat-form-specific features are limited to core features. You can add a lot of more specific features through plug-ins, and prime[31] (https://prime31.com/) has many such plug-ins.

AGASPER ANDROID NOTIFICATIONS

While the plug-ins from prime[31] cover all sorts of different features, Agasper Android Notifications plug-in (https://github.com/Agasper/unity-android-notifica-tions) focuses on just one thing: local notifications on Android. Since Unity has iOS notifications built in, you may only need Android notifications from a plug-in, in which case this is a streamlined option.

PLAY GAMES SERVICES FROM GOOGLE

On iOS, Unity has GameCenter integration built in so that your games can have platform-native leaderboards and achievements. The equivalent system on Android is called Google Play Games; although this isn't built into Unity, Google maintains a plug-in at https://github.com/playgameservices/play-games-plugin-for-unity.

FMOD STUDIO

The audio functionality built into Unity works well for playing back recordings, but can be limited for advanced sound design work. FMOD Studio is an advanced sound design tool that has a Unity plug-in. Find it at www.fmod.com/studio.

index